11-2-17

To Byron...

Very best wishes!
THE LAWyer -
Bob French

i

THE LAWyer

Robert B. French

TABLE OF CONTENTS

INTRODUCTION 1
WORTH EVERY DIME 5
TELEVISION STAR 71
THE BANK ROBBERY 91
CALVIN 152
THE ASHES 165
FRIENDS..207
THE DIRTY TRICK..234
THROWED OUT 268
THE BOOTS..291
HIT AND DRAG SHORTY 366
PAM..414
JUST A BOY AND HIS DOG 457
INTERFERENCE..461
MEET ME IN ST. LOUIS 481
DAVE AND THE DIVER..495
TWO PENHOOKERS AND TWO BEERS.............506
THE ROBING ROOM INCIDENT..........................525
THE SALESMAN 538
LAUGHED OUT OF COURT........................ 541
TOSS IT 560

INTRODUCTION

Lawyers spend at least one-third of their productive hours doing nothing more than waiting. They wait while the court laboriously plods through the motion docket, the pleading docket, the settlement docket, the arraignment docket, the plea docket, the domestic relations docket, the juvenile docket, the trial docket and on it goes. Lawyers, dressed in their finest suits and ties, must always be sure to get to the courtroom on time and then wait, wait and wait some more.

It is not unusual for an attorney to have his case set more than 50 cases down the docket. That means he must sit in the courtroom while some 50 plus lawyers handle some 50 plus clients and their cases with the judge before the attorney has a chance to do anything. It is dead time.

The courts consider reading a newspaper or a novel disrespectful of the court's time. Lawyers, as officers of the court, are supposed to be as interested in what is going on as the actual participants. They aren't. If it is not their case, or a case in which they are involved, they have no interest in the proceedings whatsoever. Yawn, yawn - boring!

After spending more than 50 years sitting in courtrooms across the country, the lawyer decided to write down some of his experiences, put them in a *law book form*, and market the work to the gentlemen of the bar. That way, the waiting attorney can appear to be studying while entertaining himself with the exploits of the lawyer.

With that concept in hand, where to begin to find stories that might be interesting to other lawyers?

When lawyers gather for any occasion, seminars, continuing legal education classes, mediation classes, criminal defense law courses, defense lawyer courses and many others, often there is a room designated as an after hours watering hole sponsored by some firm or group. This room is called the Cave of the Winds because many windy stories will be told during an evening of quaffing a few beers.

Near midnight, the Cave of the Winds becomes "Can You Top This?" The tales normally begin as "war stories" becoming louder and funnier until it is difficult to separate fact from fiction.

The lawyer has visited the Cave of the Winds and enjoyed the stories told by fellow members of the bar. Should there be a lull, or should the lawyer be asked to share an experience, the stories included here are the tales he enjoys sharing with his comrades. Each story is a true account of an actual situation. The individuals are real and the events happened exactly as articulated in this book. Most of the stories are public record. Only the names and addresses have been changed to protect the guilty.

In addition, the reader might pick up a nugget that can be used in the next trial.

The lawyer is an Alabama lawyer practicing in Fort Payne, Alabama, a small town, located in a lush valley, in the Appalachian foot hills between Lookout Mountain and Sand Mountain.

Most of the events described here involve people from the great Cumberland Plateau, or Sand Mountain. These hearty folk become involved in some hilarious events which are usually directed in accordance with their local view of reality. For the people in these stories "town," or Chattanooga, Tennessee, is less than 25 miles away. They live in the northeast corner of Alabama where it joins the southeast corner of Tennessee and the northwest corner of Georgia.

Historically, the people of the north end's ancestors were part of the people who seceded from Alabama and Georgia during the Civil War and remained loyal to the Union. They called it a rich man's war and a poor man's fight. After the war, the folks returned to the occupation most of them knew best, making white whiskey and selling it in town. These stories involve some of their great grand children.

A debt of gratitude is due Bob Stetson of the Greater Boston Area. Without his guidance, this work would have never seen print.

Sincere thanks to Cindi Brown, intrepid Court Reporter of the 9th Judicial Circuit of Alabama for the final edit of the book.

Cindi's mother, Fay Freeman, was the secretary to the Lawyer for more than 21 years. She lived through many of the experiences recounted in this book. Cindi and her sister, Lisa, grew up in the Lawyer's office. Her experiences there may have influenced her occupation. Her work was exhausting as the gramatic and auto word created more problems than they solved.

Thanks, Cindi!

Robert B. French, Jr.
Fort Payne, Alabama
March 10, 2014

WORTH EVERY DIME

The year was 1965 and the Alabama Legislature had passed the Wallace-Cater Act. This bill provided that local political subdivisions, such as cities and towns, could organize a Local Development Corporation (LDC) and float tax free municipal bonds to develop industrial plants. Towns and villages across Alabama organized the local corporations and commenced to attempt to lure industries from up north.

The small town where the lawyer practiced organized an LDC that spawned an Industrial Development Board (IDB) appointed by the president of the LDC, who was the Mayor, of course. His Honor appointed to the board a local fuel oil distributor, a couple of retailers, the owners of two hosiery mills, a steel joist manufacturer, himself the Mayor, the city attorney and an insurance agent. In all, nine members were appointed with five present being a quorum required to do business.

The group composed a full color, slick paper, prospectus extolling the virtues of Northeast Alabama and the City in particular. The brochure contained demographics of the working and trade populations, and all kinds of colorful charts and graphs. The latter were put together by some local high school teachers who had studied report writing at Jacksonville State Teacher's College.

In February of that year, dead of winter up north, they made a mass mailing to about five hundred industries located across the rust belt with individual cover letters and wording adapted for the particular manufacturer.

They told each prospect that if it would re-locate in Northeast Alabama, the LDC would build a plant to the prospect's specifications; lease the building to the prospect for 20 years at a low monthly payments; and at the end of that time sell the building to the industry for one dollar.

The idea behind Wallace-Cater was that the plant would be built; the funding would be realized through tax free municipal bonds; monthly lease payments would retire the bonds in 20 years; and the industry would receive the plant that it had paid for at the end of the term. The industry got tax breaks from the monthly lease payments and catching a smaller tax due when the industrial plant was transferred from the LDC to the lessee-industry for $1.00. In the interim, there would jobs, jobs and more jobs for the locals, as well as a prosperous economy for second and third tier suppliers trading with the industry. It was a win-win deal for everyone involved.

It turned out to be particularly attractive to snow bound, union burdened mid-western industries. These plants were old, upkeep on them was through the roof, pensioners were all over the community, while unions continued to raise wages and benefits until the plant owners could barely survive. Now on the southern horizon was a new almost free plant, new machinery, and very willing non-union employees, making up a very young work force. Plus, the owners and managers were no longer shackled to being the chosen frozen of the north.

The IDB received an almost overwhelming response to its mass mailing. It almost effortlessly landed a Van Heusen shirt factory, 250 jobs, and a lighting ballast manufacturing facility - 300 jobs. Construction was begun on both plants.

Dozens of plant industrial site location committees were asking to come to town to visit with Industrial Development Board. Some wanted to meet with the LDC. Both entities had interlocking directors and members. So it worked out well.

Right after July 4th, a third tier auto manufacturing company sent a delegation down from Pontiac, Michigan. This plant would fabricate framing and springs for automobile seats. Like the first two plants, this was a clean industry extruding wire through a heat process and forming it into springs. The framing for the springs was nothing more than a stamping and forming process. The plant was projected to employ 400 local workers. Should the owners be satisfied with the operation, there were possibilities for expansion to include welding.

With the advent of this three man committee arriving in town, the local boys did their usual. They had individual rooms for each representative at Black's Motel, the newest, and most modern third motel in town. Reeves and Mountain View were the other motels, but they were small, older, and located on Old US HWY 11, south of town. Black's was in the center of everything. It had a restaurant and a large conference room that the locals used for their power point presentations, complete with slides, films, handouts and posters.

Following the procedure employed with the first two delegations, the locals had dinner ready when their guests arrived in their rental car from the Chattanooga Air Port. After the preliminary pleasantries the visitors were shown to their rooms on the ground floor of the U shaped two floor motel that had 60 units. The office, registration, restaurant and conference room were in the building in the center of the U facing the main street. Two stories of 20 rooms made up the equal legged U with a swimming pool toward the back.

The conference room had been set up as a dining room for dinner. The very attractive waitresses came in to take orders. The guests all ordered the 14 oz. Porterhouse steak. Then it happened.

The heavyset, red faced, graying owner of the plant said, "And young lady, I'll have a double Jack Black on the rocks before dinner."

"Make that two," said his plant manager seated next to him.

"Make that three," chimed in the production superintendent.

The five locals all did a sucking sound in unison as the waitress said, "What is that? I've never had that order before." She looked thoroughly perplexed.

The owner guffawed, "Why that's liquor, little lady. Pure de ole Tennessee sipping whiskey. Don't you have that in your bar?"

The waitress looked at the Mayor for help. As usual, his Honor rose to the occasion. "Gentlemen, let me apologize. We're in a dry county here and we don't have whiskey nor beer. I'm sorry."

"So am I," said the old guy. "I think I can tell you this is going to be a short meeting. I'm sure as hell not moving to a place where I can't have a drink."

The room became tense. The Mayor continued, "Oh, don't worry about that. It's perfectly legal in your own home. You just can't buy it here. We have to buy it in Gadsden, 34 miles from here, or bring it in from Tennessee which is really illegal." Then hurriedly thinking ahead, like the old WWII veteran he was, the Mayor continued, "Just order up some iced tea and I'll have a bottle of Jack Black here before your steak arrives."

This seemed to allow the visitors to loosen up a little, but it was clear the old guy was not a happy camper. Still, getting rid of that damned union in his plant was worth almost any sacrifice. He hated the chief steward who was onto his people every day about something. Always bitching, trying to be important. He cursed under his breath when he thought of the steward.

The Mayor excused himself and went to the front of the motel where he had a policeman waiting in a patrol car just in case he was needed. "Barnes, go up to my house and tell Cynthia Ann to send down the largest bottle of Jack Daniels Black Label, Old No. 7, that I have in the liquor cabinet. I think I have a gallon jug up there. It may be a half gallon or a liter, what the hell, it's a big bottle that hasn't been opened if my son has stayed out of it. And hurry! Use your siren!" He knew that would take care of business, all the cops loved to use their sirens. He returned to the meeting and placed his order. He had the salmon on a cedar shingle.

Sure enough, by the time the food was being served, Barnes was back with the Jack

Black. The Mayor poured a round for all present and the evening became more mellow.

After dinner the dishes were taken away and the men sat back and relaxed as the men from Pontiac described their operation and talked about what the city could do for them. Fortunately, the Mayor had thought to have a box of cigars available and everyone enjoyed an Arturo Fuentes with their whiskey.

The evening dragged on until almost midnight. The Mayor told the visitors that breakfast would be served for them at 8:30 A.M. Then, they would look at some data and take a trip around the area to see the sights and meet some of the local manufacturers.

The owner of the plant kinda wrinkled his face as he said to the Mayor, "Now you don't have whiskey nor beer in this town. I suppose you are going to tell me you don't have any ladies of the evening either. You know, escorts?"

The Mayor tried to laugh it off. "No, we don't have any evening companions that openly practices their trade here. Truth be known, I'm sure we have plenty of whores. Unfortunately, this trip I'm going to have to leave you high and dry. If you'll come back, I'm sure we can take care of that need as well."

"That's what I thought," responded the boss. "Maybe we'll be back and maybe we won't.

Anyway, good night." He went to his room grumpy.

The locals returned to the conference room in the middle of the U for an evaluation meeting.

"Okay, boys, we've learned something here tonight," the Mayor began. "From now on, when we bring these Damned Yankees in here, trying to steal their industries, we have to have liquor, beer and women. Anybody got any ideas? Shit! Next we're gonna have a group coming in here wanting to gamble."

A local dry goods merchant spoke up, "Mayor, I think we ought to talk with Pete, who owns this motel, and make arrangements for us to have a bar in here - hidden - strictly private of course. Then, we can go to Gadsden, buy several kinds of liquor and beer and store it here for our guests. Then we won't get cought with our pants down again."

Everyone agreed that was a good idea and knowing how civic minded Pete was, there was no doubt the Industrial Development Board would have a fine bar for the next bunch of Northerners that came to town.

"What about the girls?" the oil man asked. "I think we ought to look into some entertainment for these gentlemen who have traveled far. If we don't, some other group will, and we will lose jobs for our people and wealth for our economy."

"Anybody got any ideas about that?" the Mayor asked. "We just don't have any ladies of the night, who'll admit they are so inclined, here in town."

A sock mogul spoke up. "I know a guy on the North end of Sand Mountain, right above Trenton, Georgia, who has connections in Chattanooga. He might be able to persuade some of the escorts up there to come down here and take care of business for us."

"Talk to him and see what you can do," the Mayor instructed. And with that, the meeting was adjourned.

The following day everything went backward for the town. The men from Pontiac slept in, breakfast was cold, the weather was bad, the men were in a bad humor, and things never seemed to get in gear the whole day. The men spent another uneventful night at the motel and left for home on Sunday morning. The older fellow, the boss, barely said good bye.

On Monday, the Mayor visited the hosiery mill of the sock mogul. "When are you going to talk with this fellow on the north end? We have another delegation coming in Friday from Wisconsin. This time we're talking heavy duty equipment. These people make conveyor belts and materials elevators."

"I'll call him right now." The sock guy looked through his card-ex. "Here he is, Harvey Steat," he said as he began dialing.

After the usual salutations, the sock mogul got right down to business. "Say Harvey, we might have a need for some of your services. We are trying to lure manufacturing plants into our area and we need some girls for our visiting firemen. Can you help with such a request?"

After being assured that Harvey could handle it, the sock man said, "Well, according to the Mayor, we're going to need at least five escorts beginning Friday night for dinner and continuing until Sunday morning. They're gonna have to be willing to do whatever."

After some questioning about details, Harvey said, "Okay, if I understand it correctly, these girls are supposed to be beautiful, well mannered, appear for dinner, satisfy your guests Friday night, play along on Saturday during the day, do a repeat performance Saturday night, and leave town on Monday morning?"

"You got it."

"Okay, then here's what I need. I'll need two double rooms for the girls. They can sleep together if any of them are left in the room, but they'll need a headquarters to dress in, bathe, go to the bathroom and such. Then, each man will need a room of his own for privacy. The girl's expenses will be picked up by your board, plus, you will pay me $500 in advance per night for each girl's performance. I'll need my payment on Friday evening when I bring the girls down. Cash is preferred."

"That's awfully high," the sock manufacturer responded. "I don't know whether I can swing that or not."

"Hey," Harvey replied, "You want beauty, you want youth, you want anything goes, you gotta pay for it."

"Well, go ahead and line it up, but understand I have to clear this with higher ups. You're talking $5,000 for this weekend, plus expenses."

"Let me know," Harvey responded. "It isn't that easy to put five good looking young ladies together on this short a notice."

The Mayor only heard one end of the conversation, but he got the picture. "Damned! That's highway robbery!" he said to the sock man.

"I know it, but what are we going to do? The board thinks we lost the spring prospect because we didn't have girls on hand. I sure don't know anyone else to ask and I wouldn't want to ask anyone else. Hell, I feel like a damned pimp just being in this crap."

"Look, you're doing it for the town. You're doing it for jobs and commerce. You know, sometimes we just have to do what we gotta do. Call the son-uva-bitch back and tell him we'll pay, but he better bring quality girls. I'll find the five G's somewhere. Then, we'll tack it on the next bond issue and recover it. I'll put it back wherever I have to borrow it and no one will be any the wiser."

Harvey assured the sock mogul that his board and guests would be very happy with the ladies he would bring to visit. He hung up not having any idea where he would fine five available young women who would fit the bill of expensive call girls. He hurriedly called his nephew Ernie Brock.

"Nephew, I have a deal working down in the valley in Alabama. The Industrial Development Board needs five whores this weekend. Can you help with that?"

"Wherein the hell am I going to find five twats?" Ernie queried. "The only whores I know are Holley and Cherry who hang out at Bud's Bar in town turning tricks for whatever they can get, sometimes just drinks. They're old and worn out. You wouldn't let your dog poke 'em. Shit, I don't know no women. I been married 17 year." Historically, folks on Sand Mountain never put an "s" on year, pound or dollar.

"Well you gotta step up. I committed to this and they're willin to pay each girl $400 a night. That's $800 for each whore for the weekend. I figured we would give the girls $600 each and you and I would walk off with a bill apiece. We'd make five hundred dollar each while the girls were getting expenses and $600. That's good money for sitting on your ass and doing nothing. Now, find me five good looking girls to make this thing work."

"I'm tellin you Unk, that's great money, I want in on the deal, but I don't know no whores. If you wanted guns, ammo, booze, even dynamite, I could step up, but where'm I gonna find five whores?"

"Shit! I don't know," Harvey said in exasperation. "Let me think about it and call you back."

"Call me back. Don't cut me out!" Brock replied, little knowing his uncle had already short changed him out of $100 for each girl each night for a total of $1,000. Now, he was persuading his nephew to do his work for him.

Thirty minutes later, Harvey called back. "Hey look here Ernie, I been thinkin. If we can't find whores anywhere else, what about you recruiting some of our relatives? I got some beautiful nieces, your cousins. There's Lou Ann, she's just 18 and pretty as a speckled pup. Then, there's Janet Kay, she's a little older, but good looking as they come. Then, there's the twins, Cindy Sue and Lindy Lou, they're seniors in high school, but they could pass for 18. Finally, there's Rachel Ray. She's 19 and just got her first job..." He paused mid sentence.

"They's our kin people, Harvey!" Ernie raised his voice. "Our kin ain't nobody's whore."

"Ernie, they's our relatives for sure. Hell, I'm all of their uncle. That's why I can't ask 'em to do it. You're a cousin. Cousin's are like that. Cousins are expected to do things like this with their cousins. Lookey here, theys not a girl among them that don't need the money. This is big money. Further, they's not a one of them that'll turn you down when you ask them. I'll guarantee it. I mean, shit, all they got to do is look good, eat some great food, drink some good whiskey, and spread 'em for some drunk industrialist from up north who probably can't get it up anyway. That beats the hell out of spreadin 'em for nothing on Saturday night for some hillbilly who ain't done shit. Give 'em nothin more'n a beer and a cigarette in the front seat of his old worn out pickup truck."

"Well, now you do make sense," Ernie said thoughtfully. "Plus, if they're throwin around money like that, weuns ought to get in on it. I mean, the family can use the money." He paused, "I'll drive over to Aunt Hattie's and see the twins first. They're wild as hell and will convince the others to go for it."

"Call me as soon as you know something."

Brock waited a few hours for school to let out and the school bus to run. Then, he remembered that it was summer and the twins had graduated. "Shit!" He wanted to kick himself in the butt. He ran out and got into his old faded dinged up blue Ford pickup and drove over to his aunt's house. The twins had just arrived home from a shopping trip in town. They were putting their purchases away, going to the bathroom, and generally trying to relax after a day of walking in and out of stores in Chattanooga. Their mother Hattie was still at work at the rug mill in Trenton and their father James was working at the steel plant in town. On the north end, Chattanooga was always referred to as "town."

Ernie walked into the house and knocked on the living room wall inside the door, "Anybody to home?"

"We're here," one of the twins answered, "I'll be right out."

Brock heard the commode flush and Cindy Sue came out, buttoning the top button of her jeans. She was wearing a soft cloth top that made a semi-circle around here neck. Her long blond hair was cascading down on her shoulders. All Steats were blonde. Ernie's mother said it came from their German heritage. The young girl had high cheek bones, a beautifully formed mouth where her lip stick had stopped working, and the bluest eyes Brock had ever seen. Her 5'9" body would stop a clock and her ample breasts indicated that she had been around the block more than once.

Brock had never really noticed his younger cousin before. Now he could not help but think how beautiful she was in flip flops with painted toenails without even trying. Then just think, he never could tell them apart. Glorioski! Her sister looked just like her. Gold strike!

"What brings you over to our digs, Cuz?" the lithesome girl asked smiling.

"I want to talk some serious business with you and your sister," Brock replied. "I may have an offer you can't refuse with some big bucks in it for youins."

"Lindy Lou, Cousin Ernie is out here wanting to talk to us," the twin yelled to her sister somewhere in the bowels of the house.

Within a matter of seconds, the other gorgeous twin emerged into the room dressed similarly to her sister only with jeans and a Georgia Bull Dog sweat shirt. "What's going on, Cuz?" The twin asked.

"Both of you set down. I want to talk with you about making some dough."

One girl sat in a brown leatherette recliner while the other sat on a beige couch. Both sat up straight as it was unusual for them to see their cousin anywhere other than a family gathering. They were young, beautiful and attentive.

Brock cleared his throat, "I don't really know how to begin. So, I'll just begin. Down there in Alabama, in the Valley, Fort Payne, youins familiar with that town?"

Almost in unison the twins answered, "Yes."

"Okay. They've got an Industrial Development Board down there that is tryin to lure industry from up north down there for the jobs. Did you hear about them gettin Van Heusen shirt factory and the flourescent light ballast plant?"

Cindy Sue responded for the two of them. "I heard they were hiring for some new jobs down there, but I didn't know what kind of plants they had."

"Me neither," her twin joined in.

"Okay, well they are bringing in these delegations from plants up north to tour the area, visit other plants and listen to presentations about the advantages about coming down south - probably cheap labor and no labor unions." He paused to make sure they understood what he was talking about. They did.

"Now these men who come down here are wined and dined and treated like royalty because they mean jobs. All these men are fairly well off, some rich, and clean industrial boss types. You know what I mean?"

They nodded that they knew and it was obvious they were wondering where he was going with the conversation.

"Well these men need to be entertained. That means female companionship. So this committee would like to hire some young women, girls, like yourselves, to come down and wine and dine with these men and entertain them"

"How we going to entertain them?" Lindy Lou asked. "We don't play any instruments or sing. We hardly know how to dance."

"Well, it's just companionship. You know, just being there, talking, visiting, like an escort service."

"You mean you want us to be like sluts?" One of the twins frowned.

"No, it's not like that. Now you might be with a man you like and you might show him a favor or two, but that is not a requirement of the job. You would just be with one man for two nights and you would be paid $600, plus food and drink. Am I making myself clear?"

"That's a lot of money," Cindy Sue responded. "For that kind of money they are going to expect us to put out."

"Well, like I say, it might lead to that."

"Hell, for $300 a throw, I'll put out every night," Lindy Lou chuckled. "I don't care who it is. But, what are we going to tell maw and paw?"

"You gone to spend the night with some of your friends, you takin a trip to Gatlinburg. Or, you'll come up with something. What'd you think about it?"

Lindy Lou paused for a moment and looked at her sister. It seemed they communicated with each other silently. "Whose going to protect us if something goes wrong?"

"Either I'll be there or your Uncle Harvey will be there."

"You could have gone all day without mentioning good ole Unk. Now we know we're being screwed and we haven't even met the Johns yet," Cindy Sue was back in the conversation. "You can count us in for at least one try, but you are responsible for our money and safety, not Unk."

Ernie had to admire their youthful knowledge. They were barely out of high school and already knew what a crook their uncle was.

"I'll be there and I'll take care of things. I will see that you are paid in advance. Or, I'll hold your money if you think you might misplace it. Irregardless, you can count on me to take care of business."

"What's Harvey paying you?" Cindy Sue asked.

"He's giving me $100 a night to take care of things," he lied.

"Okay, Cuz, when do we start making the big bucks?" Lindy Lou asked.

"This Friday evening at 4:30 slow time. But I'm going to have to get back with you on where we'll get together, how you'll dress and so on. Do you girls have evening clothes like for going out to eat in town?"

"Yeah, we've got Sunday dresses and high heel shoes, if you mean that," Cindy Sue said.

"That's what we'll need, but I'll get to that later. Right now, I want to ask you to do me a favor. We need three more girls because five guys are coming in Friday. Do you think you might talk to Lou Ann, Janet Kay and Rachel Ray? They can hire on at the same price?"

Cindy Sue thought for a moment, she put her forefinger to her right cheek. "Yeah, we might can recruit our cousins to get in on it with us, but it will cost you and dear ole Unk twenty bucks a pop paid directly to us for each of the girls each night."

"That's an extra $120 each. Why that's highway robbery," Ernie pretended to be shocked. "You people act like you have Steat blood in your veins," he grinned. "We'll come up with $10 a pop. You have to cut your cousins for the other $10."

"Deal!" The twins said in unison and stood up grinning and shook hands with their cousin.

Ernie noticed how soft their hands were. "I'll be in touch," he said as he began to leave the living room of the simple house.

In a little over two hours, Cindy Sue called and told Ernie that the other girls were on board. He called Harvey and found him at home. "Okay, I have the relatives agreement to go with the deal. I'll be right over to discuss it."

Harvey lived at the beginning of the drive way leading to the homes of Ernie Brock and his mother and father, a little over a thousand feet away. Harvey was on the pavement while Ernie had to constantly repair his driveway that washed out every winter. Although he passed his uncle's house two or three times a day, they didn't visit often. Ernie said that every time he saw his uncle, it cost him money. Brock was going this time because it was important – real money was involved.

Ernie knocked on the door of Harvey's new home, a white brick ranch style that he called the palace. He was ushered into a spacious living room complete with decorations and fine furnishings from Town and Country in town.

"All right,"

Ernie began. "Here's where we are. I have all five girls ready to go. The twins made me agree to give each of them $10 off of the other three girl's takins that we're gettin, and they are going to cut the other three girls for another ten spot. So, you got to kick in $5 and I'll kick in $5."

"Damned! What crooks," Harvey exclaimed. "You'd think they was Goddamned Steats or something. There ain't enough in it to give them more." He stood up and paced the floor.

"They's your nieces and it was the only way I could make it fly. I mean, they ain't whores, but they're willin to take it on their backs to make this money."

"Okay," Harvey said resigned to the foot he had been cut for a little more. "Did you ask them about Sunday dress up clothes?"

"Yeah, I covered that. We want them to look like those Saturday night girls in town out on a date. I'm going to get back with them and have each of them bring some short shorts, revealing tops, bathing suits for swimming, jeans, walking shoes and nighties. Anything else you think they'll need?"

"Nah. I'll drive 'em down in my station wagon, stay in a separate room, out of sight for the weekend, and bring them back."

"Okay. I'll tell them to be over here at your house at say 3:30 fast time on Friday. That'll be 2:30 in Alabama giving you plenty of time to check them out and drive them down there and get them set up in their room before the Johns, er, guests are ready for them."

"Sounds good to me. I'll call my contact and tell him it is a done deal."

"One thing," Ernie looked his uncle dead in the eye with his good eye. "When do I get my money?"

Harvey looked insulted. It was an act he had practiced for years and didn't impress Ernie at all. "Can't you trust me to give you your money on Tuesday after the deal goes down?"

"Hit ain't a matter of trust," Ernie said with all sincerity. "Hit's a matter of money and I'll take mine right after you bring the relatives down there. I'll follow you down."

"Shit! You don't trust nobody, not even your own flesh and blood," Harvey snorted.

"Deal or fold," Ernie said looking at Harvey again with his good right eye. He had lost his left eye when he was struck by lightening at age eight. The eye looked a little to the left and he could not see out of it, but it was passable.

"You know you ought be ashamed," Harvey paused. "But I'm a bigger man than that. I'll give you your money when I'm paid."

"I want the girl's money too," Ernie said in all seriousness. "I'm gettin them into this and I'm makin damned sure they're gettin what's coming to them. I ain't gonna hear it the rest of my life that I took them to do some screwing and I screwed them."

Harvey acted shocked. "I was going to pay them myself. I wouldn't take no money myself if I had to cheat my beautiful nieces out of their part."

"You pay me for them, then we'll all know they got paid."

"I'm really hurt the way you're actin," Harvey tried a last resort.

"Youins will git over hit. Deal or Fold."

"Deal."

On Friday afternoon five gorgeous young women, dressed in high heels and their Sunday best, arrived at their uncle's house. Ernie and Harvey had them stand on the front steps for a picture. "You are the best looking young ladies I have personally ever seen," Harvey gushed. "As ugly as I am, I can't believe I'm kin to you all."

The girls giggled and posed. They did look good - all young, tall, blonde and very well built. Plus, Ernie thought, "They's well dressed and clean."

After Harvey called his contact with the Industrial Development Board to be sure everything was going as scheduled, they loaded up in Harvey's blue Buick station wagon and, with Ernie right behind in his truck, the caravan headed for Black's Motel and an adventure.

Arriving at the motel, Harvey pulled into the north side of the U. Black's faced East. Soon, Pete Gilliland, the owner came out and motioned for Harvey to pull up to the unit next to the end. He opened the room with a key while the girls were getting out of the station wagon. Harvey was soon at the door with the owner.

"Let's see now, you have three rooms for us, don'tcha? That's two for the ladies and one for me."

"The board said two rooms, but if three is what it takes, here's two more keys." He looked at the girls. They were so beautiful and colorful that they reminded him of a lovely flower arrangement. "Mercy! You ladies are beautiful. I didn't expect anything like this."

The girls giggled and tried to blush. "We're just working people," Cindy Sue smiled.

"I'll bet you are," Pete responded. He turned to Harvey who was busy opening room #2. "Mr. Steat, I think the Mayor and the others will be well pleased."

Harvey looked back and smiled. "Weuns will stay here until we are needed. Tell Mr. Hale, from the hosiery mill, that I'm here with the ladies and I'm waiting for him." In other words, bring my money or there is no action.

"I'll do it." Then turning again to the girls holding their bags to enter room #1, "If you girls need anything, and I mean anything, just call upon me. Don't talk to the desk clerk nor anyone else. You just call upon me. And, don't hesitate to use the pool." He could just visualize the five in bikinis.

Then following the first three girls into the first room, "I hope these accommodations are okay for you ladies."

The twins looked the room over, Lindy Lou looked into the dressing room and bath, then back to the two double beds, "It looks fine to me," she sparkled. "Un huns," and "me toos," came from the other girls in the room.

"We'll let you ladies rest a while, Harvey said following Pete, the owner, out and pulling the door shut behind him. The other two girls had already closed their door. Door to #3 was Harvey's room and it was cracked.

"What'd you think?" Harvey asked the owner.

"Oh, I think the board will be more than satisfied. I know that the visitors aren't expecting anything like this. These ladies are really unbelievable. They could be models. You are going to have to fight the board to keep the members out of the merchandise." He laughed, but Harvey could tell he really meant it.

The Mayor and sock mogul showed up and knocked on Harvey's door. Harvey let them in. "Come right in, gentlemen. This here fellow is my nephew and assistant, Ernie Brock." Hand shakes and greetings were exchanged.

The Mayor began, "I understand you have produced some lovely ladies to help our fair city lure some more jobs and commerce to Fort Payne."

"We have done what we was supposed to do. Only we done it very well," Harvey replied. "You simply call my room when you are ready for the parade of the goodies. I will have them come in through the back door Pete showed me, down the hall and right into the conference room. Each of them will stay behind the door until their name is called. I understand you will have seats for them to eat at and all."

"We will have their seating arrangements made when we call you. Now I understand, and I have written down their names, Cindy Sue, Lindy Lou, Rachel Ray, Lou Ann and Janet Kay. Is that right?"

"That's them," Ernie responded.

"Okay, now we need to pay the freight I suppose," said the Mayor. Harvey nodded in the affirmative. "Well, I have brought it in cash. We agree that we don't want to involve paper in this transaction. Here, count it out, fifty crisp one hundred dollar bills." He handed it over to Harvey who immediately counted it.

It was all there and the townsmen left. As soon as they closed the door, "You rotten son-uva-bitch," snarled Ernie. "You cut the deck for a bill off each wad and didn't put me in."

"Hey, did I tell you to do the deal you made? You played your hand and I called. You played with the girls and they called. What's wrong? Everything is fair and honest."

"Well, I still feel like me and the girls, we been screwed."

"You'ins can still back out. I'll give all the money back and we'uns will go back to Sand Mountain. Tit for tat. We'uns will all be back where we were before the deal went down."

Ernie would like to have called his uncle's bluff and cut the deal a little closer, but he didn't have the courage. "The rotten old son of a-bitch might just call my hand and the whole thing might fall through," he thought. "Then the girls would have got dressed up for nothing, bought some new shoes and things for nothing, and I'll get nothing. Something is better than nothing."

He spoke, "Okay, you got me again. Something is better'n nothin. Plus, I did make a deal with you with my eyes open knowing that you'd cut the deck your way somewhere. I just couldn't figure out where because there is so much money involved. I ain't happy, but I'm here."

"Good. It's settled. I brought a bottle of Jim Beam. Let's have a drink and wait for the phone call. Put something on the TV."

The five member delegation from Wisconsin manufactured some heavy parts for off-the-road equipment, as well as building conveyor belts and elevator systems for mining and road building operations. This was a big deal. If their plant moved into the area, it would employ over 1,000 highly paid workers. They would usually belong to the United Automobile Workers demanding more than $30 an hour, but in Northeast Alabama there would be no union and the wages would be considerably less, plus the benefit package would be lower. Still, in 1965 dollars, the money would spur the economy no matter the wages - 1,000 jobs. Unbelievable! The Industrial Development Board had put a full-court press on persuading the company just to look at Northeast Alabama.

The visitors had checked into their individual single rooms about mid-afternoon. The rooms were already cool, and flower arrangements from Judy's Flower Shop were on a table sweetly refreshing each room.

The Mayor and board welcomed the men and showed them their accommodations. Drink preferences were made and a bottle of scotch, vodka, bourbon, tequila, or whatever was delivered to the guest's room together with preferred mixes, ice, etc. The board acted as though the town sold liquor by the drink.

The Mayor told the visitors to change into something comfortable and relax. Dinner would be served promptly at six. Their own private happy hour would begin at five. This time was set aside as a mixer for the locals to get to know their guests and vice-versa.

At about fifteen until five, the locals gathered in the conference room which now was laid out for dining. A variety of bottles and mixes were on a bar-like credenza next to the west wall.

The Mayor addressed the board. "Gentlemen, we have some fantastic opportunities for our hometown tonight. If we can land this plant, I don't care whether we get another one or not. This plant will require all kinds of suppliers - nuts and bolts - lock nuts - stampings - forgings - weaving - the works. Gentlemen, this is a home run if we can persuade this group to relocate a plant here. Our little area will blossom and bloom like a fruit tree if we can do our job."

"Now, we've spared no expense. We're going to wine and dine them like they have never been fed before. We are going to liquor them up, and then we are going to provide them with a dinner companion that they will never forget.

"So, when we start the cocktail hour, go light on the booze. Keep a clear mind. See what we need to do to win each man. Sell our area, and I mean sell, sell, sell."

The locals visited with each other for another few minutes and then pretended to drink when the guests arrived.

The locals could see that their guests were hard core, no funny business, industrialists. The leader of the group was the Executive Vice President of the corporation. He was allowed to lead because the Chairman of the Board of Directors didn't want any responsibility on the trip. The Director of Marketing and two General Foremen were brought along for whatever input they might give.

The Chairman of the Board was in his early sixties. He had been with the company 37 years and had guided its growth as president for 19 years. He was now watching the fruits of his labor pay off for the stockholders, management and the employees working on the floor of the plant. His interest in moving south was the same as everyone else in manufacturing in the Mid-West, getting rid of the union, the United Auto Workers, who were strangling the company with its work rules, pension plans, insurance and wage demands. Finally, net profits were bordering around 6% of gross. That was less than banks were charging interest on loans. It was truly a bad situation.

The Executive Vice President was the chief operating officer of the day-to-day operations of the business. He was in his forties and wanted nothing more than to match the accomplishments of his predecessor. In order to do this, he had to reduce overhead and that was not going to happen in Wisconsin.

The Director of Marketing really didn't know why he had been included in the trip, other than the fact he was a native of the state and had graduated from the University of Alabama School of Commerce and Business Administration. He directed a force of twelve salesmen with offices scattered throughout the U.S. They competed well in the conveyor and elevator business. However, the Japanese were giving them trouble keeping some of their customers who made off-the-road equipment. Still, his company was leading the field and his sales surpassed anything the company had done in the past. Each year was better than the year before. He was quite proud of his efforts. However, he too was well aware of the fading bottom line.

The General Foremen were supervisors in the plant. Each of them managed about 200 employees with three to four foremen under them. There were two other General Foremen who had not been invited on the trip. "Somebody has to watch the store," the Executive Vice President said as he announced the trip at the regular Monday morning staff meeting.

Pete had assigned his best two waitresses to service the group. One of the girls served as bartender. Soon the booze was flowing and everyone lightened up a bit. The local board members each cornered a visitor and discussed their problems as they saw them in Wisconsin. They also extolled the advantages of Northeast Alabama. Their primary selling point was that there were 17 hosiery mills, three steel fabricating plants, and a furniture manufacturer, all within a mile of the motel, and none of them were unionized. Their workforce was in their late twenties and early thirties. There was not a smoke stack in the county.

They bragged about the school system being among the top five in the state; the rate of college attendance from the school; the town's proximity to Atlanta, Birmingham, Huntsville and Chattanooga; the airport; and the fact that Interstate 59 was brand new and had just recently opened for traffic all the way to New Orleans. They talked about these things knowing that the power point presentation coming in the morning would hammer the points home.

Then the Mayor pecked on an empty glass with a knife to get everyone's attention. The room became quiet. "Gentlemen, what is a party like this with just a bunch of ole hard-tailed businessmen? As a treat, the Industrial Development Board has provided for your enjoyment some beautiful ladies to enjoy dinner with you." Then he lowered his voice, "Or anything else you might care to enjoy with the ladies."

"I have put each of the ladies' names in this hat of mine. I want each of you to draw out a name, and that lady will enjoy dinner with you. We've done this to keep from discussing business until we have worn you out. Okay, Mr. Massey, the oldest and most important man in the room, you draw first."

The Chairman of the Board was laughing; in fact, all of the visitors were laughing; they didn't know what was going to happen; but they were going to go along with it.

The Mayor held his fedora high above his head. Mr. Massey reached up into the hat and took a slip. He handed the small folded name to the Mayor.

The Mayor unfolded the slip of paper, "Cindy Sue," he called out.

The door opened and into the room stepped a vision of loveliness. The twin was wearing a very red short dress with a large belt that highlighted her full breasts which appeared to be pressing against the fabric to escape the low-cut collar and bra that were restraining them. She wore matching red high heels with a small red bow in her ample flowing blonde hair. Her lipstick matched her dress.

Mr. Massey, being the gentleman he was, stepped forward, offering his right arm, "I'm Howard Massey, Cindy Sue. What can I get for you to drink?" He guided her toward the bar in the rear of the room, which was actually near the door from which she had emerged.

There were smiles and comments all around. Cindy Sue was without a doubt the most beautiful woman any of the men had ever been that close to in person. She mixed right in smiling, smalltalking, the works. Mr. Massey was beaming. He thought it was a great gag.

"All right," the Mayor announced. "We are ready to proceed with Mr. Beamler, Executive Vice President. Please draw." He held the hat high once more.

The CEO was certainly going along if Massey was as happy as he appeared. He drew and handed the slip to the Mayor.

"Lou Ann," the Mayor said in a loud voice.

The door opened and out stepped a very tall blonde young woman dressed in a navy blue pant suit highlighted by blue high heels. The jacket was cut away and she was wearing a light blue silk blouse with a low neckline. She has a large broach on her left side and a gold and green insignia over her left pocket. She appeared to be dripping in diamonds - a sparking neckless that contained numerous jewels flowing down across her chest. Her earrings matched in three flowing strands. She wore a one-inch bracelet on her right arm that also appeared to be diamonds. Of course, all of it was costume jewelry, but on Lou Ann, it was stunning.

Beamler stepped forward, and following Mr. Massey's lead, offered Lou Ann his arm and asked for her drink order. As soon as she had her margarita, Lou Ann was introduced all around as Cindy Sue had been.

"All right, Mr. Director of Marketing - a good old Bama boy - Roll Tide! It's your turn."

Phil Semmes, originally from Mobile, Alabama, reached high into the hat and pulled out a slip that he handed to the Mayor.

"Rachel Rae," the Mayor called out.

Rachel stepped into the room in a completely black outfit - short black mini-skirt party dress, strapless, black puffy sleeves, black high heels, black patten leather belt, a small black ribbon in her long flowing blonde hair set off with turquoise jewelry all around. She appeared to be a gorgeous, seductive, alluring witch. She had a great smile highlighted with black lipstick. The first two girls were beautiful, but Rachel Rae was more than that, she was flat-out hot.

Semmes went forward, offered his arm, solicited a drink order, and they began to mix with the others. The ladies were absolutely giddy relishing the manner in which they were being received.

Bob Young whispered to Sam Hedgepeth, "I wonder what they have in store for us working stiffs? Bet we don't get anything like what we've seen so far."

"Who knows?" Sam responded. "We're about to find out."

"Okay, Bob, it's your turn. Pull a name out of the hat."

"Janet Kay," the Mayor announced.

Now a more mature woman stepped into the room. Like the others, Janet Kay was at least

5'9" tall, weighed about 135 lbs and was in her early twenties. Compared to the others, she was an older woman, but it didn't matter. Janet Kay was dressed as a forest nymph in green from head to toe. She wore a green skirt made of various shades of green chiffon interspersed with silk green streamers of different colors flowing down. All of the materials were cut in points of different lengths stopping just above the knee. The blouse was green silk with a large silken shawl of numerous shades of green draped over her shoulders. She too had a plunging neckline and she rustled when she walked in apple green spike heels. Her flaming red lipstick against the green background set her apart from the other girls. She was wearing costume jewelry that looked like jade.

The burly general foreman followed protocol and introduced himself and led her to the bar.

As the hubbub of chatter died down, the Mayor said, "One More, Sam Hedgepeth, you don't have to draw. Your number is foreordained. Lindy Lou, surprise us all!"

And she did! The door opened and the twin was standing there in all her radiant glory. Where Cindy Sue had been adorned in red, Lindy Lou had the same outfit, the same jewelry, shoes, the works, but in brilliant yellow. The men in the room did a double take. They first looked toward Mr. Massey and the girl in red, then back to the carbon copy in yellow. A gasp could almost be heard from the 14 men who were not only surprised, they were also shocked!

Sam stepped forward with a grin as large as he could muster. He was a large man also, a man who had come up through the ranks, and he had a girl exactly like the one of the Chairman of the Board. Unbelievable!

The crowd began to seriously socialize and visit. Smiles were all around. It was not just a cocktail party, this had become an event. The sock mogul sidled over to the Mayor. "I do believe we got our money's worth," he crowed.

"More than our money's worth," the Mayor responded. "After this, if we don't land this plant, we can't land any plant. Look at how happy they are."

Dinner was put on hold for a little more than an hour. Finally, after Pete insisted, because his help had to leave, they were served a fantastic meal. Their choices were Chateaubriand, Steak Dianne, Lobster Thermidor, and Chicken Alfredo.

The meal was served with the choice of wine. After dinner liquor consisted of brandy, B & B, or Grand Marnier.

The tables were cleaned as soft music played. One by one, the board members took their leave after midnight.

Mr. Massey asked Cindy Sue if he could walk her to her room as he was tired. She agreed. He walked her over to the room, profusely thanked her for being a good sport and shook hands with her, "Goodnight."

Cindy Sue went into the room, used the bathroom, freshened up, and went back to the party. By 2:00 a.m., the revelers had all left the conference room. Semmes the marketing manager walked his date to her door, gave her a peck on the cheek and went to his room to bed.

Sam and Lindy Lou walked around the block, "Just to clear our heads from the drinking." He then dropped her by her room.

Bob took the wood nymph to his room for some light conversation away from the crowd. It was not long before they were between the sheets.

Lindy Lou was dropped by the girls' room at a little after 2:30.

Rachel Rae left the room to walk around the motel. She wanted to enjoy the night air. She still appeared to be the seductive witch, lacking only the hat. Semmes came out of his room just as she was walking past. He invited her in. She came back out at 6:30 that morning.

It seemed that some of the guys wanted to play around, but they didn't want the other folks to know they were playing around.

At 9:00 a.m. on Saturday, breakfast was served. All the guys were dressed in casual wear, mostly in jeans. The ladies joined them for breakfast wearing short shorts and revealing tops. A feast of every kind of breakfast food known was laid out in a breakfast bar, serve yourself. Everyone was friendly, the board was back in full force, yet some secret glances and touches went on between the ones who had seen action the night before.

After breakfast, at 10:30 a.m. the ladies excused themselves. The dishes were taken away and the slideshow began. Slides of DeSoto Falls, Little River Canyon, DeSoto State Park, and other scenic wonders were displayed. The demographics were put up in graph form and three different plant owners discussed the advantages of re-locating in Northeast Alabama.

At noon, the party boarded vans for a trip around the area beginning with Sequoia Caverns in the north end of the county and traveling south, visiting scenic sights, until they reached Little River Canyon Mouth Park near Leesburg, Alabama. Sandwich lunch bags had been packed for the entourage. They returned to the motel shortly before 5:00 p.m. The visitors stole glances as the girls in bikinis still playing in the pool.

The Mayor went by Harvey's door, knocked, and went in. "Show time. Get the girls back on the job."

"I hear they did pretty well last night?" Harvey questioned.

"They did. They were all we could ask for and more. You have performed admirably. They don't need to be as formal tonight. Casual attire will be fine, and just send them over by six."

"I'll do it," Harvey replied. He turned to Ernie Brock, "Go get the relatives and tell 'em to get out of the pool. Its time to go back to work."

"Hell, they ought to be ready to get out. They've been squealing and giggling out there all damned day." He left the room.

"All right, Cousins, it's off and on. Off your butts and on the job. Go change into casual clothes and be in the dining room by 6:00 p.m. Stick with the same guy you were with last night."

Promptly at six, the five girls paraded through the back door of the conference room and found their "date" for the evening. Rachel Rae and Janet Kay were almost obvious in their relationship with their guys. Certainly, tonight was going to be a repeat performance of the previous evening.

As the drinks flowed freely, the noise level of the room grew. By now, all the people in the room felt as though they knew each other very well. Phil Semmes left the room to take a phone call in his room. Frank Hale took that opportunity to get to know Rachel Rae a little better.

The whiskey had loosened both of them up a bit. Hale came directly to the point. "I think you are the most beautiful girl here," he complimented.

"Well, thank you, Mr. Hale," she smiled. "It has been a pleasure to be associated with such fine people. I have really enjoyed myself while I have been here. Outstanding people."

"When all this is over, I would like to get to know you a little better. I know the fee and I'll pay the freight."

They had been friendly enough for the past two days. She liked him. He was a clean middle-aged successful businessman. Further she had just enough whiskey to say, "You got a deal. When all this is over, I'll come for you. Give me a business card." He did, and they separated as though nothing had happened.

The party and meal went on just as it had the night before. The couples who had hooked up the first night were more open about it this time and hooked up early. The Mayor went around to each girl at some time during the evening and told each one to be more aggressive.

Cindy Sue asked Mr. Massey if he would like to get to know her better. He told her that under other circumstances he might, but this trip was an important business trip and he didn't want to be sidetracked. He did get her telephone number and told her that if he was ever in the area in the near future, he might give her a call. Just to show his appreciation, he slipped her three one hundred dollar bills.

Lou Ann thought she knew Mr. Beamler well enough to put a cold proposition to him. "Do you not think I'm pretty?" she asked.

"Oh, yeah, you are beautiful and I would love to get something going with you, but you see Mr. Massey? He's doing nothing. This is a business trip for us. I'm following his lead. Thanks for the opportunity anyway. Just realize, I would love to get you between the sheets, but I can't afford to do so. Plus, I'm married to his favorite niece. So, I think we are both keeping each other straight."

Lindy Lou waltzed over to her sister and whispered in her ear, "I don't think either of us is going to get laid this weekend."

"I know I'm not," Cindy Sue responded. "Mr. Massey has already told me how it is. So, I'm going home high and dry. He did give me three bills as a consolation prize that I'll share. Have you put a hard move on Sam yet?"

"No, there's just something about him that is different. I really don't know how to approach it. He pretends to drink, but really doesn't. He watches everything that is going on around here. I just don't know. I think he may be very religious."

"Why don't you hit him hard and see what happens," she walked away.

The twin walked back over to her "date" Sam the General Foreman. "You don't drink much, do you?" She questioned.

"No, not much. My dad was an alcoholic, and I've never really been attracted to it. You have cought me pretending. I have the same drink I began the evening with hours ago."

"Are you attracted to the ladies?" Lindy Lou asked looking into his eyes with the deepest blue eyes he had ever seen.

"Sure, I'm attracted to the ladies, but I've been married 25 years, I have three children, and I try to be a good husband and father. So, although I may have fun with you and the other girls in a crowd, there's nothing else going on here."

"Well, I'm glad we understand each other," the beautiful girl replied.

"Yeah, it takes a lot of pressure off everything. You are free to do whatever you wish. I'll be here as your 'date' if you need me." He raised his glass in a fake toast flashing a big smile.

Lindy Lou responded in kind, raising her glass, thankful that she was making good money without the risk of putting out. She wondered if such a feeling was normal.

The following morning, Pete had a light breakfast for the crowd. They said their goodbyes and the delegation from Wisconsin got into their station wagon and returned to the Chattanooga Airport. There were a couple of long looks as the men left. The Mayor turned to the board members and the girls. "Great weekend, folks. Everyone did a good job. I couldn't ask any more from you guys and you girls were superb. Let's just hope and pray we land this industry. For now, that's it. I'll be in touch." He walked toward his automobile.

Harvey had started the engine of his station wagon. Ernie was still behind him in the truck. He had squared up with the girls after breakfast on Saturday. Each of them took their money and were happy with it. If anyone received a gratuity, other than Cindy Sue, nothing was said about it.

Back at Harvey's house, the relatives wanted to know when they would be asked to entertain again. Harvey didn't know, but he would have Ernie get in touch with them the minute he heard something. "In the meantime, stay healthy, keep clean, keep out of trouble, and we'll do a repeat. You gotta admit it was the greatest."

"It was!" Cindy Sue spoke up for all the cousins. "It was fine. The food was out of sight, the liquor was good, it was fun to dress up, the pool was just right, and last of all, the money was great!"

The other girls agreed. They got into their respective automobiles and went home.

Two full weeks passed before Harvey heard from Frank Hale. "We're ready to go again. Only this time, we only need three girls. It will be a do-over exactly as we did the Wisconsin people. These are bakery people from St. Louis."

"I can handle that," Harvey responded. "Exactly what we did before."

He was not going to involve Ernie Brock this time. "What he doesn't know won't hurt him."

Harvey called his niece, Lindy Lou. "Hey, niece, this is your dear ole Unk. I have another project this weekend. I need three girls. Can you help me with this?"

"Sorry Favorite Uncle, both of us are out. We start our periods on Thursday. This group may not be as reserved as the last one. So, you better get the other three."

Harvey called Rachel Rae. She could handle it personally. She would check with Janet Kay and Lou Ann. In thirty minutes she called back. All three girls were on board for the weekend - repeat performance - same money, same deal. "How come you're calling instead of Cousin Ernie?"

"Well, I as going to excuse Ernie this time. I figured we worked so smoothly last time, he's just a fifth wheel. We don't need him."

"Uncle, you know Lou Ann. She's a traditionalist. She won't go without Ernie holding the money."

"Hell," Harvey replied. "I don't think my nieces trust me. We don't need Ernie"

"Call Cousin Ernie and have him call us and solicit us to do the job. Otherwise, no deal."

Harvey knew that not a one of his nieces trusted him. There was nothing to do but call Ernie.

"Hey, Nephew, we got another job this weekend in Fort Payne. Same song, second verse, a little louder and a little worse. This time they need three girls for some bakery boys from St. Louis. Same deal, same money. How about lining up the relatives?

"I'm on it," Ernie responded. "I must admit I'm surprised that you called me to set it up. I figured that after it went so smooth last time, you would cut me out."

"I'd never do that. You know I'm an honest man. I just like to dip my beak in now and then and take a little out. Call Lou Ann, Rachel Rae and Janet Kay. Give the twins a rest this time."

"Okay," Ernie responded. He hung up and called Cindy Sue. "Uncle has another deal in Fort Payne, but he told me to leave you and Lindy Lou out this time. I just thought I would let you know in case you find out the others went on the deal without you."

"That's fine, Cuz. Uncle already called trying to cut you out. We're on our periods beginning Thursday. So the others will have to fill in. Call Rachel Rae."

"The man never ceases to amaze me," thought Ernie. "That son-uva-bitch would steal nickels off a dead man's eyes." Still, money is money, so he called Rachel Rae and set the deal up, $300 for each girl each night. After re-negotiating earlier, now he would get $100 as would Harvey, per girl per night. So this was a $600 weekend for each of them and each girl.

The weekend came and the scheme went down exactly as the first one. Only this time, all three men from St. Louis went to bed with the girls for two nights, and didn't care who knew it. At the end of the weekend, they gave a verbal commitment to bring the bakery to Fort Payne. It would employ 750 people. The townsmen were ecstatic. They became so frantic, that they did not entertain any other delegations while they worked on putting the bakery together. It was a very big project.

The group from Wisconsin called during all the furor over the bakery and told the locals that they had an offer from Chattanooga that would give them a city, county and state tax break for 7 years. The Mayor told Mr. Massey that he could get the same tax break for the city and county taxes, but he couldn't swing it for the state.

Unfortunately, it was a deal breaker and the Mayor and Industrial Development Board went back to working on the bakery. Eventually, the bakery was built and employed almost 800 people in the area. It was a great success.

It had been some nine weeks since the last visit to Fort Payne by any of the girls. Rachel Rae needed some money. She took out her card and called Frank Hale, the sock mogul, hosiery mill owner. He welcomed her call and told her to check into Black's Motel on Friday afternoon. He would run back and forth to see her as often as he could, but count on two nights, or $1,000.

At that point, Rachel Rae knew that she and the others had been cheated by her Uncle and Cousin. Or perhaps, the cousin didn't know about the thieving ways of their uncle. Regardless, now she had her own deal going and no one would be the wiser.

Without breathing a word to any of the girls, Uncle Harvey, or Cousin Ernie, Rachel Rae checked into Black's Motel at 3:30 slow time on Friday afternoon. Pete saw her and raised an eyebrow wondering what was going on.

By this time, the entire town knew about the girls who were helping lure Yankee business to the area. It wasn't even an open secret. It was wide open discussion. Several local girls said that they would be happy to work for the Industrial Development Board for half of whatever those out-of-town girls were charging.

When the girls were at the pool, it was like a parade, as the cars went by hoping to catch a glance of the female pulchritude. The restaurant at Black's Motel did its greatest business on the weekends the girls were in town. Men would sit at the round table in the restaurant for five hours just to catch a glimpse of the women. The reports were that the wait was well worth it.

So now Rachel Rae was freelancing - at Black's Motel - alone. Who would be her visitor? This was the first time any of the girls had been back to the motel alone. Her room was closely watched by motel personnel and local gossips.

A telephone call came in for Rachel's room and five people gathered around the switchboard trying to figure out who was calling. The voice was muffled and simply instructed Rachel to go to the phone booth in front of the motel and call the number on the card. She did, watched by everyone from the desk clerk to the cook.

"Hello," she said when Hale answered. "What do I do now?"

"Just sit there. Half the damned town is watching the motel to see who goes into your room. I've never seen anything like it. I've been in and out of there, no one suspects me. I know what they're doing, and damned if I can figure it out where it'll be safe. I think I'll just let you drive out here to the mill. No one will see you come into the mill if you come around to the loading dock. But you will have to drive around and lose all those saps who are going to follow you."

"I don't even know where it is," Rachel Rae whined.

"Come up the main street, the way you came in, go straight when the road bends to the left toward the interstate. Come on up and I'm on the left, just beyond an upholstery company. There's a big sign out front, green and white. It says, 'Hale Hosiery, Inc.' Go past the sign and you'll see a driveway that goes behind the mill. That road goes around to the loading dock. Follow it around and I'll be waiting."

Rachel followed the instructions. She drove out to I-59 first, and at least three cars followed her. She turned right onto the interstate, indicating she was going home, and the automobiles went on over the overpass. She proceeded up to a gravel cross over used by Alabama Department of Highways vehicles and turned back. She drove back into town, took a left on Old Valley Head Road. Soon, she saw the sign. No one was behind her. She turned into the driveway north of the mill and followed it around the building to the loading dock. Hale was standing on the dock with a flashlight.

He waved the light. "Come on in. Have you ever seen anything like this?"

"No, it's different," Rachel Rae said dismounting the automobile and climbing the stairs up to the dock. Hale kissed her and led her through the shipping department to his office in the front of the plant. She noticed that the sock mill had a distinct smell to it. There were big white spools of thread everywhere and thread was leading to machine after machine. She had never seen anything quite like it. "It must be the way socks are made," she thought.

In the office, Hale wasted no time. "Here, let me give you this cash before we both forget it." He handed her ten one hundred dollar bills. She put them in the small purse she had with her. She was wearing a red and black plaid pleated skirt, a red blouse and white sneakers.

Hale said, "Let's get a little sample. He reached under the skirt and pulled her panties down with both hands. He had a large couch in his office and they had sex on the couch. Hale was very happy with the session that lasted a total of about 20 minutes.

He was breathing hard. "Go back to the motel, and I'm going to try to sneak into your room later tonight. Otherwise, we'll work out something tomorrow morning. If you don't hear from me, call my number from the phone booth. I'll try to hang out around here so I can get your call. Like everyone else in this town, my wife is on the alert for anything out of the ordinary. I can't afford to get cought."

"You want me to go back to the motel now and wait?"

"Yeah, you'll hear from me shortly."

Rachel Rae returned the motel and went into her room. Nothing unusual. She went into the bath area and washed up from the tryst. There was a loud knock on her door. She almost jumped out of her skin. "Who is it?" She asked when she had regained her composure.

"Open up! It's the police!" came a gruff response.

Rachel opened door, wide eyed, and wondering. "May I help you?" she asked demurely.

"May we come in, Miss?" The uniformed patrolman asked.

"Sure," Rachel Rae answered. "Come in, come in. What can I do for you?" She was scared to death.

"We've had some charges raised that you may have broken the law. Do you mind if I search the room?" The officer was very businesslike.

"Go ahead, I have nothing to hide."

The officer immediately opened her purse and took out the ten one hundred bills. "You are under arrest," he announced. And removed his handcuffs.

As he placed the cuffs on Rachel Rae, she asked, "What am I accused of doing?"

"Soliciting prostitution," the officer replied.

Rachel Rae was taken to the Fort Payne City Jail, booked, dressed in an orange jumpsuit and escorted to a cell. "May I make a telephone call?" She asked.

"Sure," the jailer replied. "If you are calling long distance, you will have to call collect."

Harvey accepted the collect call from Rachel Rae. "I'm in jail, Uncle Harvey," she cried. "I need help."

"Where are you, Rachel?"

"Fort Payne."

"What are you charged with?

"Soliciting prostitution."

"Aw shit, you went down there to cut some of those local Johns and one of their wives put the law on you."

"I guess," she whimpered. "I need help."

"Well, I can't do anything tonight. I'll get you out tomorrow. Right now there's not even a magistrate to set bond. I'll have a lawyer over to see you early in the morning."

He thought, "That damned little bitch. She went around me and now I've got to pay a price for it. Shit! Oh, well I'll get her out tomorrow."

At 8:41 a.m. the lawyer's phone rang. The secretary put the call through, "There's a Mr. Harvey Steat on the line."

The lawyer remembered Harvey Steat. In April, 1965, he had moved to Fort Payne to practice law with an old classmate. He arrived on Friday and moved in over the weekend. On Monday morning, he arrived at the office to be open for business. His new partner came in and said, "It's jury trials today and we have a white whiskey man to defend. Are you up for it?"

"Sure," I've defended moonshiners before in Tuscaloosa. What's the facts?"

"This guy comes from a long line of old white whiskey makers on the north end of Sand Mountain. They think making white is legal. He was making 1,500 gallons a week in an abandoned chicken house in an out-of-the-way location."

"That's a lot of whiskey. What was he getting a gallon? In Tuscaloosa it was selling for $7 a gallon."

"You're close. He was getting $8.00 a gallon selling most of it in the Black neighborhoods of Chattanooga and Atlanta. He was making a fortune. It's hard work though, carrying those 100 pound bags of sugar through the woods. I'm going to talk to the solicitor and see if we can get him to make a deal. We have absolutely no defense. I'll be right back."

While the new partner walked across the courthouse parking lot bound for the Office of the County Solicitor (they weren't called District Attorneys in Alabama at that time), the lawyer walked into the waiting room to meet the client. He was a large, blonde, gregarious man with hamhock hands. They shook hands, "Good morning, Counselor, I'm Harvey Steat. You going to defend me today?"

"No, I don't know enough about your case, but I may assist in your defense."

They visited and drank a cup of coffee until the partner returned. Speaking to Steat, "The solicitor says he will let you plead to 7 years and the state will recommend unsupervised probation. He's willing to do this because he doesn't want to have to bring the Revenuers up here from Gadsden. I think you have to take it since you were cought cooking at the largest still in the history of this county. It's a sweetheart deal, you got to take it."

"I ain't pleading guilty to nothin. Just try the case and I'll take whatever the jury gives me."

"I'm not going to humiliate myself by trying this case. It is dead in the water. You were cought red-handed with your cooker cooking and your thumper thumping. I've worked a miracle for you, and you don't appreciate it."

"Lookey here, I paid you $2,500 to defend me in this case. I didn't pay you to plead me guilty. I want my trial that I paid for."

"Well, I'm not going to do it. And, I'm not giving you any money back because I have earned my fee."

Turning to the lawyer, Steat asked, "will you represent me?"

"I don't know enough about your case to try it," the lawyer looked for help from his new partner.

The partner spoke, "Look, nobody around here knows you. My family has been here since it was Indian Territory. I can't try a case like this. The people around here will think I'm crazy. We'll lose dozens of clients. You know enough to try it if you are disposed to do so. The man is guilty as charged. It's that easy."

"Please....." Steat was begging.

"Ah, I have nothing to lose. Let's go try it. I'll just get my feet wet my first day in DeKalb County."

It took all day to go through the dockets and finally get a jury of 12 men in the jury box. The prosecutor needed the time to get his witnesses up from Gadsden. The case was continued to start promptly at 9:00 a.m. on Tuesday.

On behalf of the state, the solicitor made an opening statement citing all the facts.

Obviously, the defendant was guilty as he was cought red-handed making illegal alcohol

When his time came, the lawyer told the jury that he was new in the county and he would not tell them any lies nor would he put on any false testimony. "We'll just have to sit back and let this case come to us. Then, I'll talk with you again at the end of the case."

A Reveneur named Hanks testified as to the chicken house where the still was located, near the Georgia line. He then talked about what he cought the defendant doing. Then he went into great detail about how the still was made, how it operated and how much profit was being made off tax-free whiskey,

At the end of his direct testimony, the lawyer asked for a short recess and the Court took the morning break. He ran across the parking lot to his new office with the defendant in tow.

Breaking through the door, he called out to his partner, "Do we have any of those TVA Quadrangle maps? I need one for Trenton, Georgia."

"Yeah, I've collected them for years. They are in the filing cabinet. That one will be under 'Trenton Quad.'"

The lawyer unfolded the mostly green colored map which was taken from an aerial photograph. It was about three feet square. So, he laid it out on the library table. Then, he searched the area closely, running his right index finger over the surface of the paper.

"Mr. Steat, show me your chicken house."

"Right here. That little oblong purple square. That rectangle thang. That's hit."

"Thanks, let's go back to court."

With the court back in session, to the witness, the lawyer continued. "Now Reveneur Hanks, you are familiar with TVA Quadrangle maps?"

"Yes."

"And they are completely accurate?"

"They are. They're taken from aerial photographs." He was proud of his knowledge of the TVA Mapping Department.

"Let me show you the Trenton Quadrangle, and I direct your attention to this little purple building right here," he pointed to the map. "That is the chicken house where the still was located, isn't it?"

The solicitor was studying the map with them at the witness stand where Hanks was seated.

Hanks studied the map carefully looking at every detail. "Here's the paved road; here's the dirt road across the field and through the woods; here's the old barn; and here's the old farm house. Yeah, this is the chicken house. Right there, right there is where he was making illegal untaxed alcohol."

"Good. Now look at the map again, you see that dashed line?

"Yeah, I see it."

"Quad sheets always have north at the top. The chicken house is on the east side of that line, isn't it?"

"Yeah, it's east of the line by a hair."

"What is that line we're talking about?" The lawyer pointed to where the line was identified on the map.

"It says it's the state line. It looks like the still was in Georgia."

The court interrupted, "Gentlemen of the jury go into the jury room. We have a matter to take up outside your presence."

After the last juror left the courtroom, the judge said, "Mr. County Solicitor, what do you say? Your witness has just taken jurisdiction of this case away from this court."

The solicitor fussed and fumed. He asked Hanks if he was sure the still was in Georgia. He was.

The court dismissed the case for lack of jurisdiction.

Steat was a very happy client. The new partner was impressed, and the solicitor called the District Attorney in Trenton and told him to prosecute Steat. He did and Steat's lawyer in Georgia proved the chicken house was in Alabama.

The lawyer answered the telephone, "Hey Harvey, what can I do for you?"

"Listen here, I got a niece in the Fort Payne City Jail for soliciting prostitution. They cought her last night at Black's Motel with a thousand dollars in cash on her. They don't know who her John was. They're just making a case. I need you to get her out."

"Okay, I'm like everybody else in the valley, was she one of our ladies of the evening that helped us get the bakery and 700 plus jobs?"

"The same. I provided all those girls and they did a great job."

"Well, they are famous around here. They say each one of them is more beautiful than the other. Five tall blondes, I hear."

"They are. This here one is Rachel Rae, as beautiful as they come. She just messed up."

"Well, something like this had to happen. The situation was just too much a subject of conversation. I'll go get her out. My fee is $1,500."

"You won't have to wait for your money," Harvey responded. "Just please go get her out."

The lawyer told his partner what had happened. The partner advised, "Just go over and tell them you are going to kick the slop jar over and stink up the whole town if they don't let her go. And, give her that money back too."

At the jail, amidst snickers by the jailers, the lawyer was led back to the cell where the girl was held. She was in an orange jail jumpsuit, but she still looked good. She had platted her long blonde hair in one big pigtail. With her hair pulled back, she had the bluest eyes the lawyer had ever seen. They were the color of the blue hole in the ocean off the coast of Belize in Central America. She had a full mouth, high cheeks, perfect chin and he could tell she filled out the orange jumpsuit in a fine fashion. He interviewed her and took notes through the bars.

She told him about the times she had been down to Fort Payne with her cousins and how they had helped the town. Then, last night, she came down on her own. She needed the money. The lawyer did not want to know the name of the local man she met. He was afraid it might be one of his neighbors or church members.

After being briefed for the better part of an hour, he left and went to the office of the Chief of Police.

The chief was a new friend of the lawyer. "Chief, I represent the beautiful young lady you have in your lockup. I want you to let her go; let me take her out of here; and I want her money back."

"Are you serious?" The chief asked. "You want me to kiss her and ask her for forgiveness for arresting her?"

"I never thought of that. I ought to throw that in, but you would enjoy it too much. I want her out and I want her out now, or I'm going to the newspaper and it's not going to be pretty. You might want to call the Mayor and tell him what I've said."

"I don't have to call the Mayor. We've already talked. If you will commit to keeping this absolutely quiet, we will dismiss the charges and let her out in your custody on condition you take her out of Fort Payne and she never comes back."

"You have a deal. Of course, I want the money back."

"You can have it. I'm only doing this because I don't know who her John was and I really don't want to know. My officer did act a little precipitously. He should have waited until the John showed up and got 'em both. Anyway, you're an honorable man and I trust you. I'll have her dressed and ready to go in 10 minutes."

The lawyer thought that Rachel Rae looked like one of the little maids from school in the Gilbert and Sullivan play, "The Mikado." When she appeared in the waiting room of the jail the plaid outfit reminded the lawyer of a school uniform.

"Did you get everything?" He asked.

"Yes. They even gave me my money back."

"Good, now where's your car?"

"Uncle Harvey had Cousin Ernie come and got it last night. He was worried, saying he didn't know what might be in it. So, it's at home."

"Where's home?"

"Up on the mountain above Trenton."

"Okay, I'll drive you up there. I need to go by Harvey's and get paid."

Although the trip was uneventful, it was a beautiful day and they enjoyed the ride. Rachel Rae was very appreciative. She had never been in jail before, let alone handcuffed. "They had me scared to death. Those law are mean men."

The pair stopped by Harvey's white brick residence. She waited in the automobile while the lawyer went to the house. Harvey came to the door.

"Okay, you got her?" Harvey was looking out to see if she was in the vehicle. "Here's your money. Does she still have charges pending?"

"No. All she has to do is stay out of Fort Payne for a while. She is free as a bird. No charges, no nothing."

"Good job. Thanks." He turned, closing the door and went back into the house." Harvey didn't acknowledge Rachel Rae. She would have to repay him several times for this favor. All of them knew that this would happen.

The lawyer put the cash in his pocket and returned to the vehicle. Starting the engine, he said, "You know, I just can't imagine. The rumor was that the city was paying $5,000 for female companionship for industrial prospects."

"We did a good job," Rachel Rae replied. "We did everything we were asked to do."

"Yeah, but I can not imagine paying $500 a night for sex. That is a lot of money for one night. Who in the world would be worth that kind of money?"

He drove on for a while in silence.

She directed him to the place where she lived. He pulled up to the simple white Clapboard house to let her out.

She hesitated after opening the door showing almost her entire left leg well above the thigh.

"There's nobody here. If you want to come in, I'll show you my appreciation for what you did and I'll prove to you that I'm worth every dime of it."

She smiled and opened a button on her blouse and raised her plaid skirt on up to where her pink panties were showing.

The lawyer took a very deep breath. He thought long and hard seeming to weigh the risks involved. Then he said, "You know Rachel Rae, I guess I believe you. Thanks for the offer. It is the best I have ever had since I've been married."

"I'm worth every dime," she said prissily walking away from the automobile highlighting her backside.

He backed out the drive and drove back to the office wondering just how good she really was.

For the next forty-odd years, about once every three to five years, Rachel Rae called the lawyer at his office, reminded him she was worth every dime, and asked him if he had changed his mind. She did that before she was married; while she was married; when she was pregnant with her two children; when she went through a divorce; before she married again; when she had a daughter addicted to drugs; and eventually, she disappeared from the life of the lawyer. He was 74 years old when he last heard from her.

Every now and then though, he could not help but wonder, was she really worth it? He concluded that she probably was worth every dime.

TELEVISION STAR

It was a beautiful sunny morning during a very green spring on Sand Mountain in the Northeast Corner of Alabama. Birds were chirping and dogs could be heard barking in the distance. Otherwise, the area was deserted.

The young man was tall, dressed in brown coveralls, blonde hair and seemingly normal. He parked his ten year old white panel van with, "Television Repair" fading on the side panels. He stopped in the drive way near the steps to the country home. The house was a white clapboard about one hundred yards off the dirt road. There were no automobiles nor other vehicles in the vacant garage at the end of the drive way.

The young man bounded up the three steps to the porch and knocked on the door. Nothing. He knocked louder. Again, no response from the house. Once more he knocked with authority. Obviously, there was no one home. He tried the rusty door knob below the dirty six glass panes and the door was locked.

He returned to his "service truck," opened the side doors and retrieved a strange looking object. It was a piece of steel about three feet long and padded with old shag carpet on each end. In its middle was a protruding lever about two feet long. For the knowledgeable, it was an old 18 wheeler truck jack that had been somewhat modified.

Returning to the door, with his back holding the screen door, he fitted the jack into the front door jamb of the home. He slid the ratchet teeth out for the fit and began to pull the handle in the middle back and forth. Soon pressure was being applied to the door facing. It was only a matter of minutes until the jack worked its magic and the front door fell open. He returned to his truck, replaced the jack and leaped upon the porch. Confident the house was vacant, he opened the door and entered the living room.

The shades were drawn, and the room was dark. He took several minutes to allow his eyes to adjust from the bright sunlight. He noticed the Zenith television set in the corner and stepped toward it. Right then, he heard a definite clicking sound.

"Hold it right there!" came a voice from a recliner across the room from the blank television set.

Startled, the young man turned to see a very elderly gentleman in blue overalls, red flannel shirt, and snuff juice running down the corners of his mouth. He was holding a 12 gauge double barrel shotgun pointed directly at the young man's body. The young man stopped and raised his hands. He knew that the clicking sound he had heard was the gun being cocked.

"Set down and shut up," the man behind the gun instructed. He motioned with the barrel for the young man to sit on the dirty couch that had an old faded quilt covering what it could of the piece of once-proud furniture.

The young man sat down, never taking his eyes off the shotgun, and slowly began to shake uncontrollably. He was so frightened that his teeth began to chatter.

The old man needed a shave in the worst way. He appeared to be in his 70's. His watery blue eyes never seemed to blink. It was very obvious to the young man that this elderly gentleman meant every word he said and one false move and he would be dead.

"I don't want to hear a word from you," the man behind the gun said. "When my daughter gets back from the store, I'm taking you to the sheriff, you house breaking son-of-a-bitch. I don't know what you broke in here for, but I know one thing, you will pay for it with your life if you move."

After that, neither man said anything. Eventually, the young man began to stop shaking and tried to relax breathing heavily. The old gentleman simply sat with both barrels pointed at the burglar.

Nearly two hours later, that seemed like a lifetime, a car drove up in the driveway and stopped behind the van. A middle aged woman, slightly overweight, wearing a gingham dress that had gaudy flowers died into it, got out of the car, retrieved a large bag of groceries and came into the house. She stopped short and dropped the bag when she saw the scene in her living room.

"I thought the TV repairman was here, Dad," she said quizzically. "The truck is outside. Why do you have that gun on him?"

"Ain't no TV repairman. This here feller broke down your front door and came into the house. I'd been sound asleep and didn't hear him until he started prying open the door with something. He was making a lot of racket. Then, I went and got ole Roscoe and prepared to let him bark. We're taking him to the sheriff. He's a robber!"

The woman turned to the young man, "You broke into my house?" She was not only questioning, but she was demanding an answer as she began to examine the damage to her front door.

The young man thought about trying to explain his way out of his predicament, but he thought better of it. He just couldn't trust that old man's trigger finger. He had absolutely no doubt the old gentleman would pull the trigger on the slightest excuse.

"Ma'am, I don't have any lies to tell," he said in a slightly northern accent. "I broke into your home to steal your television set. I didn't think anyone was at home." There, he said it. Maybe, after a confession like that, the old man would let him go.

"I'll gladly pay for the damage I did to your door. I have two hundred dollars on me, would that do?"

"Ain't nothing gonna do," the old man responded. "You're going to jail. You don't sound like you're from around here, and you're gonna learn that we don't cotton to no thieves."

"The truck has an Indiana license plate, Dad," the daughter pointed out.

"Well, we're gonna take a ride in that truck," he turned to the young man. "Helen, follow us down to the sheriff's office. I'm gonna get in the back of that van, and we're taking this thief to jail."

He motioned with the barrel for the young man to get up and go out the front door. "You so much as think about anything funny and you are dead. I shot Germans in World War II and I won't hesitate to blow you away. Now git behind the wheel of that truck."

The young man was very careful to walk slowly around the front of the old white van and get into the driver's seat.

The daughter went to her car directly blocking the van. Her father went in the side doors of the van and closed them. He put the shotgun barrel up against the neck of the driver. "Now, follow my daughter's car and you'll live for another day."

The young man did directly as he was told. He was followed into the sheriff's office by the man and daughter. He realized that he was cought and he was going to jail.

The lawyer became a little apprehensive when the judge asked him to stop by his office for a minute. Judges normally don't invite lawyers just to visit. He knew the judge was either going to rule against him in a pending matter or the judge wanted something.

"Have you heard of the young man from Indiana, who's in jail, named Tracy Storm, I believe?" the Judge asked.

"No, I'm not familiar with the name," the lawyer responded waiting for the other shoe to fall.

"He's down here from Indiana. He doesn't know anyone, and he needs a lawyer. I was thinking you might take his case as a *pro bono* appointment," he pointedly stared at the lawyer at the end as some judges do. It means, "You will do what I'm asking, won't you?"

At that time, Alabama did not compensate *pro bono*, or free lawyers. Being a Republican in a Democratic state, the lawyer had been on the receiving end of free representation since he was eight days out of law school. Without ever having been in a real courtroom, the lawyer had been appointed to one of the most despicable KKK gang rape cases of a black woman in Alabama history. He should have known in June, 1963, that case was nothing more than the harbinger of things to come. Now another freebie case looked as if it was coming up on his plate.

"What's he accused of doing?" the lawyer asked on his guard. There might be a conflict involved and he could politely, but with regrets, refuse the appointment. There were few things he needed less than another free case.

"I believe he is accused of burglarizing several homes in the Sand Mountain Area and taking their television sets. Nothing else, just television sets."

"How many television sets is he accused of taking?"

Striking a very serious tone the judge said, "I believe he accused of taking somewhere more than 50 sets."

"Fifty burglaries?" the lawyer was incredulous. "Judge, if I defend that man, there'll be 50 families that won't use me as a lawyer. I can't take that case."

"Unfortunately," the judge began, "I think you must. There is going to be publicity associated with this defense and you can handle that. If you can't see your way to voluntarily take the case, I'll have to order you to take it. I want you to take this case."

"Well, save your writing fingers, I guess I'll undertake the representation." The lawyer had been in this position many times in the past and there was really no way out.

Like so many other appointments, he didn't want the case, but he considered it paying his dues. He had been paying heavy dues for being a GOP lawyer for more than 25 years. He would like to stop paying sometime soon. Sixteen murder cases, two capital rape cases, and hundreds of lesser offenses. But, for now, he had another free representation on his hands. He had built his reputation by going all out in the appointed criminal cases he undertook. Prisoners would stand up in open court and ask that he be appointed to represent them. He did not cut a corner. If he signed on for a case, the firm went all out. Still, he would like to quit, it was a costly proposition.

The judges didn't want him to quit because he set the standard for criminal defense in the area. When either of the judges were faced with the worst case imagined in the mind of man, the lawyer could always be ordered to take it.

Now the senior judge had persuaded the lawyer to take on a client he did not need nor want.

"Thank you," the judge checked another defendant off the list he had before him on the desk. He had eleven prisoners who needed appointed, or *pro bono*, lawyers. He thumbed through his Rolodex and called the next lawyer. This time he had a nice elderly gentleman accused of child molestation for the unsuspecting young lawyer to represent. The lawyer graciously accepted. His Honor neglected to tell the young barrister that his new client had three prior convictions of rubbing little girl's anuses, and that the next 11 year old was going to testify that he did the same to her, rubbed her anus, nothing else.

The lawyer heard the conversation and thought, "That's enough."

The lawyer returned to his office, opened a file on Tracy Storm, and went to the DeKalb County Jail to visit his client for his initial interview. The two of them were allowed to sit in a glass enclosed room. The young man, dressed in jailhouse whites, was standing talking matter-of-factly. The lawyer was seated scribbling on his yellow legal pad.

"Seventy-one television sets!" he yelled. "You burglarized seventy-one homes and took seventy-one televisions? I thought it was just fifty. That's bad enough!"

He stopped writing and looked directly into the younger man's eyes. "Do you know that you have seventy-one twenty-year sentences looking at you? That's more than fourteen hundred years."

The lawyer had piercing green eyes. Thanks to Graves' Disease, His right eye was slightly larger than his left. He had hard, dangerous, threatening eyes. He looked dead into the shifty blue eyes of his new young client. "Seventy-one burglaries! I can't believe that judge would do this to me!" He was a little more than angry.

The lawyer was resigned to do the task and would do his best - seventy-one burglaries by one person was ridiculous.

Somehow Tracy Storm understood that he was looking at more than one thousand, four hundred years. He couldn't possibly do all that time.

"I didn't know about the prison time involved. If I had, I wouldn't have taken them." Momentarily, he considered doing the time.

"Then why did you take them in the first place for heaven's sake?"

"Well, it really wasn't that bad," the younger man was letting the older man in on his secret. "See, I'm from Little Egypt, south of Cairo, Illinois, in Indiana. I'd come down here, in the country, and go around unoccupied houses during the day in my television van. Most of the houses weren't even locked. I'd go up, if any body was home, I'd ask directions, or get a drink of water, or be at the wrong place to answer the television repair call - anything. If nobody was home, I'd go in and get the TV set.

When I'd get up twenty-five or thirty sets, I would head for the flea markets in Indiana. I'd sell all of them in one day at fifty to a hundred dollars a pop. I was making good money," he waited for approval of how enterprising he had been.

"Yeah, I can see the money in that kind of scam," the lawyer started writing again.

"I finally got a pipeline. I didn't even have to go to the flea markets anymore. I'd just haul ten or twelve good color sets back to some people in Indiana, you know in Little Egypt, and they'd give me a hundred a set. It was good money."

"Well, it's not so hot now," the lawyer replied. "How old are you?" he felt sucker punched by the Judge, "burglarizing several homes," my ass. This damned boy took seventy-one television sets that he will confess to. How many did he take all total? "How old did you say you were?"

"I'm eighteen, sir. I'll be nineteen next month."

"Okay, we'll ask for youthful offender. I'll ask the judge to set your bond at $1,500. Can you get up $150 to get out of jail?

"Yes sir, I have it in my wallet. I believe I had around $200 in there when they took it."

The lawyer returned to the judge, who was still appointing lawyers to indigent cases, and asked for a bond of fifteen hundred dollars. The judge agreed after hearing the boy's age.

The lawyer went back to the jail, had the boy released on posting one-tenth of the bond in cash. The young man still had enough money to live on a few days. He had his truck, and soon, with the lawyer's help, he had a job at a local hosiery mill, and he was able to rent a small two-room apartment within one hour of his release.

The lawyer ordered the young man to attend Second Baptist Church every time the doors were open. He didn't want him in First Baptist because that was the lawyer's church.

Four months went by, and the lawyer approached the district attorney about a plea deal for the young man. The district attorney said absolutely not. "Why, there are seventy-one families in this county that won't vote for me if I agree to let that burglar off."

"Well," the lawyer responded, "you leave me no choice but to apply for youthful offender status."

"Haw!" replied the DA, "good luck with that."

Under Alabama Law a person under twenty-one years of age is entitled to apply for youthful offender status. If YO is granted, the youth has his case continued while he serves a probationary term, usually two years. If he is not arrested within the two-year period, his charges are dismissed and he does not have a criminal record.

The lawyer filed the necessary papers and returned to the district attorney.

"You back again? You want me to agree to youthful offender status for Storm? That man broke into seventy-one homes in DeKalb County. We don't know what he did elsewhere. And you want me to agree to YO for him? No way." The district attorney was pacing around in front of his desk. The lawyer was sitting in the visitor's chair in the DA's office.

"Hey look," the lawyer countered, "this is just a kid. He won't even be supervised in Alabama. He'll be living in Indiana. He won't cost Alabama a thing. Put him in prison and he will cost the state $21,000 per year until he is released. Look, he has worked for four months. I have his work record right here, excellent. Never missed a day. Best worker they had in the mill. This is an apt candidate for youthful offender status." He was holding up documents trying desperately to convince the DA.

"As I told you before, if I agreed to give that young man YO status I would have seventy-one irate householders down on me for letting their burglar go. No. If he gets it, he'll have to get it through the court."

The lawyer pointed out that most of the people got brand new better television sets after collecting from their homeowners insurance.

"There's probably no more than three or four people who actually suffered a loss here."

The District Attorney was firm, "If he gets Youthful Offender, the court will have to give it to him. I'm not going to give a break to a man who broke into seventy-one homes in my county."

It was no use. The lawyer had to begin to work the system to put the case off as long as possible. After almost eighteen months, it was time. The lawyer had to get ready for a youthful offender application hearing. He would have to prove Storm worthy of YO status to the satisfaction of the judge.

He called Storm in and reminded him that youthful offender status is a juvenile protection law. A young person given YO status does not have a criminal record, is not adjudged guilty of a crime. The person is found to be a youthful offender. After a probationary term, with good behavior, he or she is released without any criminal record. The lawyer wanted Storm to really want this treatment.

The matter came on for hearing before the appointing judge. The lawyer put on the next door neighbor of Storm from his apartment complex who testified the young man didn't drink. He didn't throw wild parties, he didn't smoke, and all he did was go to work and go to church. Next, his employer testified that he was the best knitter in the sock mill. If he wished, he would be promoted to fixer and have a great career in the hosiery industry. He highly recommended youthful offender status for his worker. The pastor of his church, in his finest pastoral voice urged the judge to have mercy. Young Mr. Storm was a regular punctual member of his church. He even came to Prayer Meeting on Wednesday Night. In addition, he sang in the choir. Other people who had come to know him were called. The testimony was that he was of sterling character, practically an Eagle Scout, an upstanding citizen who would never be in trouble again.

The lawyer introduced more than twenty letters from persons urging the Court to grant YO to young Storm and extolling his virtues.

The State put on three persons who had experienced a burglary of their homes and their televisions were stolen. On cross-examination by the lawyer, two out of the three witnesses had brand new television sets courtesy of their homeowner's insurance. Plus, their houses had been repaired and were in better shape than before the burglary. The district attorney could see no advantage to continuing to feed his witnesses to the lawyer so he quit after three. "The State rests."

The judge said that he was convinced the young man had seen the error of his ways. He practically said that he was a paragon of virtue and, over the strongest objection of the State, awarded him youthful offender status.

The lawyer had already presented Storm to the probation officer. Her investigation had been concluded, and she had discussed his YO status being transferred to his home town in Indiana. The "Yankee" probation officer in Indiana had agreed to take Storm under his supervision.

By the time the judge finished granting YO status, the probation matter was complete, the young man signed out, and was ready to leave Alabama. He had taken the liberty of packing all his belongings on his truck prior to the hearing. He had parked on the street directly in front of the lawyer's office. He had extreme confidence in the ability of his lawyer.

"Let's go over to the office and let me give you a copy of your papers. You may need some of the letters of recommendation and character references I gathered to help you get a good job. I want to keep a copy for our records, but I'll give you the originals."

Tracy Storm crossed the courthouse parking lot and street to the lawyer's office in the company of his counsel.

As they walked into the office, the two front office secretaries told the lawyer that they were on their way to lunch if they weren't needed. The lawyer usually ate in and manned the office during the lunch hour. He told them to go on. All he had to do was make about twenty copies for Tracy Storm.

Tracy stood in the waiting room looking across a counter and desk to the copy machine area of the secretary's office. The lawyer was sifting through the file and making copies of documents which he thought might be of value to Tracy. As he copied the documents, he placed the originals in a manila envelope that he was preparing for his client. There were numerous documents, maybe as many as twenty-five pages. The lawyer was intently busy reading, making his selection, and doing the copy work. Tracy went to his van for a minute and came back. By the time he returned, the copy work was done and the lawyer gave him his originals from his file.

"I just can't thank you enough," Tracy said sincerely, extending his hand across the counter to the lawyer. "You gave me a second chance. You allowed me to see how things really are. I know now I can make a living without living a life of crime. I can't thank you enough, Sir."

The lawyer and Tracy shook hands.

"It was a pleasure representing you, Tracy," the lawyer said. "You did what you were told to do, and we reaped a good result. I can only wish you the best of luck." The lawyer was warmly sincere.

"Thank you again," Tracy said with a large smile on his face. He turned and left the building. The lawyer went to the kitchen of the office and prepared his lunch. He was just finishing his chicken with noodles when the secretaries returned.

"I guess Tracy Storm is a happy fellow by now," the first secretary said as she came through the back door.

"Yeah, he's headed back to Indiana. A real success story. Sometimes the system really works," the lawyer was proud of the work they had done for Storm.

The phone rang, "It's the judge," the other secretary handed the telephone to the lawyer.

"Yes, Sir?" the lawyer queried.

"How about coming over to my chambers for a minute?"

What now? the lawyer thought. "All right. Give me a couple of minutes."

It amused him that lawyers have offices and judges have chambers.

Taking a legal tablet, the lawyer was stopped by the telephone as he was half out the front door of his office building. The secretary held the phone up for him to take. He returned to the counter in the waiting room, reached across the counter, handled the receiver, and spoke into the telephone.

After returning the telephone across the counter, the lawyer started to exit the building again. Stopping at the front door, he turned and said, "Come out here, there's something wrong in this waiting room." He looked around the room slowly.

The secretary came through the hallway door into the waiting room. "The television set is missing," she said. "See the cable has been disconnected and is laying there on the table where it always was."

"I'll be damned, that TV-thieving bastard. Tracy Storm stole our TV set while I was making copies of his letters of recommendation that I got for him. Now I know why he went to his van when I was the busiest. He took our television set out and put it in his truck. That rotten son-of-a-bitch! I'm glad the system worked for him because it ain't doing much for us. We represented him for nothing, *pro bono*. We prepared an excellent case for a person who had little chance of survival. We got him out with a slap on the wrist, and he cops our television set." The lawyer was furious.

Both secretaries were giggling. The older one said, "You have to admit it's funny. Look at the headline, 'Television Thief Steals His Lawyer's Television.'" She joined her co-worker in laughing at the situation.

"It ain't funny," the lawyer said sarcastically. "I've got to go see the judge who cost us, not only our time and money, but also our television set. I can't believe it." Once more he went out the door.

After being motioned to a chair, the judge said, "Before I talk to you about a case, I want to commend you on your presentation on behalf of that young Mr. Storm. I thought it was the best I have ever seen, very convincing. I believe that young man will do well," the judge leaned back in his chair, steepled his fingers, and looked at the ceiling.

"You know, he's extremely handsome, and with a name like Tracy Storm, he might be able to get a job in television." The judge sat contemplating his thought.

"I think he's already got a future in television," the lawyer replied.

The judge looked puzzled toward the lawyer. Neither man made further comment.

THE BANK ROBBERY

The first reddish yellow, and almost purple, streaks of light filtered through the leafless trees as daylight came to the north end of the Great Cumberland Plateau. Darren, Junior and Kevin were, "sittin' on their still." Well actually, they were laying on their backs, hands behind their necks, on the ground, watching the blue propane flame, and listening to their thumper thump.

A moonshine still consists of three main parts: there's the cooker, an enclosed container where the fire is applied to the mash and where the mash boils emitting steam. The mash can be fermented corn, corn squeezings, hog shorts, or a variety of green vegetable materials that contain sufficient sugar content to rate the extraction or conversion to alcohol. Connected to the cooker is a thumper, which is an empty closed chamber pot-like apparatus that begins the condensation process of the steam coming from the cooker. Then there is the coil that comes out of the thumper and completes the condensation process. The liquid coming out of the coil will be moonshine. The reason the condenser is called the thumper is because it expands and contracts, depending upon the status of steam coming from the cooker. As it does this process, it makes a noise. In the deep woods of moonshine country it can be heard for a quarter mile or so, whomp, whomp, whomp!

Usually the moonshiner uses a portable propane eye or propane gas tank rig to fire the cooker. Since the coil is usually small, about ½" in diameter, cookers and thumpers can build up substantial pressure and sometimes explode. For this reason, a homemade still is never sealed so tightly as to be made airtight or waterproof. For safety's sake, there's a lot of leakage around a still in the woods.

Back to the boys laying back on the leafy hillside in the deep woods, about 12 feet above Pepper's Creek (their water supply), listening to their operation make white whiskey. All three men were wearing ragged bib overalls, old brown brogans without laces, and a variety of worn out flannel shirts. Each was wearing a dirty, sweat stained, baseball cap with different logos on the front. Neither of them had bathed nor shaved in several days.

Kevin got up and packed some more flour dough into the cracks around the top of the thumper where steam was escaping. Every now and then the cooker would boil the mash to the point where it generated too much steam. The steam could not reach the condenser coil to be reduced to a liquid, alcohol. The potential white whiskey would then escape around the top of the thumper.

Kevin used flour dough to seal the steam leaks of the rig for several reasons. It didn't affect the taste of the white. The thumper had to be sealed; but if it was sealed too tightly, it might blow up. Flour mixed with the water made a perfect sealer. Often, the dough would cook in the cracks and make a bread seal. The regular "Whomp, Whomp, Whomp!" of the thumper told everyone in hearing distance that the Braswells were running their still that morning. Sound travels forever on a brisk fall morning on the mountain in the woods.

Junior got up and turned the propane burner down a little with the blue plastic knob on top of the small tank. He didn't want the thumper singing that loudly. The rhythmic noise died down. Still the propane tank gave out a small roar of the gas flame going to the cooker, as the still sang various songs hissing steam and gurgling liquid. Finally, there was the sound of the whiskey running into a five-gallon olive drab army fuel tank, which was called the catcher. Once the tank was relatively full another tank was put under the spout. The white whiskey was then poured through a funnel into the new shiny one-gallon glass jugs.

"Don't turn 'er down so low she won't cook," Kevin said. He was the unofficial distiller. He made all the decisions about the run.

"If she stops, hit'll be a while for her to build up another head of steam that good."

He continued to pack dough in cracks where the steam pressure blew out.

"I ain't gonna let her go down," Junior said a little agitated, "I'm just stopping her from telling the news to Mary. Going the way she was, the law would be down here in no time."

He turned the blue knob of the propane tank up slightly. The humming still then seemed to be running to everyone's satisfaction.

Darren said, "You know what we ought to do?" He hesitated, waiting for either one of the others to respond. His eyes searched the branches of the trees above him.

"Whut?" Kevin asked.

"We oughta finish this here run, sell the makin's, then sell the still. I been thinkin about this. I figure we can get $1,800 for the whole thing. Then we'uns could buy a van and rob a bank."

"Rob a bank?" Kevin asked in amazement. "Are you crazy?"

"Naw, I been thinkin about it. I don't know about you, but I'm tard of carrin them 100 pound bags of sugar through the woods. You know, makin whiskey ain't easy work, and you don't make no money neither. I bet that we'uns don't make ten dollar an air doin this, an look at the risk we run. We git cought one time and the lawyer gits all our profit for the whole damned year. Hit jist ain't worth it. I figure we could rob a couple of banks and make as much for a couple airs work as we make bein out here at daylight."

"He's got a point," Junior said. "My Uncle Arvil Owens used to rob banks. He never got cought and lived good all the time. He'd only rob little banks, and he'd only rob about one a year."

Twenty-one-year-old Junior was a Bostic. Kevin and Darren were the Braswell brothers with Darren, age twenty-five, being the oldest. Kevin was twenty-three. None of the men had finished high school, nor had either of them ever held a job. They were, pure and simple, white whiskey people and had been making it most of their respective lives. They learned their trade from their fathers and uncles.

"You know whut they do to bank robbers?" Kevin asked. "They put their asses in the federal prison, forever! You hear that? Forever! Anyway, I like to smell mash."

Junior joined back in, "If I did it, I wouldn't figure on gittin cought. Iffun you git away with only one bank holdup a year, you could put enough away in case you did git cought. I'd go to the joint fer five year fer $300,000. Wouldn't you? Hit shore beats hell outta makin white."

Kevin began to chink the rig with dough a little slower as he thought seriously about robbing a bank. The three partners were quiet and reflective for a moment.

"Maybe we could pull it off," he said. "If we

were gonna do it, whut bank would we rob?"

"Well, you can't rob the one in Trenton. Hits done been robbed already, and every bank robber what robbed 'um is in prison. So the Bank of Dade is out." Junior rubbed his chin as he was thinking out loud.

"Them banks in Fort Payne and Scottsboro are too big to rob. They's too many workers. One of 'um might escape and bring the law right back down on you." He thought a little more.

"I guess the same goes for Summerville. We can't rob none of them banks. Maybe Stevenson or Bridgeport might be the size we could handle."

"The bank I wuz thinkin about holdin up wuz the Bank of Menlo," Darren said. "Menlo is a small town. They's three roads in and out of the bank, but only one door to the bank. Plus, I think they's only three or four employees. We'uns could throw down on the employees, herd 'um into the vault, lock 'um in, and git away."

"Hit sounds like you been plannin this for a while," Junior accused.

"I been doin some thinkin. I'll have to admit," Darren reacted. "What'd you think about it?"

"I jist wonder why'n the hell you wanna rob a bank that ain't got no money. They's no money in Menlo, Georgia. Shit! Most of the stores are boarded up. They ain't but one store open.

Them glove factories closed a couple a year ago. They may be two little shirt factories left that work hardly nobody," Junior argued.

Kevin interrupted, "Listen, let's git this run in the jugs, git this rig tore down and put away, and then we can decide what we'uns gonna do about robbin a bank."

"They's plenty of money in that bank," Darren interjected. "Otherwise, it would be boarded up too."

It seemed he made a reasonable point.

"Will you'ins help me?" Kevin said becoming aggravated.

He was doing all the work, putting up the gas tank, breaking down the parts of the still, and trying to move things to the pickup truck. The others knew he didn't need to be pushed too far. They pitched in to help.

The three men began to work feverishly. Clean gallon jugs were removed from cardboard cartons that held four jugs each. The jugs were filled with whiskey from the five-gallon tanks and put back in the boxes. Eventually, the propane torch was cool enough to be stored. The tank was put on the battered old brown Dodge pickup, a 1958 model, and the still was dismantled.

It was after noon before the men were finished. The still and equipment had been taken up the hill and hidden in an old abandoned run down chicken house. The boxes of gallon jugs filled with white whiskey were loaded on two old pickup trucks, the other being a dented, rusty, bumper-missing GMC. A tarpaulin was spread over the jugs on each truck to hide them from the naked eye. Brush, firewood, old cardboard cartons, and other trash located around the site, were loaded on top of the whiskey to hide it from the trained observer who would usually be the authorities.

Within two days, the partners had sold and delivered 178 gallon jugs of white whiskey at $8 per gallon. They had grossed some $1,400 off an $800 investment, leaving them $200 each for their labor. Realistically, they each earned about $250 a week making white whiskey. Not bad money at the time, but the work was hard and the risks were great. It was all they knew how to do, but they wanted to do something else.

After several other discussions, they decided that they would not sell the rig. They might need it again, and copper stills were hard to come by. They decided that they would trade in one of the trucks and put up $800 cash to buy the van. They persuaded Danny Sawyer to buy the van for them in Chattanooga. The old green 1958 Ford van had only a driver's seat. It had been a working vehicle. It had only two small windows in the back with two doors on the right side for easy access. It was not titled. In fact, the title was left open and deposited in the battered glove compartment that would not lock. Whoever was driving the van was its owner. The partners did not want to invest in a tag so they stopped in Rossville, Georgia, and lifted a license plate off a van parked at a restaurant.

The partners had not actually decided to rob the bank at Menlo, Georgia, but circumstances and events were slowly falling into place for the holdup to happen. They parked the van in Junior's brother's barn and closed the doors. No one had ever seen either of the men driving the van nor being around the vehicle.

They then began to "case the bank," by watching it for three weeks. They would swap times to sit in their pickup trucks, or stand on a corner, or pretend to be looking at the building boarded up across the street. Junior Bostic took a job at Butler's Standard Station next to the bank. Through his job he learned the names of the bank personnel, where they lived, who their families were, and generally what kind of people they were. The potential bank robbers learned that there were four employees working at the bank. The money was picked up by a Brinks truck each Thursday at 2:55 p.m. The bank seemed to have most of its money right after the two plants in Menlo issued payroll checks on the third Friday of each month.

The partners decided that if they were going

to rob the Bank of Menlo, they should rob it on Monday morning, following the plant's payday and the deposits of the retail beer sales on Saturday night.

After coming down the east side of Lookout Mountain from Mentone, Alabama, on Highway 110, that is Highway 48 beginning at the Georgia line, turn left at the only caution light in town and the bank was located about three city blocks up 7th street on the right. It was a small one-story brick building about 60' wide and 100' deep. It had modernized to have a drive-in window, but that was about as far as modernization had gone. It was a family owned business and had been for more than 50 years.

The bank president, Wilford P. Grooms, always arrived first for work. The potential bank robbers timed him. He entered the bank promptly at 7:53 a.m. each Monday morning, not 7:50 and not 7:55, but precisely 7:53 a.m.

Seven minutes later, at 8:00 o'clock precisely, Mary Lynn Ables, Sara Nell Smith, and Ronald Helms parked their cars, shut their doors almost simultaneously, and entered the bank. They were so automatic they appeared to have been choreographed. And, after speaking to each other, into the bank they went.

Mary Lynn immediately made coffee. Wilford P. and Ronald Helms, with coffee in hand, stood at the vault door, waiting for it to open at exactly 8:30 am. Sara Nell would proceed directly into the vault and sign out for the daily operational funds. She and Mary Lynn worked the two inside teller cages and doubled as tellers servicing the drive-in window.

Wilford P. was an aristocrat, a stuffed shirt. He was precisely dressed in a hand-tailored suit with expensive conservative shoes. Not a hair was out of place on his graying head. He was tall, slim, and very controlled. He liked things the way they were supposed to be. He tolerated very little levity and did not have much of a sense of humor. The bank and his family were his life. His idea of a good time was choir practice at the First Methodist Church on Wednesday night. His grandfather had founded the bank in 1907. His father had been its president before him, and he had been the president seven years. Before that, he came out of Emory University and was vice president for twenty-six years.

Ronald Helms had graduated from Georgia Southern University with a major in finance. He met and married Melissa Grooms while she was a student at GSU, as well. He worked at First State Bank in Atlanta for almost a year before Wilford P. became president of the family bank and needed a vice president. His new son-in-law was nominated and elected. Ronald had been vice president the same length of time Wilford P. had been president.

With a full head of almost red hair, Ronald was somewhat pallid, almost sickly looking. He was definitely not the athletic type. His sport was chess and his hobby was cooking. He and Melissa were the parents of a six-year-old son and a nine-year-old daughter. They were active members of the First Methodist Church of Menlo, Georgia.

Both Mary Lynn and Sara Nell had worked at the bank since graduating from high school. Mary Lynn had been employed by the bank for twelve years. She was in her early thirties, the mother of two daughters with a husband who worked in Rome for GE. She was not unattractive. However, she was somewhat dumpy, plump, maybe 20 pounds overweight, but well groomed, well dressed and thoroughly businesslike. Sara Nell was twenty-nine years old and the only person in the bank with any sense of humor. She was happily married to Frank Smith who worked in nearby Coosa, Georgia as the Postmaster. She was an attractive young woman, very well built, not the least over weight with blonde hair, brown eyes, a full mouth and always well dressed.

The four bank employees interacted with each other in a certain preordained manner. Wilford P. was never questioned. His word was law. Ronald could not afford to be friendly with the women for fear his father-in-law would think him unfaithful to his daughter. Mary Lynn was consumed with her children, their schoolwork and her husband. Sara Nell was an exercise enthusiast. She ran marathons and rode bicycles and could usually be seen on the Jamestown road every Saturday at 6:00 a.m. running the miles down to the Alabama line and back.

Junior reported this information and much more to his partners. Then, he quit his job.

With the case of the bank knowledge in hand, the three met at Kevin's mobile home while his wife was at work on Friday afternoon. They drank a few beers and talked about the possibility of robbing the bank at Menlo. They eventually made the decision to rob the bank the following Monday at 8:00 A.M.

The mountain boys planned to drive the van up to the front of the bank. Junior would be driving. He would drop Darren and Kevin off just as Wilford P. opened the bank. They would follow him in, throw down on him, and keep him under control until the others arrived. When the other three employees came into the bank, they would be looking down the barrel of the Braswell brother's weapons. They would be forced to follow their usual routines as normal as possible until the safe opened. Fortunately, the safe opened thirty minutes before customers were allowed into the bank. The boys from the north end figured they could intimidate the four employees and get away before the first customer was due in the bank. By that time, the employees would be locked in the vault, and the robbers would be on their way back home.

"What do we'uns say to Wilford P.?" Kevin asked. "Do we say, 'this here is a stickup,' or do we say, 'this here is a bank robbery,' or do we say, 'git em up, this is a bank robbery?'" He was genuinely concerned.

"I think if you put a .38 special Smith in his ribs, with you'ins wearin a ski mask, he'll git the picture soon enough," Darren said. "But I'm worried about this thing, a little. Suppose we'uns have to shoot one of these people? Suppose they don't do what they're told and we have to kill one or more of them? What about that?" He looked questioningly toward his friends.

"A man's gotta do what a man's gotta do," Kevin said. "Them bank workers are told not to resist a robbery. They're supposed to cooperate and let the FBI catch the robbers. Maybe they won't give us no trouble, but if I tell one to do something, they better damned sure do it, and I mean quick. Otherwise, I'm lettin that big dog bark, an his bite is a helluva lot worse than his bark." He looked knowingly at his partners.

"Look," said Junior seriously. "If we're doin this job, we're doin the job. And, we mean to do it. Let's hope nobody gives us no trouble, but if they do, eben though I'm in the truck, I got an itchy trigger fanger."

"So've I," responded Kevin.

"Me too," Darren said. "Okay, it's settled," he continued. "We go on this job Monday."

The partners then spent the next three hours planning in great detail exactly how the robbery was going to go down.

On Monday, March 27, 1967, shortly after dawn, dressed in old dirty black gym suits, which would later be called sweatsuits, the men looked like goblins dressed for Halloween.

They wore hunting boots. The partners went to Junior's brother's barn and got into the old green van.

Since Junior was going to drive, he carried a 12 gauge Mossberg pump shotgun. Kevin and Darren were carrying revolvers. Darren had brought an extra .25 automatic which he carried in his right boot. Each man wore a black ski mask with white rings around the eyes. Darren wanted to wear this mask because he thought it would be more frightening to the bank employees. Junior wore his ski mask so the guys at the service station wouldn't recognize him. They agreed in advance to call each other "Hambone," rather than use any proper names.

On the way over Lookout Mountain, Kevin asked, "What did you decide to say, Hambone, 'stick 'em up, this is a bank robbery, get 'em up,' or what?" He was talking to Darren.

Darren turned his head in order to see Kevin through his ski mask. "Don't worry about it, Hambone. They'll git the message. We'll jist be firm, that's all."

Junior drove around for ten minutes to be sure he timed their arrival precisely with the arrival of Wilford P. At 7:53 a.m. Wilford P., dressed impeccably, approached the front door of the bank with his key in hand. He didn't glance in either direction before going into the bank. He was thinking of something miles away from what he was doing. He was humming "Amazing Grace."

Junior pulled up in front of the bank just as Wilford P. was going through the door. Darren and Kevin jumped out of the van and bolted into the bank behind Wilford P.

"What the hell?" Wilford P. exclaimed. He usually didn't use slang words.

Kevin raised his revolver and pointed it at Wilford P. as Darren did the same. Neither man said a word.

"Is this a bank robbery?" Wilford P. asked in a shaky voice.

"You bet your sweet ass hit is," Darren said in his deepest most threatening tone.

"Now git over there in yore office and shut up and nobody will git hurt. Me'an Hambone are gonna wait fer the other three. Then, we'uns are gonna rob this here bank and leave here. If you stay outta our way, you'll be all right. Otherwise, Hambone's liable to blow your shit plum away. You got that?" He advanced on Wilford P. brandishing his gun toward the bank president.

"You'll get no trouble from me, nor from any of the employees," Wilford P. said pleading. "Just don't hurt any of us. Take the money and leave. All of us have families."

He didn't think the robbers would stay around for the vault to open.

"Then be sure you see'um tonight fer supper," Kevin said threateningly.

True to form, the other bankers came through the front door together. Ronald turned to lock the door without noticing the robbers. He was locking the door so customers could not get in until the bank was set up and ready for them. The women saw the robbers, stopped in their tracks, and were speechless. Neither of them screamed as they saw the men in ski masks with guns pointed toward them. This was the day they had been warned about and had dreaded since they went to work for the bank.

Under their fall coats Sara Nell was wearing a comfortable green flowered dress. Mary Lynn was more athletically dressed in a yellow mini skirt and tight blue silk blouse with white buttons.

"Jist bring it on in here, sister," said a voice

behind a ski mask motioning with his pistol.

"Oh, what are we going to do? Mary Lynn lamented.

"You'ins are gonna do what you're told and nobody gits hurt. Fuck up one time and you're dead," the threatening voice said.

"Everybody git in Wilford P.'s office. Now git!"

The women entered the president's office without removing their coats or putting down their purses. The office was on the left rear side of the building with a window in the north wall. The east wall had a door to Wilford P.'s private rest room and a storage room for banking supplies. The office had glass around the two sides facing into the bank. From his office, Wilford P. could observe everything going on in the bank. Vice President Helms did not have an office, but rather sat at a desk between Wilford P.'s glass enclosure and the front entrance. There was an empty desk on his side of the bank in case another vice president was ever needed. The actual banking operation took place on the other side of the building where there were three teller's cages and the drive-through window.

"I'm scared to death," Sara Nell said. "I may pass out."

"Don't pass out before I do," Mary Lynn responded glancing back at the masked men. "I'm afraid I'm about to wet myself."

Ronald Helms had habitually locked the door. Then he did exactly what he was told without saying a word.

"Now you'ins make yourself comfortable," the voice behind the ski mask said. "We'uns gonna wait until that vault opens, we'uns gonna take all the money, and we'uns gonna leave. You fuck up our plans and you're dead," the mask said motioning with the gun. "This here is serious business."

All the blood had drained from Ronald's face. He would like to have been a hero, but it didn't seem the time nor place to do anything. Plus, he was frightened out of his wits. The thought did cross his mind that one block over was Jamestown Road named for the small community in Cherokee County, Alabama, that was named after the family of Jesse and Frank James. They would hide out there when the law was hot on their trail in the mid-west. "Small world," he thought.

One masked man stayed in the office with the hostages. The other stayed out in the bank watching the windows and door. For the hostages the twenty-five minutes seemed like an eternity.

To Mary Lynn, everything she said sounded stupid. She knew that everything Sara Nell said was stupid.

"Why don't you folks jist git comfortable and shut up?" the masked man asked.

The blinds on the windows were still drawn. Wilford P. sat quietly and reserved at his desk, while the women sat in his two customer chairs in their coats holding their purses on their laps. Ronald stood in the corner watching the eyes in the ski mask watching him. He tried to be sure the bandit could always see his hands. He had learned that at a banking seminar in Charlotte.

At 8:30 a.m. the whirring clicking sounds let everyone know the vault was opening. "All right folks," the threatening voice said, "One wrong move and I'll kill you."

Turning toward the glass office door he said, "Hambone, git in there, put that money in that duffel bag, and git the hell out. When you got all the money, let me know. We'uns 'er on borrowed time right now. So move!"

Five minutes later a voice from the bank vault said, "I got it all, Hambone. I din't leave much 'cept a few quarters an some other change. Let's blow this joint."

"All right, ladies and gentlemen," the ski mask with the gun nearest them said. "Git in the vault!" He gestured with his gun toward the huge gray vault door.

Wilford P. came around his desk and Ronald followed him. Mary Lynn got up to be third in line.

"I'll die in there," Sara Nell whined. "I have claustrophobia. Leave me out and I won't do anything." She was pleading.

"Git your ass in that vault or die out here!" the mask said. "I ain't gonna fuck with you. Now git!"

Slowly she went into the vault. Ronald was trying to calm her. "You'll be all right, Sara Nell, there's plenty of air in the vault. Believe me, you'll be all right."

He was trying to tell her that he knew how to open the vault from the inside. He had studied bank vaults in college and knew there was an emergency release inside the workings of the door. However, he didn't want the robbers to know about it. In addition, he always carried a one-cell pen light on his key ring that was in his pocket. And he kept fresh batteries in it, just in case.

"Lock the door, Hambone," Kevin said to Darren. As he was closing the huge door, he said to the hostages, "If we'uns see a one of you before we make our getaway, you're dead, you hear me?"

The vault door closed, and Darren spun the wheel to lock it.

Kevin ran to the front of the bank. "Okay, Hambone's comin back up the street right now. Let's git the hell outa here."

The brothers waited until Junior was directly in front of the door to the bank. As he reached over and opened the passenger door, they rushed out of the bank and into the van. Junior was moving forward as the last one jumped into the van.

The men took their masks off. Junior kept driving north toward Lafayette, Georgia. He planned to double back across Lookout Mountain, through Trenton, and home.

"We made it!" Kevin screamed laughing. "We robbed the bank and got away with it. We're rich. You ought to see the money I got. I was grabbin money in every direction. If a bag even looked like it had money in it I grabbed it. Yahoo!"

"It ain't over 'til we git home and git rid of this van," Darren cautioned.

"Well, let's see it," Junior yelled. "I been drivin around while you boys havin all the fun. Let's see the haul."

"Okay," Kevin dumped the contents of the duffel bag out onto the floor of the van behind where a passenger seat might have been. There were stacks of money held together with rubber bands, there were stacks of money held together with paper bindings indicating the amount of money, there were bags of coins, bags of bills, checks, and two drawers loaded with money for the day's work.

"Look at that money!" Darren said. "Did you'ins ever see such money in yore life? Jist look at that!."

Junior turned in the driver's seat to look at the loot. "They's more money there than I've ever seen in my life. We're rich!"

Kevin was sitting on a wooden box in the back of the van. Most of the money was on an old piece of carpet that had been put on the green metal floor. Darren was squatting with his back to the side doors of the van. Kevin reached over and lifted a bills retainer in one of the teller drawers to look at the loose money under the clip. When he did, the red dye bomb went off!

The robbers did not know that the teller's drawer contained bait money under the larger bills. Once the retainer was lifted, the bomb was armed. When the pressure was taken off, the bomb exploded and red dye covered a ten-foot area. There was a 'Whoosh!' and in the van everything suddenly went red, very red!

"Goddamned! What happened?" Junior yelled, stopping the van as it went off the right side of the road.

"They wuz a bomb in that money," Kevin said. "I never heard of anything like that before." He was wiping his eyes with his ski mask.

Darren was trying to get the red dye out of his eyes with his right coat sleeve. Junior was using a napkin that had been left over from someone's meal to wipe a small place on the windshield where he could see to drive. With all the windows drenched in red dye, the van was suddenly very dark inside. Every surface was completely red. The money was red. The duffle bag was red. Everything was red.

Kevin looked at Darren through white eyes and started laughing. "You look like a tomato with big white eyes," he laughed. "You ought to see yourself."

"I don't know why youse laughing," Darren said. "You'ins look like you jist went swimmin in a catsup bottle."

Junior could barely see to drive through the small spot he had cleaned on the windshield. He saw enough to spot a dirt road off to the left ahead. It looked as if it was not used a lot. He turned a hard left.

"I'm gonna go down in here and we'uns are gonna check our damage."

A little over a mile down the road, he stopped. There were large fields on each side of the road. Lookout Mountain was less than a quarter of a mile ahead.

"What a fuckin mess," Kevin said. He opened the side doors to the van to allow the morning light in. "We're really fucked up. We're covered with red stuff, the money is covered with red stuff, the van is painted with red stuff, we gotta do some straight thinkin now."

"I think we oughtta put the money back in the duffel bag. There ain't no tellin if theys another dye bomb mixed in with the money. Now I know why I sometimes git money with red on it. Hit's been in a bank robbery," Darren said. He began to put the dye-colored money and bags into the dye-covered duffel bag.

After the partners had finished loading the money into the duffle bag they got out of the van.

"We're in a helluva shape," Junior said. "First, how we gonna git home lookin like this? Second, how we gonna git this shit off? Everywhere its dried on me, hit's like a tattoo."

"Well, shit, boys, we gotta do somethin," Kevin opined.

"Let's jist sit here until dark and drive home like white folks," Darren said. "They ain't no tellin when that vault'll open and them people will find out their bank's been robbed."

"They'll know she was robbed by now," Junior said. "They was people waiting to get to the bank when it opened. I seen 'em at the Gulf station and at the Standard Station. So, they know their bank wuz robbed by now." He tried to see his watch, but its face was red.

Darren's coat sleeve had protected his watch. "Hit's 9:10. They already know their bank wuz robbed, them people's out of the vault, and they're lookin for a green van by now. We need to git further into the woods."

"You're right," Junior said. "Let's load up and go down near the base of the mountain. Then, we'll wait till dark and go home. Maybe lighter fluid or mineral spirits will git this shit off."

The partners got back into the van, Junior

rolled down the driver's window, stuck his red head out, and proceeded deeper into the woods toward the base of Lookout Mountain.

In a matter of minutes, it sounded as if the entire valley was bursting with police vehicles. The partners could hear police sirens in every direction. They inched forward slowly.

As soon as Wilford P. and his employees had been herded into the vault, and the door closed, Ronald produced his pen light from inside his coat. He then played the light on the vault locking mechanisms. The timer would not open the door again until the following morning. Ronald tripped a small obscure lever which resulted in the wheels turning and the door opening up. The group had been in the vault less than three minutes.

Wilford P. went directly to his desk and called the Menlo City Hall. The mayor was not at work yet, but the policeman was on duty. He was dispatched by the city clerk to the bank. Chief of Police Michael Allen, the city's only policeman, knew enough to notify the Sheriff of Catoosa County in Summerville who in turn notified the FBI. By 9:20 a.m. the bank was literally crawling with law enforcement personnel.

FBI Special Agent Art Millwee was in Lafayette when he received the news that the Bank of Menlo had been robbed. With siren blaring and lights flashing he arrived at the bank 20 minutes later.

Millwee was fifty pounds overweight, of average height, red faced wearing a gray business suit with black wingtip shoes. Sometimes he snorted when he talked. He had been the agent in charge in Northwest Georgia for more than twenty years. He prided himself in knowing every crook northwest of Atlanta.

With everyone gathered around in the bank, Millwee snorted and announced to all personnel present, "Gentlemen, a federal law has been broken. This investigation is herewith declared to be a federal investigation, and I will direct it until the miscreants are captured, or until I am relieved by my superiors."

He then told the sheriff's investigators to interview the four victims in detail, taking written statements - statements that can be used in evidence. He instructed that the people were to be interviewed separately in case it was an inside job. Every statement was to be sworn to and notarized.

He and the sheriff were going to join the dragnet for the time being. "We know they were driving an old green Ford van. People at the Gulf station noticed it cruising the street earlier today. It had a Georgia tag. Since the sheriff didn't meet any van coming over from Summerville, our robbers went toward Lafayette. They didn't go toward Centre, or west toward Mentone, Alabama, because they are Georgians. So let's take about a dozen men and spread out toward Lafayette."

The sheriff designated six men, Mike Allen volunteered, a couple of game wardens said they would help, and Millwee radioed his Special Agent in Charge in Rossville to send more agents. In the meantime, ten men started toward Lafayette. "Go down every side road," Millwee instructed. "Every one. I mean don't miss any."

In a matter of minutes the bank robbers heard police cars converging from two different directions. Apparently, cars from Lafayette had come down Highway 242, Menlo Chelsea Road, the back way from the north. Millwee's men were coming hard from the south.

Junior said, "Boys, in a matter of minutes we are goin to be in the arms of John Law if we don't git the hell outta here."

"Well, which way you gonna go?" Darren asked. "They's law in both directions."

"I'm going cross-country," Junior said, as he turned the van left into an old field. The soil was hard enough to keep the van from sinking in the soft soil up to its hubs.

After almost an eighth of a mile, Junior said, "Look at this, right there's the woods, and they'll never find us."

As Junior was speaking and the brothers were looking out red colored windows in the rear of the van, the vehicle stopped. It sputtered, ran rough, and stopped 100 yards short of the woods.

"What the hell?" exclaimed Junior.

"Sounds like we'uns done run outta of gas," Kevin said. "Did you fill the tank before we left to rob the bank?"

"Naw," responded Junior. "I knowed the gas gauge didn't work. Sos I thought we'd have plenty of gas."

He hesitated thinking out loud, "Maybe I run it out of gas drivin around waitin fer you'ins to come outta the bank." He was deeply concerned.

"Well, I wouldn't worry about it too much right now," Kevin said. "In just about three minutes we gonna git a ride with Art Millwee. I'd recognize that old gov'ment issue car anywhere. He's spotted us and is coming right across the field hell for leather right now!"

"Should we'uns try to shoot our way outta this? You know, like Bonnie and Clyde?" Darren asked, reaching for Junior's pump shotgun.

"Shit naw! Bonnie and Clyde wuz shot to hell. They's more of 'em comin. Yeah, I see about six cars. Put the gun down."

Junior asked, "Should we sit here and lettum git us, or should we git out with our hands up?"

"Shit, let's jist sit," Kevin reacted. "Don't say nothin. Don't make no statements, we'uns in enough trouble as it is."

The officers dismounted their vehicles and circled the van with guns drawn and pointed at the vehicle.

"You boys don't do nothing stupid," Art Millwee yelled toward the old green Ford with red windows and missing hubcaps.

Millwee motioned for the officers to move in closer. He walked up to the driver's door which had the window rolled down and looked into the van. In the darkness he could see three red men sitting around a large red duffle bag. Each of the men smiled at Millwee. All he could see was eyes and teeth.

He laughed, "Take it easy boys," he yelled to the officers. "All we got is Little Red Riding Hood, Red Ryder, and Red Red Robin."

He broke into uncontrollable loughter and then coughing. He thought he was more funny than he was.

Sheriff Gerald Keys walked to the van side doors and opened both doors simultaneously. It was then the officers could see the bank robbers who were red from head to foot. Their shoes were dyed red. Their hair was red; their faces were red; their hands were red. There was nothing about the interior of the van that was not red.

"I know you're bashful, boys, but get out with your hands up," the sheriff said. "Uh, throw out those guns first. Easy, easy."

Junior and the brothers were so embarrassed that they threw their two pistols and the shotgun out butt first. A Georgia State Trooper ran forward and scooped the guns off the ground. He put the guns at the back of Millwee's FBI vehicle.

It was then he noticed he had red dye all over his hands and the front of his uniform shirt where the shotgun had rested against his chest.

"Shit!" he exclaimed. "I can't believe I got that red shit all over me."

The other officers laughed. From then on, everyone was careful to avoid the ubiquitous red dye.

The three partners were photographed by FBI Agents who laughed as they snapped pictures of the bank robbers.

"These look like blank rubbers to me," chortled the shortest agent with a camera. The rest of the officers joined in the mirth.

A game warden kept it going by saying, "They'd rather be red than dead."

A deputy said, "I guess we cought them red-handed."

"You gonna give them their Miranda rights?" a Lafayette policeman asked Millwee. Then he continued trying to be funny, "He said as he read red rights readily."

"Which cowboy's going to cuff these dangerous red men?" the sheriff asked.

"I'll cuff them," Millwee snorted. "I got one set of cuffs. Gimme two more.   Several officers proffered hand cuffs. Millwee took the nearest two pairs. Turning to Chief Allen, he said, "All right Chief, give each of these boys a pair of these cuffs. You know the score. You been here before. Put 'em on."

He watched as Allen made sure Junior and the brothers helped cuff themselves. Millwee continued, "Anything you say may be held against you. If you desire a lawyer, one will be appointed for you. You do not have to answer any questions, nor say anything against your interests. Now, who the hell are you?"

"Kevin Braswell," Kevin said.

"Junior Bostic," Junior said next.

"No need for you to say anything," Millwee said to Darren. "I know who you are. You're Kevin's older brother, Darren Braswell." Darren didn't say anything.

Millwee turned to the sheriff. "I'm not going to put these people in my government vehicle. They'll mess it up too bad. Unless you want to put them in one of your cars, I suggest we take some blankets and put them over the seat in the van and let one of our men drive it to Rome. We'll leave the prisoners in the back of the van. We can follow them closely. We'll cover them up. They ain't going nowhere."

"Sounds fine to me," the sheriff responded. He turned to the game wardens, "You boys got some government issue blankets in your vehicles?" He knew they had blankets.

The game wardens nodded affirmatively and went to three conservation vehicles and brought three olive drab army blankets back to the sheriff.

The FBI had completely photographed the scene, the van, the prisoners, the guns, the money, and announced that the locals could clean it up. Several deputies and local policemen took towels and grease rags to clean the red die on the steering wheel, the driver's seat, the driver's door panel, and the armrest. Much of the dye had dried and did not pose a problem. However, there were puddling areas which were sopped up by the officers. Four towels were streaked with red. A grease rag was converted from the usual bland pink to the hideous red color of the dye.

Eventually, a five-gallon can of gas was poured into the van's tank and the blankets were spread over the driver's seat. Mike Allen, the Menlo Chief of police, being its entire police department, was designated to drive the prisoners. Millwee said the collar belonged to the FBI, but they would give credit to the local police and the sheriff in facilitating the collar, whatever that meant. The sheriff declined to drive the van when offered, therefore the Menlo Police Chief would do the honors.

He handed Junior a key to the handcuffs of

Kevin Braswell. "Unlock his cuffs and thread them through yours and Darren's," Millwee instructed. "Then you boys climb into the back of the van. I don't need to tell you we have you surrounded and we will shoot to kill if you attempt to escape. Anyway, where you going to go?" He laughed heartily again.

Junior did as he was told and handed the key back to Millwee. The FBI Agent made a mistake. He reached for the key and drew his right hand back with a red spot the size of a silver dollar on it. It would be three weeks before the spot wore off. Millwee tried to hand the key to the owner of the cuffs, but the deputy withdrew his hands.

"You keep it for a while, Art," the deputy laughed.

After several more minutes, the robbers were loaded into the van, the side doors were closed, the van was started, and the group turned around in the field and headed back to the dirt road. When the van was ready to turn back toward Menlo and the Rome City Jail, where federal prisoners were detained, Millwee stopped everyone and organized the cavalcade. He put the sheriff in the lead car. A patrol car from Lafayette followed the sheriff. Then came the van. Millwee immediately followed the van. He took two Special Agents of the FBI with him as shooters in case the prisoners tried to escape. After the government issue FBI vehicle, the rest of the group joined in and followed along. In all, it was a fourteen-car convoy with sirens blaring and blue lights flashing.

The group arrived in Rome, Georgia, without incident. The prisoners were offloaded into the hands of the jailer. He told a guard to remove the cuffs and told the men to strip. Each robber was given a towel and escorted to the shower stall in the federal holding cell.

After three hours and substantial scrubbing with Lava soap and mineral spirits, Kevin Braswell was brought into the interrogation room. He was booked, photographed, printed, and told to sit down. Four FBI Agents were on hand to question him. By the time the agents were ready to interrogate the prisoners, a special agent who was a specialist in bank robbery investigation had arrived in Rome from the Atlanta Office of the FBI. He took charge of the questioning.

"We know positively that you, your brother, and your friend, were the perpetrators of the kidnaping and bank robbery at the Bank of Menlo, Georgia, a bank insured by the Federal Deposit Insurance Corporation. Are you aware that bank robbery is a federal offense punishable by life in the penitentiary?"

Kevin hardly understood a word the agent said with a very pronounced northern accent. He looked at him blankly.

"Well, what have you got to say for yourself?" the agent said.

Kevin looked at him. He wondered if this was really happening. He was sitting in Rome, Georgia, dressed in a thin jailhouse bathrobe, thin rubber flip-flops on his feet, and red dye in his fingernails and in the wrinkles around his eyes. His hair was red, his beard was red, and a Yankee was asking him questions he didn't understand. He looked at the agent with a vacant stare.

"You are demanding not to talk?" the agent asked.

Nothing.

"Do you understand a word I've said?"

Nothing.

"You can make it easy on yourself by cooperating with the Federal Bureau of Investigation. Your friend Junior is just waiting to talk to us. I suggest you cooperate immediately." The agent was very authoritative.

Kevin said nothing.

After several more tries, the agent returned Kevin to his cell and brought Junior in. Same speech, same questions, same result. Junior had no idea what that Damned Yankee was saying.

Later in the cell he told Kevin, "You know, if old Art had questioned me, I mightuv answered him, but I waddn't gonna say shit to that blue belly."

"Me neither," responded Kevin.

Since it was after midnight, the agents decided to wait until morning to question Darren.

At precisely 7:00 a.m. the following morning Art Millwee with three nondescript agents in tow entered the Floyd County Jail at Rome.

"All right Darren," Millwee snorted. "I want some answers. Who planned this bank robbery?"

Nothing.

"Who bought the van for you boys? I know you can't afford that van. Who bought it?"

Nothing.

"Who planned the job?"

Nothing.

"Do you want a lawyer?"

"Yeah. Can I make a phone call?"

"Throw his ass back in the cell. He's being smart."

After Millwee and his fellow agents finally decided that the robbers were not going to make a statement, they appeared before a magistrate and a bond was set for each of the robbers at $15,000. The families of the red men made their bonds within 30 minutes.

Junior Bostic and his father visited the lawyer the following week. "Can you do anything for this boy," Junior's father asked after Junior had told the story.

"I don't know. These folks seem to be about the dumbest bank robbers I have ever seen. They didn't know about the dye bomb In the show money. They didn't fill their vehicle with gas before they robbed the bank. And, finally, they robbed a bank in Chattooga County, Georgia. Nobody is that stupid," the lawyer looked directly at Junior.

"Okay. I ain't Alfred Einstein. can you get me out of it?"

"All I can promise you is I will do my best. Based upon what you have told me, I do not see any way you are going to get out of this. I suspect you are going to do some federal time for bank robbery. This is particularly true since Art Millwee was the agent in charge of the investigation."

"Yeah," Junior sighed. "We know good ole Art. He's chased us fer years for makin whiskey, and he ain't even a revenuer. He just does it jist fer the pure de ole fun of it."

"He's a renegade agent within the bureau," the lawyer agreed. "He is the only agent I know who gets a lead in Northwest Georgia and follows it to New Orleans. He is supposed to call the agent in charge in New Orleans for the follow-up, but Art doesn't wait for bureau standard operating procedures. He believes he is the law. And, in many ways, I suppose he is."

Junior's father paid the lawyer a substantial

fee to represent Junior in the United States District Court for the Northwestern District of Georgia in Rome, Georgia. The lawyer qualified to represent his client in the out-of-state court and began the long arduous process of investigating the case and discovering what evidence the government was going to use to try to convict Junior.

Eventually, the case came on for trial in the old federal courthouse in Rome, Georgia.

The old Victorian style building had seen better days and would be replaced by a new courthouse three years later. At the time of the trial, Judge Cantrell was holding court in one of the oldest federal courtrooms in the State of Georgia.

The lawyer had been instructed to be in court with his client at 2:00 p.m. on Monday. As he approached the large double doors to the antique courtroom, he ran into Bobby Lee Cook. Cook, a criminal defense lawyer from Summerville, Georgia, was rapidly biting an empty pipe in frustration as he held the pipe in his right hand. His left hand gripped a brief case containing his files. The lawyer could see he was agitated.

"What's going on, Bobby Lee?"

"Woman prosecutor," Cook responded biting the pipe with his teeth making a clicking noise on the pipe stem. "It's a damned female Assistant US Attorney. You ever been up against one?" He squinted his left eye at the lawyer.

"I have never even seen a female prosecutor," the lawyer said with awe in his voice. He was trying to contemplate the idea of a woman prosecuting a case.

"What kind of prosecutor is she?" he asked genuinely interested.

"Mean as hell. Ruthless!" Cook said. "She convicted the hell out of my client in four hours, and I had a good case. I was a gentleman, and she was a bitch."

"My stars!" the lawyer responded. "I'm representing a bank robber in a case where the government has a cod lock. What am I going to do?"

"Kick her in the nuts," Cook said. "Kick that bitch in the nuts, and keep kicking her until you get your client off. Don't cut her any slack just because she's pretty. She's a goddamned shark, and you're her meat if you don't act quickly."

He turned to walk away and the floor sounded of his heels and creaked as he walked. It was a cavernous building and his heels echoed as he left.

"Thanks," the lawyer said after him. "Thanks a lot. I'll do that."

He turned and pushed his way through the large double doors.

The lawyer looked toward the government

table and there she was, big as life, a beautiful woman in a hot pink business suit, a white blouse, and wearing heels to match. She was wearing a string of pearls as her only jewelry. Her fingernails matched her suit. She was tall, blonde, and exceptionally good looking. She turned toward the lawyer, and he noticed her lipstick matched her outfit.

Even without Cook's advice, the lawyer would have been put on guard by this lady. A jury might not see right through her, but he knew she was a formidable enemy when he saw her. He walked to the defense table. His client was sitting in the courtroom with the other defendants and their attorneys. The female Assistant US Attorney didn't acknowledge his presence. When she looked in his direction, she looked over his head. He could not make eye contact. The lawyer knew it was going to be a fight, and he had very little to work with.

Charlie Floyd, an attorney from Rome, Georgia, was representing Darren Braswell; and Phil Rice from Rossville was representing Kevin Braswell. Both Charlie and Phil were appointed to represent each of the brothers pro bono, without fee, by appointment of the Court. Both men were excellent criminal defense lawyers. Both had practiced extensively in the federal court system. The lawyer left the defense table in the pit and sat between the lawyers in the audience.

"Either of you ever tried a case with a female prosecutor?" he asked with a wry smile as the three men continued to eye the oddity at the government table.

The lawyer noticed she had gold buttons on her suit and three on each sleeve. "If she was wearing a navy blue suit with white buttons and blue pumps, I would be more impressed. She looks a little flashy to me."

Phil Rice was the first of the other lawyers to respond. "No, I've never seen a woman prosecutor. I went to school with women and I've worked with women lawyers, but I've never defended a case against one. Charlie and I were just wondering whether she has the killer instinct or not."

Charlie joined in, "We have one woman Assistant DA here in Rome, but she doesn't prosecute important cases. Mostly, she handles bad checks and delinquent child support. She's a pretty good ole gal, but I been warned about this one."

Six eyes continued to be riveted on the lovely woman in hot pink. She busied herself shuffling papers, talking to a male sitting next to where she was standing, and completely engrossing herself in her work. Not once did she look toward her adversaries.

"Bobby Lee Cook told me to kick her in the nuts, and that's exactly what I'm going to do.

Her ability to convict my client is just like a man's. I don't plan to show her any mercy," the lawyer sounded ready to attack the creature in pink in the pit.

"Yeah, I saw a little of Bobby's game," Charlie laughed. "He tried to be a complete gentleman with the woman and she is no lady. She attacked him like a duck with a June bug."

"No quarter asked and no quarter given, women and children last," the lawyer said resolutely.

The clerk entered the courtroom and called the bank robbery case. The lawyers and their clients went to their table. Attorney Floyd attempted to speak to the lady, but she was having none of that. She was too busily engaged in her own affairs.

The lawyer didn't know her name and didn't want to know it. So far as he was concerned, she was the prosecutor and that is what he would call her throughout the trial.

The Judge entered from behind the bench and announced, "Lady and gentlemen, we will strike the jury, make opening statements, and get as far as we can today. I hope to finish this case tomorrow."

He then asked the respective sides if they were ready, and ordered the jury brought in.

Witnesses and interested persons were moved to the left side of the courtroom while the prospective jurors sat on the right.

The lawyer participated in the jury selection without acknowledging the feminine gender of the prosecutor. He began by referring to her as the prosecutor in an effort to deprive her of any feminine advantage she might have. He believed that if he had never seen a female prosecutor, neither had the jurors.

The judge was already fawning over her. The Assistant US Attorney in pink returned the cold reception of the lawyer with icy remarks and piercing stares. It was the lawyer's time to refuse to make eye contact with the young lady. He wished he had a better case. He thought that the U.S. Attorney had sent the woman Assistant US Attorney to try this case because it was like shooting fish in a barrel.

"Oh, well," he thought, "I'll just have to take whatever she gives me. And it's probably not going to be much."

After the jury was selected and seated in the box, the prosecutor began her opening statement. She never mentioned her name or occupation. She told the jury that the FDIC insured the funds robbed from the Bank of Menlo by the three defendants. She then briefly retraced the facts of the case and accused the defendants of putting the bank employees in fear, holding them at gunpoint, stealing the bank's money, and attempting to escape.

"It was only excellent police work that

prevented them from getting away with their daytime robbery."

She tied Junior Bostic to the case by saying he drove the getaway car.

Each defense counsel addressed the jury trying to take a different tact from the others in order to distinguish his client from the remaining defendants.

The lawyer asked the jury to watch for the little things in the Government's case. "Junior Bostic's freedom depends upon the small things, the infinitesimal things that the Government has overlooked and you will find. These little things will create a reasonable doubt in your mind as to the guilt or innocence of Junior. Remember, this is a case made by the Government. This prosecutor must prove every element of the Government's case. The Court is going to tell you this is the law at the end of the evidence. Junior Bostic doesn't have to prove a thing. He doesn't have to prove this is July 10, 1967. The presumption of innocence protects the citizen accused under our system of government. Watch this prosecutor. Watch this prosecutor's evidence. Watch for the little things. Do your duty. Make the prosecutor prove the Government's case against Junior Bostic. If the prosecutor doesn't put him in this bank robbery, you turn him loose."

The lawyer didn't know what the young prosecutor might miss, but surely she would miss something that would leave a crack in her case, and he would drag Junior Bostic through it.

At the conclusion of the opening statements the Court called the evening recess. "9:00 a.m. tomorrow, ladies and gentlemen. Court's in recess."

The following morning, when court convened, the Assistant US Attorney appeared dressed in her hot pink suit once more. The lawyer wondered if she had more than one outfit, or did she press the same one she had worn the day before. She looked exactly the same -- good.

"Call your first witness, Madam Prosecutor," the judge smiled. The lawyer smiled also. The judge had bought into calling the attractive young woman, "Prosecutor."

Her name turned out to be Ellen Whitehall. She had given her name to the clerk following the opening statements.

Ellen called Wilford P. Grooms. The lawyer listened to his testimony as he failed to identify Junior. Ronald and the other employees were called each in succession. Neither of them laid a glove on Junior. The lawyer did not ask any of these witnesses any questions.

Jack Butler, the service station owner, was called to identify Junior Bostic as the casing robber and driver of the green van. Butler testified that Junior had worked for him, but he could not say who was driving the green van the morning of the robbery. He had seen the van pass by the bank several times, but he did not think anything was out of the ordinary.

On cross-examination, the lawyer forced Butler to admit that Junior was an ignorant person but an excellent employee. He would hire him again. So far as he was concerned, Junior was honest. He could not tell the jury Junior participated in any bank robbery anywhere at any time. He volunteered that he would not believe Junior Bostic robbed the Bank unless he had seen him do it. The lawyer asked if he meant that he would require clear and convincing evidence before he would believe Junior did it. He repeated that he would have to see it to believe it.

Once he had volunteered this information, the lawyer pressed him for more positive remarks. He didn't think there would be too many things favorable for Junior in this trial.

"The only thing in the world you know about Junior being involved in this bank robbery is what you have been told by others, isn't that true?"

"That's true, and there's been a lot of that," the witness responded.

"And that doesn't mean a thing, does it?"

"Not in a town as small as Menlo, Georgia. Talking is about all we do, and we talk about everything."

"If there was a doubt based upon reasonable little things in the prosecution against Junior, you would probably refuse to believe he was guilty?"

"You're mighty right about that. They'd have to show me he done it."

On re-direct, the young prosecutor attempted to rehabilitate her witness by asking, "If Junior Bostic was arrested in the van with red dye all over him and the bank money in the back, you'd believe he helped rob the bank, wouldn't you?"

"Objection," the lawyer was on his feet.

"Sustained," the judge looked over his half glasses.

The attractive young lady in hot pink stopped in her pink shoes and looked at the judge. It was clear she was frustrated.

The judge helped her. "You asked a leading question. You can't do that with your own witness. You asked a question with facts which were not touched on in your direct nor cross. You mentioned Junior Bostic having red dye on him. There is no evidence that Mr. Bostic had red dye on him. You can't do that, Madam Prosecutor."

The young woman visibly blushed, and mumbled something releasing the witness.

The Court didn't understand. "Are you releasing this witness, Madam Prosecutor?"

Visibly peeved, the young woman turned to

the judge as she was walking toward her table, "Yes, Your Honor."

"Fine. You may step down, Mr. Butler."

This episode was the most favorable thing that happened to Junior Bostic since the trial began. However, the lawyer knew that Art Millwee and the others were going to put the hat on Junior before the trial was over. He still needed lightning to strike.

The special agent in charge of the bank robbery investigation was called. His testimony was uneventful so far as Junior was concerned. Mostly he testified about the Federal Deposit Insurance Corporation, its relationship with banks and depositors, bank alarms, Brinks pick-up times, and the use of the dye bomb.

On cross-examination, the lawyer asked the agent in charge about fingerprints. "We didn't make any lifts. There was no need to. We cought these people red-handed," he laughed at his own joke.

The lawyer smiled as well. He might have spotted a small fissure in the Government's case against Junior Bostic.

The Assistant US Attorney wanted her pictures into evidence in order that other witnesses might testify concerning each photograph.

She called the FBI special agent who photographed the scene. He produced 26 color photographs. He began with the exterior of the Bank of Menlo, then the interior of the bank, the vault, the locking mechanism, and the cash drawers and the coins scattered on the floor. At the arrest scene he identified the van from a distance, its tag, which he testified was stolen, and the red interior of the van showing the red dye everywhere, the money bag on the floor, the guns and the spot in the windshield where it had been cleared of dye in order to drive the vehicle.

His last series of photos were of the prisoners. They were covered in red dye with only their eyes and teeth a different color from the interior of the van. The jurors laughed as they saw the bank robbers. It was clear they could not identify either of the robbers.

The lawyer asked the witness only one question -- did he, or anyone else, take any other pictures of the bank robbers. The witness said the only other pictures were booking mug shots of the subjects. The lawyer examined the photographs of the robbers in great detail. He could not identify Junior as one of the men. Each of them stood with their hands cuffed in front of them. They lawyer breathed a sigh of relief. Maybe the crack he was looking for was developing.

After the noontime recess, Menlo Chief of Police Mike Allen testified as to his part in the chase and arrest of the robbers. He did not identify Junior Bostic. Still, the lawyer asked him a question, "Did you notice anything strange when you cuffed the robbers?"

"Only that red dye. It was everywhere," he laughed.

"Other than that, was there anything out of the ordinary in the cuffing of the robbers?"

"Not a thing. Standard police work," the chief responded.

"Thank you," the lawyer said as he searched the face of the pretty young woman wondering if she was on notice as to where he was going. There was no sign she knew he was in the courtroom.

Good looking women, particularly nervous ones, are used to ignoring men, he thought. I might just mine a nugget here.

Sheriff Gerald Keys testified as to his involvement in the case. He made a very good witness for the Government. He identified all three men as the people he participated in arresting after the bank robbery.

The lawyer asked him about fingerprints. The sheriff said they were not taken because they were not necessary. On further questioning, he admitted he was very interested in the cuffing of the fugitives because he provided a set of cuffs that came back to him ruined with red dye.

"Did you watch each man cuffed?" the lawyer asked.

"I watched them like a hawk. I wouldn't do it because I didn't want that red stuff all over me."

"Did you carefully see all six wrists cuffed?"

"I did."

"Did you see anything unusual in the cuffing?"

"Not a thing. Three crooks, three sets of cuffs, cuffed and taken away."

"Thank you."

It was a small thing, but the lawyer hoped Art Millwee would be his only witness. Hopefully, the special agent, who was going to hit the home run for the prosecution, would take the bait.

Millwee was the next last witness for the Government. It was his job to tie up all the loose ends and separately and severally convict the defendants. After the preliminary questions, he was allowed to testify in narrative form. He told the facts of the case, he identified each of the defendants, and he told of the recovery of the money.

Due to the manner in which the defense lawyers had been cross-examining witnesses, Charlie Floyd took Millwee first. He asked a question he should never have asked: "Agent Millwee, if these robbers were covered in red, how could you possibly say my client was one of the robbers?"

The agent snorted before he replied. "First, I

asked him his name at the scene, and he said he was Darren Braswell. Second, I accompanied him to Rome and placed him in the federal holding cell. Third, I was there when he washed all the dye off he could. It took him the better part of two hours with mineral spirits and Lava Soap. It was a mess. Fourth, I questioned him and he said nothing.

"So, Mr. Floyd I found him in the van with the money, I directed the officers taking him to jail, I watched him being booked, I saw him washing, I followed him into the cell, and I went back to see him later to question him. There is no doubt your client robbed the Bank at Menlo," he snorted, concluding his sentence.

Charlie Floyd, as though hung from a tree, seem to twist slowly in the rarefied air of the federal courtroom knowing that his client was convicted. He had not intentionally hurt the case of his client. He had done his best in a terrible case, but his question to Art Millwee left no doubt with the jury that his client was a bank robber.

Phil Rice was next. He got out of Millwee that Kevin never told him his name at the van, and he had never made a statement. He was not there when Kevin cleaned the red off. He had never been back to see Kevin.

Millwee said that Kevin was arrested, he was booked, he was charged, he was indicted, he made bond, "and he is in the courtroom today." Snort, "Kevin Braswell is as guilty of being a bank robber as I am guilty of being a special agent of the FBI. The only difference is I'm legal, working for the American people, and Kevin Braswell is illegal, committing crimes against the American people."

Rice had been through enough. He passed the witness. His client was obviously going to be convicted.

The lawyer was next to cross-examine the agent. "What's so special about a special agent of the FBI?"

"We're all special. We work for the people."

"Are there any not-so-special agents of the FBI?"

"Nope, we're all special agents."

"Even the janitor in Washington is a special agent?"

"He could be."

"So there are no FBI agents that aren't special agents?"

"Correct."

"It's just a title to make you people sound more important than you are, isn't that true?"

"It's a title, like attorney. You're an attorney aren't you?"

"Yes, I'm an attorney at law, but I'm not going around calling myself 'Brilliant Attorney at Law.'"

"Well, you could."

"Right. Then we would both be claiming to

be special, wouldn't we?"

Snort. No answer. The overweight red-faced agent glared at the lawyer.

"Since you didn't answer my last question, please answer this one: Do you know Junior Bostic?"

"I do. I know his entire family. I know his brother who's a preacher."

"Fine," the lawyer said turning to Junior. "Stand up, Junior." Bostic stood at the defense table looking somewhat uncomfortable in a cheap suit.

"Is that him?" the lawyer asked the agent.

"That's him. I'd know him anywhere."

"Hold out your right hand, Junior." Bostic held out a very strange looking right hand.

Turning to the witness, "Did you know Junior when he was injured at the sawmill?"

"I knew him when he got his hand cut off by that saw. He was sixteen years old then."

"Show him your hand, Junior." Bostic turned his hand over. It was a grotesque, claw-like appendage.

Back to the agent, the lawyer continued, "Were you aware he lost his thumb and all his fingers other than his index finger?"

"I knew he lost most of his hand and they cut off his big toe of his left foot and grafted it on for a thumb," the agent responded in an authoritative voice.

"That's why his hand looks similar to a crab

claw, isn't that true?"

"Well, yeah, but what'd you expect if they grafted your left big toe on to where your right thumb used to be? He's lucky to be able to grasp anything. I think the doctors worked a miracle with him. At least he can use it."

"Did you see his hand at the time of the arrest?"

Snort, "I wasn't looking for it."

"Did you see it?"

"No."

"Did you take any fingerprints, I mean a toe print, from the van?"

The jury began to laugh, as did the judge. Junior was still standing at the table holding out his ugly claw working his index finger and great toe. He reached down and picked up a pencil with it. The jurors were straining to see Junior's claw work.

The lawyer heard one say, "How'd he do that?"

"Did you cuff Junior, Agent Millwee?"

"No reason to cuff Junior. Handcuffs would not restrain his right hand. You'd have to cuff him to something with his left hand."

"You didn't see Junior at the jail, did you?"

"I saw him. I just didn't see his claw. He was there all right."

"Well, could you identify him at the jail?"

"I didn't need to."

"Did anyone say he was Junior Bostic at the

scene?"

"I didn't hear him if he did."

"You couldn't identify the people during the booking due to the red dye, could you?"

"Not until they scrubbed up."

"But you didn't stay until the person you thought was Junior scrubbed up, did you?"

"No."

"And you didn't see his claw any time during the arrest or booking, did you?"

"I didn't notice it."

"If you didn't identify Junior, if you didn't see something as distinctive as his right hand, and if you haven't seen him since you made the arrests at the base of Lookout Mountain, you just might have a reasonable doubt Junior robbed the Bank of Menlo. Isn't that true?"

"I didn't see him, I didn't positively identify him, but it's my considered opinion he is a bank robber."

"Considered opinions are like belly buttons, everyone has one, isn't that true?"

"Well, yes."

"Agent Millwee, you can't tell the ladies and gentlemen of the jury that Junior Bostic robbed the Bank of Millwee beyond a reasonable doubt, can you?"

Snort, "No, I can't."

"And, if you can't say that he did it beyond a reasonable doubt, neither can these ladies and gentlemen, can they?" The lawyer didn't wait for an answer, and one didn't come.

The young Assistant US Attorney stood to rehabilitate Special Agent Millwee and thought better of it. "No questions," she said. "The Government rests."

"Does the defense request a recess before proceeding?" the judge asked.

Before Charlie and Phil could respond, the lawyer stood and said, "Your Honor, Junior Bostic rests." Immediately in succession Phil and Charlie stated that they also rested.

"Then the defense rests. The Court will be in recess thirty minutes while counsel prepare closing arguments. Ladies and gentlemen of the jury, do not discuss this case. I plan to get the case to you today, but you have not heard the arguments and the charge of the Court. Therefore, you should not discuss this case until it is submitted to you. Court's in recess!" Bang went the gavel.

The attractive young prosecutor returned to the courtroom with fresh makeup. She began her closing argument by rehashing the evidence. She knew that she had convicted Darren and Kevin so she concentrated on Junior Bostic.

"Bostic took a job in Butler's service station to stake out the bank. He learned the schedules of the people in the bank. Shortly after he quit Mr. Butler, the bank was robbed. Bostic drove the getaway van. He was arrested at the scene, transported to jail, scrubbed of red dye, booked, made bond, and released. He is just as guilty as his confederates." She then asked the jury to find all three of them guilty as charged.

Charlie Floyd and Phil Rice each made half-hearted arguments on behalf of their clients. They knew they were convicted beyond a reasonable doubt.

When it came his time, the lawyer asked Junior Bostic to come to the jury box and show the ladies and gentlemen of the jury his hand as he argued his case. Junior stood with his ugly claw on the rail of the box. The jurors raised up out of their chairs, some stood, and craned their necks to get a closeup view of the great toe grafted on to the half hand where the thumb used to be. Junior turned it over and demonstrated it to each of the jurors. He buttoned and unbuttoned his coat with it, straightened his tie, took out his pen and signed his name in perfect script. The jurors sat back down as did Junior.

The lawyer continued, "When the prosecutor gets back up here to conclude the Government's closing argument I want you to be thinking, why doesn't that government prosecutor explain to us why there were no finger prints taken of Junior Bostic's great toe? I want you to also be thinking, 'why doesn't that government prosecutor show us a picture of the three robbers where we can see Junior Bostic's great toe?"

He walked to the evidence stacked before the clerk and lifted the blown up color photos of the three robbers in red. Six hands could be seen handcuffed. Junior's claw was not to be seen.

The lawyer went on, "I want you to be thinking, why doesn't that government prosecutor show us Junior's claw in these pictures? Why didn't that government prosecutor produce one single witness who told us beyond a reasonable doubt that Junior Bostic was involved in this crime? What is that government prosecutor trying to hide from us? Does that government prosecutor think good looks, fancy clothes, and a glib tongue will convict Junior Bostic? Ask yourselves these things. And if you don't like the answer you get, you have a reasonable doubt and you must acquit Junior Bostic."

The lady in hot pink was genuinely frustrated, and it showed. The four women on the jury obviously didn't like her, and the men didn't trust her. Each time she attempted to respond to the questions raised by the lawyer, she fumbled, stumbled and made the situation worse. The lawyer was beginning to have some hope of an acquittal.

The Court charged the jury and sent them out to deliberate. At 6:30 p.m. the Court had called them in to dismiss them for the night. The foreman said they preferred to finish before leaving. At 9:12 the jury announced its verdict, "Darren Braswell, guilty; Kevin Braswell, guilty; Junior Bostic, guilty."

The lawyer had hoped that Junior might escape conviction, but it was too much to hope for. The evidence was overwhelming. He had used what he called cutie pie tricks to create even the slightest defense for Junior Bostic. Had an experienced prosecutor conducted the case Junior would have been dead in the water by mid-afternoon. The lawyer had been able to make a case for him because of the inexperience of a young woman who was breaking new ground as one of the first of her kind, particularly in Northwest Georgia.

Two weeks later the judge sentenced the bank robbers. Kevin and Darren Braswell were sentenced to ten years each. Junior Bostic was given a four-year sentence. He was released from the Federal Penitentiary in Atlanta in nineteen months.

The lawyer concluded that his efforts had been somewhat successful. He had trapped the lady in pink and in so doing persuaded the judge that Junior was not as culpable as the Braswell brothers. On reflection, he was satisfied. He felt he had earned his fee.

CALVIN

He had won the Silver Star for bravery in Vietnam. He was shot in the back and given a medical discharge out of the Army. He had been home almost nine months. He was still wearing his field jacket. He had "Pugh Cat" inscribed on the back of it in colorful oriental stitching. The stitching also created a fire-breathing dragon circling around the words. He had been called "Pugh Cat" by his buddies in his unit in Nam. He was proud of the jacket, and he wore it all the time.

Calvin went over to Ernie Brock's to talk with him about buying a Volkswagen Beetle Brock had for sale. It was a 1969 model, blue, in excellent condition. Brock quoted Calvin $950 for the beetle. Calvin still had some of his mustering-out pay. Plus, he had additional funds as a result of his wounds. He paid Brock in cash for the car, took the title, and drove off in it.

Several days later, Calvin was driving down McFarland Avenue and turning right on Rossville Boulevard in Chattanooga. It was around 12:30 in the afternoon. Calvin had been up drinking all night. He started the day at a little after daylight drinking beer. He was definitely drunk. He hadn't eaten and was on his way to a cafeteria on Rossville Boulevard to eat lunch.

A Georgia patrol car pulled up beside him in the four lane. The officer tooted his horn to get Calvin's attention. Calvin looked at the cop. He pointed his index finger indicating that Calvin should pull over. In his drunken fog Calvin wondered what a Georgia cop was doing telling him to pull over in Tennessee. The officer pointed again for Calvin to pull over. Calvin pretended to stop in a parking lot. Instead, when the policeman stopped his car and got out, Calvin drove on through the lot and got away down a back street.

After losing the officer, Calvin drove over to a friend's house to sober up. No one was home. Calvin sat around on the steps for the better part of an hour consuming a six pack of Michelob Light. Instead of sobering up, he became even more inebriated.

In his alcoholic fog he thought he was sober enough to drive. He got back into his little light blue beetle and started for home, the north end of Sand Mountain, the Great Cumberland Plateau, where Alabama, Georgia, and Tennessee converge. He was taking all back streets attempting to get through Chattanooga without being stopped. As bad as he wanted to take it, he didn't dare try I-24, which was his straight shot home.

As Calvin was proceeding in a very legal manner, a black-and-white met him. The officer immediately turned the patrol car around to give chase to Calvin. Apparently, the Georgia cop, who had been trying to stop Calvin in Tennessee, had alerted the Chattanooga PD to be on the lookout for a blue Volkswagen beetle with an out-of-date Alabama tag on it. The car couldn't be missed. All Chattanooga patrolmen were looking for the blue beetle. Car 91 spotted it in the downtown area and commenced to give chase.

As the officer turned to stop the beetle, Calvin whipped into an alley behind the buildings. He crossed a street and continued into another alley. He came to an open commercial garage on his right and pulled into it. He got out of his car and pulled down the overhead door. No one else was in the building. Apparently, the owner was test driving a newly repaired vehicle. The patrol car screamed by speeding down the alley. Calvin waited 10 minutes, opened the door, and once more tried to get through Chattanooga in the blue beetle without being arrested.

He continued down the side streets, taking alleys when possible, always on the lookout for cops whom, it seemed, were all looking for him in his little blue beetle. Although Calvin was trying as hard as he could in his drunken stupor to get out of town, that was not to be.

Calvin crossed Rossville Boulevard again trying to stay near the base of Lookout

Mountain. A black-and-white spotted him. He drove as fast as he could, but the radio was faster than the engine, particularly a VW air-cooled engine. As Calvin turned near a large imposing Baptist church between Chattanooga and Rossville, Georgia, he saw cops at both ends of the block. There was no way out. Calvin drove up the steps of the church. Then, he did a hard right and drove off down the side steps and through the cemetery adjoining the church. He really didn't want to knock over those old tombstones, but he had no choice, he had to get away. Now he knew at that least four different patrol cars were after him in hot pursuit. They would not back off until he was captured, and they would call ahead for reinforcements.

Calvin went out the back side of the cemetery, through a thicket on top of a hill, down a wooded embankment, finally down a steep hill to another road which he took toward home. He thought he was safe. He thought he had got away clean. The radio outsmarted him. As he was about to cross over into Georgia, on an out-of-the-way street near where Georgia joins Tennessee, he saw Georgia cops and Tennessee cops manning every escape route. He had no choice but to try to go back up the steep hill.

The cops were closing in from each end of the street. Calvin opened the little bug up for all she was worth and started back up the thicket to the cemetery. This time, there were no cops in sight. He quickly drove through the tombstones, up and down the steps of the church, into the street, and it looked for an instant like he might make it to Rossville Boulevard before they cought him. It didn't work. Now there were more than a dozen black-and-whites from Chattanooga, Rossville, Hamilton County, Walker County and Chatooga County, Georgia, in hot pursuit of Calvin.

The cops were coming from every direction toward the beetle. Calvin only had one half block to escape in. He drove as fast as he could and took a sharp left turn in behind some garages fronting on Rossville Boulevard. The patrol cars converged on the beetle. The second car skidded into the alley and collided with a utility pole. Another black-and-white entered the alley at a high rate of speed. It collided into the rear of the first unit knocking it into the pole once more.

When the second car hit with the first car the utility pole broke in two about 12 feet above the ground. As the heavy pole bent double, it split and fell onto the first car. It creased the car where it struck it down the middle sealing both doors. The patrolman had a very difficult time trying to get out of the police vehicle before something else happened. The cop in the unit colliding with the first on the scene was severely injured and could not dismount his vehicle. The two cops barely made it out alive.

When the full weight of the huge pole came to rest on the cop car, a cable which had been used to guy the pole strained against its anchor on the front of a house across the street. Willard and Wilma Ashcraft were watching an Andy Griffith re-run when the pole fell away from their home. The cable pulled the walls of their front two rooms off the house and into their yard.

Willard and Wilma were sitting in their living room watching Andy, and suddenly, they were sitting out of doors where everyone could see them. Their home no longer had a front on it. Willard was very surprised and highly aggravated. He went into the street in front of his house and, waving his arms furiously, he cursed the policemen for destroying his home.

Calvin was blocked. They had blocked both ends of the street, plus any side road opportunities. There was nowhere he could run. The cops had him. He decided to fight his way out the best he could. He got out of the beetle. As the first cop rushed him, Calvin let loose a good shot with his right fist and laid the cop out in the alley. The second cop rushing him had another rushing directly behind him. He had his billy club out, and he was hell bent on striking Calvin in the cranium with it. Calvin kicked him in the nuts, grabbed his billy club and laid him out with it. Then he turned to face the third cop coming toward him with his club in the air. Calvin cought him in the mouth with the billy club. He thought it must have had a weight in it because it cleaned four teeth out of the cop's mouth as he hit the ground in front of Calvin in a bloody pulp. He had grounded three of the men in blue, but their help was on its way.

It was then that Calvin realized there were another ten cops coming toward him. One had his service revolver out. He began to shoot the little blue beetle in the rear. He shot it six times. Another cop pulled his service revolver and shot the motor of the VW six times also. Between the two of them, they killed its engine. By the time the two cops had shot the VW down to the ground, the others were on top of Calvin. There were cops hitting, kicking, pinching, biting, stomping, and generally beating the hell out of Calvin. He fought back the best he could, but there were just too many Laws. They were all using their batons on him. Calvin was getting the shit beat out of him. But there was very little he could do to stop it.

He hollered for help, but his screams did not do any good. The cops were fed up. Although they had known of him for only a short time, they hated him. They were wild men. They were blood thirsty, and it was his blood they were thirsty for. It was more than a feeding frenzy. They were out of control. They were in such a hurry to beat the crap out of Calvin that from time to time they knocked the shit out of each other. It was not a pretty sight. There was a lot of sweat and blood flying off the melee, some Calvin's, some the cops'.

The haunting sound of the ambulance caused the cops to back off and make way for the EMT's to get to Calvin and the cops needing medical care. Calvin was lying in a bloody mess, no broken bones, next to the left rear fender of the little blue Volkswagen Beetle. The car had been shot 12 times in the motor. It was dead. The owner of the beetle had not been shot, but he had just had the living hell beaten out of him by the cops and he was being loaded on a gurney to be taken to the Emergency Room at Erlanger Hospital.

Calvin felt good on the stretcher. The cops had stopped beating the shit out of him. He was laying back asking for a pain shot. Maybe the EMT might shoot him with Demerol. He did, and it was good. Calvin then lay back enjoying the ride. He was thinking about all the people who were pulling over as his ambulance went by. As the Demerol began to take effect, he wondered if the nurses would look good when they took him in. He imagined that if he let his elbow dangle over the side of his gurney, he might be able to get a generous feel of some unsuspecting young nurse's crotch, purely accidental, of course. Calvin arrived at the ER groggy but ready.

The medical staff rushed him into the operating area of the ER. They began to clean his wounds. ER doctors dictated out loud all the cuts, bruises, abrasions and other problems with his face, neck, shoulders, and even his hands and fingers. Nurses were swabbing his cuts and hurts with gauze soaked in alcohol. It burned like hell as they cleaned his face. It hurt particularly bad under his right eye. He thought the cop who hit him with the club there must have crushed his cheek bone. He was relieved when he found the bone was not fractured. He decided to drop off into a cozy sleep and forget about trying to feel a crotch. The Demerol had taken effect, and Calvin was sleeping.

Nurses and doctors worked frantically to patch Calvin up, stop his bleeding, and clean his wounds the best they could. It took 68 stitches in his face. His eyes were very badly bruised and cut. He was removed to intensive care. The ICU nurse hooked Calvin to all the necessary monitors to be sure that he recovered. Calvin knew that he was in a quieter place, a darker place, a cooler place, and he decided to relax and enjoy it.

Without warning, the world of Calvin was turned upside down. All at once, the needles and lines embedded in his body were ripped out! The monitors were torn away! Two cops had been brought into the intensive care unit due to their condition. When they discovered Calvin was also in the ICU they rolled off their beds, crawled across the floor, and attacked Calvin in one last effort to kill him.

He began cussing them, and they were saying that they wanted to take his picture. Calvin thought that taking his picture meant beating the shit out of him while he was intensive care. He was kicking each one of them as often as he could. A nurse noticed the changes in Calvin's monitors and ran into the room and broke up the fight before the killing.

She placed the cops back on their gurneys and replaced all of Calvin's monitors and lines. It took only about 35 minutes when everything returned back to normal. The ER doctor found out what had happened and he was highly incensed. He left the ER and visited Calvin in the Intensive Care Unit. He told Calvin that if he wanted to sue the city, he would testify for him. The way the cops had acted was ridiculous.

"This is the most uncalled for, uncivilized actions, I have ever seen. And to think, these bastards are Chattanooga Police Officers. They'll not treat a patient of mine like this. Hell, I'll report them myself."

A few days later, when the officers were

released from the hospital, the doctor made a lengthy complaint against each of them. Each man was suspended, without pay, for six months for conduct unbecoming an officer.

With the doctor's concern, Calvin insisted on another Demerol shot, stronger than his first shot, and soon he was blissfully floating through the air of never-never land. As he dove off into the place of slumber, he thought, and tried to say out loud, "Fuck 'em, if they can't take a joke!"

Seven days after he entered Erlanger Hospital courtesy of Chattanooga's finest, as well as other bulls from surrounding areas, Calvin got up out of bed and went home. The chief of police had notified the officers that charges would not be made against Calvin. He was afraid Calvin would sue the city for violations of the police department pistol firing code and the beating of Calvin in the ICU. There were other unfortunate events, such as the damage to the Ashcraft home. It would require extensive repairs which had to be paid by the city. So, out of an abundance of caution, all the charges against Calvin were dropped.

Calvin appeared in the office of the lawyer wanting to sue the City of Chattanooga, Hamilton County, the City of Rossville, Chatooga County, Georgia; the City of Ringgold, Georgia; and Walker County, Georgia. The lawyer took a lengthy statement and went with Calvin to Southeast Chattanooga and took pictures of the chase route as well as the shot up beetle, with 77 bullet holes, and the wreck scene. It was shocking to see what had happened to Calvin. In addition, the front was still off the Ashcraft home. It had some heavy blue plastic hanging down over the exposed rooms to keep the weather out.

When the lawyer interviewed some of the officers involved in the altercation with Calvin, he found several of them in much worse shape than Calvin. The officers he kicked had deep dark bruises to the bone. Those he bit lost body parts -- portions of ears, nose tips, small fingers, etc. Those he whacked with the leaded billy club were missing teeth, having hundreds of stitches in the face, and broken bones.

The lawyer returned to his office and called Calvin to come in and see him. When Calvin arrived, in a clean "Pugh Cat" field jacket, stitches out, looking fit and healthy, the lawyer told him that the police officers were in much worse shape than he was in. Therefore, the lawyer would not represent Calvin in his case against the city. Although he had lost the little blue bug, the lawyer did not believe a jury would give him a verdict against the officers nor the city. It was best to write the situation off to experience and buy another vehicle.

Calvin thought about it a few minutes. He

concluded that the lawyer was probably right. Since the cops had dropped theirs, he decided he would drop his.

THE ASHES

The unshaven, disheveled, elderly man entered the lawyer's office. He declined when he was invited to sit. He wore old Liberty overalls faded from too many washings, threadbare over the left-hand bib pocket with a few strings showing where the fabric was trying to unravel. The blue overall dye had long been worn off the knees and backsides. His shirt was a red checked plaid worn flannel that had seen better days. There were places where the red and white were running together. If one said it was a worn out cheap tartan, the old gentleman would not have known what was being talked about. His shoes were old high top brown brogans that had recently been polished with Griffin's Oxblood Polish. It didn't hide the scrapes and scars in the leather. His gray hair was a little too long and curled upward under the edges of his God-awful cap. It had been white some time ago, but perspiration and use had long reduced it to a pale brownish green that had "Bullroar" emblazoned in faded dirty yellow lightning letters across the front.

The thought fleeted across the lawyer's mind wondering what the hell does "Bullroar" mean, is it some kind of new chewing tobacco? Certainly, there were tobacco stains around the corners of the old guy's mouth, and his false teeth were just a little too rounded to look natural. Additionally, his mouth looked like it had once been the victim of an overbite. Obviously, he needed to have his dentures realigned or replaced. The lawyer had heard that people called this the droops. He also wondered why the old man wouldn't sit. During the moment of silence that the lawyer studied the man standing across his desk, he waited, giving him plenty of time, for him to talk.

After a pause of several more seconds, that felt like several minutes, the old fellow began to speak. "I need a lawyer for my son in Chattanooga, and I thought you might help," he said sternly; with his gnarled hard working hands on his hips and all the while looking down at the lawyer with fierce eyes.

"What's he charged with?" the lawyer queried. He was somewhat uncomfortable because of the aggressive attitude of his prospective client.

"Arson, destruction of property, and a bunch of other smaller charges."

"What's he supposed to have burned?"

"The place where he and his wife were living. He has some serious problems."

"I don't make any money sending business away, but I suggest you hire a Chattanooga lawyer. I'm going to have to charge you too much to go up there to Tennessee and fight a case in Hamilton County. A local lawyer can do it a lot cheaper."

"I'm ready to pay. I've got to save my son. He's been in jail now nigh on to four months." The old man, still standing, now sounded a little desperate. He was no longer threatening to the lawyer, but rather intoning him to help. "I tried a lawyer in town and all he did was take my money and do nothing. I don't want nobody from town. Powerful people are involved and it seems risky. I always heard you would fight a circle saw. I need a bulldog. I want you to take the case."

The lawyer had learned long before that the kindest way to get rid of an unpleasant matter was to quote a substantial fee. The lawyer quoted a fee large enough to run most people off. Nonetheless, the man slowly reached into the bib of his overalls and pulled out a roll of one hundred dollar bills. He pulled off the amount the lawyer asked as a fee and counted each bill individually as it curled up on the desk.

"I didn't mean to take all your money," the lawyer apologized as the man placed the small sheaf of bills back into his bib pocket.

"You didn't," the old man buttoned his bib. "I still got biscuit money."

The lawyer grinned at the old man's reply and removed a legal pad from the left drawer of the roll top desk behind him. He dated the page, poised his pen over the yellow paper, and began his inquiry.

"Tell me what happened," started the lawyer.

"I really can't tell you much. As I said, he's still in the Chattanooga City Jail. I ain't been able to talk to him, except through the glass, and you can't learn nothing that way. His wife became so upset when he was arrested, and his bond was set so high, she went to her mother's with their two children. I believe she went down somewhere near Villa Rica, Georgia, and her mother ain't got no phone. About all I can tell you is a guy named Harvey Steat is involved in it some way."

"Harvey Steat?" The lawyer was genuinely surprised to hear a familiar name. "You mean the guy who lives on the north end and has a twin brother named Marvey? Last I heard Marvey was running a liquor store over on Rossville Boulevard. Is that the one?" the lawyer questioned.

"The same. He's involved someway. I don't know how."

"What about Marvey? Is he involved?" the lawyer asked.

"I've told you all I know. I wish you would get the bond set lower so we can get my son out and go to work on his case. That money I paid you didn't come easy."

It was obvious the conversation was over.

The lawyer knew Harvey very well. He had

won a white whiskey case for him when he first moved from Tuscaloosa to practice law in Fort Payne. Then, Harvey was involved in a little matter involving a lady of the evening and a member of the Industrial Development Board. The lawyer helped in that case.

Soon after the old man left, the lawyer drove directly to Trenton, Georgia. In the old ramshackled stately courthouse in the middle of town, he listened to his heels echo off the original old wooden floor as he proceeded toward the office of the Road Commissioner. There the lawyer found Harvey Steat just as he thought he would: hotdog in hand, lunching with the commissioner. There was just a hint of mustard, ketchup and cole slaw dripping from the corners of Harvey's mouth sort of like a short narrow Fu Manchu mustache. There was a bit of mustard and ketchup resting on a cheap white shirt housing a loud print tie that looked like a Salvation Army reject. These overlaid a corpulent belly protruding past a pair of brown Levi work pants.

Except for wearing a frayed old straw hat, Harvey would have perfectly fit the image of countless small town southern politicians. With his hat off, the lawyer could see that his blonde hair line was beginning to recede. Still, he had a cherubic face with large blue eyes. Blond beard stubble was protruding over most of his face. One could see that he had once been a very strong man. His beefy arms and short stubby fingers reeked of a cheap musky based cologne. It was obvious that he was a person who sweats easily with that rare tincture of metabolized Budweiser.

He seemed to be genuinely glad to see his old attorney and profusely introduced him to the road commissioner as he recounted the story about the lawyer defending him for making white whiskey. He pointed out that he had paid the lawyer's partner, who refused the defense, and the lawyer took it to a jury trial on about 30 minutes' notice and won the case.

After things quietened down a bit, the lawyer told Harvey why he was visiting. He mentioned the client's name, and there was immediate recognition.

Still emasculating his hot dog, Harvey responded, "I know that guy. I heard he was in trouble. What can I do to help?" Harvey was downright affable. Having known Harvey and some of his activities for more than five years, the lawyer was immediately on guard.

"Who can tell me something about his problems?"

"You might start with that sonuvabitching nephew of mine, Ernie Brock," griped Harvey. He almost choked on his food as he spat out the name with utter disdain.

"You think he might know something about my boy's problems?" asked the lawyer.

The lawyer thought Harvey and Marvey were close to Ernie. He was taken aback by the attitude of Harvey. After all, they were his favorite uncles. His mother had practically raised the twins along with her own son. However, they were eight years older.

"If I were you, I'd see that sonuvabitch. He may be my sister's son, but he's not my nephew, not anymore." Harvey sounded resolved.

The lawyer asked a few background questions in the form of a statement from Harvey and the commissioner. After that bit of work he drove up the winding snake-like road from Trenton to the north end of Sand Mountain. Well off the paved county road, he found Ernie Brock and his pal, Jerry Lamar. They were in Ernie's garage, presently converted into a game room, shooting nine ball on Ernie's pool table, ten bucks a rack.

After interrupting the game and taking statements from them the best he could, he visited his client in the Chattanooga City Jail. When the lawyer left the jail, he talked with the Chattanooga Fire Marshal, an insurance adjuster, and his client's landlord - a real estate agent near the Brass Register Café on the Hamilton County Courthouse Square.

Driving south toward home the lawyer was well pleased with his one-day investigation. His success in discovering the facts far exceeded his expectations. When he typed his notes that night at home, the lawyer thought he had a decent defense. At the least, decided the lawyer, he knew what had happened.

Saturday night, August 14, 1968, a little after 8:00 p.m., Harvey Steat stopped by Wright's Steak House in Trenton, Georgia. In the crowded brown wooden building on the east side of the square, across the street parking lot from the courthouse, Ernie Brock and Jerry Lamar were seated in the last booth in the back on the left. That was where they had said they would be. Each of them was tearing into what was left of Wright's Saturday night special, 20 ounces of grain-fed T-bone steak. Harvey Steat came through the side door and slid into the booth next to Jerry.

Brock was taller than Harvey, but the family tradition of hair loss had not been favorable to him as well. He was losing blonde hair in the classic manner. He wore a blue jean cloth slouch cap with its bill snapped to the front. It was the kind of cap golfers used to wear. He wore it because it was comfortable and covered his baldness. His left eye was constantly bloodshot from having been struck by lightning when he was five years old. He was standing under an open ceiling light socket when the bolt came through and blinded him in the eye. He wore jeans and a red short-sleeve shirt. His Van Dyke beard and mustache were well trimmed and blonde.

Jerry Lamar was a redhead, a little over-weight, and dressed in brown slacks and a blue T shirt. He wore the outfit to show his muscles. Jerry was not only a weightlifter, but he considered himself a ladies' man. He was clean shaven and somewhat handsome. He scored well with the girls.

"All right boys, ain't got much time, I'll get right to the point. How much will you charge me to drop the palace?"

"The palace?" Ernie asked in disbelief. His mouth actually dropped open revealing a medium rare half-chewed piece of Wright's best meat.

Harvey was a well known white whiskey maker on the North end of Sand Mountain. He came by it honestly; his father and grandfather had made whiskey. And if the truth was known, his great-grandfather and great-great-grandfather were also moonshiners on the north end of the Great Cumberland Plateau where Tennessee, Georgia, and Alabama converge, separated only by the Tennessee River. Harvey made enough money making and selling white whiskey for $8.00 a gallon in Chattanooga to build a large home on 20 acres inherited from his father.

The white brick ranch style house was typical of the homes being built in the late

1960's, only it was larger. The home was distinguished by a large rolling yard encased by a beautiful whitewashed board fence. A paved drive led some 250 feet winding from the paved county road up to the beautiful white home with the green roof. It was a stately edifice appearing to be a mansion on its unique location.

Harvey's older brother Hank had been given the 20 adjoining acres where he lived in an ugly 12X60 mobile home. Between the dents and scratches were rusty spots, and paint flaking could be seen from a distance. Some of the windows had been replaced with a different style glass pane that didn't match the others. The front door had been replaced and painted a gaudy brown that had paint brush marks in it from top to bottom. The lack of underpinning and the rickety worn faded wooden steps did not inspire a feeling of permanence. But it had been there for a while, and there it would stay. There was a debilitated large TV dish on the top near the front door which had a softball size hole at 10:00 o'clock which did not inspire great confidence in receiving good reception.

Malcolm Steat owned 80 acres of land. Upon his death it was divided equally between four of his children. Hank's 20 acres and Harvey's 20 acres made up a 40-acre tract. Another 40 acres had been given to Ernie Brock's mother and Ronald Steat, another brother. They had told their father they would be satisfied to take the property farthest from the pavement. Marvey had been given his share earlier in another area. Brock had built his house on property his mother gave him. Together, he and his mother and father lived 1,230 feet off the pavement. Their driveway circumnavigated the property of Harvey on its north side. Ronald went in the same distance next to Hank's property on the south.

Hank was a big man, 6'4" tall, weighed about 290 pounds. Except for his age, which was apparent to the eye, he could still pass for a semi-pro football player. He too was a long time whiskey maker who had sampled too much of his product. Hank had the weatherbeaten kind of wrinkled face where one could read "alcoholic" between the lines. His reddened face with rosea on both cheeks rounded out a W.C. Fields nose. The chicken feet around his overly large watery blue eyes signified that he had smoked too many cigarettes. Any doubts about his tobacco habit were dispelled by his nicotine-stained fingers and the hacking cough that was his constant companion.

Hank had six old worn out and wrecked cars up on concrete blocks, rusting around his place. They complemented the ancient old run down chicken house and large dilapidated barn with its old abandoned pigstye. Both structures had many boards missing with gaps in the walls where the wind had removed several strips of tin used to plug the loss of the lumber. Where the tin still held on, it was rusted and bent to the point of very little utility. In short, the wind had little obstruction to blowing through both structures.

Most of the neighbors thought that when Harvey built the palace he would either buy Hank out, or he would want Hank to clean up his mess. Instead, Harvey said Hank's junk yard just made his place look better. Nonetheless, when Harvey built a fence between himself and his brother, he didn't install a gate near Hank's place. Enough said.

Harvey and the rest of the family, as well as neighbors who lived in close proximity, referred to the white brick mansion as, "The Palace." Harvey furnished the palace with the most expensive furniture and accessories he could buy from the Town and Country Furniture store in town. Folks on the north end referred to Chattanooga as "town" even though they drove through the cities of Trenton, Georgia, and Tiftonia, Tennessee, to get to Chattanooga. Harvey spent more than $30,000 to furnish the palace. The T and C interior decorator, a pushy middle aged woman, who was still fairly attractive, assisted him with his furniture selections, the carpet, draperies, and appliances.

Harvey actually had no special liking for the lavish furniture. However, despite his wife having left him a couple years earlier, Harvey built and furnished the palace as one of the finest homes on the north end.

Dropping the palace meant criminal arson, an insurance job, that was inconceivable to Ernie. He could not comprehend that his uncle Harvey would consider burning the palace. It was just too damned nice.

"You really don't want us to torch the palace, do you?" Everyone in the family was proud of Harvey for building the palace. The entire clan liked to visit the plush home on Sundays and enjoy the luxurious interior. It was truly a fine place. Steat's relatives' cars would fill the driveway. The men would bring beer and watch football while the women would cook the evening meal. It was almost a tradition. They saw uncles, aunts, and cousins they didn't even know existed.

"That's what I asked you to come down here for. I want to drop the palace. A couple of year ago I insured the palace with State Farm. I got $175,000 on the house and $45,000 on the contents. I checked with an accountant in town and he said a casualty loss, like a fire, ain't taxable. I could use the money. How much to drop it?"

Ernie contemplated the job for a minute while he was strongly working his jaws on another bite of steak.

"What'd you think, Jerry," questioned Ernie, "a buck each?" Ernie meant a thousand dollars.

"Sounds fair to me," Jerry responded digging into his potato all the way. "When you gonna leave town, Harvey?"

"I was thinking about going up to Gatlinburg this weekend. I seen the weather on TV. There's a front moving in about Saturday night. I guess the palace might get struck by lightning. It'll be a damned shame, but you gotta do what you gotta do. I mean, what's insurance fer if it ain't to pay off?"

Ernie stopped chewing and looked directly at his uncle with his good right eye. "Give us half in advance," Ernie demanded as he stretched out his right hand. Obviously, he didn't trust his uncle, and with good reason.

Harvey reached into his right pants pocket and pulled out his flashing wad. He peeled five one hundred dollar bills off for Ernie and then dealt five off to Jerry. The eyes of the steak eaters flashed and widened as they looked at the crisp Franklins.

"Saturday night?" Harvey confirmed.

"You got it," assured Ernie. "We'll use coal oil, so leave the pilot lights off. And unplug all electric appliances and lights." Ernie excitedly continued instructing Harvey on all the preliminaries.

"Okay," said Harvey as he rose to leave. "I'll give your mother the number where I'll be. I'm looking forward to receiving some terrible news sometimes early Sunday morning."

"Please act heartbroken," Ernie said grinning.

"I'll probably cry," quipped Harvey, returning the grin as he turned to leave. "Hell, I might even have to go to the emergency room. I got hospitalization insurance."

Harvey waved as he left. "Good idea," he thought. "I might even score a Demerol tablet."

Ernie and Jerry, finishing off their T-bones and baked potatoes, smiled at each other. "Easy money," Jerry said through a full mouth. Ernie continued to chew his steak; his bobbing head nodded agreement in unison with his moving jaw.

On Friday afternoon Jerry drove up the long dirt drive to Ernie's house in his 1958 beat up blue Ford pickup. He had ten five-gallon plastic jugs tied together with twine in the back of the truck.

"You think 50 gallon will get it?" asked Jerry.

"Yeah, that ought to do it, if we mop it down right," replied Ernie leaning on the passenger side door. "You know, mop it into the closets, under the furniture, sopping the rugs. Hit'll git it."

"Right," said Jerry, "And let's don't forgit to check them pilots, I want to live to spend this money. He's got a propane tank back there."

Ernie and Jerry traveled down the steep mountain's curvy road from the North End down to I-59 and took the entrance toward town. They by-passed Chattanooga and went directly to Soddy Daisy, Tennessee, a few miles north of Chattanooga. They knew exactly where they could go and their purchase would not be questioned. They went to Barnette's Spur Service Station.

Barnette was an old friend. He had bought white whiskey off the North End for years. They could rely upon him to sell them the flammable fluid and forget who bought it as soon as the money was in the cash register. They hauled the kerosene jugs back home and put them in Hank's chicken coop. Hank came down the rickety steps of his house trailer when he heard his dogs barking.

Ernie greeted his disheveled Uncle Hank and said, "Me and Jerry're droppin the palace Saturday night." He meant to sound business-like and firm.

"No! Not the palace," whined Hank, his alcoholic face contorted in agony. "I don't want to live next to no burned out ruins."

He loved to look at the palace and feel part of it because it was in the family. It was a beautiful sight to watch out of his living room window, white brick, green roof, nice lawn, and all. He couldn't believe what they were saying.

There had to be a mistake.

"Yep, Harvey said do it, and she goes Saddidy night," Ernie dramatically struck a wooden kitchen match with his right thumbnail to emphasize what was going to happen.

"Tomorrow night?" Hank asked.

"Yeah, around one in the morning on Sunday, actually."

"So, you're really gonna burn her, huh?"

"No doubt," said Ernie.

"Count on it," Jerry confirmed, unloading the last jug of kerosene.

Hank was in deep thought for a minute. "How'd you boys like to make $500 more?"

"I'd like it. What'd we gotta do?" Ernie asked.

"Well, since youins are going to burn it anyway, and since Harvey is gonna git paid for it anyway, why not move some of that fine furniture over here to my house trailer and move my junk over there? I'll give you $250 each. Its all I got. You know, all the insurance company is gonna look for is burned out bed springs and appliances. So what difference does it make?"

Ernie scratched his head and thought for a minute. He thought out loud to Jerry, what difference does it make? Hank ain't never had nothin any good in his life. It's all gonna be gone by morning anyway. And he's right, the only thing the insurance company is going to be looking for is appliances, metal parts and bed springs. Why the hell not? It's $250 more. I could use the extra money.

Jerry thought a moment and nodded in agreement. "Yeah, okay, we'll do it. Get the money, Hank. Hell, hit's only moving furniture. But, weuns are gonna need help."

"I'll help, and you'll git help," Hank assured the pair.

It was a done deal. Hank went to get the $500 from his house trailer over the protestations of his haggard wife who claimed it was grocery money. However, after hearing the plan - new furniture and appliances and all - she readily agreed and took the money from a sugar bowl on the second shelf of the old scarred white kitchen cabinet.

On an overcast Saturday afternoon Jerry, Ernie, Hank, and Hank's two sons carried loads of T & C treasures, with all new appliances, out of the palace to Jerry's pickup and on down to Hank's trailer. Each time they took a load of expensive furnishings down to Hank's, they brought a load of junk back to Harvey's doomed palace.

Wynona, Hank's wife, and their three daughters, who acted as if it was Christmas, were running through the palace hoarding everything they liked and didn't want burned. They liked everything, dishes, silverware, clothes, all of it. Finally, by 9:30 p.m., they had practically moved the palace down to Hank's stuffed mobile home. It was so packed that they had trouble moving around in the dilapidated abode. It was away beyond thoroughly packed.

Hank had to put a few pretty things that Wynona couldn't get into the house trailer into the barn and chicken coop. These pieces were what they called knick knacks. The decorator had called them compotes, vases, bronze sculptures, paintings, and so on. Lastly, Hank considered taking a couple the old wrecked car bodies up to his brother's place to burn with the palace. Ernie and Jerry flatly refused.

"Forget it. A jobs a job," Ernie said in dissent. "Me and Jerry are perfessionals, almost, and leaving those old cars layin' around wouldn't be perfessional."

At approximately 12:45 a.m. in the dark Sunday morning moon-lit night, Jerry and Ernie entered the palace to do their work. It was in shambles. Ernie felt bad about it, almost. It really looked junky. The old torn couch was placed where the beautiful genuine leather couch had been. The beds were changed out with junk headboards. The closets were crammed with old ragged clothes. There was old bedding in the bed rooms, and really just filthy junk throughout. Ernie thought that although it looked like hell now, it would look pretty good burned to a crisp. The transfer had been completed.

Hank and his family put out some of the expensive lawn chairs from the palace in front of their trailer so they could watch the show. Bounty from the palace, the outdoor chairs were made of mahogany, inlaid with teak. After a few sips of Harvey's bottled in bond, to hell with moonshine, Hank and his sons soon felt bad about not helping Ernie and Jerry "slosh" down the place. They decided that they ought to go next door and help drop the palace. It was the least that they could do.

Ernie immediately took command. First he armed everyone with a new mop that they had bought on Friday. He had a half dozen good cotton swabs in Jerry's pickup. He told everyone to take kerosene and mop it on all the floors.

"Don't worry about it dryin up, it don't evaporate too quick."

Next, Hank's old worn out mattresses were split open and soaked with kerosene. Cups, the ones Wynona had exchanged, were filled with kerosene and the liquid was thrown into the cupboards and cabinets in the kitchen. Clothing in the closets was doused from the jugs. Kerosene was poured into the window casings. Holes were knocked in the gorgeous very expensive brown paneling, and wallpapered walls were hacked with Hank's axe. Then the fluid was dumped into the walls. Finally, Jerry pulled down the folding attic stairs and went up into the overhead and saturated the insulation and the rafters with a healthy dose of the flammable liquid.

After the entire house was laden with kerosene Ernie announced the house was ready to drop. "Everybody out!" he hollered.

He and Jerry then went through the house and crumpled up old newspapers throughout every inch of the floors. They threw a box of pine kindling in the central hallway and doused it with "coal oil."

If anyone had noticed, kerosene fumes could have been smelled almost a half mile away. Ernie went to the back door, Jerry went to the front, Hank went to the garage door, and one of Hank's sons went to the sliding glass doors on the deck. Ernie counted down and each of them threw a rolled up, kerosene-drenched newspaper, into the house before turning to run.

By the time they cleared Harvey's property over the fence and made it safely back to Hank's, the palace was, "beginning to show signs."

Using a hose in Hank's front yard, the men scrubbed the kerosene off their shoes, clothing and bodies. Ernie had brought a large box of Tide for them to use to clean themselves after the dousing. Then they immersed themselves in a layer of cheap cologne to hide the remaining smell. It took a good ten minutes for them to become clean and smelling good.

The women were still in their chairs calling the fire as an announcer might call a football game. "They's flames showing the kitchen. It can be seen through the kitchen window. There goes a set of curtains on the sliding glass doors. There's flame in the master bedroom. She's gonna go soon, ladies and gentlemen."

Out of an abundance of caution, Ernie brought out another surprise and instructed the men to douse themselves in a layer of more cologne. Then, they poured up a few drinks. Hank had saved all Harvey's liquor bottles that held liquor and replaced them with old bottles he had found around his barn. The good stuff would have been wasted otherwise. And although he didn't favor bottled in bond, he could make do with Chevas and Crown Royal. Jack Black didn't hurt.

After less than half an hour, staring over at the palace, with drink in hand, Ernie announced "I would say any minute now."

"Watch it," Jerry said loudly. "In just a minute the heat will really build up. They'll be vapors when that coal oil gets hot. Then, when everything is just right, she'll blow wide open and all the fire departments in the world won't be able to put'er out."

It may have been the whiskey, but to the gathering it seemed that he was bragging.

About that time, lightning and thunder announced a job well done. "Right on schedule," Ernie pronounced raising his glass. "Lightning got it sure as hell. Now what were we doing? I got it, we were partying over here and we seen the lightning strike the palace, and before we could do anything, she was up in smoke. Everybody got it?"

"We got it," several of the coconspirators said in agreement. The girls giggled and agreed. They were drinking vodka with Harvey's Irish Cream mix.

According to Ernie's watch, it was exactly twenty-nine minutes to the second when the critical mass was reached. With one great "Whoosh!" The palace went up in flames. They sat around until the flames were shooting high out of the windows and chimney. The fire lit up the night giving an eerie yellow tint to the entire area.

"You better call the fire department," Ernie told Hank as he casually poured another drink.

Hank went into the trailer and called the Trenton Fire Department; the Ider, Alabama Volunteer Fire Department; and the Wildwood, Georgia, Volunteer Fire Department. Trenton got there first.

The entire neighborhood was now lighted by the blaze. The firemen didn't unroll their hoses when they arrived. The fire chief came over to the group, which had now grown to almost one hundred people from the surrounding neighborhood, and told the family how sorry he was that there was nothing his department could do other than watch it burn and keep it from spreading. He said the fire was just entirely too hot. He had never seen a dwelling fire that hot in his 27 years as a fireman.

An hour or so later, as the blazes dwindled, the hoses from the tankers were unrolled, the pumps activated, and the firemen began their work. The chief and his crew stayed on the scene until after noon on Sunday. They found metal from the hot water heater melted down into a huge metallic glob. Other appliances were burned completely out. The house smoldered for days. The fire chief said there was still plenty of heat in the center of the house. Monday morning, he had the forest ranger come out and cut a ditch around the charred palace remains with his forest fire dozer and plow.

Soon after Hank called the fire departments, Ernie called his mother and told her the palace had been struck by lightning. She fainted. After she was revived by her husband using a cold washcloth, she called Hank's house and asked for Ernie.

"What are we going to do? Who's going to tell Harvey? This is so terrible," she sobbed.

"I guess you better call him. You're his older sister that raised him. Tell him as gently as you can. There's not a thing can be saved," Ernie responded with feigned sadness and concern.

Ernie's mother called her younger brother at the Gatlinburg number he had given her, and told him the bad news. Harvey promptly went into shock and had to be taken to the emergency room and sedated. He cried out with chest pains to the ambulance personnel and enjoyed the Demerol-induced fog the drug gave him for the next few hours.

Harvey's best friend, the road commissioner, heroically volunteered to drive up to Gatlinburg and bring Harvey and his car back to Georgia. The commissioner's girlfriend drove him up to East Tennessee where they made a short, two-hour recreational stop in Athens, Tennessee, at the Roadway Motel. Feeling better, they moved on to pick up Harvey at the Gatlinburg Hospital. They brought Harvey back to the road commissioner's house until he could find a place to stay pending the insurance paying for a motel room while the company examined the fire loss and pay off.

As soon as Harvey ran out of the hospital Demerol he had squirreled away, he declared himself recovered and drove over to his former home. He looked forlorn as he explored the ruins of the palace. The insurance adjusters were just leaving. They had declared it a total loss and expressed sympathy for Harvey's loss. Harvey pointed out that he had been so upset that he was hospitalized. He showed real remorse and appropriate comments from a man who had lost everything. He put on an act not only for their benefit, but also for the benefit of family and neighbors. After about thirty minutes, everyone had left, and he drove over to Hank's trailer house.

When he had climbed the rickety steps, he entered the mobile home. The first thing he noticed was his things packed into Hank's place. He hid his anger and aggravation by glibly asking Hank if he was enjoying the palace furniture.

"What palace furniture?" questioned Hank in mock surprise. "That ain't no palace furniture. All that furniture burned up in the fire. You wouldn't want me to tell the sheriff no different, would you?"

"I was just bragging to you about Wynona's taste in decorating," Harvey sarcastically replied. "I'm just pleased that you won so much money in Vegas you could buy such good stuff."

Harvey was derisive, but knowing his older, larger brother, he was also cautious. He was also thinking. He had always said that if you get bullshit, use it for fertilizer to grow roses.

After sitting around on his own furniture, he eventually smiled at his brother and said, "Hank, all bygones is bygones if you will take your kids and truck and go over to the palace and get the ashes and remains of all the furniture, bed springs, anything metal, and any pieces of furniture you can find and store them in your barn for me for a while." There was still some room in the barn, in the stables.

Hank rubbed the blonde stubble of whiskers on his face and finally said that he thought that was fair enough. He and his family had made the score of a lifetime. It was only right if Harvey wanted the remains, he should get 'em. He didn't know why, but it was right. And right was right.

On the following Saturday, Hank and his kids spent all day moving what was left of the burned out contents of the palace down to his barn. For the life of him, Hank could not figure why Harvey wanted to save the ashes. But, he had never been able to figure out his brother anyway. He had always thought he was a little crazy. He had always been a crook, but he was crazy too.

Within a week after his tragic loss, Harvey left the commissioner's house and moved in with Ernie's mother, pending the insurance settlement on his house. He would get a friend to forge the motel bills for his living expenses and pocket that insurance living expense money as well.

The only thing left of the palace was a portion of the white brick walls about three feet high marking the foundations of the house and the concrete pad where the two-car garage had been located. The ruins were still warm when the insurance company issued its draft to Harvey for $220,000, less, of course, the $500 deductible.

After he had received his settlement check, Harvey gave his sister $350 for allowing him to stay at her place. He claimed living expenses on his insurance and received an additional $1,850 for the time he stayed with his sister. He thought $350 was more than generous. After all, she would have let him stay with her for nothing if he had not had any money.

With insurance money in hand, Harvey decided to move off the mountain. Furthermore, after lightning had struck the palace, it began to strike a different house on the north end every Saturday night. Harvey said that it had become ridiculous. People had to get in line to go out of town while lightning struck their homes. Sand Mountain lightning became so devastating that there was talk in Trenton of asking the President of the United States to declare Dade County, Georgia, a disaster area.

Harvey went to Chattanooga and rented the south side of a red brick duplex in a downward mobile part of town. Although the neighborhood was changing radically from the average to upscale it had once been, the duplex was still in good shape. It had two bedrooms, a bath and a half, living room, kitchen, closets, and a laundry room. There was a brick front porch that he shared with his neighbor. He had his own small screened-in back porch. The carport was on the south side of the house and readily accommodated his new red Ford Thunderbird convertible.

Harvey called his portion of the duplex, "the pad." It wasn't long until the interior decorator from T and C was appraising the pad and dreaming the expensive dreams of a grandiose interior that would convert the pad into the ultimate bachelor quarters. Harvey graciously spent some of his insurance money, and the pad was transformed into a miniature palace. The decorator had some of the rooms paneled, carpets throughout, new art on the walls and the latest appliances and furnishings. Harvey would entertain many an unsuspecting young woman in the pad's fine indirect lighting and stereo system over the next seven months.

Using a different agent, Harvey bought a new renter's insurance policy from Tennessee Home and Indemnity Company for every dime the contents were worth and about $10,000 more, thanks to Harvey's persuading the interior decorator to lend him a few expensive pieces to add to the contents the agent saw when he appraised the contents of the premises prior to issuing the policy. The off-brand insurance company was unaware of his recent fire loss across the state line. The agent didn't ask, and Harvey didn't bother listing it on the application. He forgot. After all, it was a legitimate lightning loss. It certainly wasn't his fault.

Harvey parked his new Thunderbird, bought with palace insurance proceeds, in the carport adjoining his side of the duplex. Harvey unwisely applied for auto insurance with the same company that issued the check on the place, State Farm. Although the company took his automobile insurance application, it left it pending for more than a year. Harvey thought he had insurance, but he wasn't sure. He had never received a policy.

Routinely, Ernie and Jerry "borrowed" the pad when either of them had action and Harvey wasn't using it. It worked for Harvey, and it worked for them.

Almost seven months after his sad fire loss, on a Saturday night, at a little after 8:00 p.m., Harvey stopped by Wright's Steak House in Trenton, Georgia. Ernie and Jerry were customarily seated in the last booth in the back on the left. That was where they had said they would be. Again, each of them was routinely finishing off Wright's Saturday night T-bone special. Harvey slumped down in the booth next to Jerry dropping all his weight on the wooden seat.

"All right boys, I'll get right to the point," he was strictly business. "How much will you charge me to drop the pad?" He struck a long wooden match with the thumbnail of his right hand. The sulfur smell from the match head filled their noses.

"Ain't I been here before?" Ernie asked Jerry.

"Nah," Jerry smiled, "I think we're hearing an echo."

"It's that, watcha call it, deja vu all over again," Ernie kept the game going.

Harvey was impatient, "How much, assholes?"

"$1,250 each this time, only because you been lettin' us use it," Ernie said biting into the remains of his steak while striking the bargain. "And don't forgit to turn out the damned pilot lights! You know, you got a natural gas stove and hot water heater."

"That's too much," Harvey negotiated. "You didn't charge me but a buck to torch the palace, and it was bigger."

"Take it or leave it, buck and a quarter each," Ernie retorted between bites. "You know, we ain't exactly in the insurance job business. We do this as a favor to you."

"Looks like you could do me a cheaper favor. I mean, we are related," Harvey whined.

"Ain't no way. Put up or shut up," Jerry said.

"Here's six-fifty each as a down payment. Can you do it Saturday?"

"She'll be gone by Sunday," Jerry assured him.

"Oh, by the way, would you mind moving the furniture out of the pad onto a U-Haul truck before the torch, and move the ashes from Hank's in?"

The light bulb came on over his head. Ernie now knew what everyone else in the family wanted to know - the reason Harvey saved the palace ashes.

"Sure we will for $250 each in addition to the $1,250, that's a full buck and a half apiece. We ain't no movers, you know."

"Ain't that just flat robbery?" Harvey hated to be gouged.

"Torch it yourself," Ernie said, with full knowledge Harvey wouldn't do it - too risky.

"You'se nothing but crooks."

"And you ain't? Leastwise, we'll admit we're something like. Give us another two-fifty each," Ernie repeated.

Harvey pealed off a total of nine hundred dollars each. He paid the boys a little over one-half in advance.

"Leave the stuff from the pad on the U-Haul. Rent it for a week."

"Now, we gonna have to change the schedule," Ernie said. "This weekend we'll go move the stuff out of the pad onto the U-Haul.

Then, we'll haul the ashes in from Hank's barn. We won't drop the pad for at least another week. We don't want that much action going on around the place."

"Fine," agreed Harvey. "Just deliver the U-Haul truck with the stuff on it to Hank's."

From his pocket, Harvey produced the most expensive padlock Ernie had ever seen. "When the good stuff is out of the pad and on the truck, lock the truck with this lock. I'll open it at Hank's. And don't forget the curtains and rugs. Them things cost like gold in Fort Knox."

Ernie took the lock, careful to keep it open. Harvey kept all the keys to the lock.

On Saturday morning Ernie and Jerry went to U-Haul in Chattanooga and rented the largest van available. They then drove over to the pad with three teenagers they had hired in Soddy Daisy. The teens were to help load the interior of the pad onto the truck at $6.00 per hour. After huffing and puffing, straining and complaining, the truck barely held all the pad's furnishings and interior.

Just as they were putting the last sofa and cushions on the truck the young man, in jeans and white T-shirt, who lived in the north side of the red brick duplex came over to see what they were doing.

"What's going on? Is Harvey moving out?" he asked Ernie and Jerry.

"Yeah," Ernie responded. "We're ducking out

without paying this month's rent."

"Hey man, I need to do that. Me and my wife are three months behind, and she's pregnant. Since Harvey is leaving, I'm going to find another place. Ain't no way I can pay that real estate company the $900 rent I owe them. They're going to impound my furniture if I don't get out soon."

As he closed the lock in place on the orange and white van door Ernie imparted some friendly advice, "You better get out right away. They may impound your furniture any day."

In his heart, Ernie didn't want the guy's belongings to go up in flames with the pad, but a job's a job, he thought. Ernie's conscious was clear, "The fellow had been given fair warning. He should get out while he could. He was a deadbeat anyhow."

Ernie and Jerry loaded Hank's antiquated pickup and Jerry's pickup with the ashes and brought them back to the pad after dark. They didn't see the neighbor any more that weekend. They positioned burned-out box springs to replace the expensive beds. A burned-out metal table was placed where the flashy dining room table had once been. Other burned-out pieces of furniture were put around in various places. The blackened appliances were placed in order. Even some blackened metal coat hangers were put in the closets. On Wednesday, one more trip was made in Jerry's truck. The pad now looked presentable. At last, it was ready to be dropped.

On Saturday, Ernie and Jerry went back to Soddy Daisy and bought twenty gallons of kerosene. Barnette, of course, didn't ask any questions. He had the most faulty memory in Hamilton County.

"Thisun's gonna to be harder to torch," Ernie told Jerry as they headed back to toward Chattanooga. "With only the ashes in there, it ain't gonna be as easy to get enough heat in there to get it going all at once. It's gonna be hell if the firemen get there in time and find all the contents burned up and the walls ain't even singed. They ain't gonna understand that at all. They'll call it arson for sure."

"Okay, so let's be sure to slosh it down good," said Jerry. "Twenty gallon ought to do it." He was reassuring Ernie as well as himself.

When the two arsonists arrived at the pad at a little after 8:00 p.m. the neighborhood was quiet and dark. They opened the front door, the back door, and the windows. They were sloshing so much kerosene in the duplex that they had to stop and go out for air. Plus, thought Ernie, the place would go faster with a breeze.

All at once they heard loud noises nearby. Ernie pulled his .38 Smith & Wesson and asked Jerry what was going on? Jerry checked it out and learned that it was just the guy next door making a lot of bumping and scraping noises.

"What the hell is he doin?"

"Shit. I don't know. He's moving around with something."

Ernie and Jerry returned to their work. Kerosene was soaked into the closet floors. Panels were cut with a drywall tool, and kerosene was poured into the holes. They couldn't access the attic, so they mopped the ceilings with kerosene. It was dripping on them as they worked. When the overhead job was completed, they began the final mopping operation that would insure absolute destruction. Ernie wanted the floors swimming in about a quarter of an inch of the flammable fluid.

Jerry mopped near the double windows in the dining room while Ernie finished up in the kitchen near the back door.

Without any warning the fluid ignited, "Whoosh!" In a huge orange-red flash the apartment exploded! The impact of the ignition was overwhelming. The concussion almost blew the house down. The building was blown about three inches off its foundations.

Ernie was thrown through the back screen door, knocking it off its hinges. He was propelled over the back porch 2" pipe railing. He flipped in midair landing on his head on the ground. He would remember later that the grass felt soft and moist, somewhat "cool-soft." He was out for a moment, then he came to himself. Unknowingly, his body was now hairless. His eyelashes, eyebrows, head hair and arm hair were all burned away. He was also burned on various parts of his body, but not seriously.

Jerry was thrown through the double dining room windows and landed on his back in the concrete driveway. He was cut in more than 40 places with the glass. He, too, was burned and hairless.

The pad was up in flames almost 30 feet high. Jerry stumbled to his pickup truck fumbled in his right pocket, found the keys, and started the engine. The truck would be ablaze in a matter of seconds if it was not moved. Ernie, regaining his composure, with his clothes smoking, hobbled into the passenger side of the truck and threw himself inside. Smelling kerosene and scorched clothing, Jerry backed out into the street at a high rate of speed.

"We got to get the hell out of here! They can prove we'uns guilty as sin if they see us like this!" screamed Ernie over the din of a roaring fire.

As they scratched off up the street, Ernie noticed through his singed eyelids that the neighbor and his wife had loaded all their meager belongings on a pickup and were trying to load a dining room table on top of the load while avoiding the flames. Jerry now realized what the bumping and scraping noises were from next door. The guy had taken their advice. He was trying to move out.

"Drive two blocks down, and around the block, then come back," Ernie instructed Jerry.

"Hell no, we'll git cought," replied the incredulous Jerry.

"Naw we won't. I want to see what happens when the law and firemen get there."

"Look, I'm bleedin to death," pleaded Jerry with blood running down his right arm, dripping onto the floor of the truck and staining his shirt in numerous splotches.

"You'll live, drive!" commanded Ernie. "Here, dab yourself with my hanky." He pulled a dirty white handkerchief out of his right hip pocket and handed it to his friend.

Jerry, blotting blood from his red skin, drove around six blocks before he heard the sirens of the fire trucks and the noise of the loud speakers on the police cars. He then drove back toward the pad, pulling into the driveway of an unoccupied home about half a block up the street.

Two fire trucks and their crews were working desperately as only dedicated experienced firemen can work to put out the fire. Police cruisers were blocking the street. Everywhere in the firelight there were flashing red and blue lights, loudspeakers blaring, and people scurrying about. It was organized pandemonium. "Look at that shit!" Ernie screamed laughing through his parched burned peeling lips. "The cops have arrested Denny Dimwit, the jerk-off that was sneaking out without paying his rent. They think he torched the pad!"

Jerry could hear the wife of the deadbeat renter begging the police not to take her husband as they handcuffed him and put him in the patrol car. His children were screaming as their daddy was being taken away. Jerry rolled up the windows and drove the pickup down the street past all the confusion without slowing down. A fireman directing traffic waved him through. Ernie ducked down in the truck as they passed by.

This time Harvey was in the last right rear booth of Wright's Steak House. Ernie, wearing a hunter's cap with earflaps down over his ears, dressed in camouflage fatigues, slid into a seat across from him. His dark glasses barely hid the hairless space above his eyes so that his lack of eyebrows was unnoticeable. The left side of his neck was beginning to peel. He struck a long wooden kitchen match with his thumbnail.

Ernie glared at Harvey through his tinted glasses with his one good eye. "Where's the rest of our money? You're a week overdue," he said in a slow, menacing tone. This was very serious business.

"You been paid enough already," Harvey said. "I ain't gonna give you no more money." Now he was digging into a Wright Steak House special.

"You got 30 seconds before Jerry torches the T-Bird in the parking lot." Ernie smiled as he spoke and almost imperceptibly nodded toward the burning match in his right hand. In the same instant, he tilted his wrist toward himself causing the glass of his watch face to shimmer under the light of the match.

"You know I ain't got no insurance on that car," Harvey hurriedly replied. Harvey, too, moved his head slightly to take in the small flame and the watch. He frantically tried to think of a way out of the situation. The wood of the match grew blacker and halved in length.

Harvey decided to peel the balance off his show roll. As he handed over the money he said, "Don't ever speak to me again. I ain't your uncle no more."

Ernie jammed the money into his pocket, "I won't, and you ain't." Ernie slid out from his booth, stood, and dropped the still-burning match into Harvey's steak. Then he turned his back on his uncle and left Wright's Steak House.

Ernie walked out to Jerry's truck and got in

beside him.

"Is hit sloshed?" Ernie asked.

"The ground under it is soaked. I mixed gas with it. It'll be hot."

"Then drive by it slowly," Ernie said as he rolled down his window.

As Jerry pulled alongside Harvey's beautiful red Thunderbird a safe distance away. Ernie struck the wooden kitchen match with his thumbnail. It was a one-handed movement. As the match flared with ignition, he tossed it out the window in the direction of Harvey's car.

"Whoosh!" Jerry never slowed the pickup leaving the parking lot. They heard fire truck sirens as they drove past the Trenton City Limits going up Sand Mountain.

"He shoulda turned out that pilot light under the water heater like he said he would," Ernie thought out loud.

"He shoulda given us a bonus for the singe job we got," Jerry said staring at the crooked mountain road ahead of them.

"If he'd done right, he'd have paid us on time and threw in a little something extra. We couldda' been killed."

"Shit! I damned near wuz."

The lawyer finished typing his notes from the day's interviews and leaned back in his blue high wingback leather chair in his home office.

As he starred at his IBM typewriter, he thought of Harvey and Hank Steat and their nephew Ernie Brock, who Harvey now referred to as a sonuvabitch.

Ernie and Jerry's burns had practically healed, and they didn't seem to suffer any residual effects. They were none the worse for the wear. Harvey had collected his insurance again. He was lucky to get in, get paid, and get out before the fire marshal ruled it was arson.

The lawyer thought of the old man with the "Bullroar" on his cap who had entered his office at the beginning of the day. He was the father to Harvey's luckless next-door neighbor in Chattanooga.

The lawyer knew the son was innocent and would not be convicted of arson. He would have his bond set lower where the family could make it and get him out of jail. He thought he might be able to get that done the following day.

The lawyer would be working with a DA he knew and had worked with in the past. Using the fire marshal's report that had been recently completed, the lawyer should be able to convince the DA to drop the charges. And when the state dropped the charges -- when that happened, thought the lawyer, he might even hear that bull roar, or find out what it meant, whatever that might be.

FRIENDS

Billy Ray McClung stopped the old 1978 blue Ford pickup truck in front of his cousin Bobby Joe's house, on Highway 72, just north of Scottsboro, Alabama. Ancel Roy McCarver and Gilbert Gilbert were passengers in the truck with Billy Ray. Billy Ray had new money, and he wanted to spend it on a new pistol. The three had ridden around the Tennessee River bottoms all afternoon drinking beer, smoking pot, popping speed, and snorting cocaine, when they could find someone holding any kind of dope. They had many friends, and they found plenty of free controlled substances.

Earlier, they had stopped at the Riverbank Marina to buy more beer. Gravel crunched under the pointed boots of the three best friends as they crossed the parking lot. The sharp November air contrasted with the smoke-filled cab of the pickup.

Inside a back room of the marina a dice game was in progress, and Billy Ray got in it with his only twenty dollar bill. He won two bets against a pass. Then he made three straight passes himself. On his last throw, he bet five bucks and threw snake eyes. He gave up the dice, made a lame excuse for leaving, and left the game $95.00 richer. Billy Ray and his buddies then headed for Bobby Joe's to buy the pistol with the winnings.

Bobby Joe came to the front door of his double-wide house trailer in red shorts, sandals, no shirt, and a beer in his right hand. A filter-tipped cigarette dangled from the left side of his mouth. "What'd you bums want," Bobby Joe grinned. "I know you're up to no good, and I ain't got no snort."

"Have another beer, Cuz," Billy Ray said, handing a beer up the steps of the mobile home. "I came to buy that .38 you offered to sell me the other day."

"You ain't got the money to buy that gun. I offered to sell it to you at a give-away price."

Bobby Joe backed into the cluttered living room of his double-wide. His wife was at work. The three drinking buddies followed him into his home.

"I got a hundred. Bring out that Smith," Billy Ray said as he took the money out of his pocket. He counted out the $100.00 like a big shot.

Upon seeing the cash, Bobby Joe went back to his bedroom and brought back a snub-nosed Smith & Wesson .38 Special. He unloaded the weapon while walking back to the living room. He pulled the trigger several times as he entered the room where the buyer and his friends were sucking on fresh beers.

"Listen to the action of this gun. It's worth more than I'm asking for it." He handed it to his cousin, who clicked the gun by pulling the trigger several times.

"Stop selling. I already told you I was buying it. Here's the money. Throw in that load for good measure."

Billy Ray handed Bobby Joe five crisp twenty dollar bills. Bobby Joe had five rounds in his left hand. He was feeling the shells.

"Man, there's three dollars' worth of shells here," said Bobby Joe. "But I ain't got no use for 'em."

He handed the rounds to Billy Ray who placed each shell in a chamber of the black pistol. "Here, to show you blood is thicker than beer, I'll give you the leather I keep the pistol in."

Bobby Joe offered the pistol's black holster to Billy Ray.

"Thanks, man. That's real good of you," Billy Ray responded as he loosened his belt in order to slip the holster onto his right side. Once the scabbard was in place, he holstered his new gun and drew it several times in the opposite direction of his cousin and friends.

"That thing looks good on you," Gilbert joined in. "Just don't forget its loaded."

Ancel Roy McCarver was more than loaded. He had downed eleven beers, smoked three joints of marijuana, popped four speed pills, and had three snorts of relatively pure cocaine. Gilbert remarked to Billy Ray a little earlier that he should stick a fork in Ancel Roy because he was done. Ancel Roy sat in a torn and stained overstuffed chair. It was obvious he didn't know what was going on.

"A couple more beers, and he's going to be slobbering," Gilbert said, motioning toward his drunken friend with his head.

Billy Ray looked in that direction. Ancel Roy didn't acknowledge that he was being talked about.

"It's getting late, anyway," Billy Ray said. "Let's chug our beers and take him home."

Billy Ray and Gilbert turned their beer cans up and drained them. Bobby Joe joined in and tipped his beer.

Finished, Bobby Joe warned, "Be careful toting that heat, Cuz. I don't know who that gun is registered to."

"You told me last time that it ain't hot," protested Billy Ray.

"I'll tell you again. As far as I know it ain't stolen. I bought it fair and square for $120.00 three months ago."

"Okay," Billy Ray said. "We'll get going. Ancel Roy needs to be home. This life in the fast lane is too much for him. In a few minutes he'll begin to feel good enough to fight or chase women. I don't want to be around when either of those things happen."

Gilbert nodded in agreement. Billy Ray moved for the front door, using his right hand to help Ancel Roy to his feet. The three intoxicated friends returned to the pickup. Billy Ray turned the key and started toward Sand Mountain.

They crossed the Tennessee River via the Bob Jones bridge and took Alabama Highway 35 to top of the Great Cumberland Plateau. They turned right at the hilltop town of Section and headed south toward the community of Macedonia. When they came to a place called Double Bridges, they pulled off down by Straight Creek to an out-of-the-way place where they could drink one or two more beers. The place where they stopped was an isolated spot barely one hundred yards from the pavement. It was a place where lovers parked, drunkards drank, and dopers doped. Everyone knew about the wide sandy table-type area near the deepest part of the creek. Swimmers were there almost every day during the spring and summer. It had just turned dark when the young men popped their last top.

It had been Ancel Roy's insistence that prompted Billy Ray to pull over at Double Bridges. Hopelessly drunk, Ancel Roy had chugged more beer and smoked marijuana continuously since they had left Bobby Joe's place with the pistol. He was sitting between Billy Ray and Gilbert Gilbert in the cab as they had driven toward home.

Now parked at Double Bridges, between

beers, Ancel Roy said, "You know what I think about sometimes? I think that's a shitty name you got Gilbert. You know, if your parents had made your middle name Gilbert, you would be Gilbert Gilbert Gilbert. Ain't that a hoot?"

Gilbert was used to Ancel Roy's beer induced verbal attacks. Still, in a bit of a drunken stupor himself, Gilbert couldn't resist joining the contest.

"Well, it's better than Asshole Roy, which is your name," rejoined Gilbert.

Ancel Roy tried to grab Gilbert around the head, but he spilled his beer. "Shit! You made me spill my last beer."

"I didn't do a thing," Gilbert countered. "You're the one whose wanting to grab somebody in a chokehold."

"Why don't you all give it up?" Billy Ray impatiently interjected. "You're spilling beer all over my damned truck. That's good shit to drink, but it stinks in the floorboard and upholstery. Chill out!"

Ancel Roy turned his attention to Billy Ray. "Aw, you want some of it, Billy Ray?" Ancel Roy threw his left arm around Billy Ray's head placing him in a headlock.

"Hang on! What's this I feel? Billy Ray is packing heat," yelped Ancel Roy. He acted as though he was not present when the pistol had been purchased. In his beer-and drug-induced fog, he began to fumble for the pistol Billy Ray had in the holster on his belt.

"Hell no!" cried Billy Ray. He fought back, struggling to keep his pistol. "Don't fight over a gun! It's a mistake! Stop it!"

But Ancel Roy was too drunk, and the mean streak that was usually hidden when he was sober was now in full view. He fought harder to get the gun out of the holster. Ancel Roy's beer can clattered into the floorboard of the truck freeing both his hands to fight for the gun.

"Goddamn it!" Billy Ray exclaimed. "Now you've done it, you shithead. I'm gonna kick your drunk ass."

"You and how many more little short ugly fuckers like you?"

A welder by trade, Ancel Roy was a very strong man. He had his left arm around Billy Ray's neck holding him in a hammer lock. With his right hand he was fighting with Billy Ray to take the pistol from its holster. Billy Ray was fighting back with all his might. He was afraid Ancel Roy might cause the gun to go off and hurt someone.

Ancel Roy used his strength to bring Billy Ray's head down into his lap. He was hurting Billy Ray and preventing him from breathing. "Stop it! You fool!" Billy Ray screamed. "I'm going to get ugly with you. Now stop it!"

"You're gonna give me that gat. That's what you're gonna do." Ancel Roy turned the struggle up a notch.

Billy Ray still had his right hand on the gun. While holding his neck, Ancel Roy was trying to pry his hand off it. Billy Ray became angry. He jerked the pistol from its holster with his finger on the trigger. Ancel Roy struggled to get it.

Gilbert saw his friends with the gun in sight. "Hey! You crazy fools that damned thing is loaded. Stop it!"

They didn't stop. "I'm going to kill the son-of-a-bitch if he doesn't stop," Billy Ray said.

"I'm going to feed you that pea shooter," Ancel Roy said as he released the pistol and tightened his grip on Billy Ray's head and neck with both arms.

Billy Ray was being hurt by his drunken friend. With his head in Ancel Roy's arms, he couldn't see where the gun was nor what Ancel Roy was doing. He did know the pistol was pointed up in the air. He feared Ancel Roy was going to break his neck any second. He could hear cracking sounds from the bones in his neck. He decided to shoot the gun through the roof of the truck in an attempt to sober Ancel Roy. In fear and desperation, he pulled the trigger.

With his ears ringing from the gunshot, and the strong smell of black powder in the air, Billy Ray felt Ancel Roy release him. Ancel Roy slumped down forward in the seat.

"God damned! Billy Ray, You've killed him!" Gilbert screamed.

Billy Ray sat up in the seat. He still had the smoking revolver in his hand. He rubbed his neck to be sure it was all right.

"Where did I hit him?" Billy Ray began looking for the place where he had shot his friend. "I didn't mean to shoot him. I thought the gun was pointed up in the air."

"It was," Gilbert Gilbert replied. "It was right under Ancel Roy's chin. He was so drunk he didn't know what he was doing. You shot him under the chin."

Gilbert was on the verge of tears. "We gotta do something. We can't leave him like this."

Billy Ray took a flashlight out from under the driver's seat. He shined the beam on Ancel Roy. He could see a bullet hole under his chin. His cap was in the floorboard. He had a gaping hole in the top of his head where the bullet exited. There was also a jagged hole the size of a silver dollar flaring outward in the top of truck cab.

"He's dead, ain't he?" Gilbert whined.

"Yeah, he's dead and we got problems," Billy Ray responded.

"Whaddaya mean problems?" asked Gilbert.

"We gotta dead body on our hands. I don't know about you, but I'm too fucked up to figure this thing out. Right now, let's get out of here before somebody comes to see who was shooting."

Billy Ray started the Ford with the hole in

the roof and headed for the pavement. Ancel Roy's body was totally limp and weighing on Gilbert.

"Keep him off me," Gilbert said. "I can't stand this. I think I might have a heart attack." He was near hyperventilating. He struggled to push Ancel Roy over on Billy Ray.

"Shape up, man!" Billy Ray instructed. "We have to sober up and figure out what to do. We're going to Scottsboro. Prop Ancel Roy up in the seat and put his cap back on. And take one of them napkins out of the glove compartment and wipe some of that blood off the overhead. The upholstery is ruined."

The three friends went back down Sand Mountain, back across the river, and into Scottsboro. "Let's get something to eat," Billy Ray said.

"What the hell we gonna do with Ancel Roy?" Gilbert asked.

"We'll go through the drive-in window at McDonald's."

"What about Ancel Roy?" Gilbert Gilbert was begging.

"We'll buy the son-of-a-bitch a Big Mac. He don't need no fries." Billy Ray tried to bring a little humor to the horrible situation that he and Gilbert found themselves in.

Billy Ray guided the truck into the drive-in window lane at McDonald's. He stopped at the drive-in speaker.

"Welcome to McDonald's, may I take your order?" A young female voice greeted the friends.

"We want three Big Mac's, two orders of fries, and three Cokes," Billy Ray ordered.

"Why the extra Coke?" Gilbert whispered.

"We can drink that. I just don't wanna raise no suspicions. Help prop his ass up as we get the window to pick up our order," Billy Ray whispered back as he and Gilbert tried to make their friend look as natural as possible.

The girl gave them their order without noticing Ancel Roy's condition. Billy Ray paid and asked for extra catsup for the fries. He then drove the truck with the hole in its top into an adjoining shopping center. "We can park here without being noticed," he told Gilbert.

"I really don't think we ought to be eating like this," Gilbert said.

"Eat and sober up," Billy Ray ordered. "We've got to figure out what we're going to do with this body. Billy Ray dripped catsup on his fries and simultaneously unwrapped his Big Mac. Gilbert decided there was nothing else he could do, so he also began to eat as well.

When the friends finished their meals, they halved Ancel Roy's Big Mac and Coke. Then they talked.

"Here is what we are going to do," Billy Ray said. "We're going to take Ancel Roy over to Langston. I know a vacant house over there where there's a great big well. We'll put him down in the well."

"Couldn't we just weight him down with a concrete block and throw him in the river? We could do it at the river bridge?" Gilbert asked speaking through his nose.

"Nah, five days his body will blow up like a balloon and float to the top. He'll stay down in the well until he decays," Billy Ray responded.

"I just don't think I can help you throw him down in the well," Gilbert whined. He had begun to talk rather pronounced through his nose since the shooting.

"I don't want to throw him down the well. You know, 'ding dong bell, pussy's in the well. Who threw her in? Little Tommy Quinn.' I just can't do it."

"You don't have to do it. I'll do it. Just go along."

"I don't know what else I can do. I'm in your truck with my best friend dead beside me, and you're about to dispose of his body. I really wish I warn't here," Gilbert whimpered through his nose.

"Well, you're here, som-bitch. So make the best of it." Billy Ray was determined.

The three crossed the Tennessee River once again. Rather than heading up the mountain, Billy Ray turned right immediately after leaving the bridge and followed the curving river-side road toward Langston,

Alabama.

Langston is really not a town. Some say it is a state of mind. Actually, it is truly a wide spot in the lower river road between the river bridge and South Sauty Creek. Maybe 15 families live in and around Langston. The stores have long since closed and have been boarded up. If a person from Langston needed gas for their pickup truck, they'd have to drive to the Riverbank Marina almost 10 miles away.

Billy Ray turned left about a mile short of Langston onto a dirt road leading toward the base of Sand Mountain. The road was made for four wheelers, and it was used mostly by deer hunters. They were in the middle of nowhere when Billy Ray stopped at a vacant wood frame house at the end of the road. He turned the truck so the lights would shine on a large stone well covered with a tin cap.

"Okay, here's ole Ancel Roy's final resting place, 40 feet down in the cool well water."

"I wish you wouldn't do this," Gilbert said. "I'm sober enough now to think we ought to take him to the Jackson County Hospital and see if they can do anything for him. I mean, after all, it was a shooting accident."

"You gotta be kidding. Ain't no Scottsboro Law gonna believe you and me as to what happened, how he started it and all, and how I accidentally shot him in self defense. You agree with that, don't you?"

"Well, I ain't sure, you know. I don't think you meant to shoot him. But if you was innocent, it seems to me, you would have nothing to hide," Gilbert said.

Gilbert's awareness and dislike of what was happening around him had increased. "If you was innocent, it seems to me that you'd take him to the hospital. If he's dead, let his family bury him. Don't let them wear themselves out looking for him and wondering where he went."

"Don't you take backwater on me, boy," Billy Ray turned full face toward Gilbert Gilbert. "I have four more shells in this pistol, and it won't make no difference to me to leave one body here or two. You got it?"

"Don't threaten me, Billy Ray. First, I ain't scared of you, and second, without my testimony, when you get cought, you're going to the electric chair."

"Ain't nobody gonna git cought," said Billy Ray. "This body ain't gonna be found, and you ain't gonna say a word about what happened to anybody."

He got out of the truck and went over to the stone well. He lifted the tin cap off the gaping well. Then, using his flashlight, Billy Ray peered down into the depths of the abandoned well. The well was about four feet wide and a little over thirty feet down to the water. Satisfied, he walked back to the truck.

"It's okay. This is where we're going to throw

him in. Get out and help."

Gilbert refused to move. "I can't do it, Billy Ray. I just can't throw a friend I've knowed all my life down a well. It just ain't right. You'll just have to throw him in by yourself."

"You rotten yellow son-of-a-bitch. I'd help you if your ass was in trouble and you needed help," Billy Ray snarled.

"Yeah, you probably would. But I ain't in no trouble. All I did today was go riding around drinking and smoking with my two best friends. I didn't agree to kill one of my best buddies. I didn't put a hand on him, and I ain't going to help throw him down no well."

Billy Ray pulled Ancel Roy out the driver's side of the truck. He hoisted the limber body on his shoulders and struggled to carry his friend to the well. When he reached the stone top of the old well, he slid Ancel Roy over the edge. He gave his friend one last push and listened as his body splashed in the frigid water in the bottom of the well. Billy Ray looked over into the blackness of the well. Without his flashlight, he could not see anything. He could hear a bubbling noise. He assumed Ancel Roy was under the water. He slid the tin cap back on the old stone well and put a large rock on the cap to be sure the wind would not blow it off. After checking its fit, he returned to his truck.

"What are you going to do about this hole in your truck?" Gilbert asked. As he talked he stuck his right index finger through the hole in the roof into the cool night air.

"Shit! I hadn't thought about that. What the hell am I gonna do with this truck? That damned bullet hole is a dead give away. The law will arrest me before sunup." Billy Ray was turning the truck around to leave.

"Let's get the hell out of here. I gotta do something about this truck." He drove back to the Riverbank Marina and parked in the lot beside the store to think.

"I know what we'll do," Billy Ray finally said. "We'll take this truck back to Double Bridges and burn the damned thing. I'll say it was stolen and burned. I don't know how the hole got in the roof or what happened to Ancel Roy." Billy Ray thought his idea was super.

Gilbert Gilbert agreed that it sounded like a good idea to him.

"Run me by my house, and I'll get my truck so I can take you home after you burn yourn."

For the second time that day, Billy Ray climbed Sand Mountain. This time, the two went to Gilbert's home on the north side of Section.

"Don't wait, come on and follow me now," he instructed Gilbert. It was now after midnight. He moved slowly until he saw Gilbert's headlights come on.

Billy Ray then drove back down into the wide area at Double Bridges. Gilbert followed him into the remote location.

After they were both out of their trucks Gilbert asked, "What are you going to burn it with?"

"Hell, I don't know," said Billy Ray, sounding perplexed. "Shit, I'll have to siphon some gas out of the tank and burn it. I got a bucket in the back and a siphon hose."

He went to his truck and took the siphon hose out from under the front seat. Then, taking the outer shell of a minnow bucket from the back of his truck, he inserted the hose into the gas tank of the Ford. He sucked on the hose to create the vacuum necessary to siphon the gas out of the truck and into the bucket. He couldn't get any action, so he sucked harder. Finally, he gave the hose one last big pull and gulped gasoline into his mouth and it splashed down the front of his shirt and jeans.

Billy Ray cursed considerably as he filled the bucket with gas while repeatedly spitting. He then poured the gas throughout the cab of his pickup. The engine boiled and steamed as Billy Ray sloshed gas under the hood. He went to the truck were Gilbert still had his motor running.

"You got a match?" he asked.

"I got a lighter, but I ain't got no matches," responded Gilbert.

Exasperated, Billy Ray said, "Well, I got a lighter, you ain't no help a tall. Just sit here, I'll burn the damned thing myself."

Billy Ray went to the truck and opened the passenger door. He flicked his Bic and the cab exploded. The heated gas under the hood cought a spark and blew up almost an imperceptible instant later.

Billy Ray immediately realized that he was on fire. The gas that had soaked into his shirt and jeans was burning him. He ran to Straight Creek, and waded in until he quit hurting. As a child, he had spent many dusty summer days at Straight Creek and he was familiar with the swimming hole's bottom. After extinguishing the flames that engulfed him, Billy Ray waded through the cold water back to Gilbert's truck. Billy Ray's truck burned out of control and lit up the entire countryside.

"Get the hell out of here," Billy Ray screamed. "Somebody will see the light and come runnin for sure. I need to be home in bed. Let's go!"

Gilbert hit the tarmac burning rubber. He left Double Bridges as quickly as his truck would run. He took Billy Ray toward his house two miles away.

"Don't go in, and don't make no noise," Billy Ray said. "I gotta sneak in past Linda and the kids. I gotta dump these clothes and see how bad I'm burned. I know that I'm burned pretty good."

At that time he felt the pistol still holstered

on his right side. "Here, take this damned thing and throw it over the first double bridge. Maybe the son-of-a-bitch was stolen, and I sure as hell don't want it near me if the cops come around asking questions."

He handed the gun in the leather to Gilbert. Reluctantly, Gilbert took it. He turned right on a dirt road about 100 yards short of Billy Ray's darkened house. Billy Ray got out.

As an afterthought, he came back to the truck. "Look Gilbert, I'm sorry all this happened," explained Billy Ray. "You weren't involved in it. So just forget what happened."

"Okay," Gilbert Gilbert said. "But, what am I going to tell Ancel Roy's mother when she starts looking for him in a couple of days?"

"By then, all this will have blown over. You just don't remember the last time you seen him, okay?" Billy Ray was very earnest in his request.

"Okay, I hope you ain't too burned. You smell like you are burned pretty bad," said Gilbert as he swung his vehicle around and backed onto the main road.

A few minutes later Gilbert tossed the pistol off the second bridge as he sailed past before leaving Macedonia for Section and the safety of home.

Not unlike most nights, Linda was asleep when Billy Ray came home. She worked as a knitter in a sock mill in Fort Payne and was scheduled to leave for work at 6:00 a.m. Billy Ray was a carpenter, working for his uncle, and he could show up on the job whenever he wanted. On the back porch, Billy Ray took his scorched and burned, gas smelling clothes off. It was cold being outside wet and naked. Using a hoe, he buried his clothes under a burned garbage pile behind his house.

He sneaked naked back into the house, making as little noise as possible. He went to the bathroom, closed the door, and turned on the lights. He looked at himself in the mirror and was shocked with what he saw. His hair was burned off the front of his head. His eyebrows were gone. He had a large burn on his forehead the size of a silver dollar. He could see the flesh, and it was raw and oozing. His arms were burned badly, but his chest was burned worse than any part of his body. He couldn't believe how black he was where he had been burned. He looked like meat that had been left too long on a barbeque grill.

Linda saw the light under the bathroom door and heard her husband's muffled mumbling. She thought he was home late after drinking and doping again. After several minutes passed, Linda thought she might ought to check on him. When she opened the door, she screamed.

"You are burned to death! Look at you! You're raw all over your body. Here, put on this housecoat." She threw a white robe to her husband.

She turned on the bedroom light and began to dress furiously. "I don't care what you have been doing. So don't start with any of your lies. You're going to the hospital."

"I can't go to the hospital," Billy Ray responded weakly.

"You have no choice. You're going to die if you don't get to a doctor. Go get in the car." She directed Billy Ray toward her Oldsmobile. As soon as he was in the front seat she started toward Section and Highway 35. Linda McClung turned left down the mountain for Scottsboro and the Jackson County Hospital Emergency Room.

Billy Ray was admitted into the hospital with second-and third-degree burns over 40% of his body. He would stay in the hospital five days and remain under a doctor's care for three weeks. It was almost a relief to be confined to a hospital bed the first couple of days. He was helpless to face any pressures as a result of the untimely demise of Ancel Roy. Billy Ray learned no news concerning the incident during his first three days in the hospital. He had told the admitting physician that he had accidentally burned himself burning some garbage at home. He told Linda to report his truck stolen the first day he was in the hospital.

A deputy came to the hospital the fourth day

Billy Ray was there. "So, you killed Ancel Roy in cold blood, burned your truck to hide the evidence, and had your wife report the truck stolen?"

"I don't know what you're talking about," Billy Ray responded through swollen parched lips. "Who said Ancel Roy was dead?"

"Some deer hunters found his body the day after you threw him down in the well at Langston. They were out there on four wheelers and needed water. They went to the old well and found Ancel Roy. We fished him out and sent his body to the state crime lab. Although he had been shot in the head, he didn't die of the gunshot wound." The deputy paused to let Billy Ray speak.

"What'd you mean, he didn't die of the gunshot wound?" Billy Ray sat up in bed.

"He drowned," the deputy looked directly in the eyes of Billy Ray. "He was still alive when you threw his body down the well. If you had taken him to the hospital after you shot him, he would still be alive today."

"Who told you such shit?" Billy Ray couldn't believe the law had put all this together on their own.

"Gil Gilbert came to the office and reported it. As a result of his information the Sheriff has made him a deputy. He's working with us now. He's going to the police academy at Jacksonville State University next month." The deputy looked smugly at Billy Ray..

"Is that why you call him Gil?" Billy Ray asked. "The son-of-a-bitch always wanted to be called Gil."

"We'll call him anything he wants so long as he fries your ass in the electric chair," the deputy responded. "Now, do you want to make it easy on yourself and give us a statement?"

"I ain't saying nothin until I talk to a lawyer." For Billy Ray, the conversation was over.

Two weeks after Billy Ray came home from the hospital, Linda went to Fort Payne to see the lawyer. She wanted to prevent the state from electrocuting her husband. She paid a substantial retainer, and the lawyer returned to her home with her to interview his client.

The lawyer put Billy Ray in his car, and the two retraced his steps of the drunken November afternoon and night. They drove past Double Bridges, went to the well at Langston, came back to the drinking spot by Straight Creek, and eventually they finished at the site of the burned-out pickup truck. Lastly, the lawyer dropped Billy Ray back home and headed for Section to find Gilbert Gilbert.

Deputy Gil Gilbert had nothing to say to the lawyer. He said that he was working for the prosecution. His job was to see that Billy Ray McClung went to the chair. Gil Gilbert talked briefly in an important voice with a nasal twang.

The case came on for pretrial settlement negotiations in Scottsboro on February 10, 1987. The district attorney had told the lawyer that he was concerned about his case against McClung. At most, he thought he could make a mansloughter charge stick for the shooting of Ancel Roy. Conversely, he could make premeditated murder stick for dropping the man into the well. However, the DA knew it was not a strong capital case.

He was ready to make a deal. Billy Ray had two prior felony convictions and was therefore subject to sentencing under the provisions of the Habitual Offender Act which dictated life without parole due to his record. The DA was willing to agree for Billy Ray to serve life in the penitentiary. Thus, if Billy Ray took the DA's deal, he would at least have the chance of parole.

The lawyer talked to Billy Ray and the rest of the McClung family. Linda and Billy Ray's father suggested that he take the deal. With straight life, Billy Ray could get out of prison in fifteen years. Billy Ray would not take it.

The lawyer had a policy of never encouraging a client to accept a deal which resulted in his going to prison. Moreover, the lawyer left it to the client to make the "deal or die" decisions. He told Billy Ray to make up his own mind and tell him what he wanted to do.

Billy Ray told him to negotiate 30 years and he would take it. With a 30-year sentence, Billy Ray would be out in 10 years. He didn't mind doing 10 years, but he would not do a day more.

The DA refused to negotiate a possible capital murder down to 30 years. He said that community sentiment was just too strong. Billy Ray had a bad reputation and was not well liked. Most people around Macedonia were afraid of him. Plus, the DA reminded himself aloud, Billy Ray had such a bad criminal record.

The lawyer told the DA that he would have to prepare for trial, Billy Ray was not going to settle for life. He had never allowed a client to plead guilty to life, and he was too old to start now. All negotiations were off.

The trial date arrived on February 20th. and both sides were ready to do battle. Witnesses had been subpoenaed, pictures had been taken, enlarged and matted. Substantial evidence had been gathered by both sides. Nonetheless, serious negotiations began during docket call in an attempt to find a last-minute agreement acceptable to the DA and to Billy Ray. A plea agreement seemed impossible to reach.

The trial went forward. A jury was struck and put in the box. The judge swore the jury and gave the jurors their preliminary instructions.

Then, just before the opening statements started, the DA caved in. The deal was struck, 30 years, no Habitual Criminal Act. Billy Ray could be out in 10 years with good behavior.

The DA had been running a bluff anyway. Gil Gilbert was going to testify truthfully as to what happened, and the jury would probably give Billy Ray manslaughter at most. "We thought he was dead when he put him in the well at Langston. There was no intent to murder Ancel Roy."

Gil had told the DA that he was going to have to say that they were all three friends, best friends since the beginning of grammar school. They had always been closer than brothers - real friends.

The lawyer knew that the family was very happy with the outcome of the case. He thought that Billy Ray was satisfied. He was wrong. On the 20th day of February for the next eight years, Billy Ray McClung reported the lawyer to the Alabama Bar Association Disciplinary Committee. He claimed that his lawyer had failed to prepare his case, failed to try his case, and misled him as to his possibilities of being found "not guilty." In short, he accused the lawyer of serving him as an incompetent counsel.

Billy Ray McClung, like most of the lawyer's clients, was not aware that the lawyer kept detailed time logs of each minute of his day and could conclusively prove every aspect of his employment as his defense attorney. The lawyer religiously responded to each and every complaint with copies of his log notations, documentary evidence, and a signed statement by Billy Ray McClung stating that he was pleased with the plea agreement and recommended the lawyer to clients needing representation of the kind he had needed.

By the fourth anniversary of the plea agreement, the lawyer responded to Billy Ray's yearly charges by writing "See previous correspondence and proof in the file." The bar association accepted this response since Billy Ray sent the same complaint each year.

Early on, as he labored over his response to the first of Billy Ray's eight annual charges, the lawyer concluded that Billy Ray McClung wasn't much of a friend to anybody. He was released from prison exactly 10 years from the day he was sentenced. He and the lawyer never spoke again. With a friend like him, who needs......ah forget it.

THE DIRTY TRICK

When Timothy Murray was born on the north end of Sand Mountain he weighed 12 pounds 8 ounces. He was the largest baby folks around Davis Community had ever seen or heard of. His father could have called him Timothy, Tim, or some other family nickname, but instead, he called him what he was, "A Biggun." It stuck. From birth to death, Timothy Murray would simply be known as "Biggun."

They drove straight through from Trenton, Georgia, to Houston, Texas. Biggun slept most of the way in the back seat on an old soiled rumpled yellow pillow that he had brought with him. They stopped once for two hours for Frank to rest at a rest area near the Louisiana border. Biggun never offered to drive. He was content to either drink beer or sleep, whichever felt better at the time.

They arrived in Houston the following morning around 7:00 a.m. Biggun told Frank to look for a large automobile dealership with a La Quinta Inn next to it. It was somewhere near the airport exit. He said they would be staying there. Frank drove around aimlessly until he found it and Biggun gave him the money to rent a double room.

Biggun then drove the green '81 Buick, with Georgia license plates, around back of the motel and left the keys over the driver's sun visor. He did not tell Frank about this little move. Biggun had sent Frank down the block to McDonald's to get some breakfast. After breakfast in their room, they went to bed and slept until about 5:00 p.m.

After they had dressed, shaved, and got ready to go out, Biggun said he had seen about all of Houston he needed see and was ready to go to the house. Frank wondered why they had dressed, made plans to go out and all, but he said that was fine with him. He was just the driver. They checked out of the motel, and Biggun got under the wheel of the car. Darkness was falling as he turned the headlights on and pointed the automobile southwest.

The men had traveled about 45 miles down Interstate 10 when a Texas State Trooper put his blue light on them. He pulled them over for weaving in and out of traffic. Both Frank and Biggun knew they had not been weaving. They had not passed another vehicle since they left Houston. Biggun had the cruise control set on 63 miles per hour. So, they weren't exceeding the speed limit. It was misting rain. The headlights shined on the black wet surface ahead of them. The green sign on the right side of the road said, "Chambers County."

The trooper pointed his flashlight into the driver's side of the car and told Biggun to get out. He asked to see his license. He then pointed his light at Frank and asked for his license. While looking at the license in the light of his flashlight, he told Frank to get out of the car as well. Neither man had been drinking. The trooper told them to stand at the front of his patrol car, with their hands on the hood. With their backs to their car, they were illuminated by his headlights as they tried to look behind them to their Buick, where the Texas State Trooper was looking inside their car.

"What do you think I see?" the trooper yelled gleefully while his head was still inside the driver's window of the Buick. "There's a long bud of marijuana poking through a napkin over the sun visor on the passenger's side! Hey! Look here! I just found a bottle of diet pills in the driver's door pocket in plain sight!"

"Now look," he returned to the men with their hands warming on his hood. He had left his motor running. "What I have seen in plain sight so far has given me probable cause to search your vehicle."

The trooper looked directly at Biggun with a big satisfied grin on his face. "Although I have probable cause to search your vehicle, I prefer to be on the safe side. I need for you to sign this consent to search form."

He pushed an official looking aluminum clipboard with a yellow sheet of paper on it toward Biggun. Biggun thought he was asking him to sign a traffic ticket. He couldn't hear too well standing illuminated and humiliated on the side of the Interstate 10. Plus, he didn't know how to read nor write.

The trooper assured Biggun the paper was just routine, "Sign it!"

Since it was on a clipboard and looked official, Biggun scratched his name on it where the trooper's red checkmark was. He had learned to do that in the third grade, his last grade at Davis School in Dade County, Georgia.

Later, when the lawyer asked Biggun at the trial if the marijuana over the visor and the diet pills were his, he said no. He was a rumpled up very large fat man who sat slumped down in the witness chair. He said that he had no idea how the stuff got in the car. He was then asked if he had ever taken a diet pill, and he said that he couldn't, he had heart trouble. The lawyer asked what would have happened to him if he had taken a diet pill with his heart trouble. Biggun looked balefully at the jury and said he didn't know, he had never taken one. He said that he didn't even know what a diet pill looked like.

The officer returned to the Buick, opened the driver's door, and took the keys from the ignition. He walked back to the rear of the car and opened the trunk of the Buick. There, he found 200 pounds of commercial grade

Mexican marijuana.

"I thought I smelled wacky backy," he smirked. "There's little mistaking the cool raw smell of fresh hemp in the evening."

Later, at the trial, he would testify that he could smell green marijuana when he stopped the car. He said there were four air fresheners in the car, and they weren't working.

"Those Georgia Crackers smelled like a fresh marijuana patch going down I-10." The trooper chuckled as did the jury.

Biggun and Frank were arrested on the spot and removed from I-10 to Anahuac, Texas, and the Chambers County Jail.

The jail and justice system were Chambers County's main money crop. Catching, jailing, trying, convicting, and sending to prison, was the only local industry other than seizing and selling the doper's assets used in furtherance of the crime. It was within the criminal justice system that the vast majority of men and women from Anahuac, and surrounding Chambers County, were employed.

The trooper enjoyed playing what was called "the dirty trick" law enforcement was then playing on dopers in that part of Texas. The trick worked like this: A state trooper, or sheriff, would receive information from a Houston DEA Agent, whose reliable informant had given information to the DEA that a certain motor vehicle, in this case an old Georgia Buick, green and white in color, with Georgia plates, would be proceeding east on I-10.

The snitch, a Mexican named Sanchez who had known Biggun in Vietnam, pretended to sell the Sand Mountain boys the marijuana. He had been arrested and had to make a bust to avoid prison. To save his skin, he lured Biggun to Houston, and then he had told his DEA handler when the automobile left the motel. Sanchez set up the entire transaction. The DEA Agent radioed the Texas State Trooper Headquarters south of Houston, on I-10 from his car. The trooper dispatcher relayed the information to the arresting officer. So, when the boys from the north end came down the interstate, the trooper was sitting waiting for them, and only them, at the county line.

Why was this good police work a dirty trick? If the Biggun and Frank had been busted in Houston, a jury might slap them on the hand, pay a fine, usually time served and probation, maybe even a five-year sentence. But if they were busted in Chambers County, Texas, they would be looking at 10 years to life. So, the Law let the ex-white whiskey men leave Harris County and enter Chambers County before they stopped them. The Chambers County Courts had to have jurisdiction. It was automatic. When they crossed the line, that was when the trooper put his blue light on them.

The dirty trick worked like a well oiled machine. Over and over, each day, law enforcement used the trick to slow down the drug traffic coming out of Mexico.

The DEA and locals laughed about the dirty trick because 100 percent of the people who went to trial in Chambers County, Texas, were sentenced to big time, really big time. And, if the drug was cocaine, forget it. That doper's life was over. He was sentenced to the bowels of the earth, a Texas prison for eons. He would be fortunate to ever see the free world again.

The Texas Prison System was grossly overcrowded. As a result, prisoners languished in local jails until bed space was available. In Chambers County, prisoners might remain in the local lockup for up to three years. Both the state and federal government paid the county to "warehouse" the prisoners. Frequently, it appeared the individual was simply forgotten and left to serve his term in Chambers County.

These Northwest Georgia, Sand Mountain boys, didn't know what kind of trouble they were in. Because, in all truth, they did not know what was in the trunk of the Buick. Biggun knew he left the keys in the car, but his instructions were to not look in the trunk. He knew that there was pot involved. The pot had been "fronted" to him by the Mexican. In other words, he could pay for it when he sold it. Of course, the Mexican knew he would never sell it. Sanchez was buying his freedom with marijuana what some dope dealer south of the border had fronted to him.

Poor old Frank Williams said that he didn't have any idea that the grass was in the car. All he knew was that he had agreed to drive the car to Houston with Biggun. Biggun would have had to have paid more than $2,500 to hire someone knowledgeable to make the trip. He didn't offer Frank a penny. All Frank knew was that he had a few days off and that he was going to take a trip to Texas by driving Biggun to Houston. Leaving home, he did not know that he would be asked to find a certain motel, park the car, and check in. He didn't know Biggun was going to move the car around behind the motel, and leave the keys over the visor so the Mexicans could load the pot in the trunk. Frank was a trusting soul who was befriending a life-long friend.

Approximately eight hours later, at Biggun's instructions, Frank returned to the automobile, Biggun looked over the passenger's visor, retrieved the keys, and was ready to head for home. On this occasion, he spotted the 8-inch long marijuana bud wrapped in a napkin over the visor. Since he didn't smoke, and since the car did not belong to him, he left it where he found it. Little did he know, the bud was left there, in plain view, by the snitch as a setup to give the officer probable cause to search the entire vehicle. If the bud was missing, the officer could fall back on the illegal diet pills in the driver's door. If those were gone as well, the officer used, "A search incident to a lawful arrest," or some other excuse to search.

The arresting officer was not considered competent if he could not persuade the doper to sign a consent to search form. This ended all speculation that the contraband might be suppressed by the court. All the elements of the law were part of the dirty trick. It was supposed to work 100 percent of the time, and it did.

On the way home, Frank figured to get some rest and take over driving somewhere around Jackson, Mississippi.

So, after being booked and having their bonds set at $50,000 each, the boys hired a local Texas lawyer, from Chambers County. They made bond in a few days by paying a bondsman $8,000, and returned to Sand Mountain. They appeared for every docket call, arraignment, or whatever court appearance they were called upon to appear. Those Anderson County bail bondsmen were on the ball, they called Biggun and Frank personally every time before they were to appear. Finally, after numerous trips to Anahuac, over a year's period of time, their case came on for trial. A jury was struck on a Monday, and the boys were to go to trial the following Wednesday.

Frank hung around the courthouse most of Monday morning and heard people pleading to 20 and 30 years for a couple of pounds of marijuana. Some were being sentenced to even longer periods. 50 pounds got you life.

Then, all at once, his lawyer in cowboy boots, who took him into a side room, was not talking as favorable as he had been talking. He had been saying he would get both boys off with five years probation. Now, all at once, with the trial hard upon them, he was saying 20 years, and they might be out in five. Frank didn't like anything he was seeing or hearing. He was scared for the first time in his life. He was afraid he was gone for the long count.

Shortly after noon, back at the motel, Frank told Biggun he was going to back to Sand Mountain and hire the lawyer to come out to Anahuac to help him with this case. After all, he had nothing to do with the dope deal. He did not know the marijuana was in the car, he was not being paid for the deal, and it had already cost him and his family a lot of grief. He had a young wife and a child that he had to take care of. He drove his rental car back to the Houston Airport, turned it in, and cought a plane for Nashville. He called ahead for his wife and asked her to meet him there. He told his wife that he had to have another lawyer. The lawyer in Texas was going to send him to the penitentiary for life. Frank realized that Anahuac, Texas, was a strange and different land. It was a land that thrived off the misery of others. It was quaint and corrupt. The Chambers County Jail was the largest building in town. Three stories high, it was cream-colored brick taking up one city block. It was a new building. And, next to the courthouse, it was the area's most prolific money maker.

Wednesday came, and the cases were called for trial. Biggun had stayed in Anahuac. He had watched the court Monday and Tuesday as one doper after another, all victims of the dirty trick, were sent to prison for 20, 30, 40 years, or life.

His appointed lawyer, wearing cowboy boots, told Biggun that his case had gone downhill. The DA would not deal on his case. His only chance was to plead guilty and throw himself on the mercy of the Court. When the case of State of Texas v. Timothy Murray and Frank Williams was called, Frank was missing, Biggun plead guilty and the Chambers County, Texas, Circuit Judge, who was in on the dirty trick, sentenced him to 45 years. Needless to say, the judge and all the authorities in Anahuac were mad as hornets with Frank. They wanted him for their statistical analyses, which they were very proud of. The local bondsmen, who had become filthy rich off the dirty trick, were red faced and livid. Criminals didn't jump bail in Chambers County, Texas, at least, not for long.

They shipped Biggun off to Santa Rosa, Texas, where one of the state prisons was located, and he started doing his time. After processing into the system, going through orientation, taking almost 60 days, he was shipped back to Chambers County, "to await the trial of his co-conspirator." Actually, to be warehoused for the Chambers County budget six months, then back to Santa Rosa.

On Tuesday, the day before Biggun's conviction, Frank talked to lawyers in Trenton, Georgia; Fort Payne, Alabama; and Scottsboro, Alabama. The lawyers he visited either wanted too much money to go to Texas, or they told him to return and face the music with the lawyer he had already paid. All of them said that one day's notice to try a case in Anahuac, Texas, was too short. Frank decided it was time to say to hell with Texas, and head for the Big Woods.

The Big Woods is a 30 square mile area of some of the most inhospitable country in the United States. It is located on the North End of Sand Mountain where Alabama, Georgia, and Tennessee meet. It is the northern most part of the Great Cumberland Plateau, a high table land that runs from the Tennessee line to just north of Birmingham, Alabama. Sand Mountain is the most densely populated totally rural area in the world. Looking down on Sand Mountain at night from a jetliner at 35,000 feet it looks like one long sparsely populated city from Chattanooga to Birmingham. The north end is not sparsely populated; it is remote. It is famous for white whiskey and other criminal activity.

Frank went to live in a cave and sleep in a sleeping bag with only minor provisions. He stayed deep in the cave, or in its vicinity, for more than a year. From time to time his wife and children came to see him, and from time to time Frank came home and slept with his wife. However, most of the time, Frank lived the life of a hermit. When he visited home, his wife gave him new provisions which she had carefully packed earlier. She always included some little surprise hidden in the bag. He looked forward to the surprises while he remained well armed.

The authorities believed that he was in the Big Woods and searched for him on four different occasions. Each time dogs were used to pick up his scent. Even the FBI brought a team of agents into the area and looked for him. But, nobody was going to find anybody in the Big Woods if that person was not wanting to be found.

Frank could not be found, even when he

purposefully left a fresh trail for the best pursuit dogs law enforcement could find. He enjoyed the chase as it gave him something to do. He used the same tricks over and over. The dogs couldn't find him because the country was just too rough, the foliage too thick, and the canyons, or gulfs as they are called, were too deep and unexpected. A good bloodhound might follow Frank's scent to the edge of one of the hidden cliffs, but his next step might be his last. If he was not lucky enough to stop, that dog just took a 200-foot flight without wings down to some giant rocks.

Rarely would local law enforcement personnel search the Big Woods. It took one helluva party traveling in such a manner that they could all see each other constantly to even commence it. Even then, it was not safe. Three or four officers entering the Big Woods searching for a fugitive would be like fish in a barrel. The first person who saw them back in there, and could get away with it, would kill them just because they were the Law and they were where they were not supposed to be. It was common knowledge that one or two officers would not ever come out of the Big Woods. So, it was a safe place for Frank Williams to hide for more than a year.

It was a long wet, cold year. The cave was damp, and Frank had a constant bad cold. Every time he reached the point where he could relax a little, the Law came back into the woods with their dogs and trackers. He missed his family. He needed to go to the dentist. He was tired of living in the woods.

Finally, he could take it no longer. He was just too tired. He talked it over with his wife, and they decided he should turn himself over to the F.B.I. and go back to Anahuac to face the music. She promised she would wait for him no matter how long he had to stay in prison.

Frank was sure he didn't want to be seen or arrested by any local deputies. He was convinced they would shoot him on sight because his wanted poster said, "Armed and Dangerous". He had been sent a copy of the poster by his younger brother. "Armed and Dangerous," was a tag that was added to the poster because Frank was hiding in the Big Woods. Everyone knew that no one could survive alone in the Big Woods unarmed and unready.

There were various wild animals in the area including several packs of wild dogs, wild boars, bears, wolves, and rabid coyotes. All the animals were scavenging for a meal. In addition, very few people ventured into the thickest part of the woods unless they had criminal business. Many a person had disappeared on the north end and had never have been found. Conner Carter was one. For well over 100 hundred years, dozens of bodies had been disposed of in the Big Woods. There were several deep pits, abandoned underground mines and sink holes, called bottomless pits, in the deep woods.

After he surrendered in Scottsboro and was arrested, Frank waived extradition and was taken back to Anahuac, Texas. His bondsmen were the happiest people to see him. The jailer also welcomed him back. Within a matter of days, he was brought before the Honorable Carroll Wilburn, Presiding Judge, Chambers County District Court. Judge Wilburn immediately appointed Daniel Johnson, a relatively young lawyer from Baytown, Texas, to represent Frank. He set him a new bond at $150,000, one he knew he couldn't make. The judge made sure that Frank was not going anywhere.

Less than a month before the trial, the family of Frank Williams contacted the lawyer in Fort Payne, Alabama, and asked to hire him to go to Texas and try the Williams Case. Frank's wife was Geraldine Gass, the daughter of an old client of the firm. The lawyer agreed to try the case saying that he had represented every Gass by the name on the north end for the past 25 years. He even gave them a break on the fee. He lowered it down to where the family could afford it.

The lawyer thought that he might almost break even on the case if Daniel Johnson stayed involved and would handle pretrial matters in Texas. He made a call to Dan Johnson of Baytown, Texas, to be sure that he would stay in the case if the lawyer came on board. After conferring with his partners, Johnson agreed to stay on board for the fee the state was paying him, $25.00 per hour out of court and $40.00 in court.

Johnson was one of those young (mid-30's) Texas lawyers who are kind of a new breed. They seemed to lack the fear of the old guard and the temerity of the lawyers coming right out of school. They jumped right into the breech and to hell with it. They all thought they were "Race Horse" Hanes or John Ackerman. The lawyer was familiar with this new breed of Texas gunslinger and considered Johnson to be his kind of lawyer. It was balls to the wall, full throttle, all the time. Their attitude was let the rough end drag and the slick end slide, and to hell with it. They were totally fearless. He liked that.

The lawyer sent Dan a *pro hac vice* motion to be filed with the court that would allow him to participate in the case. Dan assured the lawyer that there would be no trouble out of Judge Carroll. He said that Carroll was an Ex-DA who bent over backward to be fair to the defendant because he knew that most former district attorneys or state prosecutors find that very difficult to do. Furthermore, Judge Carroll firmly believed a Chambers County Jury would convict every defendant anyway. "Give the son-of-a-bitch a fair trial before we hang him." So, Dan assured the lawyer Wilburn would be fair. The lawyer thought the situation would be fascinating if what Dan was saying was true. A rural Texas ex-district attorney, who was now a judge in a county that earned its daily bread from the criminal justice system, could not possibly be fair to his client.

Dan filed all the necessary motions and pretried the case saving the lawyer several trips to Houston and on to Anahuac. The lawyer thought that Dan was a very good criminal defense attorney. He appeared in Houston on Sunday, September 24, 1989, the day before the big event on Monday.

The lawyer was very familiar with the Houston Hobby airport. He had practically commuted in and out of the airport in his own airplane when he was on flying status. He was also very familiar with the four lane into downtown Houston. He had kept the airway hot from Alabama to Houston when he was representing Joe and Craig Cullinan during the local coal boom of the 70's.

The Cullinan brothers owned 160,000 acres of mineral rights in Northeast Alabama. The lawyer was their representative in the area. He successfully managed the properties to the point the brothers, whose grandfather, "Buckskin Joe" Cullinan, founder of Texaco, earned millions in royalties from coal mining in Northeast Alabama.

It was after dark when he arrived in Houston. The lawyer had intended to rent a car from Budget, but they were busy. So he went to Avis because he knew they gave an American Bar Association discount. He figured he would be there one day, two days at the most, so the car didn't matter. He told the girl in the red Avis uniform, "I want the cheapest car in Texas."

She said, as if she had been waiting for him, grinning big, "I mean I got it. Just for you."

He signed the rental agreement and went out to the parking lot to find his car and load his gear. He had a suit bag, a computer, a box full of law books, boots, clothing, and underwear. Damned if he was going to Texas and not wear a pair of Lucchese handmade boots.

The large Black guy on the lot said, "There's your car." He pointed a large black finger silhouetted against the street lights of the parking lot toward a very small automobile.

The lawyer, following his point into the artificial light, said, "What car?"

The big black guy said, "The little red one over there."

The lawyer squinted his eyes, "Where?"

Avis, trying harder, said, "Right in front of you."

"That?" incredulously.

"That," matter-of-factly.

"What is it?" questioningly, genuinely interested.

"A Ford," The big black guy responded.

"That ain't no Ford," the lawyer said, letting him know he was from the South. "That's a Cushman."

"It's called a Festiva," he tried to apologize.

"No problem," the lawyer told him. "It is my fault. I asked for the cheapest car in Texas, and I got it."

"You're right about that. The keys are in it."

"The girl who rented the car said she had been waiting for me. I guess she was telling the truth."

"She was," turning back toward the terminal.

As the lawyer started trying to stow all his gear in the little car, he was thinking, Oh well, it's the propulsion that counts. Propulsion is the difference between walking and riding. He called out the black guy again. He asked him one more question, "Will it run?"

"Like its tail's on fire," he gave a big toothy grin like he knew something the lawyer didn't.

He started the little engine, turned the little dude toward Broadway, out of Hobby, and noticed that the little sucker would run.

The lawyer had always lived by a rule --

when he was in a large city he always drove like the locals. He used to say, "If they drive like damned fools, I drive like a damned fool. If they drive like little old ladies, I drive like a little old lady." In Houston, they drove like damned fools, and they drove mostly pickup trucks and Suburbans. They maneuvered them in and out of traffic like those monsters were sports cars.

The first time the lawyer saw the Holiday Inn sign in Baytown he stopped. He had to use all the influence he could muster in order to get the last room in the place. He pulled out his preferred customer card, Priority Club, and everything else and finally got a room. He had no idea where the next motel might be. So he was glad to be back home in a Holiday Inn.

He called Dan Johnson that Sunday night, and everything was set for go the following morning. They agreed to meet at his office at 8:00. Dan gave the lawyer directions as to how to get to his office. The lawyer traced the route on his map that the Avis girl had given him with the car.

Dan told the lawyer that he had had a bench warrant issued for Biggun Murray and had him brought back from the Joint. While in the Anderson County Jail in Anahuac, Texas, Biggun had told the family that he would exonerate Frank by saying that he had nothing to do with the marijuana deal. And this was the truth. Biggun could have passed a polygraph as to this question. He didn't tell the family that, even though he had plead guilty, and been convicted, he was going to maintain that he didn't have anything to do with it either. The lawyer thought, Not good.

He arrived at Frank's office at 7:30 a.m. The directions had been good. The lawyer had left early enough to become lost at least once, but he felt he made it like he was, "born to the saddle."

A little after 8:00 a.m. Dan arrived in his red Corvette, complete with auto telephone. The lawyer was impressed. However, after driving that Festiva, it didn't take a lot to impress him. He figured that there was at least one consolation: If someone stole that Festiva, they would only get practice. They sure as hell wouldn't be stealing a car.

On the way to Anahuac, Dan gave the lawyer a short history of the place, the DA, and the Judge. He said that they were going to have to work on the judge. The Judge had said that he was not going to allow Williams to have two lawyers with the county paying for one. He said the lawyer hired by the family could sit at the table, but he could not participate in the trial. That didn't sound good.

Dan said, "Once he meets you he will change his mind. He just wants to make sure you are a real lawyer and not some bullshit artist brought in to smell up his courtroom.

There's been some big named lawyers come in here and lose. They have usually taken a swipe at the system and the people when that happens. The judge doesn't like that."

The lawyer and the red-headed young Texan expressed concern to each other that Biggun had told Dan the day before that he was going to say that neither he nor Frank knew the stuff was in the back of the Buick. "What the hell does he want to do that for?" Dan asked. "He has already plead guilty to it and is doing 45 years. What has he to profit by not admitting it was his deal? He set the entire thing up, and he should clear Frank and let him go home."

The lawyer told him that he would try to get with him and speak some good ole Sand Mountain lingo to him and straighten him out.

When they arrived at the Chambers County Courthouse Dan took the lawyer directly to meet the judge. The courthouse was a modern appearing building attached to an older structure located on a square in the geographic center of town. It was clear the courthouse was the economic center of the county. It was within a stone's throw of the new jail. It looked like the drug business had been good for Anahuac, Texas.

The Judge's chambers were on the second floor of the low chrome, glass and brick part of the building. The lawyers climbed the wide marble steps to the courtroom, and from there they entered the judge's chambers. The lawyer thought, Judges never have rooms or offices. Judges always have chambers. Wonder why?

The three men talked and the judge concluded that the lawyer was not the kind that would cause him any problems. During the questioning, the lawyer told the judge that he tried cases on a national basis, and that he knew how to play by the local rules. He said, "I can assure you that you will have no trouble from me. I know my business. I will protect my client vigorously within the rules."

The judge said it would be a pleasure to have the lawyer in his court.

The DA trying the case was a dan-dan-dandy. He came into court in a cutaway western suit wearing black and white boa skin boots. He was tall, dark haired, and handsome. He let everyone know that he knew he was a striking figure. He was an assistant district attorney who was paid by the federal government to try drug cases only. He had a funny sounding voice, sort of a feminine ring to it. However, he had the most arrogant attitude the lawyer had encountered in more than 25 years. It was clear he was used to winning and winning big. He gloried in preening and strutting around before the jury like a peacock. He seemed to be a Shakespearian actor speaking plain English. He elucidated each word. To the lawyer, he was sickening.

By the time the trial was over the lawyer knew why assistant district attorney was such an obnoxious twit. He knew Chambers County's main source of revenue was law enforcement. He definitely knew how to appeal to the selfish economic interests of the jurors. He was nobody's fool. However, the lawyer said that he would give the distal phalange of his left little finger to get him in a Federal District Court somewhere with a case with only a crack in it. The lawyer imagined him leaving courthouse with his boots being the largest part of him. Later, the lawyer could honestly say that the pretty preening pettifogger had tried every cheap, Mickey Mouse, below-the-belt, trick the lawyer had seen during the past 25 years. Apparently, Mr. Pretty Boy Bullshitter was used to getting away with that cheap crap in Anahuac, Texas.

He conducted prospective juror examination like the lawyer did in a capital murder case in Alabama. It took him 6 and ½ hours to conduct his voir dire. He pulled his first cheap shot early in his voir dire examination, when the lawyers question the prospective jurors. He almost got away with it. He asked the jurors if they were familiar with William McCoy, or whoever that boy was that was killed by the mass murderers at Matamoros, Mexico. The lawyer didn't know who McCoy was, but he objected at the mention of any name other than the defendant's or that of an alleged coconspirator. He asked to approach the bench and asked the Court to require the district attorney to make a proffer, or make an offer, of evidence as to what this person had to do with the case.

"You objection is well taken, but it comes too late. The question has already been followed with another question." He then looked the district attorney in the eye. The lawyer could see that the judge had little regard for the pompous district attorney. "That was highly uncalled for, Mr. District Attorney. I herewith instruct you that you will not try to pull anything like that again."

The lawyer followed up with the judge while he had the district attorney on the ropes. He wanted the DA to know that he had the killer instinct. He requested that the DA be required to ask only one question at the time in order that he might object if necessary, and he asked for an instruction to the jury venire regarding McCoy and the murders. The Court directed the DA, "Ask only one question at the time, and do not attempt to poison this jury. Do you understand me?"

The DA smirked and walked away from the bench.

The judge then turned to the jury, "Ladies and gentlemen of the jury, I hereby instruct you that you are to totally disregard any reference made by the district attorney concerning a person named McCoy, or whoever that boy was. I believe he was taken from here in Chambers County and was brutally murdered. I know his case was in all the papers when it was tried here last month. That case has nothing to do with this case. This defendant, Mr. Williams, does not know Mr. McCoy, nor is he connected with that case. You are to disregard the fact that this district attorney mentioned that name. I believe he mentioned that name only to prejudice you against this defendant. Therefore, you are instructed to disregard it. If you cannot disregard it, I will declare a mistrial. Is there anyone here who cannot disregard what the district attorney just said?"

No hands were raised, and the district attorney continued his prospective juror examination.

At that point the lawyer knew he was dealing with a cheap shot artist who would bear watching. The young arrogant assistant district attorney was so used to getting his way that he just did whatever he could get away with. So, the lawyer stopped him from getting away with very much. He still tried the case with many illegitimate tactics which practically made a mockery out of the judicial process. It seems his rule was, "if it works toward a conviction, use it." The man had no ethics. If he knew the rules of evidence, he ignored them. He was a steam roller grinding through the courtroom to convict the lawyer's client, Frank Williams.

This jerk was so bad that in his final argument he said that the lawyer had told the jury that the trooper had put the 200 lbs. of marijuana in the car. Then he contrasted the great heroic trooper with the escapee, dope running, pulp wooder, from Georgia, who was hauling enough pot to make over 300,000 joints for Atlanta dopeheads.

It was the ugliest case the lawyer had ever tried. It took both the lawyer and Dan fighting every minute with every ounce of their experience and intellect to keep the assistant district attorney from making the jury's decision for them. While examining his witnesses, he would stop, turn toward the jury, and argue what the witness had just said. The lawyer and Dan would jump to their feet and shout him down until the judge would rule and instruct him to stop making speeches. It didn't matter, five minutes later, the would do the same thing again.

"Like I say, Dan, I sure would like to meet that piece of Anahuac crap in a neutral combat zone. I believe I could actually leave slightly less of him than a grease spot. But for this trial, we're in his sandbox, and I can only sit in amusement at his sophomoric legal gymnastics. They would be funny, but I can see two jurors who are eating up his every word. All the rest are leaning toward him, including the owner of the Dock. Two of them need saliva tests; they have become mad dogs."

Dan and the lawyer had selected the best jury they could put together. Almost everyone in the jury pool was connected with law enforcement. They either worked for the state, county, or were married to people who worked for the state or county. Otherwise, they were school teachers, registered nurses, preachers, or business people. Almost every man was a volunteer deputy sheriff. The jury venire was overwhelmingly convictors.

There was a restaurant across the street from the east side of the courthouse called The Dock. It had a false front above the street made out of silver painted tin, with a porch overhanging the entire sidewalk in front of the restaurant which was about 20 feet wide. The overhanging roof was held up by pine tree trunks which had the limbs still on them about a foot to two feet long. The trees were whitewashed. People stood around in front of the restaurant hanging onto tree limbs.

The man who owned the Dock, where the sheriff and judge ate every day, was the last juror the defense intended to strike, but he slipped through the cracks and wound up on the case. Later, the juror told the lawyer that he discovered and developed chicken fried steak at The Dock. The lawyer tried it for lunch. It was a breaded chopped beef patty, deep fat fried, and smothered in sawmill gravy. Years later, the lawyer saw chicken fried steak on the menu of several restaurants in Alabama. He wondered if the secret had traveled from Anahuac, Texas.

When the jury was seated, the lawyer looked at Mrs. Boutwell, an Avon saleslady, and Mr. Patterson, who had just been working at his present job of some kind of technician for five months, and knew the defense was in trouble. It was apparent that jury service was the most important thing they had ever done in their lives, and they were going to make the most of it. At every break, all that could be heard coming from the jury room was their mouths. It worked that way during deliberations as well. These jurors were determined to convict every drug dealer in the United States if they could. And they wanted to make an example of whomever was first before them. Unfortunately, that was Frank Williams.

From time to time, Frank wished he had stayed in the Big Woods. That life didn't look so bad looking back on it from Anahuac, Texas.

The defense tried the case to the wall. It seemed like they had a chance to bring Frank back home with his wife and family, who were in the courtroom, until the DA brought out Biggun's original plea transcript. In it, he allowed the prosecutor to put words in his mouth by saying such things as, "You and Frank Williams were in this thing together, weren't you?" And, of course, Biggun said, "Yes."

The defense tried to tack in the breeze by trying to get the years reduced rather than go for "Not Guilty." It was apparent, when the transcript came in, that the defense was not going to be successful. The DA brought the entire 200 lbs. of seized pot into the courtroom and opened the bags. He placed them near the jury box in order that the jury might believe the trooper really smelled marijuana. Every person with an allergy in the courtroom, including the lawyer, began to sneeze, have runny eyes, and generally suffer a severe allergy attack. Cheap trick.

And that was just one among many.

The lawyer objected, and the judge required the DA remove the green leafy vegetable material from the courtroom and repackage it in its garbage bags. Unfortunately, the damage had been done. The lawyer knew that you can not unring a bell.

The lawyer and Dan tried the case for a full week. In the end, the jury found their man from the Big Woods guilty and gave him 20 years. They stayed out 6 hours and 24 minutes. The only sounds that could be heard in the courtroom coming from the jury room were the voices of Jurors Boutwell and Patterson.

The Judge said that it was the lowest amount of time a jury in Chambers County had given anyone for 200 lbs. of pot that he could remember. He told the lawyer and Dan that it was a win.

Of Course, in his final argument, the DA implored the jury to sentence Frank Williams to 75 years. He was not only a doper; he was an escapee. He reminded them that the years a doper got from a jury didn't mean anything about how long he stayed in the Texas Penal System. There were people who got 30 years and were out in 18 months.

The lawyer objected.

"Overruled."

The DA continued saying that he wanted the jury to send a 75-year message to the other criminals in Atlanta, Georgia, to stay out of Texas with their dope dealing ways. The jury rejected his suggestion, but it was not Mrs. Boutwell's nor Mr. Patterson's fault. Those people could be heard all over the courthouse during deliberations. They never shut up. They just wore the jury down. Twenty years were the best they could do with the rest of the jurors so they finally took it.

The lawyer hated to lose the case. It was a sad loss, but as bad as that was, he wished he had not drank the water in Anahuac. The oil waste from the Houston oil refineries traveled underground and polluted the wells in Chambers County. The people there were used to drinking oily water, but the lawyer was not.

He was sick the entire time he was there, and he was sick for three days after he returned home. "Talk about the backyard trots," he said, "I had the backyard sprints. I was not safe more than 50 feet away from a restroom."

"Oh well, that's life in the fast lane," he consoled himself. In criminal law, lawyers go home, and clients go to jail. I feel like we did our best and that was all we could do."

The old Houston DEA dirty trick had worked once more. Each year, they made thousands of arrests just like this one. The trooper working this bust testified that he had already accounted for more than 8,000 pounds of marijuana the year he arrested Biggun and Frank. He didn't even mention how much cocaine and other drugs he had seized.

"He's making a name for himself," Dan muttered.

Frank Williams spent 21 months in prison in Texas. When he was paroled, he returned to the north end, got himself a good job, and settled in with that good looking, long-legged, blonde-headed wife of his. They had three children. The lawyer never saw him again.

Biggun Murray spent more - 28 months in Santa Rosa Prison and was placed on unsupervised parole. Biggun returned home and opened a restaurant selling some of the best steaks on the north end.

Both men got out early due to the overcrowding of the Texas Prison System. They would have never been there in the first place if it had not been for the dirty trick. Biggun had never called the Mexican to buy the marijuana. He didn't have that kind of money and had never sold marijuana in his life. Sanchez had called him, trading on being old war buddies, and enticed him to come to Houston. Apparently, he had used up all the other people he knew and had to dig deep into his memory bank to remember Biggun.

Sanchez eventually went to prison himself. He was cought when a very close friend of his persuaded him to haul a load of pot to Russell, Arkansas, for $5,000. The thought never crossed his mind that the dirty trick might be in play.

Even had he considered it, he would have probably muled the load anyway. Relying upon his services in the past, he felt close to law enforcement. He had informed on so many people that he could always count on a break. He didn't think the DEA in Houston would take him down. They did. The dirty trick was just too good to pass up.

THROWED OUT

Dressed in worn out denim jeans, a jumper that had seen better days, and a faded red flannel work shirt, M.C. Winters staggered -- he actually fell -- through the door into the lawyer's waiting room.

"I need a lawyer," he said through slurred speech. He was disheveled. His clothes were dirty and had not been ironed. His shoes were worn out, run down loafers. Although he hadn't had a shave in a couple of weeks, he was clean, but he was not neat. His appearance, particularly his red face, betrayed the fact that he was a hopeless alcoholic. He was 44 years old, unmarried, and unemployed.

The secretary nervously attempted to make him comfortable. He was making strange noises. "Now, you sit right there. The lawyer will be right with you." She tried to calm him and keep him quiet. M.C. was the only person in the waiting room.

M.C. sat in an office waiting room chair with his head rolling somewhat from side to side in his drunken fog. It was the worst kind of an early morning drunk. His hangover had been so bad that he had to have a hair off the dog that bit him in order to get his sun to come up this morning. He had been using this excuse for more than 14 years. As a result of the hair off the dog, he had not had a sober day since he started drinking right after he was medically discharged from the army in 1953.

The secretary entered the lawyer's private office. He was studying legal papers. "A Mr. M.C. Winters is waiting to see you. I believe he's drunk. He looks like it, and he smells like it."

Without looking up from the papers he was studying, the lawyer said, "If that man is M.C. Winters, he's drunk." He looked up, "M.C. slightly sobers up only toward the end of the month, when his V.A. disability check is gone." He returned to his papers. "I'll see him in a couple of minutes. Believe me, he'll keep. He's pickled."

When the lawyer was ready to see the client, he thought of M.C. for a minute or so. He remembered that M.C. had won the Silver Star in the Military during the Korean "police action." A gook shot him in his left leg and his other foot froze, causing him to lose his toes, while he was waiting for the medics to find him in the snow. M.C. walked with a pronounced wobbling limp. He seemed to walk as if he were drunk, even when he was sober, if ever that happened.

The lawyer had represented M.C. in two or three small scrapes with the law, nothing serious. He remembered that he was a "Korean War" veteran as he walked down the hall to the waiting room.

"M.C., what are you into now?" the lawyer asked as he reached out his hand to shake with the inebriated man who was now on the waiting room couch.

The prospective client looked balefully up through very watery blue bloodshot eyes. "It's my sister. She's stealing my money and won't give me any. You got to do something about it."

The lawyer knew the problem all too well. Due to this alcoholism, M.C.'s sister had sought and obtained a conservatorship to manage M.C.'s business as he was incapable of doing so. These "papers" allowed her to receive M.C.'s veteran's benefits each month and control how his money was spent.

Before she stepped into his life, M.C. would receive his VA benefits check and be broke in three days. For the rest of the month he was forced to live off relatives or friends. Eventually, he wore out his welcome with his family and everyone who knew him.

Although he owned a small white house in the rural northern area of the county, on Sand Mountain, still, he began to sleep in the streets, on park benches, or wherever he might find himself when he was ready to pass out -- shelter or no shelter. His family thought this was regrettable since he was receiving a 100% disability pension from the U. S. Army. Finally, at the urging of his family, his sister stepped in, became his conservator, managed his money, and kept M.C. from being a burden to his family and society in general.

"M.C., I know you don't understand this, but your sister is helping you. She is keeping you from drinking up your check in the first five days of the month and begging the rest of the time. You should appreciate what she does for you. She's keeping beans on your table."

The lawyer was standing over his old client in the waiting room. M.C. had not decided whether he could manage standing and walking again. So, he sat, slumped over mumbling.

"I'm telling you, she's stealing my money. I got shot in Korea, my other foot got froze off. That's the way I earned that money, and she has taken it. It was my ass that got shot and frozen. I want my money. If I want to spend it on women, or give it away, that's my business. I want my money." The drunk man was becoming a little more vocal and very belligerent.

"Well M.C., you know I'm your lawyer and I'm your friend, but I can't contest your sister's conservatorship papers. If you think she is stealing your money, we can call upon her bondsmen. They will have to pay you if she steals any money from you."

"I don't need no red tape. I want my check. It's my government check, and I want it. It came in yesterday, and I want it."

"Have you talked to your sister about it?"

"I shore as hell have, but she won't give me nothing. She gave me $10 and told me to go get drunk. Hell, that ain't enough to git drunk on. I'd like to really tie one on with my friends. You know, buy some drinks, eat something good, chase some women, git laid, mebby have a few fights. You know, just have a good time for once in my life, and she won't let me." He trailed off into a whine.

"Now M.C., I imagine you've had a bunch of good times in your life. That's why your sister won't give you any more money. Why don't you just take it easy?"

"Well, if you won't help me, it looks like I'm gonna haf to go back to makin whiskey. I can't git by like this."

"M.C., you don't need to get back into the whiskey business. The revenuers are all over that mountain. They've got a new program out now. It's called, 'Operation Dry Up -- Moonshine Kills.' They're going to arrest every white whiskey man on the north end. You'll get in serious trouble this time. Stay out of the business. They've targeted Sand Mountain. They're flying choppers over it all the time. Don't get into that. You've got enough to get by."

"I know some places in the Big Woods where I can make whiskey all day long, seven days a week, and ain't nobody gonna find that still. I need the money, and I'm gonna do it."

"M.C., stay out of the white whiskey business. This is just not the time to be making white. The woods are full of revenuers. You'll drink up too much of your makings and get cought sure as today is Monday."

"Today's Monday?" M.C. asked genuinely concerned.

"It's Monday."

"Oh hell, I'm in a mess. I thought it was Friday. If it's Monday, I gotta get the hell outta here. I got people to see, and things to do."

He rose from the couch, gained his feet unsteadily, held to the door facing, twisted the knob, and started out toward his old rattle trap blue Chevrolet Nova at the curb.

The lawyer noticed there was no one else in the car. He yelled, "M.C., you are way too drunk to drive. Let me call your sister to come get you."

"I got places to be, and people to see. I gotta drive. I'm too drunk to sing."

He walked unsteadily toward the 15-year-old vehicle that was in very poor condition. It was obvious that the motor vehicle was owned by a drunk. There was barely a place around the car that was not dented, rusting, and generally falling apart. The front bumper was hanging on the left front of the car with baling wire. The tail pipe was dangling close to dragging on the pavement. It needed to be wired back up again.

The lawyer didn't look as M.C. drove away.

It was three months, one week, and two days later when M.C. and his sister visited the lawyer together. Seated in chairs in the lawyer's office, the sister spoke first, "Have you heard about him getting arrested?" She nodded disgustedly toward her older brother.

Before the lawyer could answer, M.C. joined in, "Hit was like you said, I went back to making, and they cought me. But they didn't catch the still, though." M.C. was bragging and obviously drunk.

The lawyer talked to the sister, "I have not heard that he has been arrested. I had asked him to stay out of the white whiskey business, but apparently, he didn't. How was he arrested?"

Before the sister could answer, M.C. chimed in. "They cought me selling a few gallon in town. I just had five gallon with me. They didn't get the still. I told you they couldn't find my still." He was a bragging drunk again.

"Did you give them a confession?" the lawyer asked.

Running through his mind was the fact that M.C. had been arrested in Chattanooga. The local court would not have jurisdiction if they did not find the still in Alabama. The Feds would have to take M.C. to federal court in

Chattanooga or Rome, Georgia, if he was making in Georgia.

The sister interrupted, "He not only told them all about it, he took them to his still."

She looked toward M.C. with a look of abject derision.

"He took them to the cooker and thumper?" the lawyer asked in disbelief.

"He had been drinking all his blue john, you know, the first-run alcohol down the spout. It's more than 120 proof. Then he took a load of wildcat up on Third Street in town. He was so drunk he couldn't even make change. The local law arrested him, and he told them all about it. He took them law to the still after they promised that they wouldn't destroy it."

"But they did, goddamned it!" M.C. interjected. "They dynamited it and chopped up the pieces with double-bladed axes. Sons of bitches, goddamned liars! Hit took me two weeks to build that still." M.C. was an angry drunk. He was bordering on an alcoholic rage.

M.C. Winters was a typical white whiskey man from the north end of the Great Cumberland Plateau, Sand Mountain, where Alabama joins Tennessee and Georgia. The people from the early families believed that making whiskey was the absolute right of every man. They had done it since the land was taken from the Cherokees. They could not understand how untaxed white whiskey could ever be illegal.

Revenuers, later called Alcohol, Tobacco, Firearms Agents (ATF) had a particular relationship with the whiskey makers. Neither side shot at the other. Most whiskey men were good for their word and knew the revenuers on a first-name basis.

"Where did they make the case against him?" the lawyer asked the sister.

"They charged him here, in state court in Alabama. He's going to go to trial right here. How much do you need to defend him? We'd like to keep him home, but we know its hopeless. He's going to have to cop a plea. So you aren't going to have to try his case."

The sister was seriously negotiating a lower fee. In addition, she and the family had mixed emotions. They wanted him in prison to dry out. But, at the same time, they really didn't want him in prison.

The lawyer quoted enough fee to cover his expenses, took his camera, and went to the destroyed still. After photographing the wreckage, he approached the district attorney about a plea bargain. The DA refused to discuss the case until it was called for trial in four months.

When State of Alabama vs. M.C. Winters came on for trial, the lawyer negotiated the best bargain he could for his old client. Due to five prior driving-under-the-influence-of-alcohol convictions, and four driving-without-a-license pleas of guilty, the state would not agree to a slap on the wrist. The district attorney would only allow M.C. to plead to a five year sentence.

M.C. agreed to take the deal even if he had to go to prison for a while. His sister said she wanted him home; but in all truth, it would probably save his life for him to go to prison to dry out. He was still a relatively young man, 44 years old. She reasoned that prison would add ten years to his life and allow her to save some of his pension and maybe buy him a new car when he got out. She could live in his house and take care of it while he was gone.

About three weeks after his plea was entered, M.C. came on for a hearing on his application for probation. The Court denied his application because of his prior misdemeanor convictions and the size of his still. The rig was capable of producing 700 gallons a run. M.C. was sent to Draper Prison near Montgomery.

The lawyer regretted that M.C. went to prison, but he, like the family, thought it might be good for him. He agreed with the sister that prison might add a few years to M.C.'s life. He might dry out. In prison, he had no choice, he had to dry out.

It took M.C. being an inmate in Draper Prison for six days before he began to suffer from serious heavy delirium tremors.

Additionally, M.C. had suffered from combat fatigue, or shell-shock, since the day he was wounded in the snows of Korea. Later it would be called Post Traumatic Stress Disorder. However, a combination of his maladies resulted in M.C. screaming throughout the nights. He believed he saw rats trying to eat his toes. He saw large bugs and spiders climbing around on the walls of his cell. He thought that huge scorpions were after him wanting to sting him with their ugly tails.

After the third night of DT's, the prison officials allowed his cellmate to move to another cell. They warned M.C. to keep quiet.

Two and one-half months after he entered Draper Prison, M.C. Winters was the most hated man in the institution. He was forced to remain in his cell, practically solitary confinement, for his safety. Two prisoners had attempted to kill him in the chow hall. No one had enjoyed a good night's sleep since M.C. began his bad nights. Inmates were openly planning to murder M.C. Guards were posted on his cell to keep him awake or wake him as quickly as he went into his nightmares. He was sent to the dispensary and the doctor prescribed every medicine known to man to cure the combat flashbacks and the delirium tremors. Nothing worked.

The hideous screeches and screams continued all night every night. The prison officials tried to keep M.C. in the dispensary, but he disturbed the sick inmates worse than he did the population. They put him in the hole, solitary confinement, which was near the prison administration facilities. Without windows nor light, M.C. didn't know whether it was night or day. He wound up staying awake all night and sleeping during the working shift of the prison administration.

His bloodcurdling screams ricocheted off the office walls terrifying the secretaries and white collar prison officials. The warden put up with that for two days and instructed the uniformed personnel to place M.C. in solitary confinement in his own cell.

Once M.C. could see the light of day, he began his bad nights once more. He screamed himself hoarse, but he never knew what he had been doing. He just knew what people said he was doing. He couldn't understand why people hated him. Still, each and every night, he was visited by his demons coming out of his memory and his body's demand for the poison it had been adjusted to for so many years in the past.

The inmates told the bulls, prison guards, that if M.C. was not stopped, they were going to riot. Each night when M.C. began his horrible screams, the entire population on his wing arose and beat on their cell bars with their tin cups. It was a loud noise, but it did not awaken the sleeping veteran. Night after night the misery dragged on.

Inmates became testy. Fights broke out in the recreation room, on the yard, in the mess hall, and wherever the men were allowed to congregate. The guards were having difficulty controlling the population. The hatred for the guards by the inmates reached dangerous proportions. It was only a matter of time until a guard was killed, or several taken hostage and possibly killed. Every person at Draper Prison, guards, white collar people, service personnel, and prisoners alike, knew something had to be done with M.C. Winters. His DT's were simply intolerable.

At 4:17 a.m. on a Thursday, in the spring of the year, the guards and inmates on the night shift had all of M.C. they could stand. He was screaming, the inmates were up beating on their cell bars with their cups, screaming obscenities, and the guards had to do something. The fuse had finally burned down, the prison was within minutes of exploding.

A.J. Boatwright, Captain of the Guards on the night shift decided to take action. He personally went to M.C.'s cell and opened the door. He rushed the sleeping screaming man and threw him and his mattress off the bed and into the floor. M.C. hit the concrete with a "Whomp!" sound. He was startled awake.

M.C. heard all the noise of the inmates,

squinted at his watch, looked at the captain of the guards, and said, "What the hell is going on here?"

"You're leaving," Boatwright said from a wide-stanced position with his hands on his hips. "Get up and put your clothes on."

"What for?" M.C. mumbled.

"I told you, you're leaving. Get a move on!" Boatwright kicked M.C. in the ribs. "Get up, goddamnit! I mean it. You're history. Move it!" The guard captain was frothing at the mouth.

M.C. put on his white prison uniform with "Alabama Department of Corrections" stenciled in black on the back of the shirt and pants. His black brogans had no laces and he had no socks. His only underclothes were his white boxer shorts.

He stood up in the darkness of his cell. "Now what do you want me to do?"

"Here's a paper sack. Put your personal shit in it. Now!"

M.C. put his shaving gear, a picture of his niece, and a box of matches in the sack. The Captain of the Guards pushed him out into the cell block. When the inmates saw him, they began to yell obscenities at him. M.C. Winters was called every dirty name known to the English language. B wing of Draper Prison was in total pandemonium. Guards surrounded M.C. as he was escorted out of the cell block. The inmates were showering him with personal items that they were throwing at him, trying to hurt him. He was truly the most hated man in Draper Prison.

As they left the cell block, M.C. asked one of the guards escorting him, "What're you all gonna do with me?"

Boatwright gave him the answer, "We're throwing you out of prison. You are no longer welcome here."

"You can't do that," protested M.C. "They'll arrest me for escape. I'll be sent back for a longer term."

"You ain't coming back," one of the guards interjected.

"And you ain't escaped," Captain Boatwright said. "You have just disappeared. Sorta like a you died in prison. You just don't exist here anymore. In the morning, your records are going to disappear from our files. You were never here, and you ain't coming back."

They were now at the large front gates of the imposing medieval building. "But what am I gonna do?" M.C. whined.

"We don't give a good goddamned what you do!" one of the guards said. "Just don't try to get back in."

It was still dark outside. It was cold. And, all at once, M.C. Winters was standing on the side of a four lane highway running north and south. He looked back toward the huge darkened entrance to the prison. The guards didn't bother saying, "Goodbye." He heard the gates clang shut.

"Now, what do I do?" he moaned to himself.

M.C. noticed the traffic was increasing as the sky was beginning to lighten just a little. He looked at his watch. It was 5:05 a.m. He instinctively threw up his thumb indicating he needed a ride northward. Surprisingly, the fifth car to come by, stopped and gave him a ride to Birmingham. The driver deposited him on the margin of Interstate 59 North near the airport. M.C. began to thumb again.

It was 9:38 a.m. when the secretary entered the lawyer's office and said, "There's a man in a prison uniform in the waiting room. I think he must have escaped. He doesn't have laces in his shoes."

"Who is he?"

"I don't know. I didn't ask. He's drunk, and he looks like Mr. Winters. But, I'm not sure with that haircut."

"Are you kidding?" the lawyer asked incredulously. "M.C. is at Draper."

"Not anymore. I believe the man out there is Mr. Winters."

The lawyer went into his waiting room and saw the man sitting in the prison whites, drunk out of his mind.

"M.C., what are you doing here? Did you escape?" The lawyer was excited. He could see himself calling the sheriff and delivering

M.C. to the proper authorities.

"Nah, I don't reckon. They throwed me out of the prison about 4:00 o'clock this morning." M.C. was very serious and very drunk.

The lawyer was flabbergasted. "They don't throw people out of prison, M.C. They throw people into prison. People are given parole, or released, from prison. People don't walk out of prison. There's a pound of paperwork to be filled out when an inmate is released. Now, tell me what really happened. And, how did you get drunk before you got here?"

"Hell, I don't know," M.C. slurred, "I was sound asleep when the Captain of the Guards on the night shift came to my cell and throwed me out of bed. Then, he and the guards made me dress and escorted me out of the joint. I don't get it. I wasn't that bad. I never broke none of their rules. I was trying to get out on good behavior." M.C. was apologizing for his conduct in the prison.

"They left me on the edge of the four lane, so I stuck up my thumb and got a ride. This guy was goin to Birmingham, and so was I. I asked him if he had a drink, and turns out, he was a whiskey salesman with a trunk full of Jim Beam. He gave me a couple of fifths. I killed one before Birmingham and one after. It was cold out there."

He giggled, "Hit ain't cold no more."

The lawyer was still unbelieving. He

expected the authorities to burst into his office at any minute.

"Look M.C., you can't convince me that guards throw people out of prison who are serving a sentence. Drivers, particularly whiskey company representatives, don't pick prisoners up in front of the prison, dressed in a prison uniform, and drive them to Birmingham while giving them a bottle of whiskey to drink on the way and one for the road."

"Well, they shore as hell done it this time," M.C. said with slurred speech. The second bottle of whiskey was beginning to hit him. He could not hold his head up to look at the lawyer.

"How did you get here?" the lawyer pressed him.

"Well, the whiskey man and I made good friends. We were both in the same business. He was going to go south of Birmingham, but out of professional courtesy, he took me to north of Birmingham, and let me out at I-59 North. I stood around on the edge of the interstate. Hit was a little after daylight, and I was cold. I was pulling lightly on my second bottle of Jim Beam and thumbing. This guy came along in a pickup truck and stopped for me. He was coming to a sock mill up here to fix one of them computer driven knitting machines. I told him to bring me to my lawyer's office, and here I am."

"You're sure you didn't escape from Draper?"

"I'm telling ya, they throwed me out. I got my ditty, right here in this sack." M.C. held out the paper bag he had put his personal belongings in when he was taken out of his cell.

The lawyer knew that convicts did not escape from prison with their personal belongings. If they got out, they ran as light as they could. Still it was inconceivable that guards would put a prisoner out of the penitentiary in the middle of the night, and then someone would pick up a hitchhiker in front of the prison, in a prison uniform, and take him away. The entire account was not believable. The lawyer could not comprehend M.C.'s story.

"Were you wearing anything over your prison uniform?" He was trying to figure it out.

"Nope. Wearing just what you see, just the way I am. This is the way they throwed me out. Hell, I didn't want to leave. The food was good down there. I gained nine pound. But, they kicked me in the ribs and told me to get my ass out of there. So, I did. I didn't have no choice."

"Did you have on those brogans without laces?"

"Yep. They never gave me no cheap suit nor any $3 like I thought they was supposed to."

"And still people picked you up in your prison whites?"

"Well, two of 'em did."

"And one of them gave you two bottles of whiskey?"

"Yep, I'm a Jim Beam man from now on. I ain't never tasted bottled in bond that tasted that good. Now, I'll still drink some white, but for commercial grade, I'm a Jim Beam man."

The lawyer looked at his watch. Clients would be coming in any minute.

"Look M.C., you need to come back here in the library and wait for your sister. I'll call her and get her down here to pick you up." He helped M.C. stand and guided him toward the library.

On the way down the hall he told his secretary, "Call the sister, tell her the story, and get her down here to pick up her brother. M.C.'s number is still in the Rolodex." He guided the unsteady M.C. through the door into the library.

M.C. could not negotiate a chair no matter how hard he tried. He was too unsteady on his feet.

As he was checking chair after chair in his drunken stupor the secretary came in. "His sister is on her way."

"Help me get him in a chair." The lawyer was still struggling with the man who seemed as if he did not have a bone in his body.

The secretary took the right arm of M.C. while the lawyer held his left and most of his weight. They guided M.C. toward a chair without arms. Although the chair matched the other library chairs, it did not have arms intentionally. The court reporters used this chair when taking depositions in the library.

"Okay, help lower him down. He's going to make it." The lawyer and secretary tried to help lower M.C. into the chair.

When M.C. bent his left leg and put his weight on it, the leg collapsed. He slipped out of the helpful hands of the lawyer and his secretary. M.C. fell to the floor in a heap, but not before striking the left side of his head on the library table as he went down. M.C. was knocked unconscious.

"My God!" the lawyer screamed, "We've killed a drunk prison escapee! My reputation will never survive this."

He kneeled down, looked for blood, found none, and felt for a pulse. "He's still alive. Help me stretch him out."

"He's drunk," the secretary deadpanned as she tried to pull his left leg straight. Eventually, M.C. was stretched out on the crimson library carpet. The lawyer turned out the light and closed the door to prevent other clients from seeing the prostrate man.

When the sister arrived, the lawyer came out of his office. Thankfully, his waiting room was finally empty.

"Come this way. He's in the library." He opened the door and turned on the light. "He hit his head pretty badly when we tried to make him comfortable in here to wait for you. He fell and hit his head, hard on the edge of the table."

"Oh, don't worry about that," the sister calmed him. "You should have seen him when he fell on the stove one winter. The stove was one of those big ole coal stoves, and it was red hot. He about burned his hands off. Then, he fell in the fireplace while his hands was gettin well. You know he has trouble walking when he is sober. When he's drunk, he can barely navigate. Help me git him to the car, and I'll take him offen your hands."

"But first, tell me what's he doing here. I thought he had gone off for five years. He hasn't been gone six months."

"All I can tell you is the most bizarre story I have ever heard. He said that they threw him out of prison this morning around 4:00 o'clock. A whiskey salesman picked him up in front of the prison, in his prison garb, and took him to Birmingham. From there, he got a ride with a man coming to work on some sock machinery here in Fort Payne who dropped him here at my office."

The lawyer checked his pulse again. M.C. was moaning and trying to talk. Both the lawyer and his secretary were relieved. They thought that M.C. may have sustained serious head injuries. The lawyer was sure that he had to have suffered a concussion.

The sister, the lawyer, and the secretary struggled to get the totally intoxicated M.C. into the small red compact car of the sister. M.C. passed out again as soon as his head hit the headrest.

The lawyer returned to his desk. He dialed the number of his oldest and best friend. They had been best buddies since childhood. They had been newspaper delivery boys on V-E Day and V-J Day. The lawyer felt that he had to speak to someone.

"How?" his friend answered. It was an old childhood joke.

The lawyer skipped the preliminary pleasantry. "You'll never believe what just happened."

THE BOOTS

It was a terrible crime, perhaps the most heinous crime ever committed in East Tennessee. The criminals chose a senseless act to commit for reasons known only to themselves. Morgan County was in shock. It would be several years before it would recover from the murder. It was an unbelievably cruel and senseless act. It was an outrage to the community on a personal basis, and it was not to be forgiven.

Eighty-one year old Dr. Wilburn Case was watching Hee Haw with his wife one snowy Saturday evening in December. His godson, Curtis Bagwell, the Morgan County Sheriff, was coming by for coffee. The Cases were looking forward to seeing Curtis because he had made them proud. He represented good, clean, swift law enforcement. He was the kind of sheriff Dr. Case wanted -- fair, honest, and tough. Thirty-six years old, a family man of humble beginnings, Curtis Bagwell prided himself in meeting the high standards set by Dr. Case. He was tall, well built, sandy headed, and handsome.

Morgan County, Tennessee, is coal country. It is similar to Harlan County, Kentucky. Wartburg, its county seat, is almost due south of Corbin, Kentucky. Brushy Mountain State

Prison Farm, the prison of James Earl Ray, assassin of Dr. Martin Luther King, is about three miles from Wartburg. The county's main economic stay is coal, both underground and strip mining. The area is rich with the mineral, and huge lumbering coal trucks, laden down with black gold, ply the highways of Morgan County slowly and ponderously around the clock seven days a week.

Dr. and Mrs. Case lived on Pine Orchard Road near Oakdale, a few miles south of Wartburg. Senator Howard Baker of Watergate fame, Senator Everett Dirkson's son-in-law, lived in Huntsville a few miles up the road. The Cases' spacious home was located about 1/4 mile from the main road. A winding drive led up to the conservatively built stone and brick home. About 17 acres surrounding the home were under fence.

Dr. Case had delivered, as babies, more than 80% of the people living in Morgan County at the time of his murder.

The community would not allow him to resign or refuse to run for Morgan County Chairman of the Democratic Party. He was never opposed for the job. He didn't want the job, but he did it for the people. He was a kindly, loveable, political boss with national ties through Republican Senator Baker and many others.

Dr. Case had been the Chairman of the

Democratic Executive Committee and the county's only doctor for more than 60 years. He was a good man. Some of the local citizens practically worshiped the man for what he had done for them and their families.

Dr. Case always had time. He was always good for a "loan" or a handout. He might personally be at the point of exhaustion, but he took time with the people. As a result, he was loved by thousands. He was more than a local celebrity. He was someone everyone wanted to know, or say they knew. If necessary, he would always help with a political favor if the ends were just. Dr. Case would never be refused a justifiable favor if he was asked for one. However, he had never asked for any favor for himself. He was truly a giving and much loved man.

It had snowed heavily for three days. More than two feet of snow was on the ground, and it was four to six feet in drifts. The countryside was blanketed in the white stuff. Many roads were impassable. The schools were out for Christmas. Otherwise, they would have been closed due to the snow making many rural unpaved roads impassable. Power was down in many parts of the county. It was an East Tennessee mountain country winter.

Dr. and Mrs. Case had finished dinner, she had done the dishes, and they were relaxing before a crackling fire in the fireplace. A well decorated Christmas tree stood in the corner of the den with dozens of colorful gifts under its hundreds of beautiful lights.

While Junior Samples was cracking a corny joke, as the Dr. and Mrs. Case smiled already knowing the punchline, all hell broke loose! A man jumped through their twin double hung six foot windows next to the television set. He was wearing a field jacket, a black ski mask with yellow outlines of his eyes and mouth, gloves, and carrying an M-30 Carbine rifle. Plunging through the wood and glass, he landed on the leather covered, gold inlaid, coffee table.

"Don't move!" he yelled at Dr. and Mrs. Case pointing the rifle at the doctor.

Dr. Case was an old veteran himself. He had been wounded in Europe during WWII while serving as a young medic. Although he was eighty-one years old, he leapt to his feet and charged the intruder. Mrs. Case sat with her crocheting needles poised where they had been when the glass came flying throughout the room. The gunman on the coffee table shot Dr. Case in the left shoulder spinning the doctor somewhat out of control and into the hallway to the right of the gunman. The noise was deafening, and the smell of gunpowder filled the house.

The man in the black ski mask rushed to where Mrs. Case was sitting. She screamed and began to stand up. He hit her in the right side of her seventy-seven-year-old face with the butt of his rifle crushing her right cheekbone and breaking her gold-rimmed glasses. Dr. Case seized this opportunity to crawl into his bedroom and grab his old Army Colt .38 Special long-barreled revolver that had always hung in its leather on his bed post. He then crawled back into the hallway in time to see the gunman standing almost on top of him. He raised the Colt and squeezed off a round. It hit the wall, missing the gunman by inches, who now shot him again with the M-30. The doctor convulsed in the hallway. Mrs. Case was unconscious in the floor in front of her chair.

The gunman dragged Dr. Case into the bathroom between the bedrooms and the den. He ran back to Mrs. Case and dragged her frail body, feet first, to the same bathroom. As he turned out the light and locked the bathroom door from the inside, Sheriff Curtis Bagwell knocked on the heavy wooden front door. He had tried the doorbell without results.

Someone outside the house in the waist-deep snow at the broken window yelled, "Get the hell out of there, Man! Get out now!" The second ski-masked head disappeared into the blackness from the window.

"What the hell's goin on?" the gunman stuck his head out the broken window and yelled to his confederates outside in the snow.

The man in the ski mask appeared in the window again. "It's the goddamned sheriff, man! Get the hell out of there! We gotta git!"

The sheriff knocked louder with the bronze knocker in the middle of the heavy dark oaken door. No response from within. He tried to look through the small window near the top of the door, but it was covered with a Christmas wreath. He couldn't knock loud enough with the knocker so he began to knock with the butt of his pistol.

"Hey! Doc, open up! Come on, turn that TV down and open the door!" Curtis could hear Hee Haw playing on the television set.

"You deaf old goat, open this door!"

The Cases kept the set up too loud for him. He thought that old folks must be that way. He yelled and knocked louder. Finally, he went out to his Cherokee station wagon and turned on the emergency warning system briefly. On the silence of the snow the sound could be heard all over Oakdale. The ranger at the bi-color checking station, at the entrance to the Catoosa Wildlife Management Area, heard it two miles away.

The confederates behind the home in the snow thought when they heard the sheriff's horn that they had been cought. The man with the carbine stepped back up on the coffee table, then to the window sill and leaped out into the snow.

The three of them began to run across one of the doctor's largest pastures toward the road. They were widely circling the home to avoid the sheriff. They made it to the road before the sheriff finally arrived behind the house and saw the window broken and the various footprints in the snow.

"Aw Shit!" Curtis Bagwell cried in a loud whine. He knew something had happened. He keyed the walkie talkie from his belt, "M-18, this is M-1, do you hear me?"

"I got you, Sheriff. This is M-15, coming into Oakdale from the South. I don't believe base can hear you on the walkie. What's happening?"

"Bert! Radio base to dispatch all available units to the home of Doctor Case. Something has gone on here. I don't know what, but call the ambulance and give me backup! You got it?" Bagwell was excited.

"I'm on my way, and copy your message to base. M-15 out." Bagwell could hear Bert fire up his emergency gear several miles away.

Although Curtis Bagwell knew he should wait for backup, this was the home of his godparents and, by God, he was going in. He went to the mailbox near the door. The extra key was in a magnetized case under the box. Bagwell felt for the extra key. It was there! He opened the front door and went in.

There was no life in the house. With pistol

drawn, he literally jumped around each door as if he were in a movie. When he reached the den, where the break-in had occurred, he knew all the news he would learn would be bad.

"Hey Doc, Mother Case! Where are you?" No answer.

Curtis Bagwell observed the scarred coffee table. He noticed the knickknacks and magazines on the carpet. That would be good evidence. From the puddles of water, it was obvious some snow-laden shoes or boots had been on that table. He followed the drippings down the hallway into the bedroom. There was blood in the hall floor near the bathroom. The door was closed and locked from the inside. The sheriff knocked on the bathroom door, "Dr. Case, you in there? Mother Case, can you hear me?"

He knocked louder and thought he heard a muffled moan. He dared not break the door down for fear of what he would find.

As Bagwell was deciding whether to kick the door down, he heard Bert come through the front door.

"What's happening, Sheriff?" the breathless deputy asked when he saw the sheriff.

"I don't know. Cover me, I'm kicking this door down." Bert pulled his service revolver and pointed it toward the bathroom. The sheriff launched his right black-booted foot toward the bathroom door near the lock. He kicked it hard, and the lock housing failed. The door flew open revealing Mrs. Case laying partially on the doctor looking at the sheriff in wide-eyed fear. She was unable to speak. When she recognized Curtis she began to cry. It was obvious to the sheriff that the doctor was dead.

The sheriff helped Mrs. Case to a chair in the bedroom and put a blanket from the bed over her. The wind and snow were beginning to come into the den blown through the large broken window. By the time the sheriff had made Mrs. Case as comfortable as possible, other agencies were beginning to arrive. He returned to the doctor and checked his vital signs. His first impressions were confirmed; Dr. Case was dead. The shoulder shot didn't do it, but the point-blank shot to the chest killed him.

The ambulance attendants removed Mrs. Case from the home bound for the general hospital in Harriman a little over four miles away. Every available man from Sheriff Bagwell's staff was gathering evidence at the scene. Two special agents with the Tennessee Bureau of Investigation and several guards from Brushy Mountain Prison showed up offering whatever help they could. F.B.I. agents were on their way from Oak Ridge to assist if a federal law was involved. Amid all the organized pandemonium, three game wardens came in from the wildlife management area.

Almost an hour elapsed before a detail of

officers began to follow the footprints in the snow that crossed the pasture, cleared the fence, and made it to the road. They followed the clearly distinct prints westward into the Catoosa Wildlife Management Area. They lost the prints about a quarter of a mile short of the bi-color checking station.

The station was a shack, similar to a guard shack, that was manned by park rangers who checked the color of the various passes the deer hunters had paid the state to allow them to take game from the wildlife management area.

Some of the cops knew the ranger on duty at the checking station. He had no idea Dr. Case and his wife had been the subjects of an attack. The Cases were friends of his. Doc had delivered all four of his children.

The ranger said that the only traffic he had seen since he came on shift four hours ago was four hunters who came by in an old pickup truck. His log showed it was Barney Woods in a 1958 Chevrolet truck. The license tag was shown on the log as a Tennessee plate. The plate was checked immediately and confirmed that it belonged to Barney Woods of Jamestown, Tennessee, over in adjoining Fentress County.

The sheriff, as well as almost everyone else, knew Woods. He was a superintendent with Starkfellow Mining Company and an inveterate deer hunter. There was no way he would be involved in hurting Dr. Case. He even served as an auxiliary deputy and was a member of the Sheriff's Posse of Morgan County. He was the captain of the Morgan County Mine Rescue Squad.

"Who were the guys with Barney?" Bert Watson asked the ranger.

"I donno. I knew Barney. He's in here all the time, all hours, with all kinds of different people. I've checked him and his friends a hundred times, and every one of them is legal. They buy their passes over at Jamestown. It was cold, I didn't want to go outside, and I didn't check Barney this time. I know one thing, Barney Woods is not going to be hauling any crooks or illegal people through here."

"Suppose he didn't have any choice. Suppose they had thrown down on Barney and forced him to drive them through here," Watson said more than a little bit aggravated.

"That didn't happen. I flashed my light on them. They weren't acting suspicious. Barney was happy. They were his friends. If they weren't, Barney would have given me a signal."

"He wouldn't have given you a signal if there was a gun to his head."

"Are you trying to tell me Barney came out here to hunt alone, by himself? He ain't never done that since I've been here. Those men were friends of Barney's," the ranger wanted to cover his butt.

'Well, where would Barney go to spend the night?"

"I don't know. There's a couple of hunter's cabins up near Smith Branch. I know he uses one of them sometimes. They're shown here on the management area map," he pointed the small black squares representing the cabins out to the officers. They were about three miles north of the ranger shack.

Jim Rollins, the chief deputy, arrived and came in stomping his boots and blowing from the cold. He had seen officers sitting in their vehicles with their motors running. He had seen others standing around the shack in the light of the vehicles. The shack was filled with officers and cigarette smoke. It held only about five people.

Rollins, who had been in radio contact with Bert Watson since he had left the house and started toward wildlife management area, called everyone to gather around him. He stood in the doorway of the shack where everyone could hear him. He handed out rough drawings of the management area north of the bi-color checking station.

He barked team instructions to Bert Watson and James Jernigan of the TBI. Within minutes both men had gathered their respective teams together, passed out maps, and gave instructions as to how the teams would fan out and cover every passable road in the management area.

For the rest of the frigid night the teams searched the area without success. With daylight the weather turned more foul than it had been earlier. The temperature dropped to four degrees below zero. The wind picked up to 30 miles per hour, and snow began to fall again at 6:30 a.m. By 7:30 a.m. the men, who had worked without sleep, were searching in a blinding blizzard.

The sheriff had proceeded into the management area immediately after being sure Mrs. Case was in the hospital and Dr. Case was in the funeral home. He left men in the Case home to seal up the window with plastic and secure the scene for the crime lab, while he headed for the management area. He got a full report from Rollins by radio on his way into the wildlife management area.

Bagwell had hunted with Barney Woods several times. He struck out on his own, in his four-wheel drive Jeep Cherokee going to various places in the area where he had been with Barney. Bagwell did not follow the main roads.

He turned the Cherokee off the main road, to the right down an old strip mine road about a mile toward Smith Branch. He was in the area where the old strip mine had been reclaimed. He plowed through the snow in four-wheel drive until he saw signs in the snow. It wasn't long before he found Barney Woods in his truck trying to keep from freezing to death.

Woods had driven down into the old strip mine area on the mining road that he was very familiar with. He had built the road when he had mined this area ten years before. The snow had begun to pile up quicker than he thought. His truck could not get traction, and he was stuck. He was making the best of it when Curtis arrived. However, he was more than a little concerned. He dared not leave his truck, and he couldn't turn around and climb back out. He didn't know how much deeper the snow was going to get. He knew the rangers would search for him when he didn't come out and his family inquired, but he might be dead by then. He had to be careful until help arrived.

Curtis pulled up beside Barney, rolled down his window, and motioned for him to get into his Cherokee. Barney was already a little stiff. He was having trouble moving. Curtis got out, tromped through more than knee-high snow, and opened the passenger door to the old truck.

"You all right, Barney?"

"I'm worried about freezing, Curtis. Help me get out of this mess."

Bagwell dragged Barney from the truck and helped him into the Cherokee where the heater was running well. It took Woods several moments to stop shaking. His teeth were chattering to where he could not talk. Bagwell had a thermos of hot coffee and gave him a cup. He couldn't hold the cup without spilling the coffee. The sheriff had to hold it up to his mouth for him to drink. After what seemed to be an eternity, Barney Woods was able to function normally. Bagwell maneuvered his four-wheel drive around in the hood-deep snow and started back out.

"What happened to the men with you?" the sheriff asked. "Who were they, and where are they now?"

"I don't know who they were. I picked them up just short of the bi-color checking station. They were walking with their guns. They said they had been hunting all day, and their truck had broke down. They had been to Oakdale and got a new fuel pump and was on their way back to their truck. They were nice guys. Why?"

Bagwell didn't respond to Woods' inquiry. "Who were they, and where did you leave them?" He continued to plow his Cherokee through the deep snow trying to stay in the tire tracks he made coming in. He was going uphill at a very steep angle. It was easier to get in than get out.

"I don't know who they were. They gave me their names. One of them said they were hunters from down in Alabama. But I'm not good at remembering names. I just gave them a ride to their truck," Barney said through still chattering teeth.

"Where was their truck?"

"I donno," he scratched his head through his cap. "They said it was off on the first turn to the right. You know, over there near Sawyer's barn? I didn't take them down to the barn. They told me to go on. They would walk back to their truck. I knew the barn was less than a quarter mile off the road. So I knew they would be okay."

Curtis Bagwell's mind was working like a well-oiled machine. Now, he knew what had happened. There were three murderers. The prints had shown this, and Barney Smith had confirmed it. One of them had jumped through the picture window in the den and landed on Doc's coffee table on his feet. He had, then, for whatever reason, murdered Dr. Case by shooting him twice with a .30 caliber M-3 army carbine. The shell casings proved that.

The murderers had heard him at the front door, ran across the field to the highway, turned off the main road into the management area, cought a ride with Barney Woods, and played him for a fool. They had no pickup truck. They had to have been dropped off by a confederate.

Through adroit questioning, they learned about Sawyer's barn. That's where they went to spend the night. It was shelter, near the entrance to the management area, a safe place where they could wait for their ride to come back in the morning and pick them up. Since the man who was supposed to pick them up the night before did not find them, he would definitely be back searching for them.

Bagwell hated that he had Barney with him. He wanted to get to Sawyer's barn right then, but he was stuck rescuing a witness. He radioed Jim Rollins, Bert Watson, and James Jernigan. He told them to proceed immediately to Sawyer's barn. He expected them to find the killers in that barn. He took Barney Woods to the bi-color checking station. The ranger would arrange for a tow truck to pull Barney's pickup out of the drifts when it cleared up. It was still snowing hard, large flakes. Curtis met all kinds of law enforcement on the roads in the management area.

When Sheriff Bagwell finally arrived at Sawyer's barn, the place was swarming with officers. A state crime lab four wheel drive vehicle was there. He saw Jim Rollins coming out of the dilapidated old structure.

"Did you get 'em?" he asked his chief deputy.

"Nah, they got away. They spent the night here. There's all kinds of signs in there. Don't worry, Sheriff, they won't get far. They left here going due south toward Oakdale. They are backtracking and paralleling the highway. If they stay in the woods, they'll never get across Emory River at this time of year. If they come out we're on the highway waiting for them. They won't get far. So we can take our time. We have them in a sack made up of the roads and the river."

Bagwell walked up to the barn and looked at it. It was a typical old East Tennessee barn. It was about forty feet high and about sixty feet long. There were six long abandoned stalls, still intact, which still contained hard old dried-out manure mixed with straw. Although the barn had not been used in 20 years, it still smelled like a barn. There was rusted baling wire lying in circles in various places. The ground floor of the barn was dark and dry. The big barn doors could not be closed. They had long since sagged on their big rusty hinges.

Officers began reporting to the sheriff.

"You were right. There are three of them," Bert reported. "We found three indentions in the hayloft where they spent the rest of the night. They ate C-rations for breakfast before they took off; the cans are still up there. One of them smokes Camels, one chews tobacco, and the other one doesn't have those habits."

"How big are they?" Curtis asked. "Did they leave any other signs?"

"They're a little larger than average. The crime lab guy measured the indentions in the straw and figured the shortest one was right at six feet. They left their ski masks buried in the hay pile. They also left their long guns here. I guess they didn't want to carry them. There was a pump Browning 12-gauge shotgun, an automatic Winchester .12 gauge, and the army M-3 carbine that was used to kill Doc."

"So we have recovered the murder weapon?" Bagwell was relieved.

"Yeah, the ballistics guy said he could tell the weapon had been recently fired from direct observation. Also, the twenty-round clip was two rounds short."

"I imagine the casings we found at the Case residence will fill up the clip," the sheriff responded as he approached the dark worn ladder nailed to the wall and leading up to the hayloft.

"He probably put one in the chamber just before he went in the Case house. This would account for the entire load in the magazine."

Bert walked toward his vehicle carrying the olive drab used C-ration cans in a plastic bag. He would mark the bag and deliver it to the crime lab guys.

As Curtis poked his head through the hole in the hayloft floor he could see at least six officers working in the loft. Sheriff's Patrolman Willis should have been outside securing the parameter. He had no business being up there, but Bagwell didn't say anything. When he stepped off the ladder onto the hayloft floor he walked over to the crime lab men. They were near the door where the hay had been boomed into the loft.

"What'cha got?" he asked.

"We were just looking at how they wired the hayloft door shut. Look at this wire. It has been stressed within the past few hours. They wired the door shut to keep out the wind. Then they ate their C-rations. You think they brought the C-rations with them?"

The crime lab man was wearing a long black overcoat, covering a suit and tie, with galoshes on his street shoes.

"No, they didn't think that far ahead," the sheriff responded as he looked at the snow through the cracks in the walls of the barn. "I'll lay odds Barney Woods gave them the rations. He always carries a case in the back of his truck during hunting season. He had some in the cab with him when I pulled him out of his truck a little while ago,"

The sheriff reflected. "That damned ole Barney is just too nice for his own good. Oh well, he could be the only identifying witness we'll have later on. What else you got?"

"You can see where each of them burrowed down in the hay. Frank has already photographed all the indentions before they were disturbed." He pointed toward the obvious body forms left in the old hay.

"We found the three weapons laying over near the east wall." He pointed to where the guns had been found.

He paused. "Other than recovering possible fingerprints on the weapons, cigarette butts, C-ration cans, and ballistic checks on the rifle, we've done about all the damage we are going to be able to do."

The black overcoated right arm went up as he motioned for Frank, his fellow criminalist, to wind up the investigation and, "Let's get out of here. I'm freezing my ass off."

The sheriff spoke out in a loud voice, "I want all my men up here in the hayloft. Now!"

The criminalists waited at the top of the ladder as four men climbed up to meet with their boss. Bagwell had concluded that the hayloft was the best place to make their next plan. The wind was whistling through the lower floor dog trot like a wind tunnel blowing off the snow. It was relatively comfortable in the hayloft. Although some of the flapping tin was noisy, the old barn still had its roof intact.

"All right," the sheriff started, "I want to know who has equipment necessary to take up the chase from here. Who has boots, radios, food, four-wheel drive vehicles?" he looked into the faces of his men.

"Sheriff, we aren't in any position to track these guys right now,"Jim Rollins told Bagwell.

"Those guys have at least five miles to go

through the snow, and they have to find a way to cross the river, or they have to come out to reach a road out of here. They can't do it. We've got them bottled up. The state troopers are over there on the road waiting for them. Let's go back to the office, get some rest, and start fresh."

"I agree," Bert Watson spoke up. "We ain't ready to attack the management area the way we're dressed and equipped. We'll get out there and cause more problems for ourselves than we can solve. I think we ought to go back and organize the Sheriff's Posse, they need something to do, and use every available man to catch these bastards."

Jernigan didn't say anything. He was just happy to be along and be one of the men involved. He thought, "This is what every hunter dreams of, the ultimate hunt, hunting fugitives through the snow."

The sheriff thought for a minute. "You boys are right. Shit, them bastards may die out there in those hills and woods. And, even if they are lucky enough to make it out, the direction they are going, the first thing they are going to see is a Tennessee State Trooper or a Brushy Mountain State Penitentiary Guard. Alert the captain of the guards over there to send some more men to help watch the roads. Let's go home. It's almost nine. We should get some of the posse boys on this by lunch. I don't want you guys on this chase until you've had some rest. We've been at it for more than 16 hours." The sheriff started for the ladder down from the hayloft followed by his men.

Back in Wartburg, in the sheriff's office, all shifts had been called in. Fourteen men were waiting for their boss. As the vehicles pulled into the lot beside the jail, men looked out the window awaiting their instructions. They were ready for action. All of them were disappointed that they had not been in on the original investigation. By radio they knew that their job was now to take up the chase and make the arrest, dead or alive.

The large map of Morgan County had been taken down from the back wall of the dispatcher's area of the sheriff's office. Bill Miller, commander of the SWAT team had taped a temporary enlarged map of the Catoosa Wildlife Management Area, Oakdale, and surrounding environs where the county map had been. A large aerial photo of the entire area was next to the map. The "ready room" was ready.

Jim Rollins came out of the back room and handed the sheriff the overall plan. He had enough copies for everyone. Each man studied his map and assignment. The roads in the management area were to be searched from their beginning to end. The search would seek to drive the fugitives toward the highway or the river. Either way, they were to be driven into the awaiting arms of the state troopers and prison guards. Helicopters had been called in, but the ceiling was too low for them to fly. The parameters had been secured. They would not get out, and their pickup man would not get in. All the dragnet needed was to be tightened.

"Remember men," Bagwell was gravely serious, "these men are presumed armed, and, by God, you better know they're dangerous. They've killed once, and they won't mind killing again. So be careful." He sounded like a sheriff in a Western movie, but he meant it.

"What are you going to do, Sheriff?" Jim asked. He knew better than to ask the sheriff if he was going home to rest. Nobody was going to rest until these murderers were behind bars or dead.

"First, I'm going by the hospital and check of Mother Case. Then, I'm going to go up on Turkey Knob where I can reach every unit and keep up with the chase. I want to be sure every single cave and hiding place in the dragnet is searched. I think I know where the caves and old mines are. Right now, I think I know the general area where the murderers are located. Bert's as tired as I am, but since he was on the case first with me, he'll be my driver and number one assistant. Jim, I want you to take charge of the field. I would like to send you home, but I know that asking you to go is a waste of time."

"You got that right."

"Well, you're the best man I got. I want you to coordinate all units in the search. Once you have dispatched your men, bring your unit to Turkey Knob and meet me."

The sheriff left the building. Bert Watson slid into the driver's seat of the Cherokee and pointed it toward Harriman.

Mrs. Case was in intensive care. The unit allowed the sheriff to visit with her briefly. Looking up from the semi-lit ICU bed, Myrtle Case recognized Curtis Bagwell. Behind her bandages, and with tubes down her throat, she whispered, "Honey, I wouldn't have had this happen for the world."

"I know you wouldn't. But look at it this way: Doc lived a prosperous and fruitful life. He was ready to go, and he went out with a bang."

"I should say so," she whispered. "He loved it. If he could have, he would have killed that goblin."

"And you have provided us with some evidence," Bagwell grinned at his godmother.

She looked at him unable to speak much more. It required too much effort and she was in great pain. The doctors had told the sheriff she would eventually be all right if there were no complications.

The sheriff continued, "I understand that he hit you with the butt of his rifle and crushed your right cheekbone. That means he is probably left-handed. We know there were three of them. The one that's left-handed is our murderer, and he will get the death penalty."

The sheriff smiled a grin of satisfaction as he explained detective work to a person he loved.

After a few more minutes, Bagwell excused himself and went to Turkey Knob high above Oakdale which gave him clear radio contact with Wartburg and the rest of the county. From this high point he could monitor each and every transmission coming from the numerous officers and men in the search.

First, the more experienced officers started in hot pursuit following what was left of the footprints in the snow. Hour after hour the officers slogged through the deep snow and high drifts following the vaguely defined trail of the three men who had passed that way hours earlier. The officers believed they were no more than four and one-half hours behind the subjects. After struggling through the sub-zero temperatures, through the three feet of snow, for approximately three miles, the officers began to proceed slower and more warily in case of an ambush.

This phalange of professionals were flanked and followed by literally hundreds of deputies and deputized citizens, mostly deer hunters and miners, who made up the posse, and were very familiar with the area. True to the sheriff's suspicions, the trail was leading directly southeast between Pine Orchard Road and the unimproved Snow Road. The criminals were facing trying to cross Twin Bridge Road, which was lined with officers. If they successfully crossed that hurdle, they were still facing a raging Emory River with the railroad yards and Oakdale Road on the other side. Bagwell knew there was no way out for the killers.

The phalange chase unit was called Unit One. Every quarter mile or so, its leader, James Jernigan, reported to Jim Rollins and Curtis Bagwell. Curtis had not wanted to put James in charge of the lead unit, but he knew the country better than any other man available. He practically lived in the management area. He had been a game warden before going to be with the Tennessee Bureau of Investigation. He had grown up in Oakdale.

Other groups searched strip mines, underground mines, caves, roads, and other areas on the chance there were more criminals than first believed, or they had divided up. Most everyone in the search concluded that Unit One was going to make the arrest or start the shootout.

It was nearing dark, almost 4:00 p.m. Sunday when Unit One arrived at Twin Bridge Road. It was clear the trail crossed the road in broad open daylight. Why not? There was not an officer present to see Unit One cross the road. They were now less than one-half mile from the river and less thanthree quarters of a mile from downtown Oakdale. Unit One proceeded to the west bank of Emory River. The river was almost 150 feet wide where the signs seemed to enter the water. Unit One spread out up and down the river and found no other prints.

"Sheriff Bagwell, we are on the west bank of the Emory right now. All signs indicate that the suspects forded the river at this point," James reported.

"Is there a possibility they went up or down the river?" the sheriff asked.

"Negative. They went into the water here."

"What are your conditions?"

"We're about 3/4 mile from the Oakdale Bridge. The river is rushing along near the tops of its banks right here. It is more than 150 feet wide along in here. The water varies from two to four feet deep. It is obvious the subjects went into the river. The current is too strong for them to go upstream. There are some frozen people who went down this river," James was trying to give the sheriff as many details as were available.

Curtis Bagwell made a snap decision. "Attention all units, this is M-1. Call off the search west of Emory River. The suspects have forded the river near the most eastern point of the management area, right across from the railroad yards. Attention all units near Butler's Hill. Please converge near between the middle of the rail yards and the Oakdale Bridge. Proceed with caution. I repeat, these subjects are suspected armed and dangerous. Do not run any risks, and confirm any sighting of the subjects with me. You people in Oakdale should be hot right now."

West of the river the hunters, deputies, and sheriff's posse, started backtracking in their own tracks to get back to their vehicles, warmth, and for some, a shot of whiskey. Other units joined the state troopers who were in charge of protecting the J. Lon Foust Highway to Harriman. When darkness fell the emergency lights and lights from several hundred vehicles sealed the parameter where the subjects were thought to be contained.

Curtis Bagwell stayed on Turkey Knob all night. Nothing.

With daybreak, Curtis directed Unit One to proceed back up the river, on both sides, from the Oakdale Bridge to the hill country and intercept the suspects or determine where and how they avoided capture. They were to proceed with caution.

Unit One had not slept either. Almost all the men in the chase now had been on the job 36 hours or more. Tempers were beginning to get short.

The coordinates where the subjects had entered the river had been plotted, and the possible avenues of escape had been calculated. Unit One went up river on both sides of the Emory from the Oakdale bridge. On the west, the land rose quickly upward from the river. On the east, the railroad yards stretched for two miles. Every possible hiding place had been explored. After three hours they arrived back at the bank of the river precisely where the prints entered the water. No sign.

"This means they went downriver, staying in the water. The water is too swift for them to go against the current. Let's go southeast of Oakdale," Jernigan announced.

Unit One walked the bank some three to four miles south of Oakdale. No sign.

When they arrived back at the steel bridge over the river at Oakdale, Jernigan reported to Bagwell, "No sign, Sheriff. They have vanished into thin air."

"They ain't vanished," Curtis Bagwell responded sarcastically. "We just ain't been where they been. Call it off. Those people escaped. We'll have to look somewhere else."

Curtis ordered all units back to base. He met them at his office in Wartburg and dismissed each of them with his thanks. Yes, he would call them as quickly as they were needed. Bagwell concluded that the men had stayed in the water more than five miles and got out at Oakdale ahead of the search crews.

Their pickup man had been cruising the highway between Oakdale and Harriman. He got there and found them, and they were on their way somewhere trying to thaw their feet. Bagwell was going to have to broaden the search. Right now, he was going home and get some sleep. He was near exhaustion as were most of his men.

On Tuesday morning Bagwell was up and about at around 10:00 a.m. and on his way to Oakdale. He stopped at Ben Holtzclaw's Standard Station. He went into the warmth of the gas station where it felt good. Ben was sitting in his old straight-back cane bottom chair behind his old metal desk with his credit card machine and cash register on it. He was working on his books.

"I know you have heard about everything. Do you know anything you can give that might help?"

The sheriff hoped that someone had seen the pickup man and could identify the vehicle that rescued the suspects.

"Well, I told several of your deputies who came in here, and I called your office last night, but nobody paid no attention to me. I knowed you wuz busy, but I needed to tell you something."

"What? I heard that you called, but it didn't

seem important," the sheriff was anxious. He thought, How the hell could somebody miss something like this?

"Well, it probably waddn't, but I'll tell you what it wuz. Yestiddy, around 2:00 PM, Martha, my wife, you know, saw a man she had never seen before using our pay phone outside the station," Holtzclaw pointed to the telephone on the wall near the red drink box. "She said this guy looked bad. His feet were wet, and he looked like he had been hunting. He made a call and left. She called your office as soon as he finished the call."

"Where'd he go?" the sheriff asked, hoping Holtzclaw might know.

"He left the phone and crossed the bridge and went walking toward Harriman," Ben said.

"You mean with over a hundred law enforcement officers in the area, this guy walked up to your pay phone and made a call? Right here, in Oakdale?"

"He shore did."

"Did she see anybody with him?" the sheriff inquired. He was now on notice that this was probably the shooter. If he was, this would explain how they missed catching them.

"Nope. Ain't seen nary a thing, other than what I jist told you."

The sheriff said, "Thanks," and started toward Harriman in his Cherokee.

He couldn't believe the criminals escaped as

easily as they did. They shot the doctor, walked a little, cought a ride, found out about a deserted barn, spent four to six hours resting in there, eating food provided by Woods, went cross country five miles to the river, waded down river 3/4 mile, climbed out at the Oakdale Bridge, made a call at the local service station, crossed the bridge, hid in the woods until their ride came by, and left. "What a mess. Oh well, I needed to see Mrs. Case anyway."

About a mile down the road he stopped at Kilgore's Country Store on the left-hand side of the highway. He went in and asked Kilgore if he had noticed any strangers around his place on Monday. He thought some of the officers might have already talked to Kilgore, but he learned they had not. Incompetence! he thought.

"As a matter of fact, I seen something that cought my eye, but I'm shore hit don't mean nothin," Kilgore responded.

"Let me be the judge of that, feller," Bagwell was losing patience in a hurry.

"I come down to the store right at dark last night. I mean it was right on the edge of twilight and dark. I was going to check and make sure no pipes had busted and we would be able to open this morning. Just as I was goin in the store, I seen an old tan Oldsmobile come clanking down the road with its tailpipe draggin. Inside, it was full of men all bundled up. I ain't never seen none of them before. And, I can't identify any of them. I just seen 'em. That's all."

"You say it was a tan Oldsmobile? What year? And, what kind of tag did it have, Alabama?" Curtis had fished a note pad out of pocket and a ball point pen.

"Matter of fact, I seen the tag because the tailpipe was making a helluva noise, sparks and all. But, it warn't no Alabama tag. Hit wuz a Tennessee tag from Cocke County. Betcha business hit wuz."

"Newport, all right!" the sheriff was delighted. "You are a good man, Milford Kilgore. Thanks!" the sheriff paused at the door. "You don't know nothing else, do you?"

"That's hit, nothin more, good luck. I don't know whether it means anything or not.

In his Cherokee the sheriff radioed base. "I have a lead. It seems like the suspects were picked up by somebody from Cocke County. Call Brad Wilhelm, the sheriff over there, in Newport, and give him the information and get him on it. I'm going to the hospital and see Mrs. Case, be in around one."

When Brad Wilhelm heard the facts of the situation, he told his chief deputy, "Check the local hospital. Somebody was bound to have shown up in the past few hours with frostbite, or frozen feet."

The sheriff was going to check out the Oldsmobile lead.

Wilhelm sent deputies to every used car dealer in the county to find out if any of them had sold an older model Oldsmobile in the past year. No such car had been sold. However, one deputy noticed an older model creme colored Oldsmobile at Wells Used Cars. It was for sale on the lot. He asked Billy Wells who the car belonged to.

Billy Wells had a long criminal history of mostly misdemeanors, gambling, making white whiskey, and handling a few hot cars. He had been arrested 18 times in his 42 years. He was a short overweight balding man with watery blue eyes. He ran a car lot out of his yard in front of his modest white house that was up hill from the automobiles.

The neighbors complained to the local authorities, but he continued to do it anyway. The city fathers had refused to give him a license until he moved into a commercial area. Newport didn't have a zoning ordinance, but it would have one soon as a result of this mess. When Billy Wells threatened to sue the hell out of the city, the city fathers relented and allowed him to be a used car dealer again. He usually kept four to six old clunkers around his house, sometimes in his front yard, with a "For Sale" sign out front and a small sign at the curb that said, "Wells Used Cars."

Sheriff Wilhelm called Curtis Bagwell and gave him this information. Bagwell asked

Wilhelm to wait until he could get there to question Wells. "He sounds like our man," Bagwell said happily.

"Bingo! At the hospital!" Jim Rollins reported to Bagwell. "Three men were treated for frostbite late last night at Newport General Hospital. Their names are James D. Steat, his brother, Doc A. Steat, and Glenn Hasten, all from Alabama. Glenn Hasten was signed into the hospital by Billy Wells!

"Let's go!" Bagwell said, and they were out of the office and into the Cherokee bound for Newport, Tennessee, about 50 miles northeast of Wartburg.

It was almost 4:00 p.m. when they arrived at the Cocke County Sheriff's Department. They were brought up to date by Wilhelm and his chief deputy.

"It all fits," Wilhelm told Bagwell. "There were three men involved in the murder. They were from Alabama. They were chased through the snow and froze their feet in the river. They were picked up by their finger man, Billy Wells. He picked them up south of Oakdale and brought them to Newport. I'd lay odds the deal was Billy's. He probably spotted Dr. Case as having money. He checked the worst one into the hospital. The others registered on their own and were treated and released. The two released bought boots from the Shoe Emporium and left town in a car they borrowed from Well's girlfriend. She's a waitress down at the Longhorn Restaurant south of town. She tells everything she knows to my deputies. They eat there every day. She has already told one of the boys that Billy made her lend her car to some hunters from North Georgia. They are going to Trenton, Georgia, to get it next Saturday. So, what do you think?"

"I think you're right on target. Let's see what our evidence is if we arrest them right now. First, we have a corpus delicti, Doc Case, God bless him. We got shoe or boot prints on the coffee table. We know the shooter is left-handed. Barney Woods can identify him. We know the route he took to get here. Suppose he says nothing. Suppose nobody says nothing. Where are we?" Curtis was thinking in his detective mode.

"You got a bunch of circumstantial evidence," Wilhelm rejoined. "Without a confession or a snitch, you got a hard row to hoe. I think that a good lawyer, like some we got around here, would beat your socks off. You need something stronger, like fingerprints would do it."

"There's something else," Curtis was on to it. His face was lit up, "There's something that'll convict the hell out of them! His shoes. No. He had to be wearing boots! His goddamned boots have glass in them from Doc's house, and the glass has to match the glass in the coffee table. That's a cod lock! Let's get to the hospital and seize Mr. Glenn Hasten's boots!"

Curtis was running toward the door, Bert was right behind him. The Cocke County boys were with them. They all crawled into Curtis's Cherokee. He put on the siren, the blue lights, and away they went in a mad dash for the hospital nine blocks away, due north, on the right side of the highway.

Curtis drove into the ER entrance. He was careful to get out of the way of the emergency doors, leaving plenty of room for the ambulance. He had turned off the equipment before turning into the hospital grounds.

Sheriff Wilhelm ran to the ER Staff Desk and asked the head nurse, "Kathy, where are the shoes of Mr. Hasten in 214?" Wilhelm was almost breathless.

"They ought have gone up to his room with him, Sheriff," the young pleasant nurse responded. "Wait, let me see if they were cut off him when they brought him last night."

Kathy studied the ER report on Glenn Hasten. "He was brought in at 10:05 p.m. last night. He was suffering from exhaustion and severe frostbite. His feet were swollen, blue, and he lacked feeling in the toes. Oh, here it is! He was brought into the ER without shoes. His feet had been wrapped in a sweatshirt. His pants had been split up each leg nine inches." She looked at the Sheriff and his companions.

"Damned!" Bagwell exclaimed. "He was wearing boots. They had to cut his pants. We've got to find out where those boots are."

"Well, he didn't wear them to the hospital," Kathy responded studying the report again.

Bagwell turned to Wilhelm, "You think Billy Wells might tell us what happened to those boots? It sounds like they were cut off his swollen feet. He must have been in a helluva mess."

"Billy Wells probably knows what happened. He may have cut the boots off, but you'll play hell getting him to tell you anything. Wells is an old rat in the barn. He ain't about to tell you anything that'll put his ass in a sling."

"What about his girlfriend?"

"That's the only chance. I wouldn't approach Wells. He'll spook, and you won't learn anything about anything. You don't have enough evidence right now to scare him."

"That's true, but I just gotta find those boots. That's the cap. That puts the case away. That's the tie. You know there ain't no fingerprints on those guns, unless they're on the rounds. Those guys wore gloves. Mrs. Case can't identify them. We got to tie them to the murder scene. We got to have the boots," Bagwell was excited.

"You want to go up and question Hasten right now?" Wilhelm questioned.

"Hell, no. If he is as tough as he has shown

himself to be so far, he'll just tell us good day.
Nah, put a man on his door without him
knowing it. Dress him up like a doctor. Keep up
with who comes in and out. Get pictures, if
possible. And, don't let Hasten leave. Arrest
him if you must. We have to keep him here.
Let's get down to your office and get on the
wire. I want to know the criminal history of
these Jaspers."

He waved to the nurse, nodded to the staff
he passed, and left the hospital.

Back at Wilhelm's office, Doc A. Steat and
James D. Steat did not have criminal records.
Glenn Hasten had a long criminal record,
including auto theft, armed robbery, assault &
battery, DUI, and numerous white whiskey
charges. There was a record on a Marvey
Steat, who lived in the same area as Glenn
Hasten. Curtis Bagwell concluded that James
D. Steat was Marvey Steat. He ordered his
criminal record and it tracked Glenn Hasten's,
with the exception Steat had more illegal
moonshining charges and convictions.

It was almost 6:00 p.m. when Art Millwee,
Special Agent F.B.I., walked in the door of the
sheriff's office. He was in the company of a
detective from the Chattanooga PD, Bruce
Case, who was a great nephew of Dr. Case.
Bruce spotted Bagwell, Wilhelm and company.

"Boys, this is Art Millwee. He is the F.B.I.
Agent in charge of the north end of Sand

Mountain. You all know where that is? Okay, Art can write you a book about every one of these people."

Curtis Bagwell, Wilhelm, and the other officers shook hands with the short, pudgy, large jowl, red-faced man wearing thick glasses. Millwee always snorted through his nose before he said anything. He snorted and said he was glad to meet them.

He said, after another snort, "Listen up. I've already been told about your suspects. I've been brought up to date. You're right in your thinking. Your murderers are Marvey Steat, Glenn Hasten, and the Doc A. Steat is a false moniker for Doc Anthony Worth. They said your murderer was left-handed. I already checked it out. Out of the three, Glenn Hasten is left-handed. All the guns were stolen. Here's a printout on the criminal records of these three.

"I've known them all for years. They were mostly white whiskey people who were driven out of business in 'Operation Dry Up,' a campaign we developed during the late sixties to stop illegal moonshine. When we dried them up, they turned to stealing cars and armed robbery and burglary to make easy money. I've had them on post office burglaries, bank burglaries, car theft, chop shops, you name it. They know Billy Wells through the white whiskey business. He's stealing cars too. I checked it out."

"I appreciate the information," Curtis Bagwell was genuinely appreciative. He was impressed with the work of the F.B.I. in such a short period of time with so little information.

"I still am reluctant to arrest Glenn Hasten right now. I want to see what flies that honey draws. They say he's going to be here at least another four days."

Snort, "Well, you can bet that Glenn Hasten was your trigger man. Although any one of the three of them would kill you for five hundred dollars and never blink an eye doing it."

"I need the boots Hasten was wearing. That'll tie the case together. Without them boots we are making a weak case of circumstantial evidence," Bagwell reported to Millwee.

Snort. "I'll see what I can do." Millwee left the sheriff's office bound for the Knoxville F.B.I. office. Detective Case went with him. They had ridden up together from Rossville, Georgia. Millwee's office was in Rossville, adjoining Chattanooga, Tennessee.

Five days later, when Glenn Hasten was released from the hospital, minus four toes, he was arrested and taken to the Morgan County Jail at Wartburg charged with the murder of Dr. Case and the attempt to murder Mrs. Case. Simultaneously, Marvey Steat and Doc A. Worth were arrested on the north end of Sand

Mountain above Trenton, Georgia, by the Sheriff of Dade County and SA Arthur Millwee of the F.B.I. They were placed in cells adjacent to Glenn Hasten on the second floor of the old run-down two-story Morgan County Jail. Billy Wells was arrested as an accomplice and was taken from Newport to Wartburg.

The Sheriff's Department was on the first floor under the jail. It only had eight cells. Billy Wells immediately made a $50,000 bond. His bondsmen followed him from Newport to Wartburg when he was arrested. He was booked and released. The boys from North Georgia and Alabama took three of the cells by doubling up the usual resident drunks, brawlers, and local ne're-do-wells. Neither of the four suspects made any statement other than, "I want to talk to my lawyer."

Bagwell and his wife, who cooked for the jail from time to time, tried to make friends with the north end boys over Christmas, but it didn't work. They were friendly enough, but when anything about the Dr. Case murder was mentioned, they just looked at the person blankly.

"Truly," Bagwell told his wife, "They have been around the block before."

It was the first week of January when the brother and sister of Marvey Steat walked into the lawyer's office. The lawyer had a long history with this family.

"Marvey has been accused of murder, and he needs a defense," his twin brother, Harvey told the lawyer.

"He was cought up in Wartburg, Tennessee where the Law accuses him of murdering the only doctor in the country." Harvey was very serious.

"Doc Worth, Glenn Hasten, and some other fellow was arrested with them," his sister Olivia said. "How much will you charge us to represent Marvey?"

The lawyer thought for a while. He weighed all the pros and cons of becoming involved in this defense. Of course, it was work, it was a current fee, and he would do it -- for a price.

He quoted a fee of far more than he thought they could come up with. Harvey peeled out the fee in new One Hundred Dollar Bills. The lawyer was hired.

The lawyer had a young partner whom he had known several years, Eddie Norris. When the clients were gone, he went into Norris' office, the one with the "Destroyer Man" painting, and showed him the fee and told him about the case.

"When are we leaving?" Norris asked.

"This afternoon. Pack for three days. We'll take Ernie Brock with us to do the gumshoe work, and go up and explore the case. We need our own transportation. We won't fly."

The lawyer was on his way out the back door to pack for himself.

Although Norris would eventually become a U.S. District Judge, at this time he was working his first murder case.

The three drove to Wartburg in Norris' used Dodge. Norris and the lawyer rode in the front seat while Ernie Brock rode in the back. They rode with the windows open and Brock insisted that they have a six pack of beer before leaving Chattanooga.

Brock was Marvey's nephew. It was his mother who visited the lawyer with Harvey. Brock and his Uncle Harvey did not get along.

Brock had brought a large bag of boiled peanuts with him. He passed around the first beer and then the peanuts. By the time the group cleared Chattanooga on Highway 27 North, they were half lit.

Norris noted that he hated to spend the night with either the lawyer or Brock because he expected the beer and peanuts would create blue flame flatus into the night. The lawyer opined that Norris might also have a problem with the eats since he had packed it in on top of the raisin pudding he had for lunch. The lawyer knew that Norris was setting the predicate for his relief rather than the relief of himself or Brock.

They drove into Wartburg, visited the prisoners, met the sheriff, looked at the old antique courthouse, and Norris took the picture of the lawyer and Brock under the entrance to the jail. It was the first of 1977. Over the old oval brick entranceway was written, "Crime Does Not Pay." It came out well in the photograph.

From Wartburg they went to Oakdale and to the residence of Dr. Case. The lawyer noted to Norris and Brock that the river was raging at this time of year.

Brock said, "That ain't no river; that's a creek. That's the one they waded for almost a mile."

From the home of Dr. Case the party went to the bi-color checking station in the Catoosa Wildlife Management Area. The ranger involved the night of the murder happened to be on duty. He was more than happy to cooperate with the defense. He could not identify anyone that night other than Barney Woods. If the men in jail were the ones, he didn't recognize a one of them. The lawyer concluded that Barney Woods would be the principal witness of the prosecution.

"Who is Barney Woods, and how smart is he?" the lawyer asked over and over. Each potential witness was questioned extensively about Barney Woods.

They followed TVA quad sheet maps that overlapped in the area. The land was marked at 20 foot intervals for contour lines. These maps led them to Sawyer's barn. As they walked toward the barn with cameras in hand they met a man coming back along the trail in overalls. He was walking hump-shouldered, with his hands behind his back. He was about 62 years old.

Norris asked him, "Is that Sawyer's barn?"

The old man in bib overalls straightened up bringing a double-barreled 12-gauge shotgun out from behind his back and pointing it directly at Norris, "And who wants to know?"

Before Norris could respond, Brock stepped forward and reached out his right hand to the old man, "Glad to meet you, Sir. We're here investigating the Dr. Case murder and would appreciate it if you could tell us what you know about it. Perhaps you might show us where everything was found in Sawyer's barn. That is, if you know. If you don't know, you might tell us where we might find someone who will show us the barn." Brock was good at talking fast.

"I know where everything was. I was there the morning the Law came. I went in with them in the first wave," the older man said lowering the shotgun.

"Must be an old Marine," Brock thought. "Then how about showing us what you know. You know if you don't show it, nobody knows you know it."

The old guy marched out, leading them on a path around an abandoned garden plot toward the barn. The lawyer took his picture from behind.

The old guy pointed out where the indentions were in the hay. He showed them where the guns were found. He showed where the C-ration cans were found. He showed where the three ski masks where found. He knew about the twisted wire on the hayloft door.

Brock readily assured the old guy that he was a true hero and was probably in on the chase that resulted in the lost trail. The old guy admitted that he was.

He went right up to the river bank where the footprints disappeared. "From there, they waded down river to the bridge, climbed out, walked down the road, called their pal, he came and picked them up, and they were out of here."

"Why did the murderers kill Dr. Case?" the lawyer asked.

"Don't know," the old guy said. "Some said it was dope. Others said that they thought he had over $250,000 in a safe down stairs and they came to get the safe. The car dealer guy in Newport fingered the doctor, and he hired these guys down in Northwest Georgia to come up here and do the job. It was botched because of Sheriff Curtis Bagwell. If he'd got there sooner, Doc would still be alive." The old man sounded proud of the local hero.

After a nice visit, the party departed and drove through the management area. When they reached the road's end, they returned through Oakdale to the kindly grocer down the highway. He was happy to meet the fellows. He only knew what he had told the sheriff, and he repeated it. He couldn't identify anyone.

"We're back to the testimony of Barney Woods again," the lawyer said as the party went into the Harriman Econo Lodge for the night.

After consuming more than a little beer, the investigators went to sleep. The lawyer and Norris occupied one room, and Brock had his own room.

A train went by behind the motel. Norris said, "Have you ever been a place with walls so thin? I thought the railroad ran through the middle of the house."

The lawyer responded, "What's saving us is the termites are joining hands and holding this motel together every time a large member of American transportation goes by."

The next day, Norris would accuse the lawyer of snoring too loudly for him to sleep. Then they learned that everyone in the county knew they were there, what they were doing, and who they were.

The second day in the Wartburg area resulted in a man telling the group at the local Standard Oil Station that it would be best if they stayed out of town. They were not welcome in Wartburg.

A waitress at a local restaurant had to be forced to wait on them at lunch in front of several dozen loggers and miners. When they paid, the man behind the register said, "I served you this time, but I won't serve you again. Don't come back. Dr. Case was a friend of mine."

They stopped at a local motel, and they were told to stay in Harriman. So, at the end of what they considered a fruitful day, the three returned to the paper-thin walled Econo Lodge.

Brock provided the Jack Daniels, and after dinner, the three began to become roaring drunk. At that time, Norris and the lawyer promised Brock that they would never represent a drug dealer.

"White whiskey people are one thing, but those dopers are something else," the lawyer said. They didn't know they would break their promise when the first substantial drug dealer visited them less than two years later.

The following day they scouted the area north toward Oliver Springs. They explored community sentiment concerning their client. It was bad. Not one person said Marvey Steat should not be executed.

"Dr. Case has given of himself for 81 years. Those people have done nothing but take all their miserable lives. They should be executed," said the minister of the Oliver Springs Baptist Church.

"Good Christian," muttered the lawyer to his companions.

In early afternoon they arrived in Newport. They went to the hospital and confirmed what they already knew with a lovely blonde-headed nurse named Kathy.

They drove around town and finally out to the Longhorn Restaurant where Billy Wells' girlfriend was working. She would know where the lawyer could find Billy. She told them Billy was at home.

She called him and told him they were there, and he said, "Come on out."

But first, the most important thing she could tell the lawyer was that the Law was wanting Glenn Hasten' boots bad. They had to have them to make a case. They would be willing to deal for them. The lawyer said this was great information.

After being introduced to Billy Wells, and listening to his story, the lawyer asked, "Where did you throw Hasten's boots when you cut them off his feet?"

"Look, I had to cut them off. He wuz swelled into them and wuz goin to pop if I didn't get them off. I had to cut his jeans to get to the top so I could cut them off. His feet were a mess." He was apologizing as though he had done something wrong.

"Just one question, Man. Please, answer just one question," the lawyer was insisting. "Where did you throw the boots?"

"In Douglas Lake, off the north side of the last bridge." The small round bald man looked concerned.

"Is there a possibility they didn't land in the water?" the lawyer asked.

"Could be. I was drunk as Cooter Brown."

"Let's go," the lawyer sounded excited. As Norris drove them, the lawyer said, "This is it, boys. This is what we've been looking for." They raced toward the last bridge on the lake.

As they crossed the bridge, Billy said, "Right here is where I begun to throw them."

"Who was driving?" the lawyer asked as they approached the parking shoulder at the end of the bridge.

"I was. I had stopped back up the road and cut the boots off him. They had to come off. Otherwise, he would have lost both feet to gangrene. Then, when I got down here, I threw them over the side."

Billy was out of the car and plunging down the bank to the marsh on the shore of the lake. The shoreline went out with brown and green vegetation about fifty feet. The lawyer didn't hesitate. He, Brock, and Norris were in hot pursuit. They were rewarded. They found both of Hasten's boots. They literally fished them out of the mud.

They then returned to Billy's simple home and washed them clean. They were clearly cut with a sharp instrument down the inside of each of them. The boots were knee high black working boots. They were not waterproof. Their tops folded down easily. The lawyer put them in a grocery bag and into his brief case.

They then went back to the girlfriend's restaurant, had steaks, and left the county. They didn't mention the boots. It was a joyous ride home.

James Appleman, from Jamestown, a rotund, bearded young man with large lips which perfectly held a generous cigar, was appointed to represent Billy Wells. Cecil Finwell of Cleveland, Tennessee, a brilliant young criminal defense and personal injury lawyer, had been hired to represent Glenn Hasten by the Hasten family on the north end. A young lawyer named Flick, from Knoxville, was appointed to represent Doc Anthony Worth.

The case came on for preliminary hearing. The lawyer had prepared a motion for change of venue. This case could not be tried in Wartburg. No way. All the lawyers, detectives, and interested parties representing the defendants, gathered at Harriman the night before. The Econo Lodge, where else?

The little band arrived at the Morgan County

Courthouse in Wartburg at 8:55 a.m., for a 9:00 a.m. hearing before the Honorable Judge Warren Hobson. The town was packed. They had to park two blocks away.

Hobson looked like Abraham Lincoln. Because people told him that, he tried to look even more like the 16th President. He had a mole, a little off center, but not so's you would notice. He was tall and slim and walked stoop-shouldered as everyone said Honest Abe did. He made important pronouncements, laced with traditional homilies, to the entertainment of everyone. Yet, the lawyer noticed immediately that the man was a legal scholar. He ruled hard, but he was always right on the law. Young Lawyer Flick made certain by being prepared with statute or case law. He and Norris were the bookworms on the case.

When the lawyer, who was leading the contingent of lawyers, investigators, and assistants, arrived in the quaint old Tennessee courthouse, he went directly to the circuit courtroom. He had previously visited the courthouse and courtroom when he first came to interview his client.

The lawyer could barely push his way up the stairs. There were people from door to door and lined up the stairs. In the courtroom there was no place for the lawyer to sit. He made sure of that by attempting to be seated last. He wound up sitting in a window casing. He approached Honest Abe and presented a motion to change venue and returned to the window sill.

"On what theory do you base this motion?" the judge looked directly at the lawyer and the packed ancient courtroom.

"Would your honor take judicial notice of the fact that the attorney addressing the Court, in support of the motion, is seated in the window because there is not another seat on the courthouse square of Wartburg, Tennessee? And this indicates not only a great public interest in this case, but also a manifest prejudice, etc., do I have to go forward?"

"No, you don't, Sir. The Court takes judicial notice that a fair trial cannot be had by these defendants in Morgan County, Tennessee. Venue in this case is hereby transferred to Anderson County, Tennessee, and this case will come on for all dispositive motions and preliminary matters in 45 days. The case will then come on for trial beginning May 1st in Oak Ridge, Tennessee. Court's adjourned."

Everyone got up and filed out of the building. The lawyers visited with their clients in jail for a few minutes, telling them to keep the faith, and then they went for lunch. Norris was driving, the lawyer was in the middle with Finwell at the passenger door. Appleman, Flick, and Brock were in the rear seat. They were leaving town. As they reached the crossroads there was a loud sound like a rifle shot. All the lawyers ducked. Norris swerved off the road and stopped. "Somebody shot at us!" he screamed to the assemblage ducked down in the car.

"And they hit me," James Appleman reported with a bleeding neck.

On close examination, Norris had rolled his right rear window up in a bind. It had cracked in the heat of the day with all the bodies in the car. One chunk of glass flew out and hit Appleman in the neck. The group was relieved because it was very tense for the lawyers in Wartburg.

Time went by. The lawyer visited his client on a regular basis. When he talked with Marvey, he had to visit with Doc and Glenn. He had been the lawyer for both of them in the past. He had represented Hasten's cousin and Worth's father. They had all been to the well together, as they would say on the north end.

One morning in spring the phone at the right side of the lawyer's bed rang. Doc Worth was on the line.

When the lawyer answered, Doc said, "Your boy Marvey cracked up last night. You may not have known it, but they have been questioning us with every cop in training in East Tennessee. Right after one of our lawyers leave, or a family member leaves, Curtis Bagwell and his henchmen jump on us. I've even been questioned by the pastor of his church, a scout master, and his wife. Marvey just cracked. He couldn't take any more questions. Curtis knew it. He, Art Millwee, and a bunch of goons are taking Marvey to Senator Baker's home in Huntsville, Tennessee, where he is going to confess and implicate everyone of us. And, he ain't even got a deal. He's cracked. You gotta do something!" It was important!

"I'll be right there." The lawyer called Norris and told him. "Take care of my cases today. Curtis Bagwell and Art Millwee have kidnaped our client, and they are taking him to get him to sign a confession at Senator Baker's home. I got to go right now."

The lawyer dressed hurriedly, raced to the airport, preflighted his Mooney aircraft, and headed to the airport nearest to Wartburg, which was at Rockwood, Tennessee. It was not quite warm yet. He ran the single engine at 160 kts. When he landed at Rockwood he met a young man there applying for a job. The lawyer offered to pay him $30 to rent his car for two hours.

The young man said that he could not make that much in a day, "done."

The lawyer paid him $20 up front and jumped into the ancient blue Pontiac. It was well over 10 years old and had spent its life on unpaved roads. It rattled as it went, but it ate up the pavement to Wartburg.

The lawyer burst into the Sheriff's Department and ran to the deputy on the desk. "Where's Marvey Steat?" he demanded. "He is my client, and Curtis Bagwell is violating his Constitutional rights. Do you want to be guilty too? Where is my client?"

"He wanted to go to Huntsville about 20 minutes ago. He wanted to make a clean breast of it. So they took him to Huntsville to the home of Senator Baker. They took a court reporter to record it all."

The lawyer ran back to the ugly old Pontiac, and glancing at his map, headed for Huntsville. When he arrived, he asked the first person he saw on the street where to find Senator Baker's home, and received perfect directions. He drove up the long tree-shaded, white-board fence drive to an old Tennessee home. It was plantation, but not too much so. It did not have columns, just substantial posts.

The lawyer parked directly behind Curtis Bagwell's Cherokee. He ran up the 14 steps leading to the veranda-type porch and opened the door without being asked. Deputies and agents were standing around on the front porch.

"Where's my client?" the lawyer yelled as he burst into the spacious antique dining room where Marvey Steat was sitting between Curtis Bagwell and Mrs. Bagwell at the large dining table.

He did not recognize any of the other people around the table, other than Art Millwee and a court reporter.

"I demand to talk to my client before any statement is made."

Caswell Cramer, the Morgan County District Attorney, who would later use his interest and trial of this case to be elected Tennessee Attorney General, intervened. "Sir, Mr. Steat contacted Mrs. Bagwell and told her that he would like to clear his conscious by giving a statement. We did not encourage this at all. It was the idea of Mr. Steat."

"Well, it isn't his idea anymore," the lawyer said.

Then addressing his client, "Marvey, what the hell you doing up here?"

The client looked like the cat that had eaten the canary and been cought. He also was happy to manifest his masculinity as well.

"I was just getting a free breakfast. You know, bacon, eggs, grits, juice, milk, coffee, stuff like that outside the jail. Sheriff Bagwell offered to do these things for me and he did them. I'll have to give him that. He did what he said. But then he brought me up here and I don't want to be up here. I don't know what they're talking about when they discuss the Dr. Case murder case. Make them take me back to jail."

"You heard the man," the lawyer said to the

prosecutor.

"Take him back, boys," Cramer instructed Bagwell and company.

"And don't question my client without me being there," the lawyer yelled.

"He's right!" Cramer responded. "Don't talk to his client again. We will lose the whole case. Now don't do it, Curtis." Cramer meant it. He knew his case was in danger now that he had been cought trying to pull a fast one.

The lawyer became an established hero on the north end with this act. He saved Marvey who had been brainwashed and would say whatever Sheriff Bagwell wanted him to say. He saved Doc Worth because he responded to his call. He saved Glenn Hasten because Marvey would have probably said that he killed Dr. Case and gunwhipped the old lady, which would have put him in the electric chair.

It was nine weeks until the trial. Cramer was not happy. He told Curtis that their case was only a few random circumstances. They did not have an open-and-shut case by any means. He needed evidence which would connect Glenn Hasten to the Dr. Case murder other than because he was left-handed. One left-handed person on the jury would hang that jury forever. The case was not good. They really needed Steat's statement, but the lawyer had prevented it.

"What can I do, Caswell?" Curtis asked.

"I don't know, Sheriff, but we got to do something. We ain't gonna make it with the case we got right now among those people in Oak Ridge. You know that. They're engineers and atomic energy people. They are going to make the state prove its case," Cramer looked meaningfully at the sheriff.

The sheriff called Detective Case in Chattanooga. He had always said he would help with his last drop of blood.

"Look, Bruce, we got problems with this case. Caswell says he don't have enough evidence to link Hasten, Worth, and Steat to the murder scene. The murder weapon was recovered, no prints. We're in a mess."

"What can I do to help?" the lean mean relative of the doctor asked.

"I need the boots Hasten was wearing. I can match the glass in those boots to the window glass in the table. The boots would convict him."

"Come see me, man. I think I can help."

Case called Art Millwee. "Can the F.B.I. lab identify the glass from the boots as being the same glass from the window and found imbedded in the coffee table?"

Millwee didn't snort on the phone. He was brief and to the point. "The lab can match the glass. An expert in glass technology will come from Washington and testify. It gives credibility to the case of the state. Do you have the boots? I know the table is still in place, and there is still plenty of glass at the scene."

"No, I don't have the boots, but I may have before long," the detective responded.

"Let me tell you where Hasten lives. I have had people watching his place. Nobody has been in or out," Millwee reported.

"I'll bet those boots are in his closet," the detective giggled.

"Anything's possible," Millwee responded. "I'll tell my agent to let you by."

He told them exactly how to get to Hasten's home. He then called his agent on the radio and told him to cooperate fully with the sheriff and the detective.

The three officers approached the house after dark. The agent had the crowbar that the bureau had used to gain entrance before. He pried up the window to the front room, and the three entered the house. Bagwell and Case had flashlights. They walked into the room, which was obviously the master bedroom. They looked in the closet.

"Bingo!" said Bagwell. "Look at that pair of new anklehigh boots." The new boots literally shined in the night as the lights were flashed on them.

"Don't touch," said Case, "Fingerprints."

He took a coat hanger from the overhead in the closet, unbent it straight, and lifted the boots through the pulls on their back. He put them in a plastic bag.

With the boots in plastic inside an evidence bag, Curtis Bagwell and Bruce Case drove to the Case residence at Oakdale. The auxiliary deputy on guard welcomed the sheriff. Bagwell told him to wait outside and keep watch. He and Case had important work to do. The citizen volunteer went back to his vehicle in front of the house.

Bagwell and Case took the boots into the den of the Case residence.

"There's the table, right where I left it. See, the glass is still on it. See where his boots scratched the table? Mother Case went to live with her daughter in Knoxville after she got out of the hospital."

The sheriff turned on an overhead light. His officers had hung a tarpaulin on the rear wall of the house where the window was out. There was very little light in the room.

Case walked to the broken window, climbed up, and stood in the sill. "You think they'll fit me?" Case smirked to Bagwell as he leaned against the tight tarp and removed the boots from the bag by the pulls. He had already removed his wingtips. He slid his right foot into the boot and left it unzipped on the inside. He slipped the left boot on.

"Put the table in place," he instructed Bagwell. "And leave the glass scattered on it as it is."

Curtis pulled the coffee table over directly beneath the slight detective. He then stood back as Case jumped from the window onto the table being careful to scar the table and embed glass into the soles of the boots. He almost lost his balance and fell into the floor; but regaining his balance, he jumped off the table onto the floor driving the glass from the window and coffee table into the boots.

Removing the boots and returning them to their bags, Case said, "I'll take these back to Rossville and give them to Art Millwee. He knew we were going out to the Hasten residence. He probably thought we would find the boots. He'll send them to the F.B.I. lab in Washington, and that ought to nail this case down."

Case smiled at Bagwell just before he returned to his vehicle to drive back to Chattanooga.

Bagwell stayed around long enough to take new pictures of the table. He had to be sure to remove the earlier pictures of the table from the evidence in the case. The scratches might not be the same.

The lawyer had made an earlier flight into the Wartburg area during early January. Brock went with him. He told Brock, "Hold the plane steady, Ernie. I'm going to get some color shots of the management area." He let go of the yoke.

Brock had a problem holding the plane level. It appeared the lawyer was not noticing what he was doing. Finally, Brock could contain himself no more. "You better grab this thing! We're going down!"

The lawyer reached over, leveled the aircraft, and took it up another three thousand feet before he turned another tight spiral over Oakdale. He got all the photos he thought he needed before he headed back south and home. No one would ever believe that three men trekked through the hills and valleys to the river in below-zero weather, in waist-deep snow, then waded down the river, and escaped through the tightest police dragnet in the history of Tennessee.

The case came on for trial scheduled in Oak Ridge, Tennessee. Judge Hobson ran a tight courtroom. A jury was struck using the very best jury selection techniques of the day. Every potential juror had been investigated prior to trial. Jurors were questioned for two days before they were seated. There were eleven men and one woman. She was a waitress at Shoney's.

When Billy Wells saw her, he said, "I just ate with that woman being my waitress and I told my girlfriend, 'that girl whistles through her nose.'"

Caswell Cramer was a worthy adversary

with Curtis Bagwell, Art Millwee, and Bruce Case as assistants. Plus, the chief ranger from the Catoosa Wildlife Management Area was at the beck and call of the state.

After the state's opening argument, the lawyer told the jury that Marvey Steat was not guilty and it would be up to the state to prove him guilty beyond a reasonable doubt and it could not do that. He had asked each juror if he or she would acquit if the state did not prove the defendant guilty beyond a reasonable doubt, and they each said they would. He pointed out that this was their duty. This was their oath.

"The state cannot prove Marvey Steat guilty, and I expect you to find him not guilty."

The other lawyers made similar statements. Norris did not attend the trial. He was too busy keeping the office going. Brock became lost during the trial week doing whatever Brock did. The lawyer was on his own with the representatives of the other defendants.

There was a courtroom artist from the *Knoxville Sentinel* drawing pictures of the participants in the trial. It was the first time the lawyer's likeness had ever been drawn during trial. It would not be the last.

Caswell Cramer took his time presenting his case. He devoted half a day to how fine Dr. Case was. Mrs. Case and her daughter were sitting on the front row of the courtroom. Curtis

Bagwell was the state representative seated at the state's table with Cramer.

At the defense table, Cecil Finwell, the lawyer for Glenn Hasten, sat nearest the state at the head of the large table. Hasten sat next to him. Flick was after Hasten, then Worth, then the lawyer, and finally his client, Marvey Steat. Appleman and Wells did not sit at the table because Wells refused to join the other defendants. So far as he was concerned, he was not guilty and there were no twelve people from East Tennessee going to convict an innocent man.

Wells lay on the left front spectator bench behind the defense table most of the time. Judge Hobson instructed Appleman to awaken his client three times during the trial. It didn't matter. Within a matter of hours, Wells would be sleeping again with his girlfriend looking on from behind frantically.

Cramer slowly developed the crime scene for the jury. Then, he went to the chase, the telephone call, the Oldsmobile -- possibly the one owned by Wells -- and finally the hospital. Cramer held Barney Woods back. The lawyer knew it would come down to Woods' testimony and his positive identification of Hasten, Steat, and Worth.

Three days into the trial, Caswell brought Detective Case from Chattanooga to the stand. Case testified that at the encouragement of

Special Agent Art Millwee of the FBI, he and Sheriff Bagwell went to the home of Glenn Hasten and recovered a set of boots from his bedroom closet.

The lawyer was shocked. He could not believe those boots would have glass in them. He had Hasten's boots in his briefcase in the courtroom at the time. Even the other lawyers did not know he had the boots. He asked Detective Case only one question, "Do those boots have glass in them which may have come from the crime scene?"

Case answered, "That is a possibility. Those boots were sent to the FBI lab in Washington by myself and Sheriff Bagwell. I do not know the results of that lab's findings."

The next witness was the Special Agent of the FBI from the crime lab in Washington, D.C. He testified that he had received the boots, the top of the coffee table, and fragments of glass from the window in the Case residence. He described glassmaking and the fact that each batch of glass has certain characteristics due to the sand from which it is extracted. After blah, blah, blah, building credibility, the agent testified that the glass in Glenn Hasten's boots, the coffee table, and the window of the Case residence was from the same batch. He cited the formula of the glass and put it up in large print on a posterboard.

The lawyer tried to trip him up on cross-examination, but he had been to the F.B.I. Witness School, and he was well trained. He put the hat on Glenn Hasten.

The lawyer wondered who would tie Worth and Steat to the murder scene. It had to be Barney Woods, the home run hitter for the state. That was it. Caswell Cramer had saved Woods for his last witness to make a positive identification of Steat and Worth. All three defendants were being tied together in one neat package for the jury to convict.

The lawyer asked for a recess. "Granted, 10 minutes recess."

He waited until all the people were out of the men's room. It was about eight minutes into the break. He went into the back stall, locked the door, and opened his briefcase. He did something he had dared not do before. He lifted the boots and examined the soles. There were glass fragments in the soles visible to the naked eye. He looked at the soles with a magnifying glass he always carried with him. Glass, plenty of it. He closed the briefcase, relieved himself, and returned to the courtroom.

The lawyer knew that Bagwell, Millwee, and Case, or one of them, manufactured the boot evidence with the glass. But there was nothing he could do. If he produced his boots, the state would move for a continuance to check the boots. If the glass matched, Hasten was in the electric chair. That evidence would simply be too credible. If he said nothing, Hasten would be convicted on fabricated evidence. He kept quiet and laid low. He didn't represent Hasten; Finwell did. If he wanted the boots, he should have found them. Furthermore, they wouldn't do him any good anyway.

Glenn Hasten had been identified without the use of Barney Woods. This witness would have to be the witness to identify Marvey Steat and Doc Worth.

Caswell Cramer announced on the fourth day of trial, around 3:00 p.m., that he was winding down his case. He called, "Barney Woods."

The lawyer thought to himself that if the state had cheated in one aspect of the case, they would not be above "gilding the Lily" in another aspect of the case. He simply had to wait until he might assume the gold plating was going to occur.

All the people at the defense table were wearing suits and ties. When Caswell Cramer left the courtroom to get his witness, and before Woods came into the courtroom, the lawyer told Marvey Steat to swap seats with him. He was now at the end of the table where Steat had been sitting throughout the trial.

Barney Woods entered the courtroom. He was dressed in rugged but presentable cowboy boots, relatively new jeans, and a good solid red flannel shirt. He was carrying a cap with his company's logo on the front of it. He walked to the witness stand and sat down placing the cap on his lap. He looked at every person at the tables, smiled, waved to the sheriff, and waited.

Cramer was anxious to present his star witness. He never acknowledged the defense. He filled his eyes with Barney Woods. He took a full 12 minutes of background on Woods building up his credibility. Then, he took another 30 minutes allowing Woods to describe the events of the day leading up to his picking up three hunters short of the bi-color checking station. Woods remembered everything so perfectly because it was the only time he had ever gone deer hunting alone. The lawyer thought, "Yeah, he remembers it because it was the only time he ever went hunting alone. Baloney! He remembers it vividly because he has been coached and rehearsed over and over again."

After laboriously establishing his required legal predicate, Cramer pulled his trump card.

"Do you see any of those men in the courtroom today?"

"I am sure I see one, and I'm pretty sure I see another one." Barney was scanning the defense table.

"All right. Tell the jury who you picked up that night if you can identify him," Cramer was almost strutting, and he got out of the way so Woods could identify Marvey Steat and Doc A. Worth.

Barney Woods looked very closely at the six well-dressed men to his left. Then his face lit up, and he looked directly at the lawyer at the end of the defense table. He pointed his finger at the lawyer.

"There, that's him! The one at the end of the table! He's wearing a suit and tie now, but he had on a camouflage field jacket when I picked him up. That's him! I will never forget that face, even until my deathbed. I'll never forget him! That is the man!"

The lawyer stood up and said, "Let the record reflect that the state's absolutely positive eyewitness, the only witness in this case against my client, has identified the lawyer for Marvey Steat as the man he picked up on the night of the murder. He has said conclusively that he will never forget my face. And, I'll bet he won't now."

"Don't overdo it," Judge Hobson admonished. "The jury has your point."

The lawyer knew that either Bagwell, Millwee, Case, or Cramer had coached Barney too well. They couldn't afford for him to make a mistake in identifying Steat. "He's the one on the end," one of them had told him, and Cramer didn't catch the lawyer switch in time. He was too busy preening before the jury with his star witness.

It was almost painful watching Caswell Cramer try to get his case back on track by having Barney identify Doc A. Worth. Barney was now so upset he had trouble identifying Doc as well. He was embarrassed and he stumbled around making his situation worse. Then after several painful minutes, he finally guessed right on Doc. By then he had lost all his credibility with the woman who whistled through her nose, as well as the rest of the jury. The state's case came apart at the seams like the proverbial cardboard suitcase in the rain.

The defense put on only one witnesses, Glenn Hasten's sister. She testified that the boots the state produced were bought as dress shoes and had never been worn by her brother. The soles were exceptionally clean, except for the embedded glass fragments and scarring as a result of the jump to the table. The boots appeared as though they had just been taken out of their box. It was clear to the jury that the boots had never been worn. Still, there was the glass.

The jury stayed out four hours. It was after 9:00 p.m. on Friday when they came in with a verdict. Billy Wells, Marvey Steat, and Doc A. Worth were found not guilty. Glenn Hasten was found guilty of murder and, at the jury's discretion, sentenced to 25 years in the penitentiary.

The families shouted, all except the Hasten family. The lawyers were practically dancing in the pit, with the exception of Cecil Finwell who had represented Glenn Hasten.

The lawyer started putting his papers together to leave. As it worked out, he was the last member of the defense to exit the courtroom. He had to pack his papers and evidence in separate boxes. The boots took up all the space in his large leather briefcase, which was now carefully locked.

The custodian began to turn out the lights as Curtis Bagwell and Art Millwee came through the door from the state's witness room also leaving. The lawyer walked out right behind them.

"You walked two murderers today," Curtis Bagwell turned and said acrimoniously to the lawyer.

"Aw, it was all in a day's work," the lawyer responded trying to lighten a tense situation.

Millwee stopped short. Snort. "You and I know what happened," Art Millwee looked directly at the lawyer through his thick glasses with hatred in his eyes.

"You did it. Those other lawyers didn't do it. You did it when you changed seats, and I'll get you if it's the last thing I do." It was a threat, and Millwee meant it.

As they entered the dark hallway leading out

of the Anderson County Courthouse, with their heels resounding on the marble floor, the lawyer fired off one last shot.

"I'd watch it if I were you, Arthur. You never can tell when another pair of boots might show up. You know, the real boots that somebody might have actually worn a little. Those boots might be knee-high black boots that were cut off somebody. If that happens, some folks might have a whole lot of explaining to do."

The men walked out of the building in silence.

The three men looked at each other in the light of the tall street lamps outside the courthouse. The lawyer knew Curtis Bagwell was apprehensive. He could tell he had struck a nerve with the sheriff. He had cheated and still lost.

For the moment, he wondered what Millwee was thinking. Did he really know? The agent looked blankly at him and got into the passenger side of the Cherokee being driven by Curtis Bagwell. The lawyer smiled. He had the measure of Agent Millwee, Sheriff Bagwell, and Detective Case.

He cought up with the celebrating lawyers, clients, and their families at the corner.

HIT AND DRAG SHORTY

The year was 1946. The lawyer had passed to the 7th grade at Decatur Junior High School. While he was in the 6th grade, he had been let out of school during the school day, as a news boy, to sell extra editions of the *Decatur Daily* on V-E Day and V-J Day. It was the high point of his young life. Not only was the war over, but also he had liked being able to stand on the corner of 2nd Avenue and Johnson Street and shout, "Extra! Extra! Read all about it! The Germans have surrendered!" Just like those news boys on the radio. Other than those two signal days, he laboriously delivered 360 papers on his old used red bicycle each day to earn extra money for the family. Now he had passed to junior high school. Although the word had not been attached itself to his vocabulary at that time, soon he would be a genuine *teenager*.

When school started in September, he became fast friends with another news boy who lived near the Decatur Country Club, an old nine-hole golf course with different tees for the front and back nine. When school was out that year, both boys agreed that they were tired to throwing and delivering papers. His new friend suggested that they go to Decatur Country Club and become caddies on the golf course.

"Why, they pay you $1.50 for carrying a bag 18 holes. Most golfers will tip you a quarter or fifty cents. Two dollars for three and a half hours work is not bad. Plus, those golf bags don't look that heavy."

The future lawyer agreed, and the boys visited the pro shop where they were soon hired on at the country club. They were the only white boys there, but they didn't know it. Times were different then. The hard times of the war were over, the soldiers were coming home, and it seemed like the idyllic times would last forever. The housing boom and the baby boom that would change the face of America had begun to flourish.

The big golfing days were Wednesday afternoon when the stores were closed at mid-week, and all day Saturday and Sunday. Most weekends they could catch a bag in the morning and another in the afternoon. If all the caddies didn't show up, they could manage a double, carrying the bags for two golfers - twice the money!

Monday was caddie's day. The course was closed, and caddies could play all day free while the greens crew cut the fairways, roughs, tees, and greens. The boys played golf every Monday when they could share clubs with a caddy who had some clubs. None of the caddies had a complete set of clubs. For most rounds all the friends had was a three wood (then called a spoon), an eight iron, and a putter. Within a few weeks they could score in the 80's with the three clubs. They hooded the eight iron for long iron shots and opened it up for the nine and wedge placements.

They rolled up their overall pants and looked for balls in the water hazards. The word "jeans" had not entered the lexicon at that time. They were constantly in the roughs and woods looking for lost balls when they weren't caddying. If a golfer in either of their foursomes lost a ball, they always returned to the spot after the round and searched until they found it. The good balls they found were sold to golfers for a dime or quarter apiece. They kept the rest in order to have balls for their game. Usually, if the ball didn't have a cut, called a "smile," it was sold.

Most golfers were still using clubs with persimmon heads and wooden shafts. The war effort had taken all the metal, and golf technology had stood still during that time. When the teens saw their first set of clubs with shiny new steel shafts, they could hardly contain their enthusiasm.

The members raised the funds, went in debt, and demolished the old white ramshackled clubhouse that had once served as a farmer's home. They built a new huge imposing brick edifice that they would expand several times in the future. Sometimes on rainy days, right after they moved into the new building, the old pro would take the two budding teens into the dark damp basement of the clubhouse and teach them the golf swing under one dangling light bulb. The lessons could go on for hours, the boys swinging a club on a square piece of carpet that the pro had provided. He was an excellent teacher of the game, the best wedge man either of them ever saw, or ever would see. Divorced, his sons were with his ex-wife, and he seemed to genuinely enjoy working with the two. At that time, the golf professional was also the greenskeeper. He hired the pair to work on the course when they were not carrying bags. He paid them forty cents an hour to crawl around on the greens with putty knives spading up crabgrass and other foreign growth. Sometimes they broke rocks with 12-pound sledgehammers. They cut bushes and did anything else he would allow them to do. They thought they were getting rich. Still, both of them agreed, caddying and shagging balls was where the money was to be made.

To no one's surprise, they became quite good at both caddying and golf. So good in fact that each of them had a "regular" - a golfer who played at least three times a week - and his regular caddy was expected to be on his bag. If the regular wanted to practice, his caddy would station himself at the appropriate yardage down the fairway for the club the golfer was hitting. When a caddy shagged balls, he was always the target. Sometimes the ball boy could catch the ball in the shag bag. Chasing balls paid fifty cents an hour and was easy work. Neither of the friends were ever hit with a golf ball. The closer the golfer hit the ball to the caddy, the easier the work. His friend's regular paid better than the lawyer's; but the lawyer's played faster and more often, so it about evened out.

One day, in the future, his friend would become the Chief Executive Officer of his own successful company. At that time, the future CEO was tall, slim, fair and blonde. The future lawyer was shorter, more muscular, and more dark complexioned. When a person saw one, the person saw the other. They were always together. They were tied together by not only friendship and work, but also by the game of golf.

They were always begging the pro to look at their swings. Most of the time, he was simply too busy to be bothered by the insisting boys. One day, when it was raining, the pro agreed to take a look at their swings and told them a story as they were going down to the basement:

"You boys remind me of Joe and Shorty who were best friends like you. They were playing golf, and Shorty had a heart attack on the tenth hole. Sometime later, Joe came up to the eighteenth fairway pulling Shorty by the shirt collar. People ran out of the clubhouse and learned of Shorty's condition. They called an ambulance, and he was taken to the hospital. The local pro asked Joe what happened. Joe said Shorty had a heart attack on the tenth. 'What did you do?' the pro asked very concerned. 'Oh, I'd just hit the ball and drag Shorty.

,'"

The pro broke into near uncontrollable loughter. The young golfers liked the story. It exemplified their love for the game.

The first golf club the lawyer ever owned was homemade. He searched around his rural house until he found a branch of a small tree that resembled the shape of a golf club. He cut the branch with the coping saw he had used in shop at school. Then he stripped the bark off the shaft part and shaped the head with his Scout knife. The "club" needed a face. So he tacked a Campbell's Soup tin can lid on the front of the head part of the limb as a face to strike the ball. He used the remainder of the lid, bent under the "face" as the sole of the club. It didn't look like much, but it suited his purpose. He swung it relentlessly practicing his swing.

When he was not working at the golf course, he would tee up a cheap ball, a U.S. Knobby or Firestone golf ball, on a clod in the cotton patch adjoining his home and hit the balls down the furrows of the field. He would walk through the dusty plowed ground, locate the balls, and hit them back. He would do this for hours, usually in the broiling hot sun, practicing the golf swing the pro had tought him.

When caddie's day rolled around, he took his stick to the club and played with it as a driver on the course. The other caddies laughed at him when he pulled it out of his "golf" bag, made from the remnants of an old cotton sack his mother stitched together for him, but they stopped laughing when he outdrove them. He could hit a new Titleist a little more than 200 yards with his homemade club. The other caddies tried their hand with the stick, but they couldn't hit it. His best friend could do pretty good with it, but he said it needed a grip. They bummed friction tape from the pro shop and wrapped the top of the white wooden shaft overlapping the tape like they wrapped their baseball bats. They were in business with a driver that had a grip.

The budding golfer kept the stick until he could round up the three wood, eight iron, and putter. One misty day he took his "driver" and hit three balls down the cotton rows. The cotton was up then. It had been chopped and was growing toward putting on bolls. He lost the balls among the near knee-high cotton and said "so long" to the faithful old club. He had used it an entire summer and fall. Winter was near, and the cotton would soon be ready to harvest. He really hated to throw it away. But, his buddy now had a two wood (called a brassie), a five iron, nine iron (called a niblick), and his own putter. Together, they almost had a set of clubs. At least, they had a set good enough to play eighteen holes. And the "new" clubs sure beat the homemade driver, three wood, eight iron and putter they had been using to play the course.

The summer of 1948 joined the pair to golf for life. That year they both had a complete set of used clubs with metal shafts. With their "new" equipment they began to shoot pretty good golf. There were not more than half a dozen players at Decatur who could beat them. They could easily beat the men they caddied for, but they kept quiet about it. They analyzed every swing they saw, and they were critical of every golfer's swing silently. In the future, the CEO would become club champion at Decatur several times.

They made the high school golf team; the CEO was the Captain. When they turned sixteen and got their driver's licenses, they began to travel across North Alabama in the CEO's '37 Chevrolet playing strange golf courses. Their favorite was the Jasper County Club in Jasper, Alabama, because the greens were so lush and fast.

After high school both boys were cought up in the Korean War. By the time they had finished their military service and college, they joined the workforce and found themselves going their separate ways. They still found time to play golf and keep up with each other. Weddings, best man, wives, and children came along. Still, they continued their love for golf together and they and their families vacationed together, always near a golf course. The women and children did whatever women and children do while the men played golf.

Slowly, as working young men applying the work ethics they had learned as boys, they gained some wealth, became pilots, and owned their own airplanes. The aircraft opened up new golf vistas for the friends. They began to travel the country during their time away from work, playing golf at the most well known and challenging golf courses in the country.

They played Sawgrass before the TPC discovered it. They played Arnold Palmer's Bay Hills the first season play was allowed.

Palmer had just purchased the property from Dr. Phillips. Their favorite courses were Hidden Hills near Jacksonville, Florida, now paved over as a commercial development, and Eagle-Vail where the ball went great distances in the high thin air of the Rockies. And so it went -- Doral, Pebble Beach, name it, the life-long best friends, and golf.

Once, when they were living in cities about 100 miles apart, the lawyer, at age 25, was playing the best golf of his life. He was in the pairing for his club's championship against the reigning champ, a 62 year old, who toured the course well under par, primarily because of his putting. Senior golf had not crossed the golfing mind, and golf carts hauling clubs and passengers had not been invented. The club did not have a caddy program, and the day was burning hot. Pair after pair of the first flight teed off, each golfer pulling his clubs on a cart. Finally, it was their time.

The round started off well enough. The lawyer was two strokes up at the end of three holes. It looked like he might coast to an easy win. On the fourth hole, the pair teed off, both in the fairway, hit their second shots to the green, and prepared to putt. After lining up his putt and approaching his ball, the old champ's face turned ashen, gasping for breath. He was having a heart attack near the cup on the fourth hole. He clutched his chest and fell face forward on the green, about six feet from the hole, where the green broke to the left about two inches just short of the cup. The lawyer, a robust muscular young man, who had lifted weights in college, was in perfect physical condition. He lifted the old golfer and carried him like a baby back to the clubhouse, pausing to put him down and rest briefly every now and then. He kept talking to his load praying he wouldn't die. The elder's breathing was irregular, heavy, while his fingernails were blue and his eyes were rolled back in his head. He was limp as a dishrag and very difficult to carry. When he could speak, he would thank the younger man for what he was doing.

The club pro ran out to meet them along with the crowd at the clubhouse. They helped the lawyer with his burden about half the length of number one fairway. The pro said he was going to run ahead and call an ambulance. The old guy stirred and mumbled for him not to do that. He said that he thought he would be all right if he could get a nitroglycerine tablet from his locker.

In the cool of the dim locker room, the lawyer watched as the old champ with shaking hands put a tiny white tablet under his tongue. Sitting on the locker room bench, in minutes his color began to come back. His breathing was less labored. And after a quarter of an hour and a drink of some more water, with help, he could stand up. With all the concerned golfers standing around, he finally walked a few steps with his steel golf cleats clacking on the worn red painted concrete floor. Then, instead of going to the hospital or returning home to his family, he said confidently, "I'm ready to resume the match."

The lawyer couldn't believe it. He was

exhausted. He had just saved the old guy's life. His arms were like heavy weights, he could barely lift them, and his legs were like rubber. But he resolutely ambled back across the course with the old guy, back to the fourth green where they had left their clubs on their push carts. They guessed where their balls had been and putted out for pars.

The lawyer was still up first on the tee, but his swing was gone. He sliced his drive out of bounds. Try as he might with his practice swings, he knew that he could not swing his driver. In desperation, he tried to hit a two iron off the tee. The old champ won the fifth hole. The younger man knew that he was losing his chance to win the silver cup. Long story short, the old guy beat the lawyer by two strokes and remained club champion.

The membership had a good laugh at the lawyer's expense. They began to call him "Godzilla G. Gorilla." One wag even had tees printed with the name on them and presented them to him at the appropriate moment with the appropriate crowd around.

When his friend, a youthful CEO, heard the story, his first remark, after his loughter subsided, was, "Hit and drag Shorty. You lived the joke!"

"Yeah, taint funny, McGee," the lawyer quoted from an old radio show they had listened to as kids. And, no matter how hard he tried to find the humor in the experience, it just didn't come out funny. Golf was a serious business.

Fast forward almost fifty years. The friends were in their early 70's, still living a little more than 100 miles apart, and still playing golf together whenever possible. Neither had officially retired from their professions, but they did make time away from work for plenty of golf.

The CEO still played regularly at Decatur County Club, and the lawyer played across the state at Fort Payne. Usually, they met almost halfway and played in Scottsboro where the lawyer was a member of Goose Pond Colony, one of the top five courses in Alabama. They were never allowed to hit from the golden senior tees.

As one member of the foursome said, "Hell, no. I weigh 260 pounds, I'm 6'4" tall, I'm 25 years younger than you guys, and both of you outdrive me 50 yards. Hell, no. You old geezers play from the members tees with us."

"You could show some respect to your elders."

"It ain't a matter of respect. It's all about money, and I'm tired of always giving you geezes mine."

At least once a year, the CEO took the lawyer as his guest to play at Alabama's premier golf and country club, Shoal Creek near Birmingham. The CEO was a charter member, and Shoal Creek was more than a round of golf - it was an experience. The club had made an early grab for national prominence in 1984 when it invited the PGA Championship in for its tournament. Later, in 1986, the U.S. Amateur Championship was played there.

The PGA came back in 1990. During this tournament, a reporter learned that the club did not have any black members and splashed the fact across the front pages of the country. Shoal Creek's lily white membership became sort of a national scandal. With an initiation fee of $90,000, the members were not surprised that many people did not apply for membership. They couldn't understand the furor. They didn't feel they had discriminated against anyone. However, under intense media pressure the club brought in some African-American members, but it did not invite national tournaments to return to the beautiful course designed by Jack Nicklaus.

Lying deep in a narrow lush valley, Shoal Creek has attempted to be Alabama's answer to Augusta National in neighboring Georgia. It is gated, it is shaded, with guards, caddies, and the works. It can best be described as hoi-hoi, where the very rich gather for their own kind of recreation. Truth be known, it is probably the second best kept course in America. The fairways are like greens, while the greens are like a shaved carpet, at least 15 on the stem meter. The rock work is in abundance as are the profusion of flowers, and there are seemingly endless breathtaking vistas. Even the water of Shoal Creek, and the hazards it provides, are artificially dyed deep blue. No expense is spared in keeping this treasure gorgeous. It would take Augusta National, at its best, to top it.

The lawyer had a standing invitation from his friend to play Shoal Creek as often as the rules allowed. But, as old age was creeping on, walking the long course, uphill and downhill, with a caddy, in the Alabama searing summer heat, was pushing the envelope for the lawyer. Still, he and the CEO made it at least an annual event, occasionally twice a year, but not more.

When the CEO would strongly insist, the lawyer would bring along someone from his usual foursome and they would have the once in a lifetime luxury that only Shoal Creek affords. Occasionally, the friends would stay in the Nicklaus cabin and play two days in a row. It usually took the lawyer at least three days to recover from the walk in the heat.

To stay in shape for Shoal Creek, the lawyer arose at 4:00 a.m. and walked three and one-half miles, before sunup, four mornings a week with his banker. That was not enough. Shoal Creek, with its stagnant humidity and stifling heat was a demanding and difficult mistress.

One summer, toward the fall, the lawyer was in one of the judge's chambers doing some courthouse golfing with a judge similarly inclined. The lawyer casually mentioned that he was going to play Shoal Creek the following week with his best friend.

"I'd give my front seat in Hades to play Shoal Creek," the corpulent judge opined, reclining in his large judge's chair, and allowing his eyes to search the ceiling.

"You're definitely invited," the lawyer responded magnanimously. "Be at my office on Tuesday at 10:00 a.m. We'll drive down, have lunch at the club, hit a few practice balls, and play the course."

The judge was ecstatic, "I'll be there!"

The lawyer called his friend and confirmed it would be all right to bring the judge along. He would make a foursome, as another member of the lawyer's foursome had previously been confirmed.

"Bring the Robe. We'll have fun," the CEO had responded in his usual jocular manner.

Things went as planned. Three golfers left Northeast Alabama and pointed the lawyer's SUV toward Shoal Creek right on time. The experience was as advertised. The food was fabulous. The practice tee was perfect, the practice green was excellent, and the course was typically Shoal Creek. It was a sublime experience for the three visitors.

The caddies were on top of their game, and the golfers felt like pros as they ambled off the first tee down number one fairway. Unfortunately, by the time they had played sixteen holes, the lawyer had stopped taking a practice swing. He was trying to just keep walking and keep striking the ball. However, the nineteenth hole, with scotch on the rocks and water on the side, La Gloria cigars, and the CEO telling stories out of their childhood and various golfing adventures, the day was topped off perfectly. Neither of the three men from Northeast Alabama could have asked for a more fantastic day.

Toward the end of the following year, the looming figure in the huge black robe happened to find himself alone with the lawyer in his vacant courtroom. The conversation quickly turned from the finer points of law to golf.

"How did you play at Shoal Creek this year?" the judge queried, making it quite obvious that he had not been invited back to heaven.

"I didn't have time to go this year," the lawyer replied. "I've been busy with the practice preparing for my son to come back from Montgomery and take over the business."

"Too bad," the judge sympathized. "I'd give

anything to play that course again."

"We will," the lawyer confirmed. "I'll just have to work it out. I'll let you know."

When the lawyer's son graduated from law school and was admitted to the bar, he decided to practice with another lawyer in South Alabama rather than return to his father's practice right away. Finally, after almost six years, he told his dad that he was ready to come home. He felt he was now experienced enough and qualified to live in his father's shadow. The lawyer was delighted as he wanted to wind down. Truthfully, he could see himself playing even more golf.

On one occasion, when he had given up on his son coming home, he had retired. It had lasted a total of three weeks. Too many people were coming to his home and begging him to take just one more case. His wife had said that he was going to have to return to the office, even if it was just a few hours a day, a few days a week. She couldn't handle the traffic and the phone ringing off the wall at home. He returned to the practice "part time" but he was soon working as he hard as he had when he was younger and needed the money. His son's announcement was music to the old guy's ears.

Once the son was ensconced in the practice, the lawyer played more golf, and it didn't take long for that to happen. It was almost like the old days with the CEO again. At the end of an enjoyable eighteen at Goose Pond, on Lake Guntersville, the CEO asked, "When are we going back to Shoal Creek? We haven't been in a while. You didn't even go last year."

"Yeah, the judge happened to mention that. I just don't know. I'm trying to get my son going. And when I don't play golf, it's business as usual, but don't give up on me."

"Oh, well, it's too hot to play down there right now. Plus, it has really been wet this summer. The course might not be up to par right now," the CEO mused. "However, I doubt it. That greenskeeper stays on top of things. The last time I was down there, and I don't go nearly often enough, they had installed large oscillating fans in back of every green to keep the grass cool."

The lawyer was impressed, That's Shoal Creek, he thought.

A young man, about twenty-three years old, tall, dark hair, fairly handsome, sat down across the desk from the lawyer with his overweight father. The elder gentleman was dressed in bib overalls and completely filled the adjacent blue leather English banking chair. He breathed heavily, often, and loud.

The son began, "I need you to take a

divorce case for me. My wife left home with our eight-month-old son. She won't let me see my boy. She won't let my folks see their grandchild. I feel like my son is growing up without me. I need help. I really don't want a divorce, but I got to see my boy."

He was contorting his face in anguish and wringing his hands to emphasize his point. He talked without taking a breath. He was wearing a "Dish Network" blue shirt indicating he was a satellite television installer.

When he did stop talking long enough for the lawyer to get a word in edgewise, the lawyer said, "I don't take divorce cases. My son does. He was the domestic relations master in Montgomery County for quite a while. He's an expert on divorces. Come with me, and I will introduce you."

He stood up and walked around the desk to the door. The tall young man with the problem rose to follow him up the hallway as did his trailing father, brogans sounding on the hardwood floor.

The lawyer introduced the pair to his son and turned them over to him. The son went right to work with the interview. The lawyer walked back down the hallway to his office and back to work.

A little more than a week went by. The office staff began referring to the client as "Cry Baby." The lawyer asked why the moniker?

His son responded, "He complains every day. The facts of the case are that he pushed his wife down on a couch at a party in front of witnesses. He had been drinking. She was ready to leave the party, and he wasn't. He didn't mean to push her as hard as he did, but according to witnesses, it was a forceful shove. She wasn't hurt, but she was humiliated."

"After he pushed her, she left without him and went directly to her mother's house. Her mother is a legal secretary. The next day they went to court and got a restraining order against him based upon domestic violence. He can't come within 500 feet of her by the judge's order. She won't allow his parents to see their baby. They don't have visiting rights. He can't understand why we can't get the judge to rescind his order and give him visiting privileges with his child. I can understand his dilemma, but it's his whining I can't stand. It's constant. He even sheds tears every time he comes to the office."

The lawyer began to notice that the young man was in the office at least four times a week. He didn't bother coming through the front door and waiting in the waiting room anymore. He came in the back door and stood by his lawyer's door until he could get an audience. The office telephone logs reflected that he called every day, sometimes three and four times a day.

One morning, the lawyer's clerk approached the lawyer, "You've got to do something. Cry Baby is driving us crazy. He simply can't understand why we can't get the restraining order lifted. We have it set for hearing at the earliest possible time, but we can't get it any quicker. Please get this man off our backs."

"I am not familiar enough with the facts of the case. Further, I don't want to become involved in a messy custody fight."

Days rocked on. The lawyer's son labored diligently on behalf of Cry Baby. The lawyer heard his son tell the client, "I hope you know I'm charging you for every telephone call and every visit when you come in here and complain because I can't work a miracle for you."

A few days later, the doorbell rang at the lawyer's home slightly after dusk. He went to the door, and the client was standing there. "May I come in? I have to talk to you."

"Sure," the lawyer swung wide the door. "What can I do for you?"

They went down to the lawyer's study and sat down. "I need help, and I don't believe your son is doing all he can for me. I want you to take over my case."

"I know very little about your case. I do know that your wife is the daughter of the secretary for the top divorce lawyer in this county. I do know that you have been charged with domestic violence. I do know there is a restraining order against you. I do know that this order has been set for hearing. What else do you want from my law firm?"

"I want to see my baby. I just believe that if you would step in on my case I could get some action. I want custody of my boy and I don't believe your son can get it for me."

"Neither can I. No one can. The Alabama Law presumes that a child of tender years should be with its mother. The most you are going to get is standard visiting rights, every other weekend, four weeks during the summer, one week at Christmas, and so on. You know the drill."

"I can't help it. I just believe you can do something for me. Please take over my case, please." He was pleading. Tears welled up in his eyes and ran down his cheeks.

The lawyer could see why the staff called him Cry Baby.

"Call me in the morning. I'll take a look at it. Right now, do you shoot nine-ball?"

"I shoot some stick if I get the chance."

"Then choose your weapon while I rack the balls. I've been wanting to play some pool."

The lawyer and the client shot pool for a couple of hours in the study. The case was not mentioned again. The younger man was not much competition, but it was a good workout.

The following morning, the lawyer called the

staff into his office. "This boy with the baby who is aggravating you folks, you call him Cry Baby, came to the house last night and asked me to take over his case. What do you think?"

His son beamed, "You will be the greatest father in the world if you will lift this burden from me. Please!"

The clerk joined in, "We can't handle this guy. He is the world's worst client. He is a pest. He will not listen to reason. He just whines and complains, and it's constant. If anybody can handle him, you can. We can't."

The secretary nodded assent. "The man is impossible," she said. "We're at the end of our rope. You talk to him, he doesn't hear you. He just continues to gripe and moan. Also, he cries."

"All right. Bring me the file. Son, you stay here and bring me up-to-date. I'll take it over."

Members of the staff breathed an audible sigh of relief. One said, "This calls for a celebration. Break out the Diet Cokes!"

The lawyer reviewed the file. He concluded that his son had perfectly represented the client. The facts were orderly arranged, the law was behind its tab, and the pleadings seemed they were right out of a form book. The lawyer's son spent the better part of two hours going over the evidentiary pictures and witness statements with his father. When the conference concluded, the lawyer telephoned the client and left a message on his recorder to come to the office and see him. Cry Baby didn't receive the call. He came by the office, as was his habit, less than thirty minutes after the lawyer had finished reviewing his file. This morning he had brought his dad. He wanted to know if the lawyer had decided to take over his case.

The client and his father were once more seated in the lawyer's office. The lawyer told him that he had taken the case and proceeded to review the entire file with the two men. He explained the law in detail. He told the pair how he expected the judge would rule in the case. He carefully explained that a divorce and standard visiting rights were the most the client could expect. He said that he didn't know if he could get it, but he would ask the judge for an expedited hearing as the client had not seen his baby in almost two months. Cry Baby left the lawyer's office seemingly more satisfied and breathing a sigh of relief.

The lawyer went to the office kitchen, poured up a cup of coffee, and returned to his desk. While leaning back in his chair, sipping his coffee, he thought, It's time to take the judge back to Shoal Creek. A good lawyer knows the law. A great lawyer knows the judge. He pressed the CEO's automatic dial on his telephone.

The CEO answered the telephone as they

always had since they were juniors in high school. They had been told a joke about an Indian who came face to face with the devil. The devil told the Indian, "I'll give you all the cattle you want, all the squaws you can handle, all the tepees you can use, fresh water and green pastures if you can answer one question. If you can't answer it, your soul is mine."

The Indian made a deal with the devil and agreed to the proposition, "What's the question?" the Indian asked.

"How do you like your eggs?" the devil responded. "But don't answer right now," and vanished.

Sure enough, the Indian got more cattle than he could herd. He had four wives, beautiful tepees, green pastures and pure water. He lived in absolute bliss for twenty-three years. He never thought of the devil again.

One day he was down by his beautiful babbling brook participating in his favorite pastime, fly fishing. Poof! In a cloud of smoke there stood the devil. Ole Satan raised his right hand palm upward in the typical Indian peace greeting and said, "How?"

"Fried," said the Indian.

The boys had loved this old joke that had been told to them by their favorite teacher in high school. And for sixty years they had greeted each other, either in person or on the telephone, with "How?"

When the secretary told the CEO that the lawyer was on the telephone, he answered "How?"

"Poached," said the lawyer, which was an appropriate response grinning. "I called to ask you about a visit to Shoal Creek. I've just taken a damned divorce case that is really ugly. The divorce lawyer representing the wife has a personal involvement in it. It's his secretary of twenty-plus years' daughter. He seems to be going out of his way to bend the law and use his influence with the court. He is being totally unreasonable, and I've go to do something."

"Humm," the CEO considered. "Ever think it might be his child?"

"Yeah, I thought about that because of the way he is conducting himself. You know me, I will bring that possibility up if it becomes necessary. Right now I'm trying to avoid it. The case is before our golfing buddy, the judge. I think I can make an end-around run if we can take him back to Shoal Creek, the Garden of Eden."

"Sure. Name the day. I'm looking good for the next three weeks. Just remember, Shoal Creek is hot as the hub of hell during July, down in that valley and all."

"Yeah, I know. But I need to take him right away. I'd like to pave the way for the temporary hearing in this case. That lawyer on the other side is manhandling our client atrociously, and I need to stop it. You know, I won't discuss the case with the judge, I won't even mention it. But the male bonding will be there. There is no bonding like golf buddy bonding."

"Name the day."

"Thanks. I'll be back with you." The lawyer smiled inwardly thinking, There's no substitute for trickery and deceit.

There was no need for the lawyer to file an appearance in the case as the law firm was already attorney of record for the defendant in the file. He would simply blindside the divorce lawyer by showing up at the Temporary Restraining Order hearing and kicking his butt. The judge would not know he was involved until he appeared on the day of the hearing.

"This is going to be good. Cry Baby will be a happy baby," he liked his plan.

He dialed the judge's number and issued the invitation. The judge was delighted. The date was set, and a repeat of the former trip to Shoal Creek was on. This time it would be only the lawyer, the judge, and the CEO.

The phone rang. It was the CEO. After the traditional "How?" the CEO said, "I've forgotten the Robe's first name. I know it's not judge, is it? What is it?"

The lawyer gave him the name, "I guess you know you've saved my life."

"What else is new? I've been doing it sixty

years. We're on for next Tuesday." They said "goodbye" and the lawyer went back to work on the file.

The weekend went by, and on Monday, Cry Baby came into the lawyer's office. "I've come to pick up my file. I don't want you nor your son representing me. Figure out what I owe you. I'll pay, and we're through. I don't think you have my best interests at heart. I want custody of my boy, and you say you can't get it. So I'm going to a lawyer who can get it for me."

Fired by a cry baby, the lawyer thought. "More than that, damned! Fired after committing to a golf game in the scorching summer heat. I have outsmarted myself. Oh well, it's still golf, and it is at Shoal Creek." He took some consolation.

He told the secretary to clean out the file and give it to the client. "Good riddance!"

The morning of the golf game, the CEO called the lawyer at home at 6:30 a.m. "I checked with the pro yesterday, and he said nobody is playing at Shoal Creek after starting at 8:30 in the morning. It's too hot and humid. So, I just want you to know it's too uncomfortable to play golf today. I invited Wilkey to play with us. He said, 'It is too damned hot to play golf.'"

Dr. Roger Wilkey was a mutual friend of the pair. He had played golf with them when he was a boy and they were caddies. He had also participated in their cross-country golfing trips when they were traveling to the most exciting courses in the U.S.

"Howsomever, if you are bound and determined, as I guess you are, I'll see you down there at noon."

"Yeah, we're on, for better or worse. But I'm not sure I can walk that course in this heat. Will they let you have a cart if you're over 71 years old?"

"Yeah. The membership at Shoal Creek has aged. They will let you use a cart now provided you also hire a caddy. I anticipated that you and the judge might have a hard time walking in this weather, so I told the pro to have a cart for you. Call me when you turn on Hugh Daniel Drive so I can be sure I am ahead of you to make it okay for you to get in at the gate."

"Will do. That's good thinking - the cart. I'll see you down there."

Later that morning, the lawyer stopped his SUV at the convenience store near his home to buy a cup of coffee. A friend saw him after he was back in his vehicle and came over to say hello. The lawyer pushed the button, and his driver's side window lowered. After passing pleasantries with the friend, he pushed the button to raise the window. It didn't budge. He cut off the engine and tried the button, no luck. He listened to see if the window motor was activated, nothing. He tried the other windows, all worked. He concluded it wasn't a fuse, Probably the window switch rolled over and died. Nothing to do but return home and swap vehicles. This day is not beginning on a good note. He was concerned. Bad omen.

At precisely 10:00 a.m. the judge pulled up behind the lawyer's office. The lawyer met him outside. He could feel that the heat and humidity were high. It was mid-morning, in Northeast Alabama, in the mountains, in the shade, and the day was already beginning to swelter. Shoal Creek would be, as the CEO had said, hotter than the hub of hell.

The judge was a big man, 300-plus pounds, 6'3" tall with a Teddy Roosevelt mustache. "We may need to take your vehicle," the lawyer told the judge. "You're probably too big to ride comfortably in my car."

He told the judge about the window failure on the SUV.

"Oh, that's okay. I'll enjoy riding in your car." They loaded the judge's clubs and shoes into the trunk of the lawyer's car. "I don't get to ride in a Mercedes that often."

"I'm really looking forward to today," the judge said trying to adjust himself to the seat and having substantial difficulty wrapping the seat belt around his abundant girth. He could get it around him, but he could not push it far enough to get it locked. Click it or ticket, the lawyer thought.

"I haven't played golf more than ten times since the last time, but there's nothing like going to Shoal Creek," he said, giving up on the seat belt and letting it slide back into its return at the door.

"It's going to be hot," the lawyer replied. "You know, Shoal Creek lies down in a valley that holds the moisture and temperature in. The CEO said they have fans behind every green. He also said it is too hot to play down there today. But we're on. The CEO invited our mutual friend, Dr. Wilkey, and he declined the invitation because of the heat. Wilkey always was smarter than me or the CEO."

He started the car and the welcomed air conditioning came up. He had driven a little over three blocks when the judge's cell phone rang. He answered it,

"What?

" Is he alive?

" Can you see him breathing?

" Have you called 911?

"You hear the sirens?

"Oh, they're pulling in right now?

"Okay, call me back. My phone's on." The judge looked perturbed at the lawyer.

"That didn't sound good," the lawyer commiserated.

"That was my twelve-year-old son. He's working with his grandfather this summer in his locksmith shop in Gadsden. It's my wife's father. He just fell out in the floor. All the men are out on calls, and my son had the good sense to call 911. He heard them coming up."

"Do I need to take you to the hospital? We can cancel the golf match. I have the CEO's cell number in my automatic dial."

"Nah, there's not much I can do. He's breathing. He can't talk, but he seems to be all right for the shape he's in. There's nothing I can do. Let's play golf. My phone's on."

The lawyer thought, Hit and drag Shorty. He counseled once more, "Judge, I'm perfectly willing to drive you directly to the emergency room in Gadsden if you want."

"Go on to Birmingham. I'll keep up with it by phone."

The golfers proceeded out of Fort Payne on I-59 South toward Birmingham. The Judge's telephone rang before they had traveled six miles.

"Yeah, I talked to him. The 911 people have probably already taken him to the hospital."

"Do you think I need to come home or go to the hospital?"

"The only thing I can do is ooh and aah and stand around doing nothing.

"Okay, my phone's on. Let me know."

"That was my wife. She's going to Gadsden, to the hospital. I offered to go, but she told me to go on and play golf."

The lawyer thought, Yeah, I'll bet she did.

You're going to pay dearly for this one.

He offered again to take the judge to the hospital and was declined.

Fifteen miles down the interstate, the telephone rang again.

"Yeah, I know about it.

"He's at the ER."

"I don't know what's wrong with him.

"Yeah, that would be good if you did go over there. I imagine he's all right though.

"My wife is on her way down there. You know it is her father.

"My phone is on. Thanks."

Turning to the lawyer, "That was the guy who runs the business across the street from my father-in-law's shop. He saw the ambulance over there and wanted to know what was going on. He's going to the emergency room to check on him."

The conversation changed to law, the difficult job of being a judge, golf, and more golf.

Twenty-six miles out of Birmingham the judge received a report from his wife. His father-in-law's blood pressure was 60 over 40. There was no diagnosis at that point. They had taken him to the intensive care cardiac (ICC) unit.

At Shoal Creek the guard at the gate signed them in and they drove through the luxuriant shaded grounds, on the twisting road, to the club dropoff. The CEO was waiting with the caddy master. The clubs were unloaded, the caddies were assigned, and the lawyer parked the car.

The three golfers went to the nineteenth hole for lunch. Sitting among the original paintings of famous golfers who were members of the club, they enjoyed the spread that was sumptuous as usual. All three went for the seafood gumbo which was declared to be "Out of this world." Large pieces of crab meat, lobster, shrimp, oysters, the works. The meal was fine.

During lunch, the judge brought the CEO up to date about the condition of his father-in-law. The CEO raised his eyebrows and looked knowingly at the lawyer at his left of the table. The judge rose and went to the buffet for more gumbo.

"Either he has a father-in-law like some of mine have been, or it's hit and drag Shorty, You gotta admire a man like that," The CEO said under his breath to the lawyer while watching the judge.

"I think it's the latter. Let's hit that gumbo one more time." The friends rose and joined the judge at the soup terrine.

Lunch over, the golfers walked the heavily paneled hallway to the locker room. They changed into their golfing shoes before the CEO's mahogany locker.

"I didn't see anybody hitting golf balls," the CEO mentioned, indicating the heat. "If either of you guys have a heat stroke and pass out, don't expect me to give you mouth-to-mouth resuscitation because I won't."

"I don't want you to help that way. If it comes to that, just let me die," the lawyer chuckled.

As the lawyer and the judge picked up facial towels and headed for the practice tee, the CEO went to the pro shop. The guests began to hit a few balls. On the fourth ball with a wedge the lawyer had to use his face towel. He was sweating to the point perspiration was running down his sunglasses. The CEO joined them on the tee.

"The pro has an instrument up there that calculates the heat index at 122 degrees. We have the course to ourselves. There are no tee times until after 5:00 p.m."

He took out a wedge and began to warm up forcing his face towel into his belt.

The lawyer counted them. He had personally hit fourteen balls and quit. The judge was becoming soaked with perspiration but kept swinging. His caddy had begun to give him a lesson.

The CEO hit a total four balls and said, "I'm already warmed up. I think I'll putt a couple and be ready to go." He wiped the sweat off his face with his towel.

The lawyer went to the putting green with his

friend. He could barely see how to putt the ball due to the perspiration. His golf shirt was soaking wet. His cap was wet three inches up from the band. He knew that it was going to be a hard day. The Alabama sun continued to beam down at its raging inferno like zenith.

"Hit 'em up, Judge," the CEO instructed as the three reached the first tee.

"You walking?" the lawyer asked his friend.

"Yeah, I don't think I'll need a cart. I may get one at the turn."

The first hole at Shoal Creek teases a golfer into thinking the entire course will be like it. The fairway is wide, the roughs are narrow, with tall pine trees and hardwoods bordering each side. The green is in sight of the first tee, and for a par four, the hole is not that long. A good drive and a nine iron or long wedge can reach it easily in two. The green is large with slow left-to-right undulations. It is trapped only on the right side in the front. In short, it is a beautiful easy golf hole. It is a Jack Nicklaus dirty trick because the golfer is not going to see a hole that easy for six thousand more yards. Nicholas probably wanted to give the golfer confidence at the beginning of his round with an easy par or birdie. However, birdies don't come easy, even on number one. The green is very tricky and fast as a hard wood floor

The judge teed it up, took a couple of vicious practice swings, and put his 300 plus pounds into a drive that went long. But it also went right, far right. The lawyer thought it went over the trees and out of bounds, but he had vision problems due to perspiration.

"It probably hit a tree and stayed in," Jojo, the judge's caddy, assured him.

The lawyer was up next. He hit a 280 yard drive with a slight tail end fade. He was in the right rough, but his ball stayed out of the trees. The CEO hit it straight down the middle 260 yards. After he hit he immediately walked down the middle of the fairway trailed by his caddy, Jerry. The lawyer and the judge, along with Jojo the caddy, standing on the back bumper, rode the cart with the judge driving.

The group looked for the judge's ball. Five minutes went by, no luck. They fanned out and thoroughly searched the area where everyone thought the ball might have come down. The lawyer was using his facial towel regularly.

Finally, the CEO's caddy, Jerry, announced, "I found it. It's down in this hole."

The group examined the hole. It was precisely the size of a golf cup. It appeared someone had taken the cup boring tool and cut the hole in the rough. It was about 2 ½ to 3 feet deep, dark, overgrown with grass around the edges, but a golf ball was slightly visible in its foreboding depths.

Strange, thought the lawyer wiping more sweat.

Jerry rolled his eyes, "Judge, if you want to reach down in there and get your ball, it's okay with me. But I'm afraid of snakes."

"I ain't sticking my hand in there," Jojo said.

The judge bent over and peered down into the hole, poked the ball with the handle of a club, and said, "Give it up. I'm not reaching down in there either." It was truly an ominous hole.

"Just drop a ball, Judge," their host said. "It won't cost you a stroke. We found your ball, it's just in an unusual place. With a hole like that this close to the green, it has to be grounds under repair. It's just not marked." He walked toward his ball in the fairway.

The judge dropped his ball near the fairway in such a way as to avoid the trees. He hit toward the green and faded off to the right and into the trap.

The CEO hit his ball to the green, twenty feet from the pin. The lawyer hit his ball toward the flag, but was four yards short of the green. He had misjudged the distance. To himself, he blamed it on the sweat.

The judge took the cart toward the trap because the lawyer said that he would walk to the green. He was accompanied by Jojo.

"Look here, Jojo," the lawyer said in a low tone. "I started this game as a caddy. How many times have you guys used the old 'I found your ball down in the hole,' trick?"

Jojo gave a wide missing-front-tooth smile under his Shoal Creek green cap and just above his white caddy coveralls. "I ain't saying nothing, and don't axe me."

The lawyer had his answer.

The lawyer chipped past the cup. The green was faster than he thought it was, much faster than the practice putting green. As he walked across the hot green, cooled only by the giant oscillating fan about eight feet up on a 4' green steel pole, he noticed Jerry was driving his cart back toward the clubhouse with Jojo beside him. The golfers were left alone to putt out. As he tended the flag he saw that the caddies had left three drivers laying on the edge of the green in the direction of the tee. The CEO parred the hole. The judge was given a generous double bogey. The lawyer had a bogey five.

"What's going on," he asked the CEO. "Have we been abandoned by our caddies?"

"Hell, no," the CEO responded wiping more sweat. "I told them to go get a cart for me. I can't walk this course."

The lawyer chuckled to himself thinking, Yeah, "I'll get one at the turn." He made it one hole.

The heat was indescribable. Bottled water was in ice chests on every other tee. The three men were drinking three bottles of water a hole and carrying an extra one each just in case.

The lawyer tried to stay in the shade as much as he could, but the only relief he got was when the judge was driving the cart fast and he took his cap off to catch the warm breeze. The judge sweated so much that he had to hang his glove on the left cart top strut to catch the air and dry it to some degree.

Shoal Creek carts have tailights and horns. The steering wheel of the lawyer's cart was glistening with sweat from the judge's moisture-laden hands.

Jerry and Jojo returned with the CEO's cart soon after the golfers had teed off on number two. Number two is a long par four, dogleg right with the trees and a hazard in play. Shoal Creek, or an oversized wide deep ditch called Shoal Creek, meanders among the trees down the right edge of the fairway as it falls off to a green that is partially visible from the tee.

With a second cart, the game was on.

The lawyer noticed that each time his friend approached his ball, he had to use his little thin towel. By the middle of the third hole, a par five, it was not helping him as it was soaked. The CEO didn't wait for Jerry, he wiped his ball with it on the fifth green.

By the sixth hole, the lawyer began to believe that he was the most miserable he had ever been in his life. He had experienced 65 below zero during the Korean Conflict, but this heat was unbearable. By hole seven, he had decided that nine holes, if he could make it, would be enough. But, as hot as it was, the judge was having a good time. Strangely, his telephone was not ringing. The lawyer wondered if he had decided to turn it off during the round. He kept his thoughts to himself.

Going up the ninth fairway, a very long par four, dogleg left with trees and water in play, the lawyer sidled up to the CEO. "I've had enough. Why don't we call it a day at the end of nine. This is no fun. You can't shoot good golf on a day like this."

"Wilkey said it was too hot to play golf. We should have listened to him."

"Yeah, I know. He was always smarter than we were."

The CEO moved over to the rough and walked a little way with the judge. Soon he rejoined the lawyer in the fairway.

"I broached the subject with hizzoner, and he wants to keep playing."

At the turn, the golfers were given iced towels and Gatorade approaching the tee to the tenth hole.

"Boys," the lawyer addressed the group utilizing his iced towel. "I've had enough. I can't make it nine more holes."

"Well, I'd like to play. What about you?" the judge asked the CEO.

"I'll play, but it is mighty hot. I had just as soon not."

"What about cutting across at fourteen?" Jojo joined the conversation. "You can play five holes. That way you get to play the signature hole."

At the Jack Nicklaus signature hole, the group agreed and drove the carts up the steep non-slip rubber Parque-coated path to the tee. The signature hole is at least 80 feet, perhaps more, above the fairway leading to a well-trapped green. It's a long uphill par four. 230 yards out from the elevated tee, the hole's fairway is trapped long, maybe 75 yards, on the right side to catch all slicers and faders in its bunker.

It's truly a beautiful sight to be up on the elevated tee and look out over Shoal Creek concentrating on the wide lush fairway toward the green. Then the golfer drives the ball out into the vast open space where it seems to drop for several seconds to the fairway or the bunker. It reminded the lawyer of some of the courses in the North Carolina mountains where they had played when they were young. It also reminded him of seventeen at Eagle Vail.

The group teed off from the elevated tee. Both the judge and the lawyer went into the bunker on the right. The CEO was right down the middle.

And so the torture begins again, thought the lawyer re-mounting the white cart on the passenger side.

The group finished the par five seventeenth and almost made it to the eighteenth tee before the thunder and lightning came, a typical Alabama summer thunderstorm. The lawyer was sitting in the cart near the tee when a flash of lightening appeared fairly close. He looked up and noticed that the taller trees had ground wires running from their tops to the ground. Not a good sign, he thought.

Then the rain came in torrents. "Let's make a run for it!" the lawyer yelled to the judge and the CEO.

"Let's tee off at least," the CEO said. "We can't be anymore wet than we already are."

With the thunder rolling and the rain coming down, the golfers teed off on the long downhill eighteenth hole with its green near the clubhouse. When the last ball was struck, the thunder roared! As an exclamation point, the storm horn terminating play sounded from the pro shop at the clubhouse in the distance.

"I'm picking up my ball and getting the hell out of here!" the lawyer shouted to the others above the din.

"I'm with you," the CEO screamed back, trying to fight off the rain unsuccessfully with his umbrella. He had it open and was holding it beyond the front of the cart. The rain was coming in over it and around it. However, it probably did some good.

The golfers raced down the long hill that was

the eighteenth fairway, the caddies picked up the balls and the group rode as fast as the carts would run toward the clubhouse. The rain was picking up in intensity, now coming down in sheets, the lightning was cracking and the thunder claps were louder and closer. The heart of the storm was moving directly toward the golf course. The carts were speeding across the puddles and wet grass toward the safehaven of the massive clubhouse. The noise was deafening.

All I need is to be struck by lightning after a day like this, the lawyer thought.

By the time they reached safety, the rain had increased even more substantially, if it was possible. Soaking wet, totally exhausted, the golfers went to the locker room, toweled off, put on their street shoes, and went to the nineteenth hole for drinks.

"If anybody says anything, we were bringing this course to its knees when we were driven by the weather," the CEO suggested.

"I don't know if I'm that big a liar. I shot near fifty on the front nine," the lawyer replied. "But I'll try."

The drinks were uneventful. They had the nineteenth hole and the snacks to themselves.

The pro put his head in the door, "Weather run you boys in? How far did you get?"

"We got to the eighteenth hole and had the course by the throat, but the weather killed our round," the CEO answered laughing.

"Yeah," the pro smiled. "I'll bet. Too bad the weather cought you. You'd have probably shot the course record."

An hour later, when the rain let up, the lawyer and judge packed their belongings back into the lawyer's vehicle and headed out of Shoal Creek bound for Fort Payne. They were not out of Hugh Daniel Drive when the judge's telephone rang.

"Oh, okay. I'm on my way home now.

"I'll be there in a little while.

"Aw, that's too bad.

"Well, we'll talk about it when I get there.

"My phone is still on."

He turned to the lawyer. "That was my wife. My father-in-law had a massive heart attack. He is going to have to remain in the CCU until next week when they'll do a quadruple by-pass. Sounds like it must have been serious."

"Well, at least he's still alive," the lawyer opined.

The CEO pulled up alongside them at a red light in the middle lane of Highway 280. The lawyer rolled down his window. The CEO followed suit.

"His father-in-law had a massive heart attack and has to have a quadruple by-pass," the lawyer yelled to his friend.

"That's too bad," the CEO replied sympathetically. "It was just too damned hot to drag Shorty anyway, but we came close."

The judge didn't know what they were talking about. Why should he? It was an old joke.

Twice in one lifetime, the lawyer thought. That old pro didn't know he was a prophet when he told us that joke almost sixty years ago.

Golf must be a sickness. People contort their bodies in a way nature never intended just to hit a golf ball. Yet, it gets in your blood to the point one man goes back on the course after a heart attack and another abandons his father-in-law when he has a heart attack, all for the game of golf in excruciating heat. At least, the judge kept his phone on.

The lawyer had never really considered the impact the game had had on his life. Here he was, he and his life-long buddy, both driving toward North Alabama after suffering through the worst torment imaginable on the golf course. But on reflection, the scorching sun, the humidity, the thunder storms, they really didn't matter. All the years they had played the game they had always considered it athletics played outside in all kinds of weather. He could remember playing on a day so cold they bought a butane bottle and heater to keep the cart warm. They used it to warm their hands before striking the ball on the frozen earth. "Golfers must be slightly insane."

He remembered back to when they were playing golf three or four times a week. His young wife had taken it as long as she could stand it - tournaments every weekend, lessons when there were no tournaments, travel, evening leagues. Finally she had realized that she was a golf widow.

One summer day he came in after being married less than five years out of the forty-six years the marriage would last, "It's either golf or me!" she screamed into his sunburned face under his sweaty golf cap as he came in the front door at dark from a tough golf match.

The lawyer hesitated unbelieving. He was taken aback; he was in shock. He stood there in the twilight, in the doorway, and thought for a minute. Finally, as his wife glared angrily at him, hands on hips, viewing him in total disgust, he said, "Pack your bags."

How dare her come between him and golf. Even at that moment of hesitation and life changing contemplation, he had thought about Joe dragging Shorty. Golf is not a game; it's an obsession.

PAM

His secretary cracked the door between her office and the lawyer's office for the first time that morning. He looked up from his computer keyboard to meet her glance as she stuck her head through the opening.

"A Mrs. Gayle Darwin is here to see you," said the secretary. "She does not have an appointment, and I am not sure what she wants."

The lawyer had a full catalog of interests outside of his career, and technology was on the top of his list. He was the first lawyer in town to have a computer, the first to have a fax machine, and probably the first to have an intercom system. But breaking old habits was not on his list of interests, and therefore the intercom never suffered from overuse. It seemed much easier to yell through the door.

"Darnell," thought the lawyer, misinterpreting the name given him by the secretary. "I don't know any Darnell," he said out loud. "Send her in."

The lawyer swung his high-back leather chair around from the computer toward the table desk that separated him from three blue leather English banking chairs placed for clients along the opposite mahogany-paneled wall. His chair was the command center of his fortress. The front rampart was a large, leather-topped table desk with three deep drawers. This segregated him from his clients. On the right side of the table top was his telephone and client log sheet; in the front middle was a fancy gold-plated pen and pencil set; to the left front, adjacent to the wall, was an unobtrusive University of Alabama lamp; and a small ancient bronze fox holding a platter of business cards. To his left was a small cabinet of four drawers with brass knobs. His telephone books and diary were on its surface against a wall that held some of his degrees, licenses, a few pictures, a painting of Abraham Lincoln holding a book in one hand and an axe in the other, and his own pastel rendition of the Denny Chimes at the University of Alabama.

Behind him, and against the wall separating his office from the staff, was an immense antique mahogany roll top desk made by the Derby Company in Boston in 1914.

This desk, in mint condition, held much of his work in its numerous compartments and drawers. On its top were family pictures, another University of Alabama lamp, a statue of Denny Chimes, and a radio taken from his grandfather's dairy barn in 1937. It was a Philco, tuned to WSM in Nashville, in hopes the country music would keep the cows contented and they would give more milk.

To his right was a small, modern, pressed-board computer desk, covered in brown wood grained sticky paper, and supporting the latest in computer wizardry. A small opening between the computer desk and the table provided the only entry into the stronghold. His high-backed blue leather chair rolled around on a large plastic office carpet protector.

A gnome-like, seemingly elderly, woman hobbled from the hallway through the entrance to the lawyer's office. She was way overly made up, heavy rouge and face powder, with large watery blue eyes, a pug nose, and a heart-shaped mouth filled with darkened teeth. An imitation pearl necklace rested on her dark blue blouse. The blue blouse was tucked into a conservative white polyester skirt. The woman looked toward the lawyer with anticipation. Reaching toward him with two pudgy hands, she almost dropped the flat black patent leather purse hinged under her left arm.

"Pam!" exclaimed the lawyer, jumping to his feet. He clipped through the small entrance-way and around the table. "It's so good to see you!" he said as he hugged the woman.

Only 4'9" tall, and twenty pounds overweight, she reached around the lawyer's waist and hugged him. She put her cheek against his chest and grunted loudly as she tightened her hold.

Gayle Darwin stood watching in the doorway. Tears welled up in her eyes, and she smiled at the sight of the lawyer and her sister-in-law embracing.

"Are you glad to see him?" asked Gayle.

Before Pam could respond, the lawyer said, "Hey, this is my baby. This is my Pam."

Pam glowed in the attention. She giggled and spoke with a pronounced impediment, "I knowed he would be glad to see Pam."

"Well, sit down, sit down. Come on in Gayle. It's good to see you. It's so good to see you. I thought a Mrs. Darnell was coming in. I had no idea it was Pam. And Pam looks so good!"

The two women took chairs. Gayle explained that they needed a document prepared for Pam to sign which might help Pam gain admission to a school for retarded children. She needed to write a short history of Pam's life and disability. This would have to be in affidavit form with Pam's signature notarized. This was a necessary first step for Pam to receive the admission application to a retarded children's school in Talladega where she might learn to read and write.

"She can dial a telephone, remember up to seven numbers, operate the dishwasher and the television set," Gayle bragged about the retarded woman.

"We are seeing progress every day. We've bought a small travel trailer, and next week Pam is going to move into her own place. She thinks she can take care of the place. She is very excited."

"Dats wite," Pam added in her usual choppy and slurred syntax. "If I tan learn to weed and wite, I tink I dwil be aba to funton wit uhders."

"That's great," returned the lawyer. He had spent enough time through the years around Pam to understand her language.

"I'm so happy for you. I'll just pull up a form in my computer here, and we'll take care of it right now." He swivelled around to face the computer.

"We didn't mean for you to do it right now," Gayle apologized. "We know you are busy. We just wanted to talk about it today."

"Nah, no problem," the lawyer assured Gayle as he scanned the indices on his computer screen for an affidavit form. "Here it is right now. It won't take but a minute. Pam needs that schooling."

The lawyer began to insert the correct names and phrases into the document. He made smalltalk with Pam while he briefly traced her history.

The computer sent the finished document to the printer near the secretary's desk. The lawyer went through the door to the secretary's office to retrieve the document.

"Can she sign this paper?" the lawyer asked Gayle as he returned to his office.

"I tan sign," interjected Pam. "But Dale dwil

haf to dwaw it for me fust."

"Well, let's go into the library then. We can sit at the table in there and have lots of room." The lawyer led a procession down the hall to the library.

"We'll need a pad so she can practice," Gayle said when they had reached the library. The lawyer returned to his office to retrieve a yellow legal pad.

"She will have to sign Pamela Darwin," he told the women.

"Oh, that will be almost impossible," Gayle said. She can only sign "Pam."

"What about Darwin? Can she write her last name?" returned the lawyer.

"Maybe she can, if I draw it for her first," answered Gayle.

Gayle printed in large letters, 'Pam Darwin.' She turned the legal pad over to Pam. "Do you think you can write that, Pam?" asked Gayle.

"I tink I tan, but you'll haff to hep me."

The library was one large room with shelving floor to ceiling everywhere except for the old double-windowed entrance door. Books were running over and some were double shelved, i.e., books were in front of each other. A large thick glass-topped library table, which seated eight people, dominated the maroon carpeted room. The chairs were carved wooden arm and back rest seating that appeared to be very similar to dining room chairs. The lawyer sat at the head of the table while Pam and Gayle sat to his immediate right.

Gayle helped Pam practice writing her name in a printed scrawl. She attempted to teach Pam to draw a straight line to make the first part of the P, then a small circle to complete the letter. The A was made of three straight lines, two tilted toward each other and one like a ladder. The M was two small mountains. Drawing for Pam required quite a bit of imagination.

Pam passed the practice session in labored stokes. Finally, it was time to execute the legal documents.

Pam sat up to the table and spread wide her elbows for leverage. Her face was nearly touching the paper as she tilted her head to the right. Her tongue worked slowly over the left side of her upper lip as she drew out the letters.

Slowly, ever so slowly, she traced the lines drawn by Gayle.

"Whew!" She let out a big breath when she had finished.

"Okay, she has signed the original, and we'll just run copies for the others," suggested the lawyer.

"I'm sorry she was not able to do 'Pamela,'" Gayle apologized.

"That's okay," responded the lawyer in an attempt to reassure Gayle as well as to give

Pam some confidence. "I'll notarize the document as signed by 'Pamela' even though she only writes 'Pam.' I know what she is intending to do and why."

"After I send the original off, do I need to record the document, just for safekeeping?" questioned a relieved Gayle.

"No, it won't be necessary. But, you are going to have to do several other things if you need to transfer the property in order for her to qualify for the school," the lawyer instructed.

"How much I owe you?" Pam asked the lawyer. She unsnapped her black patent leather purse.

"You don't owe me a thing, Baby," said the lawyer, "I'm your lawyer."

"I know dat. A man tum to da door the udder day an tri to start double. I tole him you my lawyer and he leff me alone."

Pam looked smug as she thought about the idea of having her own lawyer.

"Well, I sure am," the lawyer said walking with the women into the waiting room.

"Good luck, Pam. I hope you get into that school and learn to read and write."

He patted Pam on the shoulder as she left.

"Every time I see that woman I almost cry," the lawyer said as he walked back past the secretary's desk. "I'm on the verge of tears now."

"Is that the Pam you told me about?" asked

the secretary.

"Yeah, did you ever know Pam's mother?"

"No, but I heard about her," replied the secretary. She dabbed her eyes with a tissue as she remembered the story of Pam.

The lawyer returned to his office, closed both doors, sat in his chair, and thought about the life of Pam. And, of course, he thought about Pam's mother Mable, for Pam's story was hopelessly written by Mable, as Mable's life, in turn, was written by those generations before her who had come to homestead the Great Cumberland Plateau, locally called Sand Mountain.

Mable Darwin, Pam's mother, first came into the lawyer's office in 1965. Mable was a woman with a modified hairlip. She spoke in a loud tone with a speech impediment. She pointed out repeatedly that she was a college graduate. Her degree came from a correspondence school – La Salle in Chicago. Mable was very proud of her accomplishment. She had studied law as part of her selected curriculum.

Notwithstanding the legal correspondence courses, she did not know enough about the law to handle her own problem. So when the correspondence school wrote to her refusing to send her diploma, for some reason not understood by Mable, she loaded   up her daughter Pam and headed down to the valley town of Fort Payne.

Fort Payne is the county seat of DeKalb County, Alabama. Large, white-columned antebellum houses dot the valley in remembrance of once-promising ore deposits found in the early boom days shortly after the Civil War. When the deposits bore little profit, the steel industry moved South to Birmingham. Fort Payne and its empty mills floundered along until mid century when a few entrepreneurs decided to open hosiery mills in the vacant, cheap-to-rent, mill buildings. By the 1970's, Fort Payne was the self-proclaimed, "sock capital of the world."

Seated in the middle of Fort Payne is the county courthouse flanked by old homes turned into lawyer's offices. The lawyer Mable sought out had a recently made well-known name up on Sand Mountain. He had great success defending Sand Mountain bootleggers when the federal government decided to put an end to the lucrative white whiskey trade. They called it, "Operation Dry Up -- Moonshine Kills!" The lawyer had won seven white whiskey cases in a row.

When he met the two ladies for the first time, the lawyer attempted to talk to Mable's daughter, Pamela. One of the first things Mable told the lawyer was that Pam was retarded. Pam was hardly able to converse.

The lawyer soon learned that Mable had mental problems of her own. She suffered from very severe mental problems that were hidden by her intervals of lucid competence. Mable could function in society. She even had superior abilities in some areas. For example, Mable could speed read and was able to pass the correspondence school classes. But, Mable's personality wasn't exempt from heredity. After she retrieved some "misplaced" courses, with a letter from the lawyer, La Salle issued her a diploma.

Alabama was part of the Mississippi Territory in the American West when Mable's ancestors fled the boundaries encompassing civilization that had become the resulting states of the east coast. The stubborn Scotch-Irish people brought from the old country a distrust of government and a desire for autonomy.

As the cities, towns, and villages grew, they left and headed west. The north end of Sand Mountain, the part of the Great Cumberland Plateau where Georgia, Tennessee, and Alabama converge, offered freedom and independence for Mable's forefathers who were willing to work hard.

Sand Mountain offered cheap, unsettled land, and only a rare visit from the tax collector or the census taker. In return, it exacted a tough life. The sandy soil made farming a difficult endeavor even in good years. Long, hot dry summers kept farm animals skinny and unproductive.

Running north to south, from Tennessee some 90 miles to Birmingham, and from east to west some 30 miles, Sand Mountain is the most densely populated total rural area in the world.

Although some citizens joined the North or South during the Civil War, Sand Mountain remained a Union stronghold. It was a rich man's war and a poor man's fight, and the people on Sand Mountain were having none of it.

Pavement and telephone wires crawled up the edge of Sand Mountain long after running through most parts of the country. Until after WWII, the area was considered one of the most isolated areas in the United States. It was common for some wag to say, "The people on Sand Mountain know they're up there, they just don't know we're down here."

Time Line: 1897 - **Ethel Elaine Maxwell, Mable's mother was born on the north end of Sand Mountain.**

The hard mountain life commanded strict living. Communities were small, tightly-knit, and wary of outsiders. The farm offered no rest and no time off. A few snapped under the strenuous tedium of Sand Mountain life.

In addition, there were outlaws, bootleggers, and other unsavory characters going about who were mostly unchecked by lawmen. Up until the late 1950's the Sheriffs of DeKalb and Jackson Counties would not proceed north of Ider, Alabama, into the area called the "Big Woods" for fear of their lives. Folks in that area had the reputation that they shot first and asked questions later.

For those who chose to lead a "good life," there was no rest and no escape from the taxing banality of raising a family on the mountain. The one single exception was church on "go to meetin' day." Sunday was more than a day of rest. It was a social gathering, a place where boy met girl, and a place to vent for the little spoken, hard working, mild mannered farmers.

Time Line: 1927 - **Mable was born in the family home, on the Maxwell Farm, near Henagar, Alabama.**

Luther Maxwell, Mable's father and Pam's grandfather, was somewhat of a strange man. Working from sunup until sundown, he was a dirt farmer during the week and a fiery evangelist on the weekend. As a young girl, Mable watched her father, an average man with thick cropped black hair and a ruddy complexion, dressed in faded and worn overalls, sweat silently under the relentless Alabama sun doing backbreaking toil day in and day out. The family did not have running water nor electricity. Mable used an outhouse all of her life. At night, when Luther came in, he said little as he washed up in the wash bowl, ate his supper, and went to bed.

But on Sunday, Preacher Luther Maxwell was a different man. In his worn out brown suit, in an old white shirt, with a frayed collar, and a tie with gravy stains on it, Mable hardly knew him. As a child, she would cling to her mother's leg from the first pew as her father ranted, and screamed and danced and sang. He clapped his hands and fell to his knees. He looked to the sky and shook his head. He trembled, and he cried. Finally, when he was completely worn out, he would sing in unison with the congregation.   They said that he preached so hard that churchgoers could smell the fire and brimstone from the gates of hell. Then, on Monday he was sane again.

Time Line: 1934 - **Susan Jane, Mable's sister was born.**

Although deathly afraid of him due to his Sunday escapades, Mable dearly loved her father and was very close to him. Susan, seven years younger than Mable, was closer to their mother.

Time Line: 1940 - **Mable's father, Luther Arnold Maxwell, died of cancer at age 67.**

Mable was only 12 years old when her father died. She was in the 6th grade at North Sand Mountain School. That was the last year that she would attend public school. She had to stay home and take care of her mother and younger sister who had become dependent upon her to do the housework, cook meals, and generally do whatever needed to be done to keep the three females going.

They lived in a small two bedroom, living room and kitchen, "shotgun" house. That's the kind of house you can open the front door and shoot a shotgun through the house and the shot would go out the back door. It was a common house built by Mable's father and grandfather out of roughcut lumber from the sawmill they put together on the farm. They first built the barn, tool shed and pigsty. Then, while building the elder Maxwell's house, they built the same house for Mable's father. It was located about 60 feet from the first house. Neither of the homes had ever been painted, but after forty years in the weather, they were passable. The parents had always occupied one bedroom, and the girls slept in the same bed in the other bedroom.

Water for both houses came from a shared "freestone" well between the houses. However, each residence had its own outhouse. Although the houses sat on the north side of a very well traveled road from Henagar to Valley Head, Alabama the road was not paved until 1961. The homes sat on sixty acres that had been homesteaded by Mable's father's family and had been passed down from Chester Arthur, President of the United States, by way of a land grant.

Despite Mable's care, her mother rejected her, and remained loyal to the baby, younger sister Susan.

Whenever Mable would displease her mother, she would tell her to "go out behind the barn and get religion."

The feeling of insecurity suffered by Mable at her father's death, the feeling of inability to please her mother, and the great responsibilities hurled upon Mable as a mere child, would have lifelong effects on Mable's psyche.

Time Line: 1944 - Mable marries Harold Darwin.

To get out of the living hell in which she was involved, Mable married at age sixteen and had a son Danny one year later in 1945. She and her husband worked in a hosiery mill in Fort Payne while her mother kept their infant son. Her mother became very close to her grandson and offered Mable and her husband the other family home on her property. This was the house where Mable had been born and raised.

When Mable's grandfather had passed away, as a widower, Ethel and Luther had moved into his house as Luther was the only heir, and the furniture in that house was better. This house was a mirror image of the home where Mable had lived, only it was further off the road by about twenty feet. The Darwins were glad to have this accommodation as they didn't have to pay rent, and they were close enough that Ethel Maxwell was readily available for keeping Danny.

Mable's mother had a will drawn equally dividing the Maxwell property between Mable and Susan. The younger daughter got the property where the older house was located, and Mable was given the property where she was living with her family.

The Darwins did relatively well during the period immediately after WWII. Both were employed bringing home a check weekly. They did not have to pay rent, and they could truck farm on the property behind the house bringing in extra money from produce they grew.

Time Line: 1950 - Pam was born to the Darwins.

The birth of Pamela in 1950, resulted in Mable being forced to leave her job. Immediately following the birth of Pam, Mable began to experience great feelings of nervousness. She suffered from post-partum depression. Although she was able to return to work while her mother kept both children, she was hospitalized on numerous occasions between 1953 and 1955 for nervousness and exhaustion. She had a hysterectomy in 1955.

Money was tight, and Mable continued to work when she could which was most of the time. She worked in hosiery mills until 1964 and worked in a glove mill for three months in 1965.

Time Line: 1965 - **Mable visits the lawyer for a second time.**

With two children and a chronically ill wife, Harold became a typical hosiery mill Romeo. That is, he kept himself clean, looked as good as he could, flirted with as many women on the job as he could, and scored with the ladies on a regular basis. He grew distant from his family.

Mable learned that her husband was having an affair in 1965. She visited the lawyer stating that she wanted a divorce. The lawyer met with her and her husband Harold and persuaded them to reconcile. Unfortunately, Harold could not stay away from his mistress, and he and Mable went through an uncontested divorced.

Time Line: 1967 - **Mable and Harold were finally divorced.**

The divorce seemed to emancipate Harold, and he began to move from woman to woman in the hosiery mill society. As a result of his romantic inclinations, Mable's ex-husband wanted little to do with his children Danny and Pam. Mable worked at various jobs in hosiery mills, school lunchrooms and mill-town cafeterias attempting to support herself and her children. She returned to the lawyer time and again to take Harold back to court and force him to pay his child support and provide medical care for Pam.

Mable's mental problems progressed and she could not keep a job long because she would get into very loud arguments with co-workers or supervisors. Fortunately for herself and the children, she usually worked for a time long enough to continue drawing unemployment compensation. Other times, she had to quit her job because her mother would quit babysitting Pam. Danny was old enough to fend for himself. Pam was a different matter entirely.

Time Line: 1970 - Mable is seriously injured in an automobile accident.

While on her way to work on the evening shift, a drunk driver swerved into Mable's lane and hit her head-on. She suffered a broken right leg and a collapsed lung. She could not work during a long convalescent period. When she recovered well enough to get about, she visited the lawyer, who took her case. After several months, he was successful in recovering a $35,000 settlement for her. This was a lot of money at that time, and it allowed her to pay off debts she owed and participate in some modicum of enjoyment – a new car, new clothes, and everything Pam could possibly need.

Interestingly, Mable had her little house covered with imitation brick. That was rolled roofing material with bricks imprinted on one side. When it was applied properly, it looked like real brick from a distance. Mable's siding was not applied properly and looked like an old house with imitation brick roofing material nailed up on it all around. But it did keep the house a little warmer in the winter and a little cooler in the summer.

When Mable went back to work, her mother rarely did more than a six-week stint as day care provider for Pam before quitting. Mable was moving job to job due to her inability to get along at work. The family's life continued in this mode until Mable was forced to quit working at the shirt factory known as Sand Mountain Manufacturing Company in 1972. It would be the last time she would ever work.

Time Line: 1972 - Mable diagnosed with anxiety reaction and chronic colitis.

In 1973, Mable was 47 years old. Susan was 39 and had been married to an engineer with TVA in Chattanooga for more than 15 years. Pam was now 23 years old and hopelessly retarded.

Mable had never allowed Pam to go to school. When the truancy officer came to Mable's house, she would not budge. Danny had insisted that his mother allow his sister to at least try school, but she would not. She initially claimed that Pam was sick and could not go to school. Finally, Mable was taken before a judge who ordered Mable to put Pam in school.

For five days Pam rode the school bus with Danny to the country school. Danny fought with foes as well as friends for those five days. Pam looked normal enough to the other children but her sputtering voice subjected her to unusual childhood torture.

On Pam's first day, Danny attempted to sit with Pam, translate for her, and help her with the simple tasks handed out to a first grader. Of course, the teacher would not hear of Danny skipping his own studies to sit by Pam all day.

Mable couldn't stand her baby being away at school. And so on the second day, Mable came to the school and visited Pam's first grade class. Mable screamed at the teacher for the next three days. Investigators came out to Pam's house and were satisfied that Mable was telling the truth about Pam's mental condition. Mable talked for Pam the entire time; and, as a result, the truancy officer and the teachers agreed that Pam could be kept at home with her mother. That was the end of Pam's educational experience, five days. Five days of torment for Pam, first because of the students, then because of her mother.

Danny still spent as much time as he could entertaining Pam after school and on weekends. They would take long hikes around the farm and through the adjoining woods. Mable would stand in the back doorway and watch Danny and Pam, two small figures walking through the tall grass to the cow pond, one figure with a fishing pole over his shoulder. Pam would sit beside Danny and babble aimlessly while Danny cast and re-cast his line.

Pam also enjoyed the little animals Danny cought in his traps throughout the farm. After examining the squirrels, rabbits, opossums, and other small animals himself, Danny would pass them to Pam. Pam was usually too rough with them, and they would leap from her hands to freedom. Danny laughed loudly at Pam's feeble attempt to run after an escaping critter. He laughed even harder when Pam would give up, turn around to face him, and say, "nudder one," before laughing herself.

Danny graduated from high school with high marks. He got a job in a hosiery mill as a fixer. He was a young man on his way up. As he had grown up, Mable had became more and more mentally ill. Unfortunately, Pam grew more dependent on Mable for entertainment and companionship.

Back In 1970, since Pam had become an adult, Mable came to see the lawyer about a petition for her to be Pam's legal guardian.

Pam was now twenty years old, and Mable demanded to be her legal guardian. "I want it legal," she said.

By 1975, Mable's mother was now 77 years old and suffering from a variety of maladies. She became more and more infirm; and she had less and less patience with Mable, Pam and their problems.

Mable liked living on the farm where she had grown up as it provided a safe nest for her and her children. With Danny married and living away, the old farm grew up around Mable's house and her mother's house. Mable and her mother never became friends. As Mable's mother aged she became so disgusted with Mable and Pam that she would no longer speak to either of them. Ethel would not evict Mable and Pam, but she told Mable that if she came on her property again, she would call the law.

Mable had been making her mother's life miserable by constantly coming to her front door, or up to her porch, and screaming incoherently at her. Ethel didn't know what she was talking about, and neither did Mable. It was the screaming and ravings of a maniac.

After her mother's warning, Mable would go to what was known as the "dividing line," the center of the driveway between the two houses, and yell to her mother. Mable would do this each and every time she saw her mother out of doors, particularly when she was sitting in her swing on her porch.

Ethel enjoyed sitting on her front porch swing and waving to the neighbors and church members driving past. However, Mable's tirades made this nearly impossible to relax and enjoy anything. Finally, Mable's mother had a neighbor-church member nail up 3 sheets of 4' X 8' X ½" plywood on the side of the porch facing Mable's house. Then she could sit in her swing, and Mable couldn't see her. She wore house slippers and oiled the porch swing chains so Mable could not hear her nor know she was there.

Still, if a car's horn blew, or if Mable saw someone wave, she would proceed directly to the dividing line and scream, "I know you're out there, you old hag! You're going to die and roast in hell! Your tongue will be cut out by the devil himself!" And on and on it went until her mother would go into the house and slam the screen door so Mable would know she was gone.

Danny came by as often as time permitted to check on his mother and grandmother. Mable would be on her best behavior when he came. He would make minor repairs on each of their houses. During these visits, he paid special attention to Pam. Pam never failed to relish Danny's visits. She always giggled in anticipation when she heard his pickup turn into the driveway.

Danny suggested sending Pam off to school every time he visited, but Mable would either ignore him or go into one of her mentally deranged tongue-lashings. Danny even visited the lawyer on his own, and on one occasion he asked if there was anything that could be done to have Pam sent to a school where she could learn to be self-supporting.

The lawyer informed him that, with Mable as her guardian, as long as Pam's basic needs were provided for, there wasn't anything that could be done. "Besides," explained the lawyer, "Pam leads a happy life and things may as well remain status quo as long as Mable is able to care for Pam."

Danny didn't like it, but there was nothing more to be done.

The lawyer often had visits from Mable and Pam. He felt remorse for both of them. However, it appeared that Mable was doing the best she could to take care of Pam.

Mable drove her old car from place to place always with Pam in the seat beside her looking out the window. Mable talked constantly to Pam about whatever was on her mind. Often, Mable's voice would grow louder and louder into a screaming crescendo before Mable would suddenly return to her normal tone of voice. Pam would just sit in the seat beside her silently, looking out the window.

By 1976, Mable was in serious trouble financially. Her ex-husband had never regularly contributed by paying the court-ordered child support. Danny had his own family and was unable to help out. Mable had become so irritable that she could not work around others.

She decided to visit the lawyer for help in getting social security disability benefits. Mable had suffered a back injury during her last employment at the garment factory in 1972 while cutting cloth. She claimed to have several ruptured discs, but her doctors couldn't find any, and thus Mable had been denied benefits when she applied. She asked the lawyer to apply for an appeal hearing before an administrative law judge.

When Mable came into the lawyer's office to inquire about the appeal, Pam was, as always, with her. While Mable raved on to the lawyer about her injured back, Pam sat totally quiet.

"Stop jabbering so much, Pam," the lawyer teased the young woman.

Pam smiled a dark toothy grin. The lawyer always teased Pam a little, and she expected him to say something to her. He didn't know how far he could go with the girl, so he was careful. Additionally, the lawyer knew Mable didn't appreciate his aggravating her poor retarded daughter.

After gathering all the medical and work

history of Mable going back to 1944, the lawyer told Mable point blank that she could not get social security benefits based upon her back trouble. She had simply not suffered a disabling injury. The lawyer then carefully broached a sensitive subject with his old client.

"How bad do you need the benefits?" he asked, looking directly at Mable.

"We've got to have it. I can't work no more. My mother won't tend to Pam. I can't leave Pam alone. Danny tries to help when he can but he's got his own family to think of. We're drawing some welfare based on Pam's disability, but I have to have more money. We can't live through another winter without help."

The lawyer knew Mable had been diagnosed with anxiety reaction and colitis since 1973. He had watched her over the years and knew that she had been sinking further and further into mental illness.

"Well, if you really need it, I can tell you how to get it. You may not like it, but it is the only way you can get the benefits."

"How? I'll do anything for Pam. If only her daddy would help out, but he won't."

The lawyer looked over at Pam. She was silently looking around the office as she always did. The lawyer felt sincere compassion for Pam. What? he wondered, was going through her demented mind as he and her mother were talking.

"If you'll do anything, you can get the benefits," said the lawyer. He hesitated. He truly hated to say what he was about to say, but he felt that he had to give his client every opportunity to collect the benefits that she was entitled to receive.

"You'll have to have a mental evaluation by a psychiatrist. I believe he will say you have been and are mentally deficient to the point you'll be entitled to Social Security disability benefits."

Complete silence enclosed the room as the lawyer waited for the explosion, and it wasn't long in coming.

"I'm not crazy!" Mable exclaimed. "How dare you think I'm mentally deficient. I have a college degree. I will not lie to get money. Me and Pam will starve first." Mable was indignant.

The lawyer thought she would walk out. She didn't, but she was fuming.

"Look Mable, I'm your lawyer. Talking to me is like talking to yourself. I would never ask you to lie or mislead anyone for money. But I have represented you for more than 20 years. I got your divorce. I got you damages from your wreck. I had you appointed guardian for Pam. I can go on and on. But, Mable, I think you have severe mental problems. Now think about it, who do you get along with?"

Mable stopped fuming and thought long and

hard. After several minutes, with her semi-hairlipped lipped accent she slowly said, "I guess Pam is the only person I get along with. My sister hates me. My mother stopped talking to me some time ago. My son doesn't come around no more. The people I worked with don't like me. People always misunderstand me. My preacher asked me to stop coming to church. Can you believe that? A preacher asked a church member, who tithed all she could, not to come to church. No, I ain't got no friend in the world. I donno, I guess Pam is the only one who likes me."

"Mable, it's not the people. Everyone can't be wrong. It's Mable. Now, what do you say? Can I make an appointment for you and appeal your social security case?"

"Well, I guess so. I don't like it one bit. But, I'm desperate. I do get nervous sometimes, and I do have bad dreams, and I can't keep my mind on anything for any span of time. I even have trouble reading now," Mable said aloud.

The lawyer nodded his head sympathetically.

"Okay," Mable finally said, "If you think it will get us the benefits, go ahead."

The lawyer filled out the necessary forms, made an appointment for his client with a psychiatrist, and generally began to prepare a new social security claim for Mable Darwin.

Mable did as she was told. When her

appointment time arrived, she spent four long hours with the psychiatrist. When he filed his report with the lawyer, the psychiatrist reported that Mable was bipolar schizophrenic, and hopelessly insane. The doctor was surprised that she was passing in society. He stopped just short of saying she was a clear and present danger to herself and to society in general.

The psychiatrist noted that Mable had unmet dependency needs, a desire to be taken care of by others, and felt threatened by her husband's divorce and by her retarded daughter's dependency upon her. The psychiatrist also noted that Mable felt inferior to some people but attributed this to their attitudes. Of course, during the examination, the psychiatrist also got a taste of Mable's temper and her ability to misconstrue what people were saying.

The lawyer reapplied for benefits based upon this examination. The hearing before the Administrative Law Judge on the back injuries was dismissed, and the new claim was set for reprocessing.

After several months, the lawyer and Mable went Gadsden, Alabama, to meet with a social security examiner regarding the new filing. Pam rode in the back seat of the lawyer's automobile. She didn't say a word during the trip. Mable carried all the conversation. She would start on one subject until her voice reached it's raging heights, and then she would turn to a new subject and repeat the process all over again. The lawyer found it to be a little nerve-wracking.

Out of curiosity and some degree of boredom, the lawyer would sometimes ask questions designed to set Mable to screaming. Or if Mable was already screaming, the lawyer, would try his hand at calming her. In the heat of one of Mable's louder moments, the lawyer thought he could hear Pam in the back seat humming a modern popular tune, but he thought that he must have been mistaken.

Pam was calm in her apprehension as the three arrived at the Social Security office. Pam stayed in the waiting area while Mable and the lawyer went forward and met with the examiner. His desk was one of about 30 in the room where other examiners and staff were working.

After the examiner began his interview with Mable, he cought the lawyer's eye. He seemed to be asking the lawyer what was going on with his client. The lawyer produced the medical records which he had prepared in booklet form. On top of the book, he had placed the record of the psychiatrist.

The examiner took a few minutes to read the top documents from start to finish. Mable talked incessantly while the examiner was reading.

Sometimes she laughed, and sometimes she broke into tears. When the examiner finished reading, he asked Mable to wait in the waiting room while he talked with her lawyer.

Mable didn't like it. She thought something was going on. They were planning against her. However, after persuasion by the lawyer, he escorted her to the waiting area.

Returning to the examiner, the lawyer waited.

"Your client is certifiably insane, isn't she?" he asked the lawyer.

"I hate to say it, but I've known her more than 20 years, and she's crazy as four o'clock. She rarely has a sane thought in her head. Years ago, she would have an occasional lucid interval, but those are few and far between now."

"Well, after reviewing her application for benefits, reading her doctor's reports, reading the affidavits you provided from the people who know her, her so-called friends and acquaintances, then interviewing her, and talking with you, I am going to recommend that she be given benefits without any further processing. This woman's history and present condition proves that she is permanently and totally disabled."

The examiner smiled as the lawyer thanked him and got up to leave.

The examiner walked him out into the waiting area. He shook hands with Mable, "I'm recommending benefits for you, Mrs. Darwin," he said as he looked at Pam.

"That's my daughter, Pam. She's retarded," Mable responded.

After studying Pam briefly, the examiner turned to the lawyer, "I guess this confirms my decision, doesn't it?"

"I suppose so. The apples don't fall far from the tree," the lawyer replied. He shook hands with the examiner and guided Pam and Mable toward the door.

Never without some legal problem, Mable told the lawyer about her home heater stove on the trip back to Fort Payne. Although the stove was never taken out of the box, it had a crack in the bottom rendering it unusable. Danny unsuccessfully attempted to fix it. Subsequently, he went to Prestwood Supply Company and attempted to have it replaced - again unsuccessfully. Mable was unable to afford to buy another stove and the winter was fast approaching. The lawyer once again saved Mable when he was able to have the stove replaced by merely writing a letter to Mr. Prestwood and returning the defective heater.

Time Line: 1983 - Social Security benefits begin with substantial back pay for Mable.

The lawyer would help Mable two more times before the Social Security Administration during her life. Twice, the Social Security Administration decided Mable's disability had ceased such that she could return to work. Fortunately for Mable and for Pam, both in 1985 and in 1987, the lawyer was successful in having the benefits continued.

Time Line: 1986 - Mable's mother died.

When Mable's mother died, Mable and her sister, now a middle-aged woman, needed to divide the 60 acres that they had inherited from their mother.   Susan was well educated, married into money in Chattanooga, and wanted little to do with her Sand Mountain heritage.   Still, she wanted her share of the family farm where she was born and raised.

Mable wanted to find fault with her sister during the property division, but Susan Jane and her husband successfully avoided any conflict with her.   Susan was well aware of Mable's temper and well aware of Mable's resentment of her closeness with their mother. Whatever Mable wanted, the sister agreed, so long as she received her half that her mother had left for her.

Mable visited the lawyer concerning the property division. He suggested that to avoid probate she and Susan should have it surveyed.

Mable almost drove the surveyor to the brink of distraction when he tried to survey the property. Mable walked the lines with him; she ranted and raved; inspected every flag he planted; and generally attempted to influence the survey any way she could. She definitely wanted the property line to start at the driveway between her shack and her mother's. She would give Susan their mother's home, but she wanted to take more land on the back, away from the highway. The surveyor made sure the survey reflected an even distribution, but Mable looked for problems. She didn't seem to be able to allow the property division to be settled without conflict. She searched and searched and finally found a problem: The property didn't start at the right place. She returned to the lawyer's office.

"I've been cheated! I knew my sister and her husband would do this to me and Pam. She and her husband have all the money and land in the world, but now they want what is rightfully mine," Mable had tears in her eyes.

"What's the problem?" the lawyer asked. "I looked at the survey, and it looked exactly like what your mother set out in her will. Show me the problem," the lawyer was genuinely interested in satisfying Mable.

She unrolled the large survey sheet on the desk of the lawyer. "Look here where the land line begins. It's all wrong. I don't get my driveway. See, if they had started at the pob, I would have gotten what I was supposed to get. But, no, they wouldn't do that," Mable was wringing her hands and whining in agony.

The lawyer didn't want to embarrass his highly emotional client. "It sure looks okay to me," he said studying the drawing.

"Look here at this arrow. It's all wrong."

"The arrow is pointing out the southeast corner of the southeast quarter of the southwest quarter. There's nothing wrong with that."

"That's where he started, and it's off. It's the pob that's right. If they had started at the pob I would have gotten what I wanted, what was supposed to be mine. Now, I don't have a driveway." Mable was in anguish.

"Pob? What in the world is a pob?" asked the lawyer as he studied the survey once again.

"Wait a minute. Let me talk to my abstractor," he took the survey and went into his library and called Annette, his abstractor.

"Mable is about to have a fit back there. She thinks she has been cheated, but I can't see anything wrong with this map. Take a look at it, and see if you can find the pob. She says that if the surveyor had started the land line at the pob, it would have been all right."

The abstractor smiled looking at her boss. "You don't get it either. The pob is the Point of Beginning."

The lawyer knew that property descriptions often start at points not actually part of the property. This is merely for the purpose of having a good reference position from which to describe the land. But, the lawyer had never heard the letters "P.O.B." found on almost every land survey, actually spoken as the word, "pob."

"Oh, thanks. I was about to be as crazy as Mable," the lawyer said to his abstractor. "Now how in the world do I explain that to her?"

"Just tell her how it is," Annette replied leaving the library.

The lawyer returned to Mable in his office. "Look, Mable, the survey does start at the pob. Go out there and look on the ground. I promise you that you'll find an iron pipe with an orange flag in it. That is the Point of Beginning."

"I know where that is," Mable said jubilantly. "Is that were my land line begins? If it is, I'll be happy. That's where its supposed to start, at the pob."

"Believe me, that is the Point of Beginning. The pob is the Point of Beginning."

Mable left the office smiling with Pam in tow. Now all problems had been solved. She was satisfied.

Six years passed. Mable came into the lawyer's office with Pam. "I'm dying of cancer. I want to check my will and be sure that Pam is cared for. Make me a new will leaving everything to Pam."

The lawyer joked with Pam as he drafted the will on his word processor. He really didn't want to believe Mable was dying, but he could tell by looking at her that she was in serious trouble. She handed him a medical report stating that she had colon rectal cancer in its final stages.

The lawyer finished the will, Mable signed it, and she and Pam left the office. That was the last time the lawyer would see his old client alive.

Time Line: 1992 - Mable Darwin died.

When Mable died in 1992, her son Danny brought Pam to the lawyer's office to file the will for probate. Since Mable had transferred everything to Pam prior to her death, other than the real estate, the lawyer suggested that the brother and sister avoid probate. He told them that without a will the property passed to them in equal parts and Danny could execute a deed deeding his portion of the property to Pam. That would carry out the terms of the will without going to court. Or, if he and Pam so decided, they could deed the property to whomever they pleased if Pam could understand the nature and quality of her acts.

Danny said he didn't know whether she could or not, but he would make a deed to Pam which would carry out the terms of the will.

The lawyer told Danny that he was being smart as the costs involved would, other than the real estate, far outweigh the benefits Pam would receive.

With his children gone, Danny moved Pam into his home with him and his wife, Gayle. Pam had no other place to go, and she needed constant care.

Time Line: 1993 - Pamela is subjected to testing by psychologist.

Gayle took Pam to a psychologist in Chattanooga and had her tested as to her various abilities. The battery of tests required the better part of a week.

After the test results were certified to Danny and Gayle, they called the lawyer for an appointment. When they arrived, Danny opened the conversation. "You know that Pam is now living with us?"

"Yeah, I heard she was very happy with you folks," replied the lawyer.

"She is. She is improving every day, but I have something terrible to tell you," Danny said. He looked concerned, and Gayle was quietly sobbing.

The lawyer wondered what was going on. Perhaps there was more of a problem than the Darwins were willing to admit.

"What is it?" he asked.

"You won't believe it," Danny started. "We had Pam tested with every conceivable test known to modern psychology."

"Yes?" the lawyer wanted him to go on. He

was very interested. He expected terrible news. Perhaps Pam was more than retarded. Maybe she was borderline intellect. "Is she borderline?"

"No Worse than that."

"What then?"

"She has a certifiable IQ of 110." Danny smiled.

"Isn't that above average?" the lawyer asked.

"It is 10 points above average. Pam was never retarded. It was always Mama," tears welled up in Danny's eyes.

"You mean Mable treated Pam as retarded, said she was retarded, and held her out of school. Pam has developed into a 40-odd-year-old woman who totally acts retarded, and isn't?" the lawyer asked with astonishment.

"I mean it," Danny said. "It was always Mama. She had it in her demented mind that Pam was retarded; and she convinced everyone, including Pam, that she was retarded. I always thought I had a retarded sister. She always acted retarded, but she always has been just as normal as you and me."

Tears were rolling down Danny's cheeks. Gayle was still quietly sobbing.

The lawyer thought he would not be able to hold back the tears.

"This is absolutely terrible," he said. "Pam

Darwin is just as sane as you are, and yet she is in her 40's and can't read or write or speak plainly?"

"That's right," Danny said. "I didn't think Pam would ever be able to sign any document. I thought she was out of it until I saw her trying to control the television set. She was given the remote, and within 45 seconds, she could switch channels to the program she wanted to watch. I told Gayle, 'Pam is not retarded.' That's when we decided to have her tested."

"And she couldn't talk plain because she was imitating her mother with the speech impediment," Gayle interjected.

"That may be one of the saddest stories I have ever heard no, ever participated in," the lawyer replied. Where do you go from here?"

"We don't know. Right now, I'd like to see her learn to read and write. She's 46 years old now. She has a lot of catching up to do. She still acts retarded."

After talking to the family a little longer, and consoling them as much as possible, the lawyer showed the Darwins out of his office. Gayle said that she and Pam would return soon to fill out papers to be admitted into the retarded children's school in Talladega.

The lawyer told her, "Any time, just drop by."

He went into his secretary's office and told her what had just happened. She cried as she heard what a sad thing had happened to Pam.

The lawyer truly regretted that Pam had lived most of her life as a retarded person, but he was happy that she was on her way to true reality.

At birth, Mable did not give to Pam the irascible mentality of her forefathers. Nonetheless, Pam did not escape her Sand Mountain heritage.

The lawyer turned out the lights in his office and clicked off the computer. The room dimmed as the screen faded to black. Gathering his briefcase, the thought ran through the lawyer's mind, The lost has been found.

Five weeks later Gayle was back in the lawyer's office to have Pam's real estate title checked and certified. The first thing the lawyer asked was what kind of progress was Pam making.

"She has been living by herself for a month now. She is in the literacy classes, but she is not making great strides. She's just making progress, very slow," Gayle sounded disappointed.

"Is she trying hard enough?" the lawyer asked.

"I think she misses her mama," Gayle responded. "She doesn't apply herself like we think she should. Maybe she just doesn't have the ability to try any harder. But it sure is slow," Gayle sounded as if she was about ready to give up.

At the school in Talladega, it seemed that Pam liked being with the children so much, she would not take the time to learn herself. She was too busy playing with the retarded children. The teachers attempted to stop her, but they were not successful. Pam helped several students learn to read and write, but not herself. It was as if she refused to learn while encouraging others to apply themselves.

After almost a year of frustration, Gayle and Danny were ready to give up. They decided to allow Pam to live her own life and go at her own speed. She was still living in the small mobile home in their yard. She could operate all her appliances and entertainment equipment without any problem. She was doing her own laundry and helping Gayle clean the Darwin house once a week. It was still impossible for her to pass in public alone. She would get lost in Wal-mart and almost panic. Being unable to read caused her great difficulty.

Eventually, overcoming all her challenges and hardships, Pam became a very happy individual who was more or less whatever she wanted be. Remarkably, Pam never met a person she didn't love.

JUST A BOY AND HIS DOG

It was supposed to have snowed during the day, but it didn't. It just turned cold.

Over dinner, the lawyer said to his wife, "You remember Donnie?"

"Sure," she responded. "We knew him when he was growing up, knew his entire family. I saw him at Wal-Mart the other day."

"He was in an accident."

"Really?"

"Have you heard about the new drug task force?"

"Yes, but what does that have to do with Donnie?"

"He's either on it or wants to be on it. I heard he was wearing an earring."

"Which ear?"

"I'm not sure. He doesn't wear it all the time."

"Is he an undercover narcotics officer?"

"He's looking scroungy enough. You should see some of the others. They look like a pretty raunchy, rough bunch."

"Do all of them look that bad?"

"Most of them."

"What happened to him?"

"He went out on a drug raid right after they got this new drug dog."

"What kind of dog?"

"It has a funny name. The drug task force

bought it in Belgium. It's a big dog, a big expensive black dog with a funny name."

"What happened?"

"Donnie took this big dog out on a drug raid, they call it a bust, with him and the rest of the bunch."

"That's what they bought it for; right?"

"Yeah, that dog is supposed to sniff out the drugs saving the narcs' time."

"What did Donnie do with his dog?"

"They put on all their fatigues and stuff, and went out to a person's home whom they suspected was dealing in drugs."

"What do they call themselves? Drug officers?"

"No. I think they are going to call themselves the Drug Task Force, but I don't know whether that has been made official."

"Well, what did they do?"

"Donnie, along with the rest of them, burst into the room with this big dog, yelling and hollering like they do. All of them were cursing and hollering. I suppose this is to intimidate the person they are after. Regardless, they're loud."

"Like they do on TV?"

"Worse. TV can't curse the way they do. They use the worst language imaginable."

"You mean, curse like a sailor?"

"Worse. They use language that I never heard during the Korean War."

"Okay. They ran into this person's home yelling and cursing. What happened?"

"Well, he goes bursting into this house yelling and hollering like they do."

"Really making a lot of noise?"

"A lot of noise. And the dog got excited, and it attacked Donnie."

"You mean his own dog bit him?"

"His own dog bit him. Bit his right forearm pretty bad, I heard."

"Is he hiding his arm?"

"I think he's hiding, period. Everybody is laughing about it around the courthouse. The drug bunch went out and bought an electric collar."

"For Donnie?"

"No. For the dog."

"What does that do?"

"Shocks hell out of the dog if he starts to bite Donnie again."

"Does Donnie keep the button?"

"He'd better. That dog is not going to tolerate all that crap."

"Are they thinking about getting rid of the dog?"

"No. The dog cost almost $5,000. They're thinking about getting rid of Donnie. Good drug dogs are hard to find."

"Sounds like they're expensive too."

"You're right. They can always find some idiot who'll put an earring in his ear, look funky, and play narcotics officer."

"They have to grow a beard and fix their hair disheveledly?"

"Some of them. They even curl their hair?"

"Sounds like a scroungy hippie group to me."

"Some of them are. It seems like being a narc is a license to be a slob."

"We should buy them all dogs."

"Right."

"With or without electric collars?"

"No collars with earrings."

"Right. How has the dog reacted to all this?

"He still doesn't like Donnie."

"Smart dog."

"Yeah. Donnie has the button."

"Smart Donnie."

"Yeah. Pass some more of those delicious English peas."

INTERFERENCE

Lister Ray Caffee was a genuine hero of the Korean Conflict. He won the Silver Star with several Oak Leaf Clusters. He was shot up pretty badly in the right hip on Porkchop Hill and easily slid into alcoholism while he was recovering from his war wounds in Japan.

When he returned to his home on Lookout Mountain, in Fort Payne, Alabama, he was drawing a 100% disability from the Veteran's Administration. He moved back to the family farm with his mother and father and promptly began to do what he did best, make white whiskey. People said he drank up all his profits, but that was not the case. Lister Ray did quite well selling white for $7.50 a gallon. Every time he made a fifty-gallon run, he ran out and had to make another one. His thumper rarely stopped singing.

Due to Lister Ray's quality merchandise, and his 50 cents below market price, many a mountain man spent his paycheck with Lister Ray before he got home on Friday night. Several mountain women began to complain to the sheriff that Lister Ray was bootlegging out in the open and that he had gone public.

Everyone within thirty miles knew Lister Ray was bootlegging. If a man needed a pint or a quart or even a gallon, he drove up to Lister

Ray's house on Fruit Farm Road and bought it. Nothing was hidden about the transaction. "Money talked, and moonshine walked."

In response to about six complaints, the DeKalb County Sheriff decided to spring a trap to catch Lister Ray selling untaxed whiskey.

Lister Ray knew, and was friends with, almost all the deputies. The sheriff knew that there was no way he would fall into a trap with the officers he knew. Plus, the sheriff was not exactly sure his men would go along with trapping a genuine war hero.

Secretly, with only his knowledge, the sheriff brought in a deputy from an adjoining county to try to buy a quart from Lister Ray. The sheriff didn't have an interest in putting Lister Ray in prison. He just wanted to slow him down or put him out of business entirely. More than anything else, he wanted the wives and mothers off his back with their complaints.

The deputy, dressed in overalls, went to Lister Ray's house early one Saturday morning. It was a rather large white clapboard house sitting back from the road with an expansive eight-acre fenced-in pasture between the home and the pavement. It was neat, and the lawn was closely mowed.

Lister Ray's father had been a successful farmer, and his mother, Juanita Caffee, had operated a bakery in Fort Payne for more than 20 years. Together they had bought the large white, nine room house, sitting on 49 acres of land. Lister Ray had his own little apartment in the rear. In an earlier era, Lister Ray's living area would have been the servant's quarters - small, clean, and comfortable.

The undercover deputy asked Lister Ray's mother where he might find her son. She told the undercover man that Lister Ray was in Fort Payne and would probably be there all day.

"Feller, if you have any business with Lister Ray you can probably find him at the barber shop or pool hall. That's where he usually hangs out." She sounded a little exasperated.

The deputy trickled off the mountain and drove directly to the pool hall on First Street, near the railroad tracks. There, just as his mother predicted, he found Lister Ray sitting in one of the chairs in the dark, on a raised level, a foot off the main floor, up against the wall. He was intently watching the bright red balls of a game of snooker, which he had a bet on.

The deputy recognized Lister Ray from the file photographs. He sat down in the old chipped wooden theater seat beside him.

"You don't know where a fellow could get a quart of shine today, do you?" He murmured to Lister Ray as the game was finishing up.

"I don't know," Lister Ray seemed deep in thought, contemplating an idea that was foreign to him. "As soon as my nephew gets through winning this game, he might know something, I don't know."

No matter how much the officer talked, Lister Ray never looked around nor took his eye off the game.

The nephew, whom Lister Ray called Tadpole, won the game. Lister Ray collected $10.00 from the man shooting against Tadpole because Tadpole was too young to gamble. The boy was only fifteen.

"That's enough for me," the loser said. "I've had it. That boy is just too good."

Lister Ray said, "He sure is," as he counted 12 ten dollar bills, folded them together and put them in his pocket.

Tadpole racked his cue, he always shot off the wall, joined his uncle, and the man he didn't know - the deputy.

"This feller is looking for some shine. I told him I didn't know anything about it, but you might have heard something through the boys around here," he looked at Tadpole to be sure he understood the code.

"Well, sure," Tadpole confidently assured the men, "I know where a feller can find a quart for $9.00."

"I'll pay it," said the deputy, pulling out a ten dollar bill. "Here, you keep the change." He pushed the bill toward Tadpole.

"Now, I'd be careful dealing with that boy, if I was you," Lister Ray warned. "He's a juvenile, and I ain't seen nothin."

Tadpole told the deputy, "Here, hold my shoes I just bought. I'll be right back."

The deputy took the shoebox from the boy as Tadpole hurriedly left the poolroom.

"Well, listen, Pal," Lister Ray said. "I've got to get on. Nice to see you." He got up and hobbled out of the darkened pool room into the late morning sunlight.

The deputy looked at his watch. It was 9:30 in the morning, a Saturday. At 10:10 the deputy looked at his watch again. "Tadpole should be back any minute."

All the DA would have to do is prove that Tadpole was working for Lister Ray, and he would have the case locked up.

Near 11:00 o'clock, the deputy approached the pool hall cashier. "What happened to that boy they call Tadpole? He said he would be back in a couple of minutes, and it has been more than an hour."

"Ah, he might not never come back," the cashier said. "He lives in Chattanooga and is a juvenile. He tricks people at pool and illegal liquor. He probably won't even come back."

"Well, he has to come back," the deputy said lifting the box. "He left me his shoes that he had just bought."

"I still wouldn't count on it," the cashier warned. "If I were you, I would go about my business. You may never see Tadpole again. Nobody around here even knows his real name. Lister Ray claims he is related to him, but folks say that ain't true either. You want to leave his shoes here in case he does come by in a couple of weeks?"

The cashier reached out for the box.

"Ah, yeah, I'll just leave them here. First, I'd like to see what kind of shoes he bought."

He removed the lid from the box revealing a quart jar of white lightening!

The cashier laughed. Obviously, he had seen the act before.

"First time I ever saw shoes with 'Mason' written on them." He continued to laugh as his volume filled the entire pool hall.

If the man had not lifted the lid, the cashier and the boys would have had that quart of shine. So he had to play his other card. "You want me to pour that out for you, Mister?" he asked in his most honest manner. He once more reached for the box.

"No. I wanted whiskey, and I got it. I'll just take it along." The deputy replaced the shoebox lid over the jar with "Mason" written across its front.

When the deputy reported to the sheriff on Monday, they agreed that they had been tricked. Lister Ray had ten dollars of the county's money, and all they had was a joke. After a taste test for quality, they poured the white whiskey down the drain.

"Don't tell anybody about this, and I won't

either," the sheriff cautioned. Both knew they had been played for fools. "I'll get Lister Ray another way."

The sheriff put a tight surveillance on Lister Ray. He wanted to know what he did and where he did it.

The tight surveillance called for the officers assigned to the surveillance to find Lister Ray at least once every day and keep the time and place entered in a log on the subject. If they saw Lister Ray more often than once a day, they noted it in the log entries. If they conducted a loose surveillance, they would find Lister Ray once a week and do the same thing.

With his tight surveillance working, in thirty days the sheriff knew all he needed to know about Lister Ray Caffee. He knew that each and every Saturday night, Lister Ray went to the VFW Club in Rainsville, Alabama and became roaring drunk. He would walk, rather stagger, out of the VFW, to a friend's house half a block away. He would sleep there and drive home on his motorcycle the following morning.

The sheriff was receiving more and more pressure from the lovely ladies living on Lookout Mountain whose husbands were supporting Lister Ray's lifestyle. Some women called him as many as three times a week to see if he had arrested Lister Ray. With the political pressure building, the sheriff felt that he had to do something.

In desperation, he told one of his favorite deputies, whom he could depend upon, "Go out there to that VFW Club in Rainsville and arrest Lister Ray Caffee. I know he is selling white whiskey out there. I want him in jail before church on Sunday morning."

"What if I can't make a case against him?" the deputy asked.

"I want him in jail by church on Sunday morning! I don't care what he's doing. I want him arrested. Do you understand?" the sheriff was more than emphatic.

The deputy had been on the surveillance. Therefore, he knew exactly when Lister Ray would arrive at the VFW Club.

As Lister Ray approached, the deputy put the blue light on Lister Ray's motorcycle and pulled him over a block before the VFW. "Let me see your license."

Lister Ray knew the deputy, but he went along with whatever was happening. He handed the officer his license to operate a Motor Driven Cycle.

"What you got in the saddle bags?" the deputy asked when the license was in order.

"Well, that's for me to know and you to find out, Henry. I fought for my Constitutional rights, and I know what they are. You didn't, and you don't. If you ain't gonna arrest me for something, you ain't got no right to search me."

"Maybe I am going to arrest you for something, Smartass," Henry responded.

"Well, you better make it stick Buddy Boy, 'cause I'll sue your ass, if you lose," Lister Ray believed in telling people how things are.

The deputy pondered a moment. "All right. Get your ass into the VFW and get drunk. I know that's what your going to do."

"You're right about that." Lister Ray started his engine and rode on up to the VFW Club.

He kicked down the kickstand, parked his motorcycle and went into the club.

When Lister Ray staggered out of the VFW Club at a little after one in the morning, Henry was still waiting for him. The instant Lister Ray stepped off the VFW property, Henry walked up to him and arrested him. He put the cuffs on the weaving Lister Ray Caffee and put him in the back of the patrol car. Lister Ray cursed Henry all the way to the jail. He called the deputy every name he could remember from his military days and then some. The deputy ignored him. He was told to have him in jail before church, and, by God, that's where he would be.

Lister Ray was booked and put in the county jail drunk tank. He was not a happy camper. He was sleeping off six straight hours of hard drinking on the concrete slab, a bench around three walls of the cell. It was the bench where drunks could sleep without sleeping on the floor. There were no bed clothes, no blankets, no pillows, just a concrete bench. Drunks had to make do. They didn't feel much anyway.

The jailers were instructed to forget about Lister Ray until Monday morning. Of course, the inmates fed him, but he was otherwise held incommunicado until Monday. His leg didn't feel a bit good after being on that concrete slab for two straight nights.

The sheriff told the assistant district attorney handling misdemeanor cases that he wanted Lister Ray prosecuted to the limit -- no the fullest extent of the law.

The assistant district attorney was an overweight, red-faced, gray-headed, retired navy man. Obviously, in his younger days, he had been blonde. He had served 30 years in the Navy and retired as a Commander. He never rose to the higher ranks because of his interests other than the Navy. First, he had asked to remain at sea as much as possible. He was unmarried and would remain so throughout his life. His family was independently wealthy, and he used his military service as an opportunity to purchase art, antiques, and very expensive collectibles.

When his ship hit port, he didn't head to the red light district. He went straight for the museums and most expensive shops in the area. As a result of his constant search for bargains, he became quite well known in the various ports of call of the U.S. Navy around the world.

Then, after he had served his 30 years, he was forced into retirement. He moved to Fort Payne, Alabama, because it was his mother's hometown.

For several years, he was thoroughly occupied building a very large home to maintain his collections. Once the interior decorations were in perfect order, and they had to be moved around several times to suit him, he became inexorably bored. For the first time in his life, he had absolutely nothing to do. He didn't fish, golf, hunt, nor visit. He relished the solitary life at sea and the strange ports of call, and now all that was gone.

The commander had a law degree that he had never used. He spent a little time and became a member of the bar just to say he was a member. A little later, he asked his friend, an old high school chum, now the Circuit Solicitor (District Attorney), for a job. He didn't care whether he got paid or not. He just wanted something to do. He was given the assistant's job at the starting salary.

By the time the Commander attended the bond hearing of Lister Ray Caffee, he had been an assistant prosecutor for five years. When the sheriff asked him to prosecute Lister Ray to the fullest extent of the law, he was more than happy to oblige.

The arrest slowed Lister Ray down a little. He knew if he violated the terms of his bond, although it was only $300, the sheriff would lock him up until his trial date. So, for about four months, the sheriff had relief from women complaining about Lister Ray Caffee selling white to their thirsty husbands.

About a week before he was to come for trial before the county judge, Lister Ray visited the office of the lawyer. When the secretary showed him in, he was grinning from ear to ear, sticking out a big right hand to be shaken, and drunk out of his mind. The lawyer could smell white whiskey on his breath when he came into the room. He shook hands with Lister Ray. The two had known each other at least 10 years. Although he had not served in actual combat, the lawyer was a Korean War Veteran as well. He had been assigned to watch the Russians which took him to some strange places - mostly very cold places.

"What is it now?" the lawyer asked, looking into Lister Ray's bloodshot blue eyes.

"Wail, you know I was shot up in Korea and can't walk straight?"

"I know that."

"Wail, back in April, I was leaving the VFW Club about one in the morning, and old Henry Boggus arrested me for PD, public drunk. Can you believe that? I had been in the VFW Club, but I hadn't had a drop all night. I was sober as a judge."

Lister Ray had concocted a pretty good defense. He did walk with a limp, and it was his word against the officer's.

When Lister Ray told the lawyer about the deputy trying to arrest him earlier, before he went into the club, the lawyer knew his drunken client had a decent defense.

Lister Ray paid the fee, and the lawyer went to work. After investigating the case, he went to talk to the assistant circuit solicitor. The retired naval officer had snow-white hair. Looking at his reddish age-splotched complexion, one would conclude that he might even have been red-headed rather than blonde earlier in life. As it was, he was portly and a bit arrogant. But otherwise, he was all right.

"How about letting Lister Ray pay a $50 fine and costs, and let's be done with this case?" the lawyer thought he was offering the prosecutor a very reasonable plea bargain.

"Can't do it," the assistant shook his head negatively and pursed his lips.

"Okay, $100 and costs," the lawyer countered.

"Sorry. Can't do that either," same response. "Lister Ray has been thumbing his nose at law enforcement for several years now. I am going to prosecute him to the limits of the law." This was more than a threat; it was a promise.

"My stars!" the lawyer exclaimed. "This is

Lister Ray Caffee, it's not Charlie Manson!" He couldn't understand the assistant circuit solicitor.

"I don't care. Lister Ray is going to trial. No deals!" The commander was adamant.

The lawyer didn't waste his breath any further. He would definitely take the matter up with the judge at the appropriate time.

Lister Ray was unhappy that the lawyer could not make a deal. He went across from the courthouse and employed another lawyer to help the lawyer. The new lawyer was the state legislator for the county. Lister Ray thought he would have more influence with the assistant circuit solicitor than the lawyer he had always used.

The state representative went to see the former commander and obtained the same result.

"We're going to have to try this pissy assed case," he told the lawyer.

"I'll move for a pre-trial conference with the Court. Maybe the judge can deflate the commander's sails. He sure does have a bee in his bonnet about Lister Ray."

The judge set the pre-trial conference the day before the trial. The assistant circuit solicitor, the lawyer, the legislator, and the judge were present.

The state legislator took the lead. "Judge, we're representing Lister Ray Caffee, a highly decorated veteran who draws 100% total disability from fighting for his country who is charged with Public Intoxication. We've offered to pay a fine and costs, and the prosecutor is putting us to trial. It's a waste of the Court's time. You aren't going to do any more to Lister Ray than we're willing to pay without bothering the Court with this disabled vet."

He was a politician, the lawyer thought.

"What about it, Mr. Prosecutor?" the judge asked the assistant circuit solicitor. "You well know that the Court has more important things to do than try a public drunk case. This should have been disposed of in a municipal court long ago. Furthermore, I know Lister Ray, and I know that he walks with a limp from old military wounds. You ought to appreciate that. We're all veterans here."

The judge had been an officer in the U.S. Army during the Korean Conflict. He had been in the artillery.

"I do, Your Honor," the commander responded. "I appreciate any service to one's country, but Lister Ray Caffee was publicly falling down drunk and should be prosecuted to the ends of the law." He was emphatic.

"Well," the judge drew the word out. "I don't intend to hear a public drunk case. If you wanted to prosecute him to the limits of the law, you should have done it in city court."

Turning to the lawyer, he asked, "What is

the defense willing to do?"

"One Hundred Dollars and costs," the lawyer quickly responded.

"Sounds fair to me. Have Lister Ray in court tomorrow for sentencing. Tell him to bring the fine and costs." The judge looked pointedly at the assistant circuit solicitor for a reaction.

"You aren't even going to give the state a chance to prosecute?" the commander whined.

"Not in your wildest dreams. Appeal me if you don't like it." The Court was firm.

"But this is just not right," the commander intoned.

"Right or wrong, that's how it is. 9:00 a.m. tomorrow, Gentlemen. Now if you'll excuse me." The judge stood up from the table indicating it was time to leave.

"This is just not right," the assistant circuit solicitor bemoaned as he headed for the door. "The state should have its day in court." He looked backward over his left shoulder toward the judge.

"The state will have all the days in court it wants," the judge assured him. "Bring me a good old axe murder, and I promise you it will have all the time you can handle. But you will not have a public drunk case day in my court." It was the Court's parting shot.

Lister Ray was waiting in the lawyer's office to find out what happened.

"Okay, we got your deal," the legislator told

the client. "$100 and costs, you can't beat it."

Lister Ray was happy. "I guess I'll celebrate this. When do I pay up?"

"You have to come for sentencing at 9:00 a.m. tomorrow. You must be here on the dot. And don't lay out all night drinking. You need to be sober tomorrow," the lawyer cautioned.

"Yeah, don't drink none tonight," the legislator backed up the lawyer.

"Yeah," giggled Lister Ray in his usual alcoholic fog. "And does the Pope wear a funny hat? You know I'm going to celebrate this."

He stood on his wobbly legs and staggered out of the office.

The following morning at 8:57 a.m. Lister Ray Caffee staggered into the lawyer's waiting room. The lawyer had been pacing the waiting room floor for fifteen minutes hoping Lister Ray would show up.

"Good morning!" Lister Ray shouted through his alcoholic fog. The fumes of his white whiskey breath filled the waiting room.

The legislator was seated on the couch. He had been anxiously awaiting Lister Ray with the lawyer. "My God!" he exclaimed. "He's as drunk as a hoot owl!"

"Yeah! And what's it to ya?" Lister Ray rejoined.

"All right," the lawyer took control of the situation. "Lister Ray, when we go in that courtroom don't you say a word. You understand? Not a word!" He looked Lister Ray dead in the eye.

"I got it," Lister Ray seemed serious, he didn't grin. Maybe he had it.

The legislator joined in. "Look, Lister Ray, the lawyer is right. If you say a word up there you're going to be in more trouble than you are just trying to get out of. You understand?" He was almost pleading with Lister Ray.

"I got it!" Lister Ray assured the lawyers. "I won't say a word."

"Okay," the lawyer told the legislator. "When we get up there, you stand on one side of Lister Ray and I'll stand on the other. I will do all the answering. You watch Lister Ray and make sure the commander doesn't suspect he is drunk out of his mind."

"I got it," the legislator sounded like Lister Ray.

The three of them went out the door toward the courthouse.

"State v. Lister Ray Caffee," the Clerk intoned. The lawyer, the legislator, and Lister Ray Caffee went to the defense table. The commander and Henry went to the state's table.

"Come on up here," the judge motioned the group forward to stand directly in front of the bench. The judge was at least two feet higher than the courtroom, and his bench was a huge brown mahogany desk-type piece of furniture that was about seven feet long and at least four feet wide. It had a huge writing surface behind a little barrier and went around three sides of the bench.

The Court read the entire colloquy required to be read to each defendant pleading guilty. "You are knowingly entering this guilty plea because you are, in fact, guilty?" the Court was asking.

To each of the Court's questions, the lawyer responded affirmatively. Lister Ray was looking around the courtroom. The legislator was holding Lister Ray's right arm. The lawyer was on his left.

"In conclusion," the Court finally said, "I accept your plea of guilty to Public Intoxication and fix your fine at $100 plus costs. Are you prepared to pay that today?"

Before the lawyer could answer, Lister Ray said jubilantly, "I got it!"

White whiskey breath filled the courtroom.

"Very well. See the clerk. Next case," the judge moved on.

The lawyer and legislator began to usher Lister Ray toward the robing room door, the quickest way out of the courtroom. The door was just to the left of the Court's bench.

The commander pointed his internationally, well-trained nose, into the air, and sniffed long. Then he ran to the three attempting to leave the courtroom and tried to smell Lister Ray's breath. As the three men were walking arm in arm, the assistant circuit solicitor began jumping around before the men, sniffing the air in front of Lister Ray, and trying to slow them from leaving.

As they reached the door, "Wait a minute!" screamed the commander.

"Judge! Did you see what they just did? He is drunk as a skunk right now, in this courtroom, in public, and one of them is holding him up and the other one is running interference for him. I can smell it on him, Your Honor. That man is drunk right now. This is a travesty of justice!"

He ran back across the courtroom and was now directly before the bench flailing his arms about. His usual paled face was now blood red. He looked as if he was having a heart attack.

"Oh, don't get carried away, Mr. Prosecutor," the judge remonstrated. "Lister Ray has a bad leg. They're just helping him out. Calm down. Get ready for your next case."

The lawyer, legislator, and Lister Ray made it out of the courthouse.

"I told you not to open your mouth, Lister Ray," the lawyer said highly irritated.

"I got it!" Lister Ray beamed.

MEET ME IN ST. LOUIS

At 8:32 a.m. on July 10, 1985, Jerry Barksdale called the lawyer and asked him to go with him to visit Lame Deer, a Sioux Indian Medicine Man, in St. Louis. After a brief conversation, the lawyer agreed to go. Barksdale, one of the lawyer's oldest and dearest friends, looked forward to making the trip with the older man.

So on July 12, 1985, the lawyer arrived at Barksdale's apartment in Athens, Alabama, where he spent the night before the trip. His friend had just gone through a divorce and was living alone. The following day, the men drove to St. Louis with Barksdale under the wheel of his Buick. They were anxious to meet the famous Souix Indian Medicine Man.

Barksdale had talked with an Indian named Raoul in Santa Fe, New Mexico, earlier in the year. Raoul wanted Barksdale to come to St. Louis to meet with some of the elders of the Nation and help the American Indian Movement any way possible.

The purpose of the gathering in St. Louis was to set up a vigil for Leonard Peltier. Leonard Peltier had been in prison for more than 10 years as an accomplice for aiding or abetting the murder of two FBI Agents at the Pine Ridge Reservation in North Dakota. It was alleged to have been the last shootout between the white man and the Indians.

This was the incident where the two agents burst into an Indian camp. There was a cross-fire, and the two agents were killed along with one Indian. Leonard Peltier ran into the forest and later escaped into Canada. According to the Indians, he was extradited back to the United States on government-concocted manufactured evidence. The Indians claimed that the agents shot each other in the excitement. This is almost a foregone conclusion due to the fact the FBI Agents were killed with bullets which were not of the same caliber as the weapons held by Peltier and the other Indians.

Two years after the St. Louis trip, the lawyer was hired to do some work for Leonard Peltier. Supporters wanted him released from prison. The lawyer visited Peltier in Leavenworth Prison, near Kansas City. Then he went on to Pine Ridge Reservation in South Dakota and did a thorough investigation of the facts of the case. At the end of a week, he concluded that the government had a better case than the folks in St. Louis had been led to believe.

The "Rainbow Family" had been invited to help set up the vigil and participate as they so desired by Peltier. The people making up the Rainbow Family were the last remnants of the hippie generation. They met once a year. This year, they met somewhere in the Ozarks Mountains of Southern Missouri and Northern Arkansas. They left their meeting to join the Indian vigil in St. Louis.

The Rainbow Family has to be the scraggliest, dirtiest, trashiest bunch of human beings on the planet. Talk about rugged individuals, they are the most. Some of them try to see how dirty and raunchy they can become. The lawyer saw some folks dressed only in pieces of leather wrapped around them. They all appeared to have very sterling character, but he thought that they worked at being filthy. They did smell ripe for human beings. The lawyer told Barksdale that he had smelled bears in the North Woods of Canada that smelled worse, but not by much.

When the two lawyers arrived in St. Louis at approximately 3:30 p.m. on Saturday, they drove directly to the United States Courthouse. Across the street, in a small park, they found the Rainbow Family and others. The Courthouse was the home of the Eighth Circuit Court of Appeals. Peltier's case was up for a hearing on Monday before the Eighth Circuit.

Earlier, the Rainbow Family had set up their vigil across the street in the public park. They erected scroungy signs, and there were 9 or 10 scroungy people sitting around. The lawyer hated to refer to them as filthy and scroungy because they seemed to be nice people.

However, he was a firm believer that anyone can stay clean.

He told Barksdale, "I've been president of a coal mining company, and my mining employees stayed cleaner than those folks."

The men from Alabama met and talked with members of the group in the park, and they told them to go out to the campground at Totem Pole Park. There they could meet with the AIM (American Indian Movement) people and maybe find Raoul or Lame Deer out there.

The lawyer thought it was appropriate that the Indians were staying in Totem Pole Park.

First though, the lawyers had to locate hotel accommodations. After trying several places without success, they finally located a double at the Radisson. The battle for Number One in the National League between the St. Louis Cardinals and the San Diego Padres was being played that night. The city was packed. Busch Stadium is located in right downtown St. Louis.

Later, the lawyers told some of the hippies about their difficulties in finding reservations. "You should have just camped out with us," a bearded ragged man told them.

That was an idea which held absolutely no attraction whatsoever for either the lawyer or Barksdale. In fact, the thought of it was totally repugnant to them.

They used the hippie's directions to find the

camp. As Barksdale drove west they past the old fairgrounds.

"Isn't that where they held a world's fair?" the lawyer asked.

"I don't know. The place where the Indians are camped is beyond the fairgrounds."

They located Totem Pole Park, a large park on the outskirts of the city.

As they walked through the portion of the park where the Rainbow Family camp was located, they noticed the entire area was a hodgepodge of rag-tag squalor.

The Rainbow Family rode around in old dilapidated buses which made a Mexican work bus look like a Cadillac. Some of their pickup trucks had giant barrels on them. They had medicine show trailers and houses. They had cut-down cars. Some of them lived in their cars. The entire scene was almost beyond description. Every direction a person looked there was total squalor. It looked like the movie set of a road warrior film.

The lawyer concluded that the Rainbow Family, for whatever good they did, were a moving slum. It didn't bother him how they lived. However, he was sure it was a mistake for him to be around them.

As they went deeper into the Rainbow Family's camp, they asked where the Indians were and were directed to about four Indians in tents over on one side of the camp. The

Indians were camped in regular U.S. Army pup tents. One of the Indians came out to meet the well-dressed men. His name was Ken Irwin. He introduced himself as the brother to the man in charge, Louie, or Louis Irwin. Ken told them that Louie was the keeper of the pipe. The white men didn't seem to appreciate the importance of this announcement.

They were told that in the Sioux religious tradition the only religious symbol used is the pipe. Being the keeper of the pipe is another way of saying the person is a Medicine Man. So the men became anxious to meet Louie Irwin. Ken Irwin continued to visit with them but did not offer to introduce them to his brother. After talking with them about 30 minutes, he told them to have a cup of coffee.

The lawyers went over to where the hippies were cooking coffee in a cast-iron pot and began looking for a cup. They then learned why the hippies carried their cups on their belt. There were no extra cups.

Barksdale remembered that he had two empty Hardee's coffee cups in his car. So they walked a little more than a quarter of a mile back to the car and got their paper cups. On the way back to the camp Barksdale threw his cup away.

He said, "I don't want any of their coffee. If you get a cup, don't offer any of it to me. I don't want to be embarrassed 'cause I don't want to drink it."

"Fine," the lawyer said. "I'm going to try it out."

When they arrived back in the cooking area, he put a Sweet'n Low that he had in his pocket into his cup. He then went to the coffee pot, which was the large cast iron kettle with a lid on it and a metal dipper in it. He dipped that coffee out, and it looked like it could stand on its own two feet. After dipping it out and tasting it, he discovered it was not all that bad. It was just very, very strong.

The Rainbow Family made the coffee by starting the water early in the morning and adding coffee grounds to it all day and a little more water as it was consumed. The grounds generally settled to the bottom of the pot, so, for clear coffee, all that was necessary was dip off the top avoiding the lower grounds. The large cast-iron pot was sitting on an open fire.

The lawyer told Barksdale, "It's a little rough going down but entirely drinkable. Of course, it will stain your teeth."

Barksdale decided he wanted a sip and pronounced it, "All right." But, he did not want any more than a sip. He said it would give him heartburn.

The pair went down the way to find some water to get rid of the strong coffee taste in their mouths. In the public restroom, the hippies were bathing in the fresh water. They had tied a hose to the water fountain in the restroom and were using it as a shower. The lawyers waited until the last hippy had bathed off and then got a cup of water. They then returned to where the Indians were and sat down on a log about 50 feet away from their tents.

Barksdale and the lawyer had sat on the log about half an hour when a young brave, or warrior, came over to them and introduced himself to them as the nephew of Louis Irwin. He wanted to know their business. They talked with him for a while. He had fresh scars where skewers had been put in his flesh right above each of his nipples. Then they had been pulled through the flesh at the sun dance. The lawyer had read about the rite and was somewhat familiar with the ceremony. After visiting with him for a while, the lawyers concluded that he was a very wise young man.

Eventually, their host went over to his uncle's tent. The uncle was sitting on a blanket on the ground outside the front of the tent. Various and sundry people had come to the tent and sat on the blanket with the uncle while the men had been sitting on the log. The younger man talked in Sioux to his uncle for a while, and then the uncle came over and shook hands with his visitors and invited them to sit down in front of his tent on his blanket.

When they sat down, the lawyer noticed

Louis Irwin didn't have a blanket. Instead, he had a striped commercial bed sheet. Barksdale sat at the edge of the sheet on the ground. As they visited, the lawyer thought that one could say that they were having a pow wow. After they talked for some time, he began to feel that they were visiting Irwin in his living room. His house just did not have any walls.

Louie told his visitors that the Elders and the Medicine Men would be in very shortly. He reminded them that there were several different kinds of time, Eastern time, Central time, Mountain time, Pacific time and Indian time. So he didn't know when they were going to arrive. They were as close as Kansas City, and they were going to stay at this camp in St. Louis until sometime in September, which would be Leonard Peltier's birthday. Louie said Leonard would be 41 years old.

When the Indians had set aside an area for the Elders, it was apparent they were very security minded. Everything turned on security. Irwin talked about security several times. He said that the Rainbow Family was also security minded.

The attorneys visited with Louie Irwin for more than two hours and had a very enjoyable time, a very good conversation. Louie apologized for being with the Rainbow Family, for the way they looked, and the way they acted.

The lawyer told Barksdale later, "You are in a hell of a mess if an Indian has to apologize for being your company. Indians will put up with anything."

Barksdale laughed off and on for 30 minutes over that observation. He said that description adequately described the Rainbow Family.

When the visit was concluded, the men returned to their hotel to sleep. It was 10:00 p.m.

The following day they got up and had breakfast. Then they started looking for the Indians again. They found the Rainbow Family where they had been the day before at the park across from the Federal Building. Toward mid-day they also found some remnants of the Rainbow Family at the Totem Pole campground. However, they could not locate any Indians. The tents were either struck or vacant. Since they were dealing with Indian time and living in the white man's world, they decided that they had best return to Alabama.

They had received no directions, no instructions, and they could not find any of the people who had talked Barksdale into coming to St. Louis. The lawyer observed that living on Indian time is difficult for the White Man. Indians have very little organization and practically no direction.

Barksdale said, "I guess you could say, they are not goal oriented. At least, this meeting was a total disaster, so far as goals were concerned."

The lawyer thought that overall it was a good trip. He particularly enjoyed meeting Louis Irwin. Irwin had invited them to the Sun Dance of Leonard Crow Dog at Pine Ridge Reservation the first few days of August. The dance was scheduled to last for four days because to the Sioux, four is a sacred number. They do everything in fours. Louie said the reason for that were the four directions, the four seasons, and nature appreciates fours.

"Another example is the woman is on her moon for four days," he said.

Barksdale said that he could not work the Sun Dance into his schedule. The lawyer told Irwin that he didn't know whether he could go or not. Irwin explained to them that each Medicine Man generally holds a Sun Dance once a year. It is a big religious festival. "What you do for four days is look into the sun from morning to night. A dancer never takes his eyes off the sun. There's a funny thing about it, after you have looked at the sun for a while, you see that the center of the sun has a beautiful blue circle. Once you see that circle, you can see the past or future, or whatever you want to see. The dancers do not eat nor drink water for four days while they are doing the Sun Dance. Some of them will put skewers in their flesh and rip them out at the appropriate time. It's a real good time. I wish you could come."

The lawyer thought that he had learned quite a bit of Indian lore from Louie. He and Barksdale had agreed to do some legal work for the American Indian Movement if they would let them know what they needed.

The trip had been a valuable learning experience for both men. They had learned a little about the Indian religious traditions and a little about how Native Americans think. Both men agreed that they had always admired the Native American because of his love for nature and the environment. They are fine people and probably the most religious people on the continent. They live very near to the soil. They realize their kinship with everything from a bug to a blade of grass. They waste nothing. Unfortunately, the white man has subscribed to another set of values. They are the wasters, the destroyers.

The Indians have a name for the white man, they call them "Fat Takers." The lawyer thought that this was an apt description.

He told Barksdale, "We rush around going nowhere, burning up everything we hold precious, while fearing our deaths. What a mess. We buy things we don't need, to impress people we don't like, with money we don't have. I am not a good White Man. My soul will always be with the Indian."

Louie had told them about an Indian who lost a foot in an industrial accident. Louie said, "He was paid $15,000. When he received his money all of his friends and relatives came to his house and lived with him. They ate, drank whiskey, bought new clothes, and generally had a great time for 10 days. When the money was about gone, they bought some old scraggly steers and butchered them on the lawn and had a big party. When the money was all gone, they left.

Now a white man asked the injured man, 'you sure wasted your money, didn't you?'

'No,' said the Indian, 'I just wish I could cut off the other foot so they will come back.'

I guess that story about sums it up. There is a difference."

On the trip home, Barksdale and the lawyer agreed that they would help Peltier or the AIM if the occasion ever arose. Both of them agreed that they had enjoyed the mysticism of the trip. They wished they could have met Lame Deer, or the event could have been more organized, but they were satisfied with Louis Irwin and his nephew.

"Well, at least we went to St. Louis and met Louie," the lawyer said.

"What do you mean?" Barksdale queried.

"You know, 'Meet me in St. Louis, Louie?'"

"Give it up."

"And we met him at the fair. That's the other

eight bars of the song."
    "Once more, give it up."
    "Okay."

DAVE AND THE DIVER

Dave Johlson had been in a boat wreck near Charlotte, S.C. Actually, it was on the lake at Rock Hill. He and his wife Susan were cruising up the channel of Lake Wylie in their speedboat just as darkness fell. Another boater came out of a side slough from the left, at a high rate of speed, and struck Dave's boat broadside with its bow.

There were numerous serious injuries suffered by the people in the other boat. Eight people, including Dave, were thrown into the lake. Susan stopped Dave's engine just before his boat sank. Dave suffered a broken back and was saved by his life preserver. Eventually, the Coast Guard picked up all the survivors and removed them to the hospital at Rock Hill, South Carolina.

Almost two years later, the injured passengers in the other boat filed suit against Dave and the pilot of their boat. Both boat owners had liability insurance with different companies. Dave was concerned about the tact the insurance lawyers representing him were taking. He was a computer programmer, a natural worrier, a nerd that he referred to as a "typicalpropeller head." And, although Dave had insurance, he did not feel his attorneys were being aggressive enough so far as his defense was concerned.

Dave had done some computer work in Fort Payne, Alabama. He was familiar with a lawyer who practiced in the small town. He hired the lawyer to defend him personally against the plaintiffs, his insurance carrier, and counter-sue the owner and operator of the boat at fault for his damages, which were considerable.

After a cursory investigation from 300 hundred miles away, the lawyer told Dave that he needed additional evidence to proceed. Although they had pictures of his boat showing a gaping hole in the left side of the front of his boat, they needed the other boat to prove that the prow of that boat had, in fact, collided with Dave's boat. The folks in the other boat claimed that Dave's damage was due to him sideswiping their boat. Both boats had sank the night of the wreck. Dave's boat had been raised while the other boat had been abandoned in more than 50 feet of water.

Dave now lived alone in a modest A-frame home on Paradise Point on Lake Wylie near Clover, South Carolina. Because of the abundance of friends constantly coming and going from his home, Dave called his place on the point the, "Paradise Hilton." He went so far as to have T-shirts printed with a picture of his three-bedroom A-frame with "I was a guest at the Paradise Hilton," printed around the home on the front.

After much conversation, the lawyer drove to

the Paradise Hilton on a sunny weekend in May to look for the responsible boat in 55 feet of water. He arrived a little after 1:00 A.M. and promptly found eight other people sleeping in various places around the Hilton. Dave had saved an upstairs bedroom for the lawyer and himself.

Before going to sleep, Dave told the lawyer that he had hired a professional diver to dive for the boat and raise it the following day.

"He'll go down and tie bags to the boat. Then we'll inflate the bags, and up comes the boat," Dave beamed.

"We'll then have the pictures and the boat. That should sink their case and make mine."

The following morning, Dave left the Paradise Hilton early. The lawyer slept in the best he could with almost a dozen people cooking breakfast and eating down stairs. He knew there were young people present because the rock and roll music on the stereo was playing loud, very loud. Still he slept fitfully, off and on, into the noon hour and beyond. Finally, everyone left the house and went down to the lake.

The lawyer was in deep sleep in the middle of the day when Dave awakened him and told him, "The diver we hired is going to be ready to look for the boat in 30 minutes. We need to leave."

The lawyer jumped up from his bed, washed

his face, and in a matter of minutes, he was dressed and ready to leave. He and Dave tooled over to the public dock across the lake in Dave's new speedboat. There, sitting at a public picnic table, was the very professional diver. His name was Mike. He was a muscular young man dressed conservatively in dark blue slacks and a white shirt.

Mike had only the best equipment. The lawyer thought his equipment looked like something from outer space. He came equipped with every piece of the latest equipment down to a marker and a buoy. His marker flag was a nylon red field and a diagonal white stripe signaling a diver is underwater.

When the three men arrived at the site of the sunken boat, Dave dropped the anchor overboard. Once the boat was stable, Mike the diver, slipped out of his street clothes, neatly folded them to avoid wrinkles, all the while wearing blue and white striped spandex briefs. Then he slithered into a black and yellow wetsuit.

But first, standing on the rear of the boat, near the boarding ladder, Mike dropped his "Diver Down" marker buoy overboard. Unfortunately, he had too much weight on the end of the line. The red flag with the diagonal white line promptly sank out of sight and down to the bottom of the lake.

Dave, forever the worried optimist said, "Was that supposed to do that?"

He looked at the surface of the lake as if the marker was going to pop back up on top of the water.

"It ain't supposed to do that," the diver said dejectedly. "I just lost my fucking marker."

Dave's face dropped. His deadpanned freckled face couldn't hide his anticipated fear of failure. He looked knowingly at the lawyer sitting on the right side of the boat.

The lawyer thought, Oh well, what the hell? Just another shitty day in paradise.

Dave, a proficient amateur scuba diver, had been planning to dive with the pro and help search for the boat. He had brought all his diving gear that he stowed in the front of the boat.

When Dave told Mike of his plans, the diver told Dave, "This is a professional dive, and you will not be allowed to dive along with me. I can't be responsible for an amateur. You wouldn't be covered by our insurance."

Dave said that he understood, but the lawyer could tell he was disappointed and didn't like not being able to help look for the boat.

The lawyer wondered if either Dave or his insurance carrier was actually paying the diver 100 bucks for this day. He felt better when the diver took out all of his space-age diving equipment. He had top of the line scuba diving gear. The lawyer was impressed as the diver brought out more and more NASA looking items from his gear bag.

Then, after rummaging through his bag three or four times, obviously searching for something, the diver told Dave that he had forgotten to bring his regulator, the thing that space-age divers breathe through.

Shit! the lawyer thought. A diver without a regulator is just another rock.

Dave beamed as he said, "I have saved the day. I have borrowed a professional diving regulator from a friend."

Then the diver had to eat a little humble pie. He asked Dave if he could borrow his friend's regulator. Dave was happy to accommodate. He wasn't allowed to dive anyway.

Mike looked good in the wet suit with his flippers and watch and other things divers have attached to their belts and other parts of the wet suit. He meticulously checked out his space-age equipment. Regulator worked, check. The face mask was tight, check. The air tanks were working perfectly, check. It was time to go to work.

The diver checked out all of his equipment one more time with just a visual check, including Dave's regulator. As he looked things over very carefully he announced that he was ready. He was sitting with his back to the water, and all at once tumbled backward into the water with his flippers disappearing last.

As he took his last look at the diver, the lawyer thought he looked like Buck Rogers in all his space-age technology. He even had a clear plastic nose cover. Too bad he had forgotten the most important part - the breathing apparatus.

Idiot! he thought. However, he was glad Dave had brought a regulator. Otherwise, he would have made the trip to South Carolina for nothing.

Dave had a big red buoy stowed in the bow of his boat. He threw the big red buoy overboard tethered to the end of a nylon line. It didn't have any weight on it. Dave began to drag it behind the boat as he slowly circled the area where the diver was down. It wasn't long before the lawyer realized Dave was following the bubbles of the diver.

"Why are you following the bubbles?" he asked Dave.

"I don't want anyone to hit the little guy if he comes to the surface unexpectedly. After all, he doesn't have his marker anymore." Both men chuckled over that maneuver.

As a consequence of following the bubbles, Dave eventually entangled the line of the big red buoy in the propeller of his boat. Plus, he discovered he was dragging his anchor.

"Shit!" Dave exclaimed, as he took off his

shirt to dive overboard and disengage the buoy line from the prop.

The lawyer thought, Oh well, everything is working out all right. Dave finally was able to dive. That's what he wanted to do anyway.

While Dave was swimming around underwater at the rear of the boat trying to untangle his buoy line, the lawyer reclined in one of the plush seats under the canvas canopy of the boat. The lake breeze, the sun, the water, the other boats going by, the beautiful day -- what more could anyone ask to enjoy? It was almost perfect.

He smiled to himself as he reflected, What a way to earn a living! just another day at the office, looking for sunken treasure. We are looking for this boat that hit Dave because it resulted in him having horrible damages. This means money from Dave's lawsuit, in his pocket and in mine. If we find the sunken boat, we prove our case and laugh all the way to the bank. Yes, it was a day to enjoy and remember fondly.

After several attempts, Dave retrieved the buoy and retied the buoy line. He discovered that it had been cut in several places by the propeller. Dave decided to stow the big red buoy and its line on the diving platform at the rear of the boat.

The diver surfaced first after about nine minutes. He didn't find the boat. After that, he began to surface every three or four minutes. Dave tracked his bubbles slowly and closely. He said he was doing it for the diver's safety. Plus, he was comfortable doing it now. The buoy was on the platform at the rear of the boat.

When he would surface, the diver would say a few words to Dave, then he would dive again. Five minutes later, the diver surfaced again on the right side of the boat.

He yelled to Dave, "Hey, that was some search pattern. I made a perfect square. I was doing about six kicks each way, covering about 25 feet with each kick. And, I wound up exactly where I was supposed to, at the boat!" he glowed.

"I've been tracking your bubbles with the boat," Dave said morosely, puncturing the diver's bubble. The diver immediately sank below the surface again.

The lawyer told Dave he should have told the guy, "Hey, that was some perfect pattern. You're a fantastic diver." Then the little guy would have gone back into the water like a shark. As it is, we have one slightly dejected diver flopping about in the murky depths of the lake.

After another dive, the professional came up and attempted to rehabilitate himself.

He told Dave, "That was a great dive."

"Oh, you found the boat?" Dave responded

expectantly.

"No," said the diver. "It was a great dive. I found a tree trunk."

Dave said under his breath to the lawyer, "We paid him to find the boat. I mean, that's the only good dive, the one where you find the boat, not a damned tree trunk." Dave was visibly skeptical.

The lawyer agreed with Dave, but he pointed out that they didn't have the best diver in the world.

"What did you expect from a professional diver who forgets the most important part of his equipment?" He was trying to lighten the situation for Dave.

After two more hours, and numerous dives, the diver came up and told Dave, "I'm not going to find that boat. The area is just too big, and the visibility is less than two feet with this good light." He demonstrated his space age spotlight by shining it in Dave's face blinding him momentarily.

"Okay, okay," Dave hastily agreed shielding his face from the light with his hands. "Come around back, and I'll help you back into the boat."

The lawyer's anticipation of big bucks dropped like the diver down buoy of the space age failure. Dave looked at the lawyer dejectedly as the diver got back into his clothes revealing a cotton undershirt with "Gamecocks" emblazoned on it.

"Sorry," he said looking toward the lawyer.

Can't expect much from a South Carolina fan, the lawyer thought as he slowly shook his head from side to side. All the high hopes of his trip had been dashed. The sun was disappearing behind the western hills of the lake. The boats on the water were quiet. The entire area had an eerie cast to it. Dave turned the boat toward the public dock to return the diver to his automobile. The lawyer looked toward the darkened point where Dave lived. Tiny sparkles of light glimmered there.

Another shitty day in paradise, he thought, but it beats whatever comes in second. He enjoyed the cool evening breeze as the boat cut through the water bound for the Paradise Hilton.

TWO PENHOOKERS AND TWO BEERS

Conrad Finnell, a trial lawyer in Cleveland, Tennessee, called the lawyer, who was an old friend of his.

"Hey, I got a client for you. He's a cattle trader, been in a wreck, had some trailer and truck damag -- not much, in the rear mostly -- and he had around a thousand dollars in medical bills. His name is Ford Wear," Conrad took a breath.

"Is this cattle trader the same thing as a penhooker?" the lawyer asked.

"What's a penhooker?" Conrad asked genuinely interested.

"They're yard lizards who lay around cattle sales barns and trade for cattle before the beef is offered for sale by the auctioneer. They pay the farmer in cash, move his beef to their cattle trailers until they think the market is right, and then they'll bring the cattle inside and hope to make a half-cent a pound or even a better profit. If they can make one or two cents a pound, they've had a great day. Farmers don't like them because they consider them to be crooks. Still, they get plenty of business from people wanting to sell their stock and leave rather than having to take a lot number and wait. Plus, a lot of farmers don't want to pay the sales barn's commissions."

"Well he's something like that, maybe on a grander scale," Conrad responded. "He buys at Alabama cattle sales, or on their lots, wherever he can get the best price. Then he hauls the cattle up here to East Tennessee and sells them. He tries to sell them the same day he buys them. He doesn't want to feed them. So I'd say that maybe he is a grand-scale penhooker."

"Okay. As long as we know where we are," the lawyer said, "send him on down."

The old friends visited on the telephone, swapped yarns, disclosed family stories, and generally enjoyed each other for 30 minutes more.

The following day, at 11:05 AM, Ford Wear sat across the desk from the lawyer. "I'm the guy Conrad told you about. I was in his office when he called you."

He was wearing jeans, a blue and white checked western shirt, dirty boots, and a brown Stetson. He was middle aged, overweight, and red faced. He had all his hair with very little gray. In short, he was a man in his prime.

The lawyer sat at his computer keyboard and asked questions. As he questioned Ford, he wrote an account of the interview.

Ford Wear and his son Scotty are cattle traders. They aren't cattlemen because they do not raise or breed cattle. They can't be called cattle buyers because they don't buy cattle, fatten them for several months, and sell them at a profit. They are cattle traders because they buy cattle in the morning and sell them in the afternoon. They own the cattle only as long as the animals are on their cattle haulers.

The name of their business is Wear and Son Cattle Farms. The title is a little misleading, since they do not own a farm. In fact, they live next door to each other on the south side of Cleveland, Tennessee. Ford and his wife Gloria, Scotty's mother, were in their fifties and devoted most of their spare time to Scott Junior, their only grandchild.

Ford and Scotty have been in the cattle business for four years. Their only assets, other than cash, are two red, late-model dual rear-wheel, Dodge pickup trucks with gooseneck cattle trailers that will hold twenty-four cows each.

The Wears start from Cleveland early each morning and drive into central Alabama or Georgia. They go to cattle sales and purchase as many as forty-eight head of cattle. They will then drive the cattle to Cleveland, Athens, or Knoxville, Tennessee, and hope to sell them at a profit. Sometimes they drive as far north as Johnson City. If they can clear as much as ten cents a pound, they have had a very successful day. On their bad days, when the price of beef does not change drastically from Alabama and Georgia to East Tennessee, maybe 2 cents a pound, they might make as much as $900 after cattle barn commissions. On good days they may gross as much as $3,000. They trade cattle five days a week.

If the prices do not hold up for the 150 miles they usually cover, the Wears lose money. If good cattle were not available down around Birmingham, or south of Atlanta, the Wears return with only a few head of cattle, or no cattle at all. Regardless of how they do, they have a rule -- never keep the cattle overnight.

It is overnight that too many bad things can happen. The cattle have to be fed, watered, and doctored. When they ran the risk and did keep cows overnight, almost always one or more of the animals died from the shock of the ride. The secret of their business is to buy low, sell high, and never buy if they cannot make a profit.

While the Wears were gone trading, Gloria Wear called each local market every two hours to check beef prices. Ford or Scotty would contact her by cellular phone from the sale barn before they bought. Her information lets them know the amount they were safe to bid for the cattle or pay the farmer in the yard. They would then call her again when they started toward Tennessee to determine where the best price for beef was in East Tennessee. If prices had declined to where they could not make a profit, they would try to dump the animals in a North Alabama market at cost. This would at least save fuel on the way home.

It was not an easy way to make a living. It was very hard work, chance taking, high risk, great profits and terrible losses. Each of the Wear families usually experienced net earnings of at least $75,000 a year. It had never been discussed, but the father and son were equal partners. Lois, Scotty's wife, kept the books for the partners and wrote the expense checks, co-signed by Gloria, of course.

On Monday, April 13, 1992, at 1:12 a.m. Wear and Son entered the north ramp of I-59 at the Noccolula Falls Exit north of Gadsden, Alabama. Scotty was leading. He had all the animals they had left from that day's business, seven heifers and one bull. Ford was going home empty. They had bought cattle late in Childersburg, south of Talladega, and the price had dropped on them. About three times a year East Tennessee would get the drop in cattle prices before the news reached the cattle sales in the south. When Gloria told Ford the news, that the market had dropped, he radioed Scotty on the CB, "We need to dump our cargo. There are problems at home."

Scotty knew exactly what this meant. They had pulled off at Gadsden, went to the sale a little after 3:30 p.m., and sold 28 head that they had bought at Childersburg. They made one and one-quarter cents a pound overall. So they had grossed a little over $500. This had covered their operating expenses for the day's trading with a tiny profit. They had seven head left. There was no interest in the remaining cattle in Gadsden.

They decided to kill time and make it to the Fort Payne Cattle Sale by opening time at 6:00 a.m. If they got there early, they would catch some shut-eye in the trucks.

Entering the interstate Scotty said on the radio, "I'm not in any big hurry to get up the road. I'm gonna run about the limit. How'm I lookin' back there?"

"Yeah, a big 10-4 on the cruise," Ford raised his headlights to high beam for a good look at Scotty's rig. "You look good. It was a good idea to pen them all in the front stall. It's a little crowded, but they're doing all right. We'll give them more room when we get up the road."

Ford sipped at his steaming cup of black coffee. He was hoping that the market had not dropped out overnight. They needed to at least break even by selling the rest of the animals at Fort Payne.

Ford was a little over a mile north of the exit, six truck lengths behind Scotty. He was continuing to drop back to give Scotty relief from his headlights.

He was at a place where the northbound lane of the interstate is at least 100 feet higher up on a cut in Lookout Mountain than the southbound lane that was not cut into the mountain.

All at once, WHAM!! It felt like an explosion! He grabbed the wheel tighter. The truck was veering dangerously across the darkened interstate toward the left shoulder and median! He regained control of the truck and trailer just as the right wheels hit the gravel off the shoulder. Slowly, he steered the vehicle and its tow back onto the highway.

"What's going on back there?" Scotty screamed into the CB.

Ford could not take time to answer. He was too busy trying to control the truck and figure out what had happened. He continued to work and look in each direction. He had been hit by something, hard! What was it?

"Dad!" Scott yelled. "Are you all right?"

He stopped his truck with the cattle on the right shoulder of the interstate.

He had been looking in his rear-view mirror when he saw a vehicle with one headlight veer off the highway, into the median, and disappear down an embankment. Shortly after it went out of sight, there was a flash! A fireball rose out of the gully between the lanes. It lit up the night sky for miles. Then BOOM! The explosion! The vehicle had blown up!

After frantically searching, Ford had seen a vehicle's left headlight in his left mirror. It was the car that had rammed him. The driver had to be drunk. Ford watched transfixed as the car started toward the left median and never stopped. It went over a high hill and crashed into a deep gully, still above the southbound lane of I-59. Ford stopped his truck on the shoulder of the left lane of the interstate. He knew that the car was gone. He was worried about the driver. Before he could completely come to a stop, the explosion and fireball went off.

"Did you see that?" he screamed to Scotty.

"Dad, for God's sake, are you all right?"

Scotty could see the lights of his father's truck, but he could not understand what had happened.

"I think I'm okay," Ford said. "That poor bastard that rear-ended me is dead. Did you see that explosion?"

Scotty was backing his truck and trailer back down the interstate toward his father. He was good. He never wavered as he backed his truck and trailer down the right northbound lane.

"I called the State Troopers on the police band. We are right near the Gadsden Post. There'll be a trooper here in a few minutes. What happened?"

"I don't know," Ford said. "I'm not feelin' all that chipper. That guy knocked the hell out of me. I always heard about it, and I guess I got it -- whiplash! I feel like my neck is broken. This seat belt saved my life."

"Don't move," Scotty said. "There's an ambulance on the way. You may have broken something. I'm almost there."

"Okay," Ford grunted. "I'm leaning back in the seat. I'd like to look at the trailer, but I ain't feeling that good. I'm just going to stay here a few minutes, okay?"

"Yeah," Scotty replied. "I'm here, shutting this radio down. Put yours on the police band in case they try to contact us."

The younger man parked in the emergency lane, left his motor running, the emergency brake on, and the truck out of gear. He ran to his father's truck. He climbed into the passenger side of the vehicle, left the light on, and looked at his father. Ford was obviously in pain, but he was taking it well. He was leaning back in the seat, still under the wheel, with his eyes closed.

"Are you going to be all right, Dad?" Scotty asked concerned.

"Yeah. I'm getting' better all the time. Give me a few minutes, and I'll be okay," Ford didn't open his eyes.

Scotty looked into the right rear-view mirror. He could see the blue reflection of trooper lights enter the interstate at the Noccolula Exit a mile or so back. Soon he could hear the warning sound of the State Trooper Cruiser. He glanced at his watch. It was 1:37 a.m.

He thought, that was quick. "The trooper post must be nearer than I thought," he said under his breath.

"I can hear the fuzz," Ford said with eyes remaining closed. The trooper's noise was getting closer.

"Yeah. He's almost here," Scotty said, getting out of the truck to meet the trooper.

The headlights and blue light remained on after the trooper pulled up behind Ford's vehicle. Scotty was there to meet the officer as he got out of his car.

"What happened? What's this about a car exploding?" The trooper looked at Scotty. His flashlight was on.

"I don't know exactly," Scotty replied, "Let's ask Dad. He was the one that was hit."

"Yeah," the trooper responded flashing his light on the rear end of the cattle hauler. "Hey, this thing is damaged!"

He played his light over the noticeable damage which had been done to the cattle trailer. The rear gates were totaled. They bent double at impact and were knocked onto the floor in the middle of the long cattle hauler. It was as if the trailer had never had gates.

The trooper could see that a motor vehicle had gone up into the cattle hauler at a very high rate of speed. The unused gates were still in their place against the side walls of the trailer.

The trooper and Scotty left the trailer and went toward the front of the truck. Ford was getting out. He stepped down to the ground and steadied himself against the truck with his left hand.

"It's like this, officer: I was doing the speed limit, sixty-five on the cruise control, following my son. In my mirror, I saw headlights coming up to me at a high rate of speed. I thought the guy would pass me. I gave him plenty of room on the left. I noticed he didn't dim his lights. I was concentrating on the road due to him blinding me when he hit me. He must have been going more'n a hundred miles an hour," he stopped knowing he was exaggerating, but there was no one to contradict him.

"What happened to the car that hit you? Is that the one that exploded?" the trooper asked.

"Yeah. After this guy hit me, he lost it, his car went off into the middle back there where that big dropoff is in the median."

"That's deep," the officer turned back toward the area where the car burned. He walked back down the shoulder.

"I can see some fire still burning down there," he strained his eyes into the night as the sound of the ambulance came over the horizon from Gadsden with lights flashing.

The trooper was accompanied by Ford and Scotty back to the point directly above the place where the car had exploded. He waved to the ambulance with his light, the driver complied and pulled off the interstate above the fire. Other officers arrived from the Reece City Police Department and took control of the traffic on the interstate.

The EMT dismounted the ambulance. "Nobody lived through that," he said looking approximately one hundred feet down to what was left of the automobile as it continued to burn.

"Let's go down and look, Jimmy," he said to the driver.

"I'll go down with you," the trooper said, walking to the side of the ambulance.

"I only have one harness," the EMT said. "Jimmy is going to play me out. If I need you, you can come down my rope."

He hooked his nylon rope through an eyelet on the side of the ambulance. Jimmy allowed slack on the line. The EMT went over the side into the gulch or ditch with his flashlight shining down the embankment toward the fire. The drop was extreme, but it was not a shear wall. It was a very steep grass-and-brush-covered descent. The EMT backed down the embankment as Jimmy played out his line through the hook on the truck.

When the EMT approached the fire, he yelled up to the trooper, "Nobody survived this! The driver's body is either blown to smithereens, or he is up on the bank somewhere. There's nobody down here."

"You sure there's nobody down there? What about passengers?" the trooper yelled from the shoulder of the interstate.

"There's no life down here. No signs there ever was life here -- no blood, flesh, nothing. That guy was blown to bits. Pull me up, Jimmy." The EMT left the burning wreckage and began to climb up the steep embankment as Jimmy and Scott pulled on the other end of the rope.

"I don't know about this," the trooper told Ford. "We're going to have to wait until daylight to find the driver's body. He was probably thrown out the windshield when the car went over the edge. We'll find him."

The trooper turned to the EMT who was back up on the shoulder of the highway. "Was the windshield still in the car? I can't tell from up here."

"Nah, the front of the car is completely gone. What's left of the engine is in the rear seat. That car was mashed. It looks like it has been through one of those car crushers that you see in junkyards. By the way, it's an '86 Buick. I copied down the license plate for you." He handed the trooper the paper.

"Thanks," the trooper said.

Turning to Ford and Scotty, "Like I said, we'll find the driver at daylight. You guys can go on after I finish the wreck report. Come on over to the patrol car. By the way, do you need that ambulance?"

"I think I can make it. I'm in one helluva lot of pain. Maybe that EMT can give me something. Otherwise, I'm going to try to make it home to my family doctor."

The EMT overheard the conversation as he was recoiling his rope. He gave Ford two pills and a bottle of water. "That'll take care of the pain later," he assured Ford.

The Tennesseans climbed into the cruiser. The trooper asked Ford about the wreck again. He listed Scotty as a witness. Completing the report took about 20 minutes. When he closed the aluminum form holder, he said, "Somebody will be in touch with you. The only thing I lack is the amount of damage done to your vehicle. Let's look it over."

By now, all three men had powerful flashlights. They examined the gooseneck. "I believe that is a little bent," the trooper said.

"Yeah, it does look bent forward," Scotty agreed. "You think it'll make it to Cleveland?"

They had been joined by a wrecker driver. He chimed in, "Yeah, it looks all right to me. I'd be careful with it."

"How much damage has been done to the truck," Ford asked the wrecker driver. "You know more about it than we do."

"Looks like about $1,800 damage done to the truck. I looked it over while you were filling out the accident report. Now, the cattle hauler is pretty damaged on the rear. The front looks okay. I'd say the trailer has about $3,500 damage to it."

"I'd think it is more than that, Ford said. I looked it over, and it looks pretty well totaled to me."

"Nah," the wrecker driver responded. "All that can be fixed. $3,500 would fix it like new."

"Let's look at it again," Ford said shining his light on the damage of the trailer. He stepped up into the trailer and looked at the interior. He was facing toward the front. "Yeah, this thing is seriously damaged. Come here and look at it. From the inside, the rear end looks like an accordion."

"I still say, 'no problem,'" the wrecker driver replied. "As long as there is no damage forward of the wheels, the hauler can be fixed for little or nothing."

"Well, I'm going to check," Ford said. The pain pills had not kicked in, and he still had a nagging pain in his neck and shoulders. However, he knew that it was important that the wreck report reflect an estimate of damages as high as possible. He didn't figure the drunk driver who hit him had insurance. He would have to claim uninsured motorist coverage on his own policy with State Farm. He decided to look the front of the carrier over carefully.

The wrecker driver, the trooper, and Scotty came up into the hay and tangled metal of the cattle carrier. The vehicle was lit up well with five flashlights. The EMT joined them last and stepped up into the cattle hauler.

There was a large amount of hay in the front of the trailer. There had been hay throughout the cattle hauler before the wreck. The cows ate it and it absorbed animal waste and made the trailer easier to clean. All flashlight beams flashed on the hay in the front of the trailer.

"What the hell is going on?" a strange voice demanded. "Who in the hell let you bastards in my bedroom?"

A very disheveled man staggered up out of the hay steadying himself on the side of the cattle hauler. He appeared to be disoriented. He thought he was in his own home.

"Who the hell are you?" the trooper demanded.

"What the hell is it to you?" the man responded angrily.

"You are the driver of that '86 Buick, aren't you? You are drunk as a skunk. You hit this cattle hauler, drunk outta your mind, you went through the windshield and landed in the hay in this truck as the back gates were broken away by your bumper," the trooper was accusing.

"That's true, isn't it?" The trooper wanted a confession.

"I mighta had two beers, but I ain't drunk,"

the confused man responded. "I do have an '86 Buick, but I don't know where it is." He looked around as if he was looking for his car.

"The Lord takes care of drunks and fools," the trooper told the crowd.

"Goddamned!" exclaimed the wrecker driver. "This is one for the books."

"Here, let me look at you," the EMT said reaching for the man's pulse.

"Two beers. That was all I had," the drunk kept saying.

"Was anybody with you?" the trooper demanded.

"Nah, I was by myself," the drunk rejoined. "My old lady threw me out earlier. We had a helluva fight, and I went down to Frank's Lounge in Attalla and had a couple of beers. I was headed back to Collinsville. I don't know what else happened," the drunk had slurred speech.

"There's something wrong with my head."

"There sure is," the Emergency Medical Technician said. "You have a severe concussion, but you're lucky to be alive. Let me clean that cut on your forehead."

He began to treat the drunken driver once more.

"I can't believe this," Ford told Scotty. "Test him," he turned to the trooper.

"No need to test this guy,' the trooper said. "He does not meet one single aspect of the field sobriety test. There are a dozen witnesses who can testify this guy is loaded drunk and damned lucky to be alive."

Turning to the drunk, the trooper said, "You're under arrest. What's your name and address?" He had his aluminum pad with him again.

The lawyer turned away from the computer and faced Ford, "This is one of the strangest stories I have ever heard. That guy went through his own windshield and was thrown into the cattle trailer and was saved by the hay."

"I guess that's about right," Ford said. "Here's my insurance policy and the wreck report. Naturally, the guy doesn't have insurance."

The lawyer took the papers and allowed Ford to go and join Scotty in their business. Three weeks later, he sent a $14,800 check to Conrad in Cleveland with releases for the Wears to sign. Conrad made the disbursements, returned the executed releases and the lawyer's portion of the fee.

Among other things, his cover letter said, "I certainly appreciated working with you on this case. Your efforts on behalf of our cattle trader clients were exemplary, as usual. I look forward to working with you again. I have another case I will refer to you later this week."

The lawyer looked at the check which was

his part of the fee. Then he re-read the accompanying correspondence.

He chuckled as he finished the letter and muttered to himself, "I hope, whomever he sends, it's not another bunch of penhookers.

"Cattle traders, my foot. They're penhookers to the bone, and that drunk only had two beers."

THE ROBING ROOM INCIDENT

Friday marked the end of a very difficult trial week for the local bar association. Jury trial after jury trial had proceeded through the court system ending Thursday at around 3:00 p.m.

The lawyer hurried into the dimly lit robing room of the third-floor courtroom. He could hear the judge calling the day's docket through the closed door. He quickly looked at his watch, "9:00 a.m., he's starting right on time, as usual."

He slipped quietly into the crowded courtroom and found a seat in the pit near the south wall that was lined with other lawyers.

It was DR-Day, domestic relations trials. Terrible divorces, volatile child custody cases, and all manner of visitation problems were the fare of the day. There were petitions to modify divorce decrees and petitions to collect delinquent child support. There were petitions for temporary restraining orders and petitions to cite violators for contempt. It was a painful mix of cases that would be heard by the Honorable Circuit Judge.

The judge was usually a jolly personable fellow who was good company wherever he might be. However, as every member of the local bar knew very well, he had a very short fuse, little tolerance for disorganization, and no patience at all for delay. He totally disregarded bombast, and he was reluctant to accept any excuse, no matter how valid. Still, he was acutely aware that he was a politician, elected by the people; and although he might not run again, by habit he always played to the members of the jury and large audiences. However, he was most judicious in utilizing the Court's time wisely.

Friday's audience was loaded with distrought women, nervous husbands, angry mothers-in-law, worried grand-parents, selfish deadbeat dads, and more than a usual number of children of various sizes and ages. Families were sitting together around the courtroom in clumps.

The substitute court reporter was in place recording the judge's every word. She flexed her fingers now and then, cracking her knucks over her machine. She checked and rechecked her tape recorder. She checked her paper and made sure her computer was on. She stayed ready.

The local domestic relations bar sat around in the chairs inside the pit. Others were at the party tables, and several were sitting in the jury box. All were paying close attention and following along as the Court called the docket. The state sat in its usual seats at the state table. Department of Human Resources representatives and the assistants to the assistant district attorney sat inside the rail ready to assist and consult.

It was obvious to all that the judge was strictly business this last day of trials. He was actually very tired. The week had been a criminal docket, and he had to remain alert throughout every aspect of every case. It had been very stressful and something he could have easily handled as a younger man. But now, after 26 years hearing lawyers pontificate and witnesses prevaricate, he was a bit exhausted.

The judge's attitude established his power and authority over the witnesses and parties that he would pass judgment for or against. His overall demeanor frightened the audience into complying with every word proceeding out of his mouth. He continued to call the docket as announcements were made in response to his queries by various members of the assemblage comprising the circuit court. It was not pleasant experience for the lawyers.

The lawyer had quickly and very quietly closed the robing room door and had taken his seat in the chair next to the door. His opposing counsel in the only case he would try that day sat in the penultimate chair.

The lawyer whispered to his opponent, "Has he called our case yet?"

"No, and don't say anything when he does," the opponent whispered back.

The judge's courtroom deputy looked at the two whispering lawyers while the judge was addressing a party seated in the audience.

The opponent continued, "Look at that muscle jump in his jaw. He is in rare form this morning."

The lawyer could see the judge's right masseter muscle flexing and unflexing his mandible as he went frustratingly down the list of the business at hand and cases set for trial.

The lawyer quickly looked around the courtroom as he listened to the tone and impatience in the judge's voice. It was cutting, tolerating little, very businesslike, moving things along. He knew the opponent was telling him that he should simply answer that he was present, rather than telling the judge their case was probably for trial. If the judge was in a foul humor, and if he was told that he might have a trial rather than a settlement, he would snap back and tell the lawyer publicly that he had not negotiated that day. From then on, times would be hard for the lawyers and parties further down the docket.

The judge called the case involving the local bar commissioner. The opponent sitting next to the lawyer was in that case also. He answered, "Ready."

The client of the bar commissioner answered from the audience when the judge asked if he was present.

"Where's your lawyer?" the judge asked.

"I don't know. I haven't seen him today."

The judge instructed the courtroom deputy to call the bar commissioner and tell him and the other six lawyers missing docket call that if they were not present in the courtroom within 10 minutes, the sheriff would escort them to the courthouse. "And report back to me."

"Yes, Sir." She left the courtroom quickly.

At the close of the docket call, the judge was obviously short tempered and extremely aggravated. It was a propitious time to stay out of his way. He abruptly stood up and walked off the bench, through the robing room, out the hallway, into the Court administrator's office, and peered out the third floor window at the darkened law office across the street from the courthouse. He briskly walked back into the robing room where the local bar had assembled to negotiate and hear instructions from the Court. As he entered, all talking ceased. The lawyers, assistants, and court personnel stopped and looked at the judge. The court reporter looked anxious to work. Everyone else looked genuinely concerned as a result of the judge's demeanor.

The lawyer could remember another occasion when the robing room contained the same group. On that occasion, he and the district attorney were agreed that they were not exactly ready to try a case scheduled for trial.

The lawyer approached the bench and presented a motion for continuance. The judge read the motion, worked his jaws, stormed off the bench, calling the district attorney and the lawyer out into the robing room. With a red face and an impatient voice the judge said, "I am tired of running this court like a circus. There's a jury sitting out there waiting to try a case. Now, all of a sudden there's no case to try!"

He stomped out of the room slamming the door leading up the stairs to his chambers. Suddenly, he wheeled around and came back through the door and said to his courtroom deputy, "I want you to organize this docket. I don't have the patience to work with these clowns. Call me when the first case is ready." He again slammed the door in a flurry of flowing black cloth.

The district attorney smirked to the lawyer, "Well, shake hands, Emmett Kelly. My name is Bozo."

"Bozo does the court thing," the lawyer laughed.

Then the two men laughed for a moment after being referred to as clowns by the judge.

The lawyer thought that the present moment might be a bit more serious than the time the judge told his deputy to send in the clowns. He decided to become like a rope on the horizon - make a very low profile.

The judge was muttering under his breath as he re-entered the room, "I looked at his office across the street and it looks like the lights are off. He may not be practicing law today."

He was fuming about the missing lawyer, who had the first case, and two other early cases on the docket.

The clients were present, the opposing lawyers were present, but the missing lawyer was absent without word. The judge was fit to be tied.

"Come with me," he instructed the courtreporter and re-entered the courtroom bound for the bench. She followed him cracking her knuckles. The members of the bar looked at each other. The assistants and representatives looked at each other. No one said a word.

About that time, the missing lawyer walked into the robing room in an open double-breasted suit. Instinctively, the bar moved to the opposite side of the dim lit room for self-preservation.

"Do I have the scurvy?" the missing lawyer asked.

"No. You are just on top of the list, and we are afraid lightning may strike where you stand," the president of the bar responded for the group.

The judge came back out of the courtroom with the court reporter in quick pursuit. The courtroom deputy had been dispatched to call some other poor missing member of the bar who had left at the end of the docket call.

The judge spied the missing lawyer, and said sarcastically, "Oh, I thought you had quit practicing law."

"No. Sorry I'm late, Judge. My client is in the courtroom." He tried to smooth it out by saying something positive.

"I know that," the judge responded testily. "He answered when I called the docket, and you didn't." He stared the missing lawyer down.

He literally spit out the next sentence, "Get in there and negotiate with your opponent. Your case is first up for trial, and I'm ready to try it. All these people are waiting and you're late. Get to work!"

The missing lawyer joined his opposition in the jury room to attempt to negotiate a settlement. Another lawyer started to leave. The judge yelled, "You have a case here today! Do not leave this room!" The lawyer meekly returned without a word.

Grumbling to himself, the judge re-entered the courtroom to take a settlement which had been announced at docket call. Immediately after the settlement he came back into the robing room and began to question the bar association about what they were doing to settle their cases.

"What are the chances your case will be

tried? How long will it take? And, I don't want any discovery during trial. If a case is going to be tried, I want the attorneys to stay directly on the issues. I have heard it all before, perhaps a thousand times. I only want to hear jurisdictional matters, grounds, the amount of the property involved, income, and what is recommended as the best interests of the children by each of the parties. I don't need any jury-persuading histrionics, passionate pleas, nor attempts at cutie pie tricks. The facts, shown briefly, without accumulation, with as many stipulations as possible, will be sufficient. Is there anyone who does not understand?" No one said a word. The lawyer thought the judge sounded a lot like his DI during the Korean War.

"Have you heard from the bar commissioner?" The judge continued. "He is the second lawyer to have a case on the docket, and he's not here. Why do we schedule court if the lawyers aren't going to show up?" He asked anyone who was listening. No one answered.

He looked at his docket. He made a notation, he paced the floor, and he fumed because the bar commissioner was not there. He confirmed with the other side that they were ready for trial. Then, as he was looking at his watch again, the bar commissioner walked in.

The bar commissioner had reddish hair, a

full beard and mustache. He was wearing jeans, old sneakers without socks, and a blue denim shirt opened at the neck. He stopped right after he came through the door. He was looking eye to eye with the judge while the entire bar was standing meekly mute behind the judge.

The judge looked the bar commissioner up and down. He became so angry he was forced to bow his head in abject derision and frustration. With red face, through clenched teeth, without raising his head, he exploded in measured tones, "Are you aware you have the second case on the docket?"

Before the bar commissioner could say anything, the judge answered his own question, "Of course not! You aren't dressed for court. You are not ready. Your client is here, your opposing counsel is here, his client from out of state is here at great expense, and you aren't ready!"

The bar commissioner appeared to look at his honor in total amazement. His eyes became large, his voice low, and he began, "Well, I can't blame your clerk, because I got notice of the trial set for today. I can't blame my secretary because she did not pick up the trial setting notice, I did. I can't blame our docket clerk for this case failing to be put on the schedule, because I never gave it to her. I picked up the notice, took it to my office, got busy on something else, and it fell through the cracks. What else can I say? It is totally my fault. I apologize to the Court for any inconvenience I have caused anyone, but I simply made a mistake."

Without raising his head, which he had been shaking from side to side as the bar commissioner gave his excuse, the judge said through clenched teeth, "That's not good enough. You have held up the Court, you have cost opposing counsel money, and you have caused great inconvenience and expense to the opposing party."

"Well, I didn't know a thing about this case being set until my secretary called me this morning as I was leaving to go hunting. She said I had 10 minutes to get here, and I came like I was. I am not prepared to try this case. I apologize." He sounded sincere. At least he was telling the truth and taking the heat for it.

"You had better tell me something better than that," the judge remonstrated.

"Okay," said the bar commissioner thinking fast, "It was the lawyer's fault."

The judge still didn't look at the bar commissioner. "What has the lawyer got to do with it? He was here on time, and he is not even in your case. This had better be good."

"He's a Republican."

"What?"

"The lawyer is a Republican. It has been my

experience that all bad things that happen in this country are caused by Republicans. I mean, look at Newt Gingrich. The lawyer is the only Republican I know. Therefore, my misplacing my docket and missing court today must have been the lawyer's fault."

The judge didn't look up. The bar was tittering in awe at the temerity of the response. Even the lawyer, who said nothing, was silently laughing. Finally, His Honor began to laugh. He still didn't raise his head. It was as if he was trying to hold the loughter back, but he couldn't hold it.

Laughing so hard tears were streaming down his face, as he raised his head, the judge said, "That is singularly the worst excuse I have ever heard in all my life."

The members of the bar continued to join in the glee. Certainly, the bar commissioner had been on his toes. He had defused a very serious situation and saved the day for the bar.

From then on, the judge was in good spirits, the bar was in good spirits, and not one single case went to trial. Every case was settled with the exception of the bar commissioner's case, which was continued, and one other case that needed a 90 day period to dispose of some issues before the final settlement. It was one of the most pleasant days in court in many years.

It was a great day when everyone at the bar was fully competent, cooperative, and thoroughly enjoyed their profession. Each and every member of the bar had a win-win situation. Each member looked good all day and settled cases. The judge cleaned up his docket and generally enjoyed visiting with the bar and the parties all day.

Upon quiet reflection, the lawyer thought that if a Republican caused the bar commissioner to miss the docket call, then the Republican might as well claim credit for the good day. There was no one he could brag to. In celebration, he bought two tickets to a GOP fundraiser featuring the Republican Attorney General.

THE SALESMAN

It was right at sundown. The lawyer was washing up for dinner when the doorbell rang.

"Sir, my name is Kevin Hale. I'm a college student at the university. I'd like to talk to you just a minute."

"Come in, Kevin."

"Hey, Mister, you have quite a grip."

"I know. What can I do for you?"

"You have two children at the university; right?"

"Yeah, what are you selling, Kevin?"

"Well, Sir, I wanted to talk to you about your children at the university."

"What are you selling, Kevin?"

"That's what I am trying to tell you, Sir, if you will just let me."

"I'll let you. What are you selling, Kevin?"

"Well, it is the greatest book in the world."

"You're selling Bibles. Right, Kevin? I have Bibles, Kevin."

"Everyone has a Bible, Sir. I'm not selling Bibles."

"I'm not interested in any religious books, Kevin."

"Sir, I'm not wanting to sell you a religious book. It's not just any book."

"Good. I have plenty of religious books, Kevin. What university to you attend?"

"The University of Tennessee."

"Oh, that's it, Kevin. I'm a Bama alumnus. You're history. Goodbye."

"Sir, you'all have beaten us for the past five years. What do you want?"

"We're supposed to beat you 10 years in a row. You win one, and then we beat you 10 more. I hate the big orange. I despise the Vols. Next to Auburn, I hate UT most."

"You can't hold that against my book."

"You must be kidding. I hold that against you, your book, the air you breathe, and the horse you rode in on. Sorry you're leaving, Kevin."

"I can't believe you're throwing me out, Sir."

"I'm not throwing you out, Kevin. I am escorting you out. Why don't you just pretend you're leading a parade, and I'm the brass band?"

"You won't even look at my book, for your children's sake? I use it every day in my studies at UT."

"Goodbye, Kevin. My children buy books at Bama."

"I hope we beat the hell out of you people this year."

"Aha! So you didn't make a sale for your book, and now your true orange and white colors come out, eh, Kevin?"

"They were always there, Sir. I hope Bama loses every game."

"Spoken like a true Vol, Kevin. Roll Tide!"
"Go Big Orange!"

LAUGHED OUT OF COURT

It was shortly after 9:00 o'clock on a cloudy Monday morning.

"There's a guy in a wheelchair with a plaintiff's collar coming in," the secretary announced to the lawyer.

He listened closely as he heard the chair's wheels clicking down his hallway. He heard a bump, muffled cursing, as the person pushing the chair bumped the injured man into the wall. The lawyer stood up and walked out into the hallway to greet the potential client.

"Bring him right on in here," he said to the freckled-face teenage boy pushing a young man in the wheelchair. The lawyer gestured toward his office door and hastened to move a chair near the door in order that the teen might accomplish his task. The man in the chair continued to grumble under his breath.

Once the chair had been turned to face the lawyer's desk, the teen sat in the chair the lawyer had moved to accommodate the wheelchair. The lawyer looked at the prospective client. He was in his mid-twenties, clean cut, cast on his right leg, all the way up to the hip. There was a cast on his left arm bent at the elbow with a prop running down to his rib cage to support the arm. Then, there was that plaintiff's collar holding his neck in place.

Stitches were showing in his face where it

was stitched in several places. The wounds were still red, and the stitches were still visibly in place. He had a gash under his left eye, across the forehead, and a half moon cut on the left side of his nose.

"Went through the windshield," the lawyer thought.

The man in the wheelchair began his labored story. "I'm in the Army, stationed in Vietnam. I've been home on a furlough for 17 days. I had 30 days before I was going to be reassigned. So I got 13 days to go.

"Anyway, last Saturday night I was in a wreck; broke my leg in two places, crushed a vertebra in my neck, fractured six ribs, broke my forearm, and cut my face all to pieces.

"I'm an E-6 in the Army. I've been in eight years. Now they're going to cashier me out because I have these non-service connected injuries. I called my C.O. and he is going to get me some treatment, but it looks doubtful I'll be able to make a career out of the Army. I want to sue the hell out of the people who did this to me."

"Do you happen to have a wreck report?"

"Nah, they said it would take a week to get it from the P.D."

"Okay. Tell me what happened." The lawyer hoped it was a good case. Certainly, the soldier had the injuries for a healthy settlement or verdict. The questions running through his brain were, what about liability? and, is there a defendant who can pay?

There are three legs to successful litigation: 1. There must be liability; 2. There must be damages; and 3. There must be a defendant who can favorably respond, i.e., pay.

The soldier began, "About eight, Saturday night, we were coming from out in the county into town. I was driving my brother's car. We topped this hill. I was running about 55 miles per hour, which is the speed limit out there, and these headlights were directly in my lane. I swerved off the road to avoid a head on collision and hit a damned car up on jacks that I couldn't see. Some niggers were changing a tire."

The lawyer interrupted, "We can do without the racial slurs. I believe people of color prefer to be called Black today."

"Look," said the soldier squinting his bloodshot left eye, "In Nam they call themselves niggers. They call us honkies, and we call them niggers. These niggers were on a nigger weekend -- 24 hours of fighting, 24 hours of fooling around, and 24 hours of tire changing." He tried to laugh at his racial joke, but the pain in his face only allowed him to snicker.

The lawyer was repulsed by the tone of the conversation, but he was more worried about there being insurance or a defendant who could pay in the equation.

"Was there insurance? Obviously, the African-Americans probably did not have insurance?"

"Not a dime," replied the soldier. "But that damned woman who was driving a pickup truck, blocking my lane, has Farm Bureau. And she's the one who was really at fault. She was blocking the road with her bright lights shining right in my eyes. The niggers were off the road doing what they had a right to do. So, the way I see it, they ain't at fault anyway."

"How do you figure that?" The lawyer asked.

"Well, I wouldn't be in this shape if she had stayed in her own damned lane. She was blocking my lane. You hear me? She was blocking the fucking road!"

The lawyer's secretary came into the room with a client-attorney contract along with three medical authorization forms. The contract was signed setting out a contingent fee agreement to prosecute a case against Mrs. Caldwell, the woman driving the pickup truck.

The lawyer questioned the soldier about his injuries, identified his medical providers, filled out a client data profile, identified witnesses, and suggested that they go to the scene if the soldier was up to it. He was.

The lawyer got his camera, measuring tape, legal pad, and helped the teen remove the soldier out to a pickup truck parked at the curb.

The wheelchair was put in the back while the soldier held on to the door jamb. After the chair was secured the best it could be with the brakes on and bricks chocking the wheels, the two men lifted the complaining soldier up into the truck and carefully reseated him in his chair.

"Don't drive too fast, I can't stand all this leaning," the solder said trying to adjust his casts to a comfortable position in the chair.

The lawyer followed along in his Pontiac Tempest. Although his driver attempted to be as careful as possible, the lawyer could see it was a miserable ride for the soldier.

When they arrived at the wreck scene, the Fort Payne - Valley Head Highway. After they got out of their vehicles, the teen pointed out all the landmarks to the lawyer. The soldier remained in his wheelchair. There was an obvious impact point on the right shoulder of the road coming toward Fort Payne.

The wreck scene and debris were photographed. The lawyer drove down below the hill and photographed the highway to show that the solder could not have seen the lights of the pickup truck until he topped the hill. Then it was too late to avoid the wreck.

After goodbyes to the soldier and his young friend, the lawyer went to the junkyard and photographed the soldier's brother's totaled Plymouth Valiant. Then he photographed the old Chevrolet he had rear-ended. He then went to the police station and talked the desk sergeant into giving him a copy of the wreck report which had not been officially filed because it had not been signed by the investigating officer. He returned to his office and dictated letters requesting medical records from the medical providers of the soldier.

He studied the unfinished wreck report. Mrs. Caldwell was employed as a school bus driver. She was 47 years old. She was driving a blue '68 Ford pickup truck. She was in the wrong lane of traffic attempting to provide light for the men changing the tire on the disabled vehicle. When she knew the soldier was topping the hill, she attempted to back up into her correct lane of traffic.

She claimed to have successfully returned to her lane when the wreck occurred.

After his brief investigation, the lawyer thought he might have the three legs of a successful plaintiff's law suit: damages, liability, and a defendant who can pay.

Eventually, he attempted to settle with Farm Bureau, but the insurance company would pay no more than the soldier's medical bills and pay for repairing his brother's automobile to the lowest possible repair estimate.

True to his suspicions, the soldier was not welcomed back into the Army. He did receive treatment for his injuries at the Fort Bragg

Army Hospital,

; but once he reached his point of maximum medical improvement, he was discharged. No more Vietnam excitement for him. He went to the VA Hospital in Birmingham to recuperate.

The lawyer was proud of his client, particularly after he learned he had been awarded the Bronze Star and Purple Heart. He prepared the case with great zeal.

During discovery, Mrs. Caldwell said that she was in fact a school bus driver, and had been for 16 years. She had never had a ticket nor a wreck. On the night in question she was simply trying to be a Good Samaritan. She had taken a group of school children to the skating rink in Fort Payne for a skating party.

After the party she was driving the kids home when she came upon two black men, Robert Lewis and Leroy Grant, pushing a flat tire along the side of the road. She stopped and asked if they needed help. They did. They needed a ride to a service station. Their car had a flat tire, and they didn't have a spare.

They had jacked up the car, taken the flat tire off, and they were pushing the casing to a service station where they might put a tube in it. Although Mrs. Caldwell was going home to Valley Head in the opposite direction, she offered to take the men back to town and bring them back.

The men were thankful for the ride and

climbed into the back of the pickup. Mrs. Caldwell drove them about two miles to the service station, waited while they put a tube in the bad tire, inflated the tire, and loaded it back on the truck. She then drove them back to where their car was up on the jack.

When they arrived at the disabled auto, it was dark, and the men couldn't see to replace the tire on the lugs. No one had a flashlight. Mrs. Caldwell offered to shine her headlights on the left side of the Chevrolet while Robert Lewis replaced the tire on the left rear hub. Leroy Grant was not helping. Mrs. Caldwell did not know what happened to him. She did not see him until after the wreck.

The lawyer thought he had an excellent case and prepared it without flaw. When the jury was selected, he was confident he was going to get a policy limits verdict and then some.

The counsel representing Farm Bureau Insurance Company was seated at the defendant's table with Mrs. Caldwell. His name was Jim Wilson and was the local insurance defense attorney. He had an excellent won-loss record and was considered to be the best legal mind in the county. He represented one of the banks, the city, the county, the hospital board, the board of education, and all the major corporations in the city. In short, Jim Wilson was a very skilled, highly competent, "silk stocking" counsel. It didn't hurt his reputation that more than two-thirds of the populace in the county had Farm Bureau Insurance.

The lawyer thought he might get a record verdict off ole Jim this time. He certainly had it coming as Jim did not settle any Farm Bureau Insurance Company cases no matter the fault of his insured or the injuries of the plaintiff. If the attorney for the plaintiff didn't take some Farm Bureau policy holders as jurors, the case would have to be put off and a special jury called. This took several years.

Later, the lawyer learned that there were only 1,400 local citizens in the county jury pool, and a majority of them were dead. That meant that a blue ribbon jury of about 450 men were trying all the jury cases, and almost all of them had Alabama Farm Bureau Insurance. It was a terrible situation.

Desperate times call for desperate measures. The lawyer arranged to get appointed to a criminal case. He immediately appealed, challenging the jury venire system. Rather than allow the case to go to the Supreme Court, the Alabama Court of Criminal Appeals conferred with the legislative leaders, and the jury system was changed throughout the state. The new law even allowed women to serve on juries. From that time on, everyone who had a driver's license, or was on a voting list, was put into the selection process. Ole Jim didn't fare so well after that.

That would come much later. Now, after the selection process, although there were some Farm Bureau policy holders in the box, the all-male jury looked pretty good to the lawyer. His opening was persuasive.

Jim told the jury that the soldier was speeding and contributed to his own injuries and for that reason could not recover. In Alabama, contributory negligence, no matter how slight, was an absolute defense. In the area where the wreck occurred, if the soldier was driving 56 miles per hour, he could not recover.

The lawyer put on his witnesses, read his doctor's depositions, introduced his pictures, measurements, the medical records, and the soldier's lost career earnings. By the time he was through, he had put damages on the board totaling more than $250,000. He was more than confident when he rested.

The investigating officer as well as the jury were obviously on the side of the Bronze Star, Purple Heart, winning Vietnam Vet.

Jim called Mrs. Caldwell. She tried to persuade the jury that the soldier was speeding. On cross-examination she was destroyed. The lawyer thought it was like shooting fish in a barrel. He was going to clean up Farm Bureau Insurance Company this time.

He had heard that Mrs. Caldwell had employed private counsel who had put Jim on notice that Farm Bureau should settle within the policy limits of $50,000. Jim refused. By law, this made Farm Bureau liable for all damages the jury might award. The lawyer thought he was going to break the bank.

By the time the plaintiff had put on his entire case and Mrs. Caldwell had been destroyed on cross, Jim was beginning to rethink his decision to try to prove contributory negligence on the part of the soldier. He had one witness left, Robert Lewis. Leroy Grant had moved on to greener pastures and could not be located for deposition or trial.

Jim's last witness, Robert Lewis, boogied into the courtroom when he was called to testify. He was wearing yellow shoes, purple trousers, a green jacket, and a pink shirt. He was tall, 6'2", and he floated up to the stand in a rhythmic manner as if he was moving along to music only he could hear.

He was sworn by the Clerk and slid into the witness chair. He was missing a few teeth, but several front teeth were lined with gold. He smiled as he sat down.

Jim began slowly. This was it. He was very concerned that his decision not to settle had possibly been the worst choice he had made in more than 25 years of practicing law. After eliciting the name, address, and lack of occupation on the part of Robert Lewis, he asked the judge for a short recess. The judge gave him five minutes. The lawyer went to the restroom. Shortly after entering the toilet, he was joined by Jim.

"What would you think about $35,000?" Jim asked the lawyer.

"I wouldn't think much of it," the lawyer replied at the urinal.

"I can't get any more authority than that," Jim said with concern in his voice. "The adjusters believe that your man was speeding."

"I think if we were going to settle, we should have settled before the trial had come to this point. Right now, I think I'm going to hit you a strong lick. So, until you offer the policy limits, plus your med pay, we aren't interested."

"Okay," Jim replied feeling somewhat sorry for himself. He had an all-white southern jury with all his hopes riding on a Black man, Robert Lewis. He didn't feel much like urinating, but he did.

The Court reconvened with Robert Lewis in the witness chair smiling a big gold-toothed grin toward some friends in the audience. A family of about nine African-Americans had come to see him testify. He was still moving a little to the music he was hearing in his head waiting for Jim to go forward.

"All right, Robert Lewis, tell the jury where you had been on the Saturday in question."

"Well, say, er-uh, you know, Missa Jim, me and Leroy been up in the nouth end of the county since early in the maunin. Long bout dark, we cided to go home. Bout two mile outta town, we done had a flat on the leff rear. I don't have no spare. So, me and Leroy cided to take off da wheel and roll it inna town and put a tube in it. We had the money for a tube."

"Then what happened?"

"Well, say, er-uh, Missa Jim, you know, I jacked it up and took the lug wranch to it. The car was offin the road and jacked up purty high. Me and Leroy made sure it was okay, and we started rollin dat wheel down da road toward town. After we done gone bout a quarter, dis white lady come along in a pickum-up truck wiff a bunch of kids in da back. She stopped and offered to take us to town to git dat tar fixed. We wuz right happy to jump in da back wiff dat tar. It wuz a helluva lot better dan walkin. Mrs. C. took us to da Amoco station an we paid $3.45 for a tube. The man put it in dat old tar and filled it wiff air. Mrs. C. waited on us and took us back to da car.

"Then what happened?"

"Well say er-uh, Missa. Jim, you know, we got out offen dat truck an I done told Leroy I would take da lug and put dat tar back on. Leroy said he had to..... You know?"

"He had to what?"

"He had to.....You know. He had to... Uh,

you know, bleed his lizard."

"What?"

"You know, piss? There I said it, but I didn't mean nothin by it." Robert Lewis looked at the jury sincerely apologizing.

"Then what happened?"

"Well, say, er-uh, Missa Jim, you know, I couldn't see no lugs to put da wheel back on. We din't have no flashlight, and Leroy wuz sorta dancin around looking for a place to do it. Bout dat time, Mrs. C. hollered out dat she'd shine her lights on da car sos I could puts da tar on."

Jim didn't know what else to say, so he continued, "Then what happened?"

"Well, say, er-uh, Missa Jim, you know, with dem lights shinin on us, Leroy wuz getting on pretty bad. He needed to do it right then. He'd done drunk some beer during da afternoon and he's needin to git rid of it. But, we got dis white lady wiff a truck load of white kids tryin to hep us out. So we couldn't say nothin."

"Did you ask Mrs. C. to help you?"

"We never axed that white woman nothin, Missa. Jim. She done did it on her own free will, outta the goodness of her heart."

"Then what happened?"

"Well, I squats down to put the tar back on while I got light to do it. Leroy is on da other side of da car looking for a place to take a leak."

Jim decided this was the time to make out his case of contributory negligence. "Was it a clear night, Robert Lewis?"

"Well, say, er-uh, Missa Jim, you know, yeah. I guess it was clear. It warn't rainin or anythin. But it was sure a black night out there outa town."

"Was the wind blowing, or any other noise going on while you were putting the tire back on?"

"Well, say, er-uh, Missa Jim, you know, no. It wuz quiet except for Mrs. C.'s motor wuz runnin."

Jim made his move, "Immediately before the impact did you hear anything?"

"Well, say, er-uh, Missa Jim, you know, no. I din't hear nothin."

Jim decided he would lead a little. "Did you hear the car coming before it hit your car?"

"Well, say, er-uh, you know, naw, Missa Jim. I din't hear nothin. It wuz just wham!" Dat's it. I ain't got no car no more. You know what I mean? Wham! Dat man knocked the livin hell outa my car. It just flew offa dat jack."

Robert Lewis' eyes widened as he remembered the impact. But, each time he said, "Wham!" he would tightly close his eyes as if he were remembering the incident photographically.

"And you didn't hear the car coming before the impact?"

"Well, say, er-uh, Missa Jim, you know, naw. I ain't never heard nothin."

Jim had to press it. He could see his case coming apart like a $3.00 suitcase. "Robert Lewis, if you didn't hear the automobile coming before impact, did you see it before impact?"

"Well, say, er-uh, you know, naw, Missa Jim, I ain't never seed no car before da hit."

"Robert Lewis, when your motor vehicle was struck by the oncoming vehicle, what did you see."

"Well, say, er-uh, Missa Jim, you know, Missa Jim, I'm just sorta hunkered down twisting dem lug nuts back on dem bolts tryin to git dat tar back on befoe somethin happens. Cause I knows dat Mrs. C. is doin us a favor, but she wuz runnin a risk bein in da wrong lane an all."

Jim could feel his heart sink. His pulse was beating fast. He knew he had no chance of surviving this trial without a substantial verdict. How would he explain it to Farm Bureau? He was breaking on the edge of being panic stricken.

"Robert Lewis, I want you to take a minute and think this thing through. If you didn't hear anything immediately before impact, tell the jury exactly what you saw immediately before impact. Did you see any headlights?"

"Well, say, er-uh, you know, Missa Jim, I ain't seed no lights."

Jim was exasperated. "Robert Lewis surely you saw something. What did you see?"

"Well, say, er-uh, you know, Missa Jim, it wuz wham! All of a sudden, WHAM! Dat car wuz done gone. I looked up and I seen Leroy. He wuz standin over on da other side of da car, or where da car once wuz. He was standin over dare shaking his hickey. He hadn't been able to wait. You know, one minute da car is dare and the next minute, WHAM! It ain't dare no moe. Dat car is done gone, knocked right down da road."

Jim thought he might make his case by the distance the jacked vehicle was knocked down the shoulder of the road.

"How far was your car knocked at impact, Robert Lewis?"

"Well, say, er-uh, you know, Missa Jim, I don't know. It wuz a pretty excitin time, you know, dem lights, dat car, dat jack, lug ranch, an dat WHAM!" Squinted eyes again.

The lawyer noticed that the jury had been hanging on every word of the Robert Lewis account of the accident. They had not paid much attention to the testimony of Mrs. Caldwell. The lawyer felt the jury did not believe Mrs. Caldwell. However, they were believing Robert Lewis. He was a fully believable witness. They were also beginning to smile and chuckle as Robert Lewis told his story. They were warming to the point they were laughing with Robert Lewis as he continued on the tract he was on.

The lawyer was concerned.

Jim pressed on. "Okay, Robert Lewis, tell the jury what happened next."

"Wha'd you mean?"

"After the WHAM! What did you see?"

"I seed Leroy."

"What did you say?"

"I sayed, Leroy, where's da car? Leroy was shakin off, and he said he din't know whered da car went? Miz. C. wuz backin up, an I'm still squattin at where da tar wuz."

The jury began laughing uproariously. One juror was almost out of his seat. The judge turned his chair to the wall in order that the jury would not see him laughing. The courtroom deputy was laughing, the court reporter was laughing, and the audience was laughing. Everyone in the courtroom was laughing except the lawyer and the soldier. The lawyer knew the seriousness of the peril his case was in at that moment.

"We're being laughed out of court," he whispered to his client.

"Robert Lewis, what happened to the lug wrench?"

"Well, say, er-uh, you know, Missa Jim, I ain't seed dat lug ranch to dis day."

Loughter once more filled the courtroom.

The lawyer tried to recover. There was no

need to cross-examine Robert Lewis. He was telling the truth, and nothing was going to change his testimony. He put the client back up in rebuttal. The courtroom became serious again, but the damage had been done. The jury had forgotten everything about the trial other than the star of the show, Robert Lewis.

During closing arguments, Robert Lewis came back into the courtroom and joined his family and friends in the gallery.

At that point the jury completely fell apart with loughter once more. The lawyer knew his case was in serious trouble. He was right. After 15 minutes deliberation, the jury was still laughing when they returned a verdict for the defendant.

TOSS IT

J.K. Watts was an old white guy who went along with just about anything. He was an infinitely kind person, not very well educated, but he was very considerate of others. He was one of those older construction workers who didn't shave every day. However, he would allow anyone in need to hang out at his very large house.

If a husband beat his wife and ran her off with their two month old baby, she would be taken in by J.K. Watts. If a guy had been hurt on the job and workmen's compensation wasn't paying, J.K. Watts would help him. If a person's lights had been turned off, his car was almost out of gas, he had no groceries, J.K. Watts would take him in and let him live with him. For example, if a person was down to his last dollar, and he had but one thing left to sell, J.K. Watts would buy it. His home was truly a home for the homeless.

James Kenneth Watts lived on the Eastern margin of Lookout Mountain Parkway, South of Dogtown on Lavender Creek. He had always worked in construction, as a mechanic usually, but he was also a carpenter, brickmason, plumber, painter, whatever.

Although, his wife would come and go as she pleased, J.K. had been living separated from her, off and on, for more than 25 years.

During that time, he had constantly built on to his house.

The original construction of the monstrous home began simply enough. J.K. had been somewhat of a petty criminal during his early years. He was convicted of two different charges of automobile theft in 1975. He and his uncle had bought two stolen Chevrolets in Georgia, repainted them, and sold them. The nephew and uncle were charged in the United States District Court for the Northern District of Alabama with Dyer Act violations. Both men plead guilty to the two different charges and were sentenced to five years in the federal prison. J.K. served three years and was released on parole.

When he was released, J.K. left Alabama, moved to Georgia, and there he began to follow one of his earlier trades, that of being a brickmason. Later, he was in an accident on the job and received a fairly large settlement from his employer's workmen's compensation carrier in the amount of $80,000.

After J.K. received his lump-sum settlement, he began to have a lot of people hanging around him in Georgia. He didn't have the ability to ask them to leave. However, he knew that he needed to get away from them. He moved back to the family property South of Dogtown on Lookout Mountain.

Using questionable judgment, J.K. took his

settlement money and began to build on to the family home. He created the huge rambling three-story house which went in no apparent direction. The garage adjoined the screened-in back porch. Outside stairs went up to a deck on a carport. Additional steps on the carport deck then led up to a smaller deck outside a southerly door on the third floor. All of it overlooked Lavender Creek and the valley it had created over millions of years of following the path of least resistance.

The main living area downstairs consisted of one huge room with a very large towering stone fireplace. There were couches, recliners and coffee tables located in three different sitting areas of the room. The room was split into three levels. There was a long one-step riser going up to the dining room. There were two longer steps going up to the kitchen from the living room and one riser going into the kitchen from the dining room. The ceiling of the living room followed the octagon pitch of its roof, was at least forty feet high and painted black. As a result, the room always appeared very dark.

After entering the room from the East side of the house, the foyer area was on the level with the kitchen, two steps above the living room floor. A large flight of stairs on the west wall went directly up to the second floor which had a balcony encircling the living area below.

Bedrooms and bathrooms opened onto the balcony. There was an additional narrow stairway that went on up to J.K.'s third-floor living area.

Once inside J.K.'s bedroom, there were the sliding glass doors to the balcony on the left. On the immediate right was a door to a bathroom and with a large pink Jacuzzi, which was in the shape of a heart. That was J.K.'s favorite place in all the world. On the far right was J.K.'s private kitchen.

The rambling heap of a home had been begun with the workmen's compensation settlement. J.K. used the money he received, rather than having a back operation that he so desperately needed. As a result, he lived in constant pain. His back hurt him terribly resulting in all kinds of problems. He rarely had a good night's sleep. He could barely sit down, and he usually was forced to stand almost all the time.

His pain was so severe he could not sleep until he was at the point of complete exhaustion. An old worn out recliner in the corner of his bedroom allowed him to be as comfortable as he could become. When he could, he usually slept in that old overstuffed chair.

The property where the house had been built had been given to J.K. by his older sister Nita. She had bought it for him when their parents died. At the time, he was in prison for the Dyer Act violations. J.K. wanted to pay his sister for the property. However, Nita told J.K. to pay her whenever and whatever he could, when he could. He paid her every week until she said that he had paid enough. When Nita was satisfied, J.K. recorded his deed.

J.K. then executed a deed to his land to his two daughters and son in equal parts. Those were Susan, Donny, and Christie. But he did not deliver the deed. Instead, he left the deed in the safekeeping of Nita. As a result, the property always legally belonged to him.

When relatives came to live with him, he made them work on the building of the place. As a result, J.K.'s house had grown to three stories high, 12 bedrooms, a huge 40' X 50' living area, three fire places, an enormous kitchen, five balconies, a four-car garage, and so it went. The huge edifice rambled helter-skelter on two acres of land fronting on the creek and parkway.

J.K. made good use of the creek. He built a meandering stone patio covering more than half an acre fronting on the creek. It was complete with a huge sandstone bar-be-que grill accompanied by sandstone tables with benches.

Some people became so comfortable in the house that J.K. couldn't run them off after they had worn out their welcome. When this happened, J.K. would put up signs. He would throw tantrums and demand that they leave. Unfortunately, often these mechanisms didn't work. He couldn't insult the moochers, and he didn't have the heart to become violent with them.

In an act of self-preservation, J.K. took the food out of his kitchen and locked it in his bedroom on the third floor. There he had another kitchen with a padlock on the door. He went to great lengths to prevent the poor, the criminal, the crazy, and the homeless, from eating him out of house and home once the individual's emergency had passed. Once he had helped someone, J. K. wanted that person to, "Get the hell out!"

Unfortunately, many of the needy J.K. helped did not appreciate his gifts. They stole everything that wasn't nailed down. Some of the "guests" took cassocks and other furniture and sold that.

The home became so inundated with people that on one occasion J.K. tried to have his home exterminated. The exterminator came, but it was impossible to do the job due to the number of people living there. The exterminator could not reach the places that needed to be treated to get rid of the bugs because of the filth and junk.

The situation frequently reached the point where J.K. had no privacy, not even in his own bedroom. People he didn't know were living in his home wherever they could find space. Some of them, especially their children, enjoyed one of his three hot tubs.

One day, when the confusion was reaching a crescendo, J.K.'s 32-year-old daughter Susan came home and moved in unannounced. She ordered some of the riff-raff out of one of the bedrooms and put her stuff in the closet.

She was incredulous that J.K. was allowing so many people to live off him. He was the only person living under his roof who worked regularly. Susan was determined to run the people off whom she did not know.

After she moved in, she replaced the regular moochers with her friends, and things became worse. Cocaine addicts, marijuana or potheads, and several pill poppers followed her into the house from Georgia. Susan had some very bad habits.

J.K. discovered what was going on and went around the house putting up signs saying **"No drugs by order of J.K. Watts."** These signs were in response to all the druggies hanging out at his home.

Many of the boys hanging around didn't work nor pretend to work. Before Susan came home, J.K. had worked and accumulated an inventory of motor vehicles. He had always had a garden. As long as the dopers could steal parts off J.K.'s vehicles to sell, or even sell the tomatoes out of his garden, they had what they wanted. If they could find enough money to buy beer or dope, they were happy to lay around J.K.'s home at Susan's drug-induced beck and call all day every day.

J.K. checked his bedroom every day to be sure the padlock on that door was in place because he was afraid people were stealing his things right under his nose. He had to lock all his watches, coins, rings, and personal papers in a safe that he kept in his bedroom. He also had a steel workbox at the foot of his bed. It was a homemade construction toolbox measuring 2 ½ feet in width and 6 feet long. He kept most of his guns and other valuables in the box. He kept the box locked with a very expensive padlock. The combination to his safe was secured by being stowed in the steel box.

His private bedroom, on the third floor, was a large room, 30 feet by 25 feet. Plus, it had a kitchen off to one side and a small balcony on the other side overlooking the valley formed by the creek. He had a spectacular view that he could enjoy from the balcony or through his eight foot glass sliding doors leading out to it.

A young woman, 20 years the junior to J.K., came to his home early one Saturday morning. She told J.K. that her husband had put her out the night before, she had no place to go, and she was pregnant. Her name was Marsha, an attractive twenty-six year old.

Marsha moved in, and strangely enough, she got along famously with Susan. She cleaned the house spic and span. She was even able to clean up after the addicts who were sleeping and eating all over the lower floor. She threw out a heaping pickup truck load of junk, old clothes, cans, beer bottles, and other trash.

Marsha wore gingham dresses without bras or panties. She didn't own any. Her husband kept all her clothes. She got out with a small suitcase when she ran away. Standing in the sunlight, one could see everything about her. She was young, she was beautiful, she was well built, she was a good housekeeper, and she was what J.K. liked.

It was a little over a month before Marsha moved into J.K.'s bedroom and began to live with him. Soon Marsha was able to get the key to J.K.'s box. One day, J.K. realized that he did not have access to his own safe and box. But, being J.K., he didn't say anything. He just hoped for the best. J.K. was an eternal optimist.

Although J.K. was still legally married, Marsha took over being the matron of the house. J.K.'s real wife, Betty, was living in Mississippi with her relatives. She had decided to leave Lookout Mountain and J.K., most recently, when after a month-long visit, she realized that she had lost control of her home due to the "white trash" J.K. was allowing to hang out there.

As more and more people began to live, or sustain themselves, on J.K.'s premises, J.K. became sick and could not rest for days. He missed work. His friends didn't know what he was doing. His life was out of control, and he was being directed about by others. He was hallucinating; and at times he became completely incoherent. It was obvious J.K. was having a nervous breakdown. That's when the riff-raff said he was having a big fit.

His sister Nita heard about his situation and came to his rescue. Nita dearly loved her brother. She had helped deliver J.K. when their mother had birthed him. J.K.'s daughters called her Aunt Ni-Ni. As things were reaching a critical mass, Nita would drop in on J.K. every Sunday after church and bring food for him and whomever was sharing his private room. When the situation became critical, Susan kicked some folks out of one of the cleanest rooms and moved Aunt Ni-Ni in.

Betty heard about J.K.'s condition and came for a visit. When Betty was there, she, Nita, and other members of the family would have a great visit.

Any time Betty was living with J.K. she bought groceries and paid the bills. She kept the house as clean and orderly as she could, under the circumstances. It was a constant battle but one that she usually won.

About a year before Susan had decided to come home unannounced, Betty knew that she had to leave. She could not tolerate the effect that the "white trash" were having on J.K. When she ran people off, J.K. would allow them to sneak back. When Betty cleaned her home, the "guests" would return and trash the house. They left the McDonald's take-out bags and paper wrappers wherever they finished eating. There were dozens of empty beer bottles in the great room. There were bottles on the tables, next to the chairs and sofas, in corners, and on the fireplace. Name it, and there was a half-empty beer bottle on it or near it. Betty finally gave up and returned to her mother's home in Tupelo, Mississippi.

Several years prior, shortly after J.K. had returned to Dogtown, it was discovered that his brother, Doug, was dying of kidney failure. He was quickly progressing beyond the aid of dialysis. J.K. immediately volunteered to give his brother one of his kidneys. Doctors found they were a perfect match. J.K. gave Doug a kidney and, in so doing, gave his brother life. Doug never forgot the importance of the gift of J.K. He truly loved his brother, and his brother loved him as well. Realistically, the Wattses were a large old family whose members were devoted to each other.

J.K. was finally forced to seek help for his back. By the time he was released from UAB hospital in Birmingham, there were so many people coming and going at his house that strangers wandered up with their dirty children and stayed a few days at J.K.'s. They didn't know him, and neither did he know them. It was a roof overhead, a dry place to sleep, and one could always find beer money somewhere.

No one knew the occasion, but Wayne McCullough came to stay in one of the bedrooms downstairs off the great room. He was such a bully that when he came to J.K.'s to "visit," he ordered whomever was occupying "his room" to vacate immediately. On one occasion, he made Jerry Blackburn sleep on the floor.

Walt DeMazio, or as he was called, "Little Toy," also stayed there. There was Little Toy and his older brother, Jack DeMazio, or "Big Toy." The brothers were first cousins of J.K.'s. Both of them made his home their own. They shared a room on the second floor. They put a large padlock on their door to keep the other "guests" out. They were directly under J.K.'s heart-shaped pink hot tub. They could hear the water pumps running while they tried to sleep.

Marsha had originally come over to stay at J.K.'s from her home in Mentone, Alabama.

The first time was after her husband Wayne Walters had lost his job, and she was pregnant. Two weeks after she moved into J.K.'s house, she had miscarried.

There were a number of people there that Nita had never seen before, and they changed from week to week. The house was crowded.

All it lacks is a few roosters, then it would be a perfect chicken coop, she thought.

When Nita learned that Marsha was staying in the room with J.K., she confronted Marsha and told her in no uncertain terms to leave. After a screaming match, Marsha left with no place to go, other than returning to her abusive husband.

Stanley Garrett came to J.K.'s with a case of cold beer. He drank all the beer himself, passed out on J.K.'s couch in the living room, and stayed there, on that couch, for four weeks.

When J.K. asked him who the hell he was, he told him that he was a mechanic that came there to work on the old junk cars J.K. had out back. J.K. asked him if he was working on any of the cars, and Stanley said he was working on a Chevrolet Impala. J.K. knew the Impala. He had bought it from a guy who was down and out for $175. It was a tan '72 model. J.K. was glad to have the cars being worked on by a real mechanic so he allowed Stanley to stay, as long as he looked busy and stayed greasy.

Later, J.K. discovered that Stanley Garrett had been stealing him blind. He was removing good parts off the old automobiles and selling them in Collinsville at Trade Day each Saturday. After selling the parts, he would head to the county line and buy three cases of beer. He would stash his beer to keep from sharing even one bottle with anyone.

J.K. had heard that Stanley had threatened Susan behind her back. If Susan found out about the threat, she would attack Stanley head on. Susan was crazy that way. Although Stanley was intent on leaving J.K. told him that he was interfering with his family and stealing and he was to leave immediately. Stanley was tired of pretending to work and staying greasy. He had stolen everything he thought he could get away with. He disappeared.

Shortly after Stanley left, Marsha came back. Her husband Wayne had given her a another severe beating. This time he took a mop handle to her, and she went to J.K. for help. J.K. thought that if Marsha would just shut her mouth when Wayne was drinking, he'd probably leave her alone. However, Marsha went right to work cleaning the house, and helping Susan every day.

After she had been there a little over a month, she and J.K. got back together. It was heart-shaped pink hot tub time. The DeMazio brothers could hear the pump running right over their heads. They popped a couple Xanax tablets, called "purple footballs," washed them down with beer, and promptly passed out. The pump stayed on for a long time. J.K. came to know Marsha a lot better this time. Within days, she had the keys to the box and everything else in the house.

Nita said that after Susan returned, more people came and went at J.K.'s house. Some folks bought groceries; others bought paper products or something else that was needed. Some had no money and just hung out there living off whatever was going on. There were people who cut wood or helped out with the junk. Relatives and friends following Susan increased the problems at the home of J.K. Watts.

Nita said that when Susan arrived, she knew she was the apple of her daddy's eye, and she took every advantage of it. After she had settled in, she ran several unknown members of the riff-raff out of the house.

Soon the entire place belonged to Susan and her friends. Her friends brought in other people, and slowly J.K. Watts lost control of everything he owned or held sacred. His sister Nita said that J.K. just couldn't make the decision to put them out. Most of these people were Susan's friends from Georgia. As many as twelve people at a time lived there, but twice more than that would be hanging out there at all hours of the day and night.

Nita said that sometimes she felt sorry for the white trash who had children, and she brought groceries in on Sunday for them to eat during the ice storm that winter.

Some of the people would get too drunk. There would be fights, particularly around the pool table in the game room off the West side of the great room. They would gamble, cheat, refuse to pay up, hit each other with pool cues, and pull knives. Then they would break up the furniture and leave their half empty cans, bottles, and trash everywhere around the house. Wayne McCullough was involved in almost every fracas. Sometimes he got the better of it, and sometimes he didn't.

Marsha stopped working on the house after she had settled in and J.K. had taken her back. Her job became girlfriend, and she performed it well. Susan spent all her time partying with her friends, getting into fights with friends and relatives, and hanging out with Marsha. With Betty gone, Nita moved back home and rarely came by.

Marsha was serving as girlfriend, and no one ever cooked nor cleaned house. They just made bigger messes. Men full of beer urinated just outside of doors around the house when they could have easily gone to one of the three available bathrooms. But that was too much trouble. The places around the doors began to smell of rancid urine. The ones who did use the facilities never raised the seat nor flushed the commode. The bathroom on the first floor became filthy, rank, and eventually stopped up. They had to keep the door closed to keep it from stinking the house to where it was uninhabitable for them.

Nita said that there were a number of guys, some looking like teenagers, who came into the house and went straight to Susan's bedroom where they would close the door.

"And who knows what goes on behind closed doors?" Nita certainly didn't know what was happening in there, but she had a good idea.

Nita said that after a while, Susan had a bunch of girls coming over there to the house and spending too much time. Nita confronted Susan saying that lesbians were hanging out over there at J.K.'s. Susan denied it.

Later Susan told Nita that she had heard that her favorite Aunt, Ni-Ni, was saying that she was bringing bad boys and drugs over to J.K.'s. She wanted Ni-Ni to know that she was not bringing drugs into J.K.'s house.

Nita said, "It doesn't matter to me what you do or did, but I reserve the right to talk about anything I know, whenever I wish, and to whomever I please." End of conversation.

Marsha's husband showed up again and

asked Marsha if she was ever going to come back to him at Mentone. She said she was through with him and getting a divorce as soon as she could raise the money. She had already talked to a lawyer. She asked her estranged husband if he would like to paint J.K.'s hotrod so J.K. could sell it and pay her lawyer fee. The rod was worth about $2,500. J.K. would pay $750 for him to paint it.

Wayne put a cot in the garage and moved into J.K.'s downstairs while he painted the hotrod. He lived with the hotrod and a keg of beer. All the while his wife was living with J.K. upstairs. Their children were with her mother in Mentone.

Stan Black, whose daughter had married a Townsend, came out to the house with Toy Benefield. Benefield was the third person named Toy to move into J.K.'s house. This Toy was a thief. He stole things out of the house and refused to pay his pool losses. As a result, Toy Benefield was beaten up by Wayne McCullough and some of the people on the first floor.

The following morning, J.K. learned that the Townsend girl was rumored to have AIDS. Absolutely no one would have anything to do with her. J.K. allowed her to stay. She needed help, and he didn't worry about AIDS. He had one of the rooms on the balcony vacated, cleaned out, and given to her.

J.K. was raised like a son by his other older sister Sybil from the time he was 10 years old. When J.K.'s daughter Susan was growing up, Susan loved her Aunt Sybil. She was like a grandmother. But Sybil said that Susan began to change so that there was no one on earth who could get along with her. Susan became hyper, like a maniac. She was nervous and would go for days without sleep. Then she would sleep for two days straight. When she became angry, Susan would knock all the dishes off the island in the middle of the kitchen, or she would throw glasses into the sink and break them.

On occasions she would go up to strangers and say "Get out of my house, or I'll show you what tough is."

Frequently Susan would punctuate her instruction with a swift kick in the groin, or a sharp slap in the face.

Sybil asked her husband, Wallace, to go down to J.K.'s and see how Susan was acting. He moved into the cleanest second-floor bedroom. Susan came into the room drug induced raving incoherently. Uncle Wallace immediately grabbed her and physically took her to her bedroom and threw her across her bed. He yelled into her face, with snuff breath, that she was out of control and needed to straighten up. Everyone there knew she was a speed freak. Wallace told her that he would handle her. He was going to fight her like a man.

For a couple of weeks, Susan calmed down and acted in a civilized manner. Wallace went back home. After he was gone, Susan began to do speed again.

Doyle Watts showed up one day and occupied a room on the second floor. His father, and J.K.'s father, were first cousins. Doyle and J.K. had always hung out with each other both as relatives and as friends. Doyle was a family man who attended church.

Doyle and J.K. would do projects together and help each other. For example, Doyle took chert rock and went over to J.K.'s with his dump truck. He graveled all the driveways leading up to and around J.K.'s house. Doyle also helped J.K. put in a second septic tank when the lower bathrooms became stopped up due to foreign items flushed into the main septic tank from the house. Doyle would also take firewood to J.K.; and he would use J.K.'s saws, torches, and other equipment. They used each other's tools as though they both owned all the tools. They seemed to own all their things together. Doyle later said that he never saw any dope being sold by J.K. He just saw J.K. being J.K.

John McCorley stayed with J.K. almost five months. He was an alcoholic who drank a lot of beer and stayed to himself.   McCorley's mother was Christine Guest McCorley. She came around J.K.'s now and then, lived a few days, and moved on.

Reba Etheridge was another semi-permanent guest of the rambling home. She was the daughter of Edwin, J.K.'s older brother. Reba was worried about the stuff that was going on at J.K.'s and wanted to come down and help take care of him.

She was there during the second Drug Task Force raid. She was the one who had diet pills on her, in a pill bottle, that had an expiration date three years old. She was arrested because of the drugs during the bust. The charges against her were later dismissed.

After Betty, Susan, and Marsha had stopped preparing meals, Reba took over cooking for J.K. and Marsha. She began to do all his washing and cleaning, but she could not get ahead of the riff-raff. So she did most of her work in J.K.'s bedroom, kitchen, and bathroom on the third floor.

Larry Watts was J.K.'s nephew. He was J.K.'s brother Timmy's son. Larry told J.K. that he would take care of things outside. He was supposed to be taking care of the place for J.K. while he was away. Larry also told J.K. that he would run everyone off, and he genuinely tried to stop the madness. But he couldn't stem the tide. There were just too many aggressive freeloaders and moochers.

Larry was sincerely bothered by what was going on at the house. He said that it hurt him to know everything that was happening at his uncle's house. When Marsha found out that Larry knew what was going on, she tried to pick a fight with him so J.K. would run him off. Larry refused to fight. Like so many of the others, he had no place to go.

Billie Watts moved in. Billie was the mother of Larry. She was a good Christian woman. She was Sybil's sister-in-law. Her husband, Timmy, and Sybil, were J.K.'s siblings.

Big Toy and Little Toy were Sybil's sons by a former marriage. Big Toy was about 43 years old. Because he was one of J.K.'s nephews and lived on the first floor, Big Toy started raising hell about the fact that nobody was looking out for J.K. when J.K. wasn't there.

He accused everyone of stealing from J.K. Some of the other people said he was stealing from J.K. Those were fighting words, and there were several fights between the two Toys and other people about the place. Little Toy became involved in most of the fights. He was married to Nita's cousin for a while between his prison terms. He was still on parole, and he was at the house all the time.

Little Toy was once married to Sparkle Dean Candy. From time to time, Sparkle Dean moved into J.K.'s house with her small son. Usually, Sparkle Dean worked as an exotic dancer at the Pussy Cat A-Go-Go Club in Atlanta. When she could make a little money dancing, she would move back into a mobile home behind her father's house a quarter of a mile up Lookout Mountain Parkway from J.K.'s. They lived toward the four-way stop at Dogtown.

On one occasion, Susan shot hot pepper sauce into Sparkle's eyes when they were having words. Susan said that she was just sticking up for Little Toy when he was arguing with Sparkle.

Jackie, whose last name was unknown, had moved in and was living there during the time Susan and the Toys were fighting with everyone who would take offense to their actions, attitudes, or cursing. Jackie was a large man and often broke up fights. Jackie, last name unknown, remained at J.K.'s for a little more than two months and disappeared. Nobody knew who he was, where he came from, nor where he went.

Brenda Kennedy came to live at the house because of the abuse she was suffering from her husband Burford. He began to hate everyone at J.K.'s and came to the house armed demanding that his wife go home with him. J.K. asked him to put the gun down or leave.

Before he could make up his mind which to do, Big Toy hit him in the head with a tire tool saying, "Now he won't hurt anyone."

Burford lay on the floor bleeding for two days. People just stepped around him.

Brenda borrowed money from J.K. twice and paid it back. When Buford was released from the hospital, she returned to him. And after that she was rarely seen over at J.K.'s house. No one ever saw Burford again.

Seth Adam Bell was J.K.'s youngest son. He has born of J.K.'s affair with his mother 17 years earlier. All his life Seth knew J.K. was his pap, but very little was done about it. Now, Seth wanted to take his father's name of Watts. His mother was a drunk named Myra Joyce McAdams. She said she would sign any papers necessary to give Seth J.K.'s name. Seth had just turned 16 and was living in a camper out behind J.K.'s house. Soon he got a room on the first floor. He had always lived with Cotton Bell, who was one of J.K.'s friends and had raised Seth.

Seth had to ask Cotton to allow him to move back into his home soon after school started. People had stolen all Seth's belongings at J.K.'s, including his clothes, and school books. It was vicious on the first floor. Two weeks after school started, Seth Adam Bell quit school and took a job as a knitter in a sock mill.

People in the crowd staying with J.K. began to say that Susan had become too moody. She had begun to bring in the bad stuff, dope that had been "cut" with something harmful. Once she chased a guy, who no one knew, through the house with a knife. The people said that J.K. was afraid of his own daughter.

She said one day, "Now he's got me; he's stuck with me. It's my house. I can do what I want."

After she got into the hard stuff, she became very close to Marsha Martin. Unknown to J.K., after they had begun a lesbian relationship in the heart-shaped pink hot tub, they plotted to sell J.K.'s house, personal property, little things, and land. When confronted with this conspiracy, Susan said that if J.K. tried to run her off then she would fix it so he would get busted.   J.K. heard about it and said he couldn't get busted since he wasn't doing anything.

Several of the religious neighbors living around J.K. decided that his home was a den of iniquity. Many of the people in the area had moved to Dogtown following an itinerant tent evangelist named Duval Thomas. This preacher, who by his own admission was totally illiterate, preached to the people from Pennsylvania to Iowa that the end of time was at hand, that the Antichrist was ready to appear.

Evangelist Thomas had seen in a vision that after a certain period of time, certain people in the United States could be saved from the persecution of the Antichrist by living in a secluded area of Lookout Mountain near Dogtown, Alabama. He didn't even know where the place was. He just had this vision that it was Dogtown on Lookout Mountain. It was wild theory, but it worked for himself and a lot of other people. His followers, from all over the United States, sincerely believed Brother Thomas, and moved to Lookout Mountain to avoid the holocaust to come.

Several of the saints of this new religious sect, the "End Time Prediction," called, or went to see the County Sheriff complaining that J.K. Watts was living in sin. He had young people drinking and hanging out at his place. He had substantial traffic coming and going from his home at all hours of the day and night. People were fornicating over there. No one over at J.K.'s made any attempt at being a good citizen of the community wherein they resided. They did not go to church. They did not bother to contribute to religious endeavors. Some of them urinated in the yard for all to see.

These fine folks, who watched for Jesus to return by the hour, intended to see that J.K. was busted. They wanted the riff-raff gone with him because they were all guilty. So one by one they called the sheriff and complained about J.K. They were effective.

The sheriff called the director of the Drug Task Force and discovered that they were observing the residence and suspected that methamphetamines were being sold at J.K.'s house. They suspected that Susan was a habitual user, that Big Toy and Little Toy were bonafide drug dealers, and that J.K. and Marsha were not only users of methamphetamine, but they were also sellers.

The sheriff called in the members of his staff who were also members of the Drug Task Force.

"I don't want to know what you know," he told the officers who worked for him. "I want J.K. Watts arrested for trafficking in drugs, if he is in fact selling drugs. Does everyone understand what I want?"

He looked at each of the four deputies directly in the eye. Each of them knew their jobs were on the line. Without a salary from the sheriff's department, they were no longer on the Drug Task Force. All nodded affirmatively.

Gary Wade, a process server, had known the sheriff the longest. "Sheriff, J.K. is an old white whiskey man. I think that he has gone from bootlegging to dealing in methamphetamines. I think we can bust him in a matter of days."

He looked at the other officers for support. All had affirmative remarks in support of the contemplated arrest of J.K. Watts.

Within the hour the director of the task force

called all the members into their meeting room in the district attorney's office on the fifth floor of the courthouse.

"Gentlemen, it's time to take J.K. Watts down. The community out there is up in arms, the sheriff is demanding action, and all the while J.K. is running wide open. He's selling drugs. You know it, I know it, everybody knows it. Let's do our job. Let's take down J.K. Watts!" He unveiled an easel with an enlarged aerial photo of the property of J.K. Watts. The resolution was so good, one could almost read the car tags on the numerous vehicles around J.K.'s house.

"Listen up! I want your input in formulating the plan to take down Watts."

For the next three hours, red Magic Marker marks were made on the photo with notations. Many were erased with a damp tissue. Finally six notations and red arrows remained. The plan was then dictated for the secretary to transcribe the following morning.

Sixteen loose-leaf notebooks were made for each member of the task force. Each notebook contained the officer's name and assignment. Inside the notebook there were 12 photographs of J.K. Watts' house. Inside and outside doors were clearly identified. Windows were highlighted. The plan was set out in large bold type. Thirty-two mug shots of the persons known to frequent J.K.'s home were laid out with a short biography and criminal record of each person pictured. A summary of the surveillance of the residence was in the rear of the book. Each officer knew his job, the people to be encountered, the habits and potential of each person, and the time frame to be used by the strike team.

On October 14, 1995, the raid began with a sheriff's patrol car pulling into J.K.'s driveway. J.K. happened to be in back of his house feeding his dogs. He saw the car and went over to the officer.

"Hey, Alvin, whatcha doing?" he asked smiling recognizing the decoy deputy.

"I need to serve a paper, actually a warrant, on one of the DeMazios. Are either of them here?" the deputy asked returning the friendly manner.

He got out of the car and leaned against the driver's door. The deputy acted casual, but he was ready to draw his weapon in an instant.

"I think Big Toy is in there asleep," J.K. said as he lit a cigarette. "You want me to get him?" J.K. was more than cooperative.

"I'll get him," Alvin responded heading toward the back door. J.K. began to follow him along. When they entered the house, the other members of the task force strike team came out of the bushes, around the corners of the house, and pulled up in other squad cars. As five men rushed into the house in full SWAT gear, the commander began to shout through the public address system which was mounted on the second patrol car.

"This is a raid! We are police! Don't move nor resist! We have a legal search warrant, and we are going to search this place! Everybody get on the ground! Keep your hands where we can see them!"

He could be heard a quarter of a mile away by some of the End Time Prediction people. Other SWAT officers rushed the house and every man, woman, boy, and girl was forced to lay down on the floor or the ground wherever they were found.

Alvin was joined by his point leader, Jimmy Dan Boydston. "On the floor, J.K.," Jimmy Dan shouted. "Don't move, and shut up!"

He handed J.K. a copy of the search warrant.

J.K. had followed Alvin in and had started toward his bedroom. He was forced to lay down on the landing at the top of the steps leading to his bedroom. Marsha was ordered to lay down on the bedroom floor. Susan was put down on the bathroom floor near the pink heart-shaped hot tub. Big Toy and Little Toy were taken down with 12 other people in the living room, recreation room, and dining room. Several relatives were immobilized in the kitchen.

People were rounded up outside the house.

In all, 28 people were taken into custody at the beginning of the raid. As other people drove up to see what was going on, they were also detained by the officers.

Once everyone was immobilized, the search began. The officers systematically searched each room slowly and thoroughly. Carpet was lifted, beds were taken apart, drawers in cabinets were jerked out into the floor, pictures were removed from the walls, and chairs were overturned and inspected. Draperies were pulled down. The searchers ripped the house apart and didn't bother to replace anything.

The people were searched. Pocket books, purses, and wallets were seized and searched. Books and papers were taken in case they were drug records. A couple of joints of marijuana and a small quantity of methamphetamine were found in the pillowcase of Little Toy. He and Big Toy were arrested and handcuffed because they occupied the room where these drugs were found. In addition, the officers had a warrant for Big Toy.

When the officers began to search J.K.'s bedroom they methodically explored every possible hiding place and found nothing. They emptied every drawer, overturned every box, and broke down every piece of furniture. Still, they found nothing. Eventually, they came to the jobbox which was padlocked.

The Drug Task Force was going to knock the lock off and break into what they called the "locker," then get the combination of the safe.

As expected, one officer later made an affidavit that he took the key to the locker and combination to the safe off J.K. Watts. He did not. The keys and combination were found in Marsha's purse where they had remained while she and Susan conspired to sell J.K. out.

Saying they took the keys to the locker and combination to the safe off J.K. strengthened their case in that whatever was found inside the safe and locker belonged to him. They exercised an old police procedure to place blame on their target. Marsha didn't have a criminal record so she was in the position to contradict the illegally obtained evidence.

Boydston had asked J.K. for the key early on. Otherwise, he said, they would have to take a sledgehammer and knock the lock off the metal container. They searched J.K. and concluded he did not have the key. They searched Susan without favorable results. Finally, when they searched Marsha they located the locker key, and subsequently, the safe combination.

When Jimmy Dan opened the safe, he found what they had been looking for -- four ounces of crystal methamphetamine laid out in plastic baggies in four-gram amounts. An electronic scale had been located in the bathroom. Short straws and razor blades were found in a drawer of the vanity in the bathroom. The drugs and paraphernalia were put together on the bed. Jimmy Dan found $3,400 in cash in the safe. This money was fanned out on the bed, along with J.K.'s guns and jewelry. Pictures were taken of all the 'contraband' to be shown to the press and the jury later on.

Reba Ethridge, J.K., Marsha, and both Toys were taken to jail together. Susan called various family members to help make the bonds. J.K. and the others were bonded out and released by approximately 2:00 a.m. Several members of the family were on hand to take them home.

Six days later J.K. and Marsha visited the office of the lawyer in Fort Payne.

"You remember representing me in 1965?" J.K. asked after the preliminary pleasantry.

He and Marsha were seated across the table from the lawyer.

"I was a young man then, running a honkey-tonk out on Lookout Mountain out there near Derwood Jenkins. Do you remember that?"

"Yeah," the lawyer responded lost in thought, trying to remember. "There was a stabbing out there, and the cops found out you were running illegal booze and an illegal dance hall?"

The lawyer furrowed his brow as he tried to bring back to his mind events 31 years in the past.

"I believe they called your place the 'Bloody Bucket,'" the lawyer remembered.

"Yeah," J.K. said. "There was a stabbing out there. They did close me down, and you did represent me when they charged me with bootlegging. You got me out of it."

The lawyer responded, "You were a young guy then."

"Yeah! That's me! We were both young." J.K. was happy to be recognized.

"What brings you here?" the lawyer asked affably.

"You may have read in the papers where I was busted." He didn't stop. "Well, I was busted. They came into my house and took down everything out there. I couldn't believe it. It was like an invasion. They absolutely destroyed my home." He paused.

"I know what you mean," the lawyer responded. "They make a lot of noise and rip things apart once they get started."

"More than that," Marsha said. "They all cussed real bad. It was, 'Motherfucker this and Asshole that.'" She winced as she repeated the favorite words of the Drug Task Force.

"Anyway," J.K. interrupted, "I need a lawyer. And there ain't nothing better than an old lawyer."

"We'll have to see about that," the lawyer replied. "Tell me about your problem."

"Okay!" J.K. took a deep breath. "I was out there at my house, with a few relatives and friends of mine, when they brought down a SWAT team on me and arrested me for distribution of a controlled substance."

"What was it?" the lawyer asked blankly.

"Methamphetamine, crystal," J.K. responded. He sounded important.

"How much?" the lawyer asked.

"A little over an ounce," Marsha responded. She was trying to get agreement as to how much was involved. The cops would have an accurate amount that they seized. Or at least what remained of what they got.

"Something like that," J.K. growled in a very low voice through unshaven jowls.

"J.K. had taken $3400 from the bank, the remaining accident proceeds, and bought a trailer," Marsha said.

J.K. interjected that before he could pay for the trailer that the cops took this money. "They claimed it was drug money."

J.K. described where all the members of the task force were, what they did, and what they said.

"I had just sold a car. The cops found the purchase money, $1,700, and took that. They also took all my jewelry, guns, personal records, and an old blunderbuss shotgun that had belonged to my great-great-granddaddy. I want that back."

J.K. was hacked off for being treated as he had been by the cops.

"They were badassed people, but I could handle whatever came along. If you can't stand the heat, don't come into the kitchen," he quoted Harry Truman philosophically. "Well, I need to get out of this. I'm a two-time looser. You remember that I got convicted during all that Dyer Act stuff back in the early '70's?"

"I remember something about it. How many cars were you involved with?"

"Two. And they made two different cases, one on each car, in the Federal Court down in Birmingham. I did three years on it after I got two convictions. Another conviction, and I'm up for the Bitch."

"Yeah, you would be. That's life without parole if you are sentenced under the provisions of the Habitual Criminal Act."

"Now you know why I got to get out of it?" J.K. was serious.

"Yeah, I got you," the lawyer then quoted a fee. J.K. paid $4,500 down on the fee and assured the lawyer the rest would be forthcoming.

The lawyer remembered that J.K. had paid him on time when he defended him for running the Bloody Bucket.

"That's fine. Let's get out to your house. I need some pictures."

The lawyer followed J.K. and Marsha out of

Fort Payne, through Dogtown, South down Lookout Mountain Parkway to the End Time Prediction community where J.K. lived, and the believers had moved in on him. When the two vehicles turned into J.K.'s drive-way, the lawyer said to his young law clerk, "Dope dealer's property."

"How do you tell?" the clerk questioned.

"All the signs," the lawyer's right hand swept the horizon in the windshield. "Wrecked cars and good vehicles mixed together, plunder in every direction, yet wealth can be spotted. Over there is a new ATV four wheeler; there's a relatively new Waverunner, a good Harley Davidson, a new welding outfit as well as new spray-paint canisters. And then there's the dogs and the cars with the out-of-state tags. Then look at that monstrosity of a house. You know what it looks like?"

He waited for the clerk to answer.

"It looks like it was built without any planning whatsoever. It rambles in every direction, including upward. Look at it. It's a helluva mess," the clerk thought he had put his finger right on it.

"That's all true," the lawyer assured the younger man. "What it looks like is a man who had quick money. He bought stolen building materials and needed to get them up as quickly as possible. He had more money than he knew what to do with. So he built the house all over the place. If he had an idea for a porch or balcony here or there, he put it in. Yes, too much money too quickly. One hell of a lot of it is in that house. More of it is in all these vehicles and mobile homes around here." The lawyer was almost lecturing.

The two lawyers followed J.K. and Marsha through the back door into the darkened rambling house. As each man fired questions toward J.K. and Marsha, the lawyers made notes and took pictures. After an hour, they returned to the office. Two weeks later, they thought they had a handle on the case, a good defense, and they might be in a position to pressure the state into making a favorable deal for J.K.

They never considered going to trial. A guilty jury verdict would result in J.K. spending life without parole down in Alabama State Prison down South in Elmore County. J.K. couldn't take a third conviction, unless it was part of a deal to avoid the Habitual Criminal Act that criminals called, "The Bitch."

As the weeks went by, J.K. continued making payments on his fee. The lawyers had booked the case. This meant that the applicable law had been copied and placed in a trial notebook. The facts had been typed, three-hole punched, and put in its section of the book. Motions had been drawn and placed in the pleading section awaiting filing. Voir dire examination questions for the jury had been put into the book under the jury section where the juror profile continued to grow and change. Although they were not planning on going to a jury, they had to prepare just in case.

The lawyer was bothered when he ran into an old white whiskey man at a self-serve gas station one afternoon after work.

Bill Bently came over, "How's J.K.'s defense going?" he beamed to the lawyer.

"Pretty good," the lawyer smiled. He had represented Bently more than 25 years. "You know anything I need to know?" He felt that Bill wanted to tell him something.

"He's back out there running wide open," Bill grinned over his wire-rimmed glasses. "You know what I mean?" he winked at the lawyer.

"You mean he's blowing and going?" the lawyer asked.

"He's smoking," Bill responded. "I told him that if he gets cought, they're going to revoke his bond and put him in jail. But you can't tell him nothin. He's strung out on his own stuff."

"Man, I could have gone all day without this," the lawyer said dejectedly. "What can I do?" he wanted to know.

"There's nothing anyone can do," Bill said affirmatively. "He's gone on that meth with that young snapping twat. You can't get a man off that."

"He'll get cought again," the lawyer

reminded him.

"No doubt. Whatcha gonna do? The man won't help himself."

The lawyer secretly hoped Bill was exaggerating, but there was nothing he could do other than inquire. He called J.K. and asked him if he was selling dope. He told him that he had heard on the street that he was running wide open. J.K. denied ever selling any drugs. The lawyer hung up relieved. He truly wanted to believe J.K.

The grand jury went into session, and J.K. was indicted for trafficking in a controlled substance, Methamphetamine. The sheriff ordered a deputy to serve J.K. with a copy of the indictment and an arraignment notice. The deputy drove up to J.K.'s about dusk and blew his horn. J.K. saw him outside and ran out on the balcony of his upstairs bedroom and hid a plastic baggie under a shingle he could reach on the overhanging roof.

The deputy decided to forget about the indictment and arraignment notice. He dropped them on the dining room table, ran up the stairs to J.K.'s bedroom, told J.K. and Marsha not to move, and went out on the deck. He lifted the shingle and retrieved an eight-ball of methamphetamine.

He returned to the bedroom and placed J.K. under arrest. J.K. voluntarily put his wrists out and allowed himself to be handcuffed. The deputy then searched J.K. and found three illegal narcotic pills in his shirt pocket. J.K. was taken downtown and booked.

J.K. called the lawyer at home. "This is J.K. I'm in trouble again. I'm down here at the jail."

"What are you charged with? Can you make a bond?" The lawyer didn't want to go downtown after working all day.

J.K. asked the jailer, and he was told that he had two more trafficking charges. A bond had been set at $5,000. The lawyer told J.K. to make that bond and get the hell out of there as quickly as possible.

J.K. made the $5,000 property bond in less than 20 minutes and was released. The lawyer thought it was a miracle.

Six weeks later an assistant district attorney moved to revoke J.K.'s bond and the judge set it for hearing. After a three-hour presentation by the defense proving that J.K. was not a flight risk, the judge revoked his bond and ordered him to jail pending his first trial.

The judge said, "I'm not about to allow a man out on bond for trafficking in methamphetamine to stay out when he is arrested again for trafficking in methamphetamine. Bond denied."

Bang went the gavel, and J.K. was taken back to his cell.

The lawyer approached the district attorney about the possibility of J.K. Watts entering a plea. The district attorney said, "No way. J.K. caused problems in this county 20 years ago and got away with it. Now he's back causing trouble again. The best I can do for him is life. I'll run all three of his new charges with one life sentence."

"You know I can't plead a man to life," the lawyer reminded the district attorney.

"Well, that's all you're going to get. He'd better take it. I have three shots at him. If he's convicted in any case, he gets life without parole. Does he understand that?"

"Sure he knows that. He's 57 years old. You give him 15 years to serve, and that is life without. He'll die in prison. Give me something where he can see the light of day."

"You know that J.K. is an old white whiskey man. He did a little time for car theft, but he's like all white whiskey men. They never believe a jury will convict them. Well, I believe a jury will convict him this time. I might be wrong. I've been wrong before, but I believe this time we have J.K. Watts. If he doesn't take my offer, I'll prosecute him three times. I'm bound to win one of the cases. It's pure and simple-- he has to be stopped. The task force came down on him, and he was back selling methamphetamine within 48 hours. He didn't miss a beat. No, this time, J.K.'s got to pay."

"I guess I might as well get ready for trial," the lawyer said dejectedly as though he was a failure.

'Muscle it up," the district attorney smiled. "It won't take long to try it." He was letting the lawyer know he had made him his best offer.

The lawyer redoubled his efforts preparing a defense for J.K.

J.K. denied the dope was his or that he even knew it was in the house. The best defense was to blame the dope on Marsha. She had the key. She lived in the bedroom. There was a presumption the dope belonged to her. She repeatedly told the lawyer that the dope was hers. She was not selling it. She was just storing it. She did not have a criminal record. The lawyer believed that if she could testify before a jury as she testified to him and his clerk, she would be believed and J.K. would not be convicted.

The case came on for trial in five weeks. The DA would not back off his offer of life. J.K. would not even consider taking the deal.

"I'll never plead to life. I might as well have life without parole. I'll be over 70 years old when I'm eligible for parole. Forget it."

When the case was called for trial, the lawyer went to the district attorney once more. "Give me something that my client can take, and we won't have to try this case for a week."

"Okay," the DA said resignedly. "We met last night and came up with the very best offer we can make – years. He can be out in 10."

"That's still life for him," the lawyer argued. "Give me something just a little sweeter."

"All right, I'm going to overrule my staff, my investigators, all of law enforcement, the neighbors, and the citizens of this county -- 25 years, take it or leave it. If he is convicted of anything, I'm asking the Court for the Habitual Criminal Act sentencing enhancement. He had better take this. He can be out in 8 years."

The DA was trying to sell the lawyer on the deal. That was unnecessary. The lawyer knew well the seriousness of J.K.'s situation.

The deal was presented to J.K., and he promptly dismissed it. The lawyer had a policy of never recommending a deal to a client. He subscribed to the saying that clients go to jail, and lawyers go home to dinner. He tried to arrange plea bargains for all his criminal clients. He felt it was his duty to give his clients as many options as possible. It was similar to settlement offers in a civil case. He always allowed the client to make the final decision. It would be the same with J.K. up to a point.

The lawyer went back to the DA and told him no deal.

"Yeah," the DA responded. "I expected that. Old bootleggers never believe they will go to prison for any length of time. They always think something will come along to save them. Well, it won't happen this time. Let's try it."

"No way out," the lawyer responded. "He took his jury list and began to prepare to examine the jury array for the trial.

The Court called the case for trial. The jury venire was examined by the state for prejudice and examined at length by the defense to test feelings and predispositions toward the defendant's guilt. After more than three hours, interrogation, twelve jurors were selected with two alternates. The alternates were selected due to the anticipated length of the trial -- at least one week and perhaps as many as eight or nine days. After the jury was seated in the box, the Court recessed for lunch.

The lawyer and his clerk decided they needed some more pictures of J.K.'s property. They asked Susan and Marsha to go with them. The clerk was driving. On the way, the lawyer told Marsha he was going to examine her as he would examine her before the jury.

"Think before you answer. Listen to the question, and then answer the question slowly and honestly. Answer as briefly as possible, and stop talking. As long as you tell the truth, you can't be tripped up on cross-examination. Now, I want you to answer some questions exactly as you are when you testify. You understand?"

She said that she did.

Twisted to his left and looking over the front seat to the rear of the vehicle, the lawyer began. "Did you have the key to the locker?"

"Yes," Marsha sounded confident.

"There was dope in that locker?"

"Yes, there was."

"Who did it belong to?"

"J.K. and me," Marsha answered innocently.

The lawyer thought she might have not understood the question. "Did you ever see J.K. sell illegal drugs?"

"Oh, yeah, all the time. He and I have been selling drugs for about four months."

"I thought you told us since the beginning of this case that the dope was yours and that J.K. never sold drugs," the lawyer could not believe what he was hearing. His defense was coming apart with his most material witness.

"Well, I did tell you that. But now you say I've got to tell the truth," Marsha said innocently. "I'm going to lie when I testify. I'm not about to say J.K. sold any drugs nor knew the drugs were in the job box or safe. I'm going to lie like a rug." She sounded proud of herself.

"That's not going to happen," the lawyer sounded firm. "I'm not about to put a witness on the stand whom I know is going to lie. You have just taken yourself out of the loop to testify."

"But I told J.K. I would save him because I don't have a criminal record," Marsha whined.

"The best way you can save him is to leave

town right now," the lawyer instructed. "If the state finds you, your testimony will absolutely convict J.K."

"Well, I'm sorry. I want to help," Marsha continued to whine. "I'll leave town tomorrow."

The lawyer turned further and looked over the front seat at Susan, "See that she gets out of town right now. There's no need to go to the house again. We're done. J.K. has to take a deal."

The clerk turned the car around and started back toward town.

When court reconvened at 1:30 p.m., opening statements were made, and the trial began.

Only one witness, a member of the Drug Task Force, was called prior to the overnight recess. This witness was examined on direct by an assistant district attorney. The lawyer cross examined the deputy at length. It was apparent no quarter would be given by the defense. The deputy was impeached on a number of factual issues. The defense believed this witness did not hurt them and perhaps hurt the state.

The lawyer had in his pocket a love note written by a male member of the Drug Task Force to a female member of the task force. The investigator had accidentally left the note with the search warrant when he hurriedly served the warrant on J.K.

Marsha brought the note to the lawyer and asked him what it meant. He very well knew what it meant. His suspicions were confirmed. An investigator with the district attorney's office was having an affair with a female deputy from the sheriff's department. The note proposed a meeting and pledged his love and money to the deputy.

"Will you use the note?" the clerk asked.

"I am the trigger man," the lawyer grinned. "As soon as I get him on cross, I will confront him with his love letter. He's a married man. He shouldn't be arresting our clients while he is chasing another man's wife. This may destroy the task force," he chuckled in anticipation of using the only positive fact he had in this terrible case.

The following morning, the Court asked the state if it was ready. It announced ready. He turned to the defense before he brought the jury in, "Is the defense ready?"

"Give us just a minute to talk with the district attorney, your Honor," the lawyer asked.

"Okay. Fifteen minutes," the Court said leaving the bench.

The lawyer approached the DA and his two assistants, "Give me 15 years, and I'll sell it," he whispered to the three men as they stood near the state's table.

"Let us talk about it," the assistant district attorney whispered back. He knew the state had been hurt by their best witness, and more days of testimony were coming. The representatives of the people went through the door into the robing room and on into a witness room.

The judge returned to the bench. The 15 minutes were up. The defense still waited while the state debated in a witness room.

The lawyer approached the impatient judge, "Give us just a few more minutes. We may save you seven more days' trial."

"Okay," responded the judge. "But give me immediate notice when progress is no longer being made."

"What's going on?" J.K. asked. He had been busying himself earlier talking to various members of his family and friends whom he had missed while staying in jail. The courtroom was filled with J.K. supporters and relatives.

"The state is about to make us a final settlement offer," the lawyer responded with hope in his voice.

"I'm not pleading guilty for a bunch of time," J.K. said. "I spent over five years in prison. I'm not interested in going back. I'll take my chances with the jury."

"Well, I don't think you really understand what you're up against," the lawyer said. He hated to spring the Marsha stuff on J.K., but he told his client he no longer had any defense whatsoever.

"We can't put you on the stand. We can't put Marsha on the stand. We have no defense. Even if we could somehow win this case, the state has two more chances to give you life without parole. This is their weakest case. Their strongest case is the one where the deputy saw you hiding drugs under the shingles and found the illegal drugs in your shirt pocket."

"What about illegal search?" J.K. asked.

"The search was legal. It was an incident to a lawful arrest. Once the deputy was at your place legally to serve the grand jury indictment and arraignment notice and saw you hiding methamphetamine, whatever he did on the premises was legal. We're stuck with those drugs."

About that time the state re-entered the courtroom. The young assistant DA motioned to the lawyer to come over.

"We've had to do some real soul searching, and we have finally agreed to give you the 15 years. What we really want to accomplish here is community stability. Punishment is not going to change J.K. This agreement will be sure that he is out of the community at least five years. So we'll combine all three cases and give you your 15 years. Now sell it to J.K."

"Thanks," the lawyer sounded relieved. He crossed the courtroom and took his clerk and

J.K. aside. "I've got you 15 years. You'll have to serve 5 to get parole. If you stay out of trouble and get institutional good time, you'll get 75 days off for every 30 days served. You could be out in 3 years."

"I don't want to plead guilty," J.K. responded.

"It's not a matter of what you want; it is what is best for you. This is a sure thing. It gets rid of all the cases against you. If this jury convicts you, you get life without parole. If you win here and they try you again in three months on the methamphetamine charge, you could get life without parole. If they lose there, they still have the illegal drugs in your pocket that you haven't been charged with. I don't see how you can possibly win this case. Once again, if convicted, you get life without parole. You've got to take this."

"I'm not going to plead guilty," J.K. said once more.

The lawyer motioned for members of J.K.'s family to come up to the group. Almost 20 people crowded around as the lawyer told the family what the dilemma was. The family and friends were on the audience side of the divide, while J.K. and the attorneys were on the Court side of the divide.

The state was still waiting at its table. All three prosecutors were standing. The impatient judge was standing behind his high-backed chair on the bench looking at his watch. He wanted the jury to be working. What little judicial patience he had were just about gone. He was doing his usual fuming and fidgeting. The family, to the person, told J.K. to take the deal. He still refused.

Doyle, Susan, John McCorley, Little Toy, Big Toy, Reba Watts, Larry Watts, Brenda Kennedy, Seth Adam Bell, Cotton Bell, Bill Bently, Nita, Sybil, and the rest of the Watts Clan shifted to crowd around J.K. Each of them begged J.K. to take the deal. Some of his close family members were crying as they insisted he take the deal.

The judge was closely watching all the people bunched around the defendant and his lawyers. He asked the lawyer, "Are you making any progress?"

"Give us just a few more minutes, Judge," the lawyer replied. "We had to wait more than 15 minutes to get the offer. We've been talking a little over five minutes."

"I'll give you five more minutes," the judge said stepping off the bench and out the door once more.

Nita told J.K., "Hon, you have to take this. You'll never get a better offer than this. You really need to take it. I just can't stand the thought of you getting life without parole. Please take it."

Dabbing her eyes with a handkerchief, she was wringing her hands pleading with her brother to take a sure thing.

J.K.'s brother Doug, who had J.K.'s kidney, was there along with his family. "Brother, you really need to take this deal. I can't stand to think of you being in prison the rest of your life." He pleaded with J.K. to take it.

Susan was there with a couple of her friends. "Dad, you need to strongly consider this and take it. Everyone agrees that you ought to take it."

"I just can't plead guilty," J.K. said.

"Well, this judge is not going to give us any more time. You must make a decision," the lawyer said. "Tell us to try the case, and we'll go to work. Tell us you'll take the deal, and we'll do that. Just tell us something."

"Flip a coin," J.K. said.

"You're going to let your entire future turn on the toss of a coin?" the lawyer asked incredulously.

"Yeah. You got a coin?"

The lawyer fished a quarter out of his pocket and showed it to J.K. and the crowd.

"Toss it," J.K. said. "I'll do what the coin says. Heads, I take the deal; tails, I go to trial."

The lawyer flipped the coin praying it would land on heads. He flipped the coin with his right hand and cought it in his left. He covered the quarter with this right hand. "Heads!" the lawyer exclaimed showing the coin to J.K.

"Tell 'em we'll take the deal," J.K. Smiled.

"Are you ready?" the irascible judge had returned to the bench.

"Yes we are, Your Honor," the lawyer responded. The DA's took their seats at the state's table. The lawyer told the young assistant, "You've got a deal."

"May we approach the bench?" the assistant asked.

"Come up," the judge said.

"We have a plea bargain," the lawyer told the judge.

"Put it on the record," the judge instructed.

"J.K. Watts will plead guilty to the charges and be sentenced to 15 years in the penitentiary. The Habitual Criminal Act is waived and will not be used to enhance this sentence. All other charges will be dismissed with costs remitted."

The judge called the jury in and excused them with the explanation the case had been settled. He then sentenced J.K. Watts to fifteen years to serve in the state penitentiary.

Although the family cried when J.K. was taken away, everyone agreed that J.K. had to take the deal. Everyone was happy.

As they left the courthouse, the clerk asked the lawyer, "I know I'm new practicing law, but does it happen often where a man places his entire life on the toss of a coin? I really can't believe it."

"Well, I've been in the business 33 years,

and I saw it happen once -- when you did," the lawyer responded. "I sure am happy that coin landed on heads."

"Did it really land on heads?" the clerk asked. "I thought I saw tails when you first cought it."

"It was heads when J.K. saw it," the lawyer grinned. "No doubt about that."

"You palmed that quarter?" the clerk accused.

"A man's gotta do what a man's gotta do," the lawyer smiled. "Let's take the rest of the day off."

J.K. was rewarded for his good works. He had just been released from orientation into the prison population. He was going toward the main section of the prison when he ran into the warden and several officers.

The warden was saying, "I want a non-violent offender, who is a master automobile mechanic, to drive me around and keep my vehicles in running order."

J.K., in shackles, stopped briefly and said, "I'm your man."

After discussion, record reviews, and further interviews, the warden took J.K. at his word. J.K. never went into the population. Instead, he was given a room in the warden's garage apartment at his home.

He kept the warden's vehicles in perfect shape and drove him to work every day and waited for the workday to be over and drove him home. Usually, the warden had to travel during the day, and J.K. drove him wherever he needed to go. Other than that, J.K. was the warden's errand boy, assistant, or gofer.

J.K. enjoyed his job and his relationship with the warden. He died of a heart attack after serving three and a half years.

Made in the USA
Columbia, SC
29 September 2017